Guide to College Reading

ELEVENTH EDITION

Kathleen T. McWhorter
Niagara County Community College

PEARSON

Boston Columbus Indianapolis New York San Francisco Amsterdam
Cape Town Dubai London Madrid Milan Munich Paris Montréal Toronto
Delhi Mexico City São Paulo Sydney Hong Kong Seoul Singapore Taipei Tokyo

Executive Editor: Matthew Wright
Program Manager: Anne Shure
Development Editor: Janice Wiggins
Product Marketing Manager: Jennifer Edwards
Executive Field Marketing Manager: Joyce Nilsen
Media Producer: Marisa Massaro
Content Specialist: Julia Pomann
Media Editor: Kelsey Loveday
Project Manager: Donna Campion

Text Design, Project Coordination, and Electronic Page
  Makeup: Lumina Datamatics
Program Design Lead: Heather Scott
Cover Designer: Tamara Newnam
Cover Illustration: Beach Mountain/Getty Images
Senior Manufacturing Buyer: Roy L. Pickering, Jr.
Printer/Binder: RR Donnelley/Crawfordsville
Cover Printer: Phoenix Color/Hagerstown

Acknowledgments of third-party content appear on page[s] 488–494, which constitute an extension of this copyright page.

PEARSON, ALWAYS LEARNING, and MYREADINGLAB are exclusive trademarks owned by Pearson Education, Inc. or its affiliates in the United States and/or other countries.

Unless otherwise indicated herein, any third-party trademarks that may appear in this work are the property of their respective owners and any references to third-party trademarks, logos, or other trade dress are for demonstrative or descriptive purposes only. Such references are not intended to imply any sponsorship, endorsement, authorization, or promotion of Pearson's products by the owners of such marks, or any relationship between the owner and Pearson Education, Inc., or its affiliates, authors, licensees, or distributors.

Library of Congress Cataloging-in-Publication Data

Library of Congress Control Number: 2017
Names: McWhorter, Kathleen T.
Title: Guide to college reading / Kathleen T. McWhorter, Niagara County
   Community College.
Description: Eleventh edition. | Boston : Pearson, [2017] | Includes
   bibliographical references and index.
Identifiers: LCCN 2015036207 | ISBN 9780134111711 (alk. paper) | ISBN
   0134111710 (alk. paper)
Subjects: LCSH: Reading (Higher education) | Study skills. | Reading (Higher
   education)—Problems, exercises, etc.
Classification: LCC LB2395.3.M39 2017 | DDC 428.4071/1—dc23
LC record available at http://lccn.loc.gov/2015036207

2   16

http://www.pearsonhighered.com/

Student Edition ISBN 10:   0-13-411171-0
Student Edition ISBN 13: 978-0-13-411171-1
A la Carte Edition ISBN-10:   0-13-410514-1
A la Carte Edition ISBN-13: 978-0-13-410514-7

Brief Contents

Detailed Contents

Part VI: A Contemporary Issues Mini-Reader   432

MyReadingLab™: Improving Reading Through Personalized Learning Experiences

In an ideal world, an instructor would work with each student to help improve reading skills with consistent challenges and rewards. Without that luxury, MyReadingLab offers a way to keep students focused and accelerate their progress using comprehensive pre-assignments and a powerful, adaptive study plan.

Flexible Enough to Fit Every Course Need

MyReadingLab can be set up to fit your specific course needs, whether you seek reading support to complement what you do in class, a way to administer many sections easily, or a self-paced environment for independent study.

Learning in Context

In addition to distinct pre-loaded learning paths for reading/writing skills practice and reading level practice, MyReadingLab incorporates numerous activities for practice and readings from the accompanying textbook. This makes the connection between what's done in and out of the classroom more relevant to students.

NEW! Learning Tools for Student Engagement

Create an Engaging Classroom

Learning Catalytics is an interactive, student-response tool in MyReadingLab that uses students' smartphones, tablets, or laptops, allowing instructors to generate class discussion easily, guide lectures, and promote peer-to-peer learning with real-time analytics.

Build Multimedia Assignments

MediaShare allows students to easily post multimodal assignments for peer review and instructor feedback. In both face-to-face and online courses, MediaShare enriches the student learning experience by enabling contextual feedback to be provided quickly and easily.

Direct Access to MyLab

Users can link from any Learning Management System (LMS) to Pearson's MyReadingLab. Access MyLab assignments, rosters and resources, and synchronize MyLab grades with the LMS gradebook.

Visit www.myreadinglab.com for more information.

Preface

Guide to College Reading, Eleventh Edition, is written to equip students with the basic textbook reading and critical-thinking skills they need to cope with the demands of academic work.

NEW TO THE ELEVENTH EDITION

Numerous changes and additions have been made in this eleventh edition to give more emphasis to the reading process, to focus on reading larger units of text, and to introduce a new Think As You Read feature.

1. **New! Emphasis on Longer Readings.** Because students must develop skills to read lengthy textbook chapters, the focus of the mastery tests has been changed to offer full-length readings, instead of short paragraphs and brief passages as the basis for skill application. In each chapter, Mastery Tests now feature longer, full-length readings with accompanying activities and exercises.

   In Chapters 2 through 10, Mastery Tests now have more extensive pedagogy to help students read and interpret longer readings. Of the 19 mastery test readings, 11 are new to this edition, and more than half of the readings are now textbook excerpts. New topics include species preservation, corporate social responsibility, paying forward, hunger on campus, communication through objects, the practice of veiling, lottery winners, the trend to remain single, medical practice and the Internet, the right to die, and vigilantes. This emphasis on longer readings is reinforced in the Contemporary Issues Mini-Reader, that contains eight additional full-length readings and in the Fiction Mini-Reader that contains four fiction readings, providing a total of 31 reading selections.

2. **New! Reorganization of the Apparatus for the Full-Length Reading Mastery Tests.** Both mastery tests now emphasize reading as a process and include before-and after-reading activities, as presented in Chapter 2. Before-reading activities include previewing and activating background activities. Students are directed to preview the reading and answer a set of questions; they also predict content and connect the ideas to their own experience. Following the reading, students work through extensive apparatus, now including an Academic Application exercise that guides students in paraphrasing, outlining, or summarizing the reading.

3. **NEW! Think As You Read Feature.** Students are often passive readers, allowing ideas to pass in front of them without subjecting those ideas to examination and analysis. The second mastery test in Chapters 2-10 now contains a unique interactive feature that demonstrates the type of thinking that should occur as students read and encourages them to interact with the text. Students are directed to highlight topic sentences and key details, as well as useful transitions, thereby focusing their attention on structure and meaning. While reading, students encounter marginal questions that model the thinking that active readers do as they read. These questions encourage students to examine the flow of ideas, recognize connections between and among ideas and images, and think critically about ideas. The categories of questions include the following:

- **Examining Features** questions ask students to consider the writer's choice of supporting details, examine the writer's main point, or determine the function or impact of the introduction or conclusion.
- **Factual Recall** questions ask students specific facts about the reading to strengthen their understanding.
- **Critical Analysis** questions require interpretation and evaluation of the author's ideas.
- **Word Meaning and Choice** questions ask students to consider the choice of words used in the reading and/or the positive or negative connotations of those words.
- **Visual or Image** questions ask students to consider the meaning and relevance of the visual or image that accompanies the reading and consider other appropriate choices.

4. **New! Issues and Readings in the Contemporary Issues Mini-Reader.** The Contemporary Issues Mini-Reader has been revised to include two readings on each of four issues. The new issues are celebrities and athletes as activists, marketing of human organs, and the Internet and technology. Pro–con viewpoints on the issue of reviving extinct species is retained from the preceding edition.

5. **Revised Chapter 2, "An Overview of College Textbook Reading."** This chapter has been refocused to include greater emphasis on the reading process and has been reorganized to focus on before, during, and after reading techniques. It begins by discussing textbook aids to learning and then focuses on previewing, developing guide questions, reading for meaning, testing recall, and reviewing. The chapter unifies the reading and learning strategies it presents by showing students how these skills, when used in sequence, form the SQ3R reading/study system. The chapter is built around a textbook

reading excerpt used for skill demonstration and application. This chapter also includes a section on understanding graphics and visual aids, an essential part of textbook reading.

6. The chapter on "Organizing and Remembering Information" has been moved to earlier in the text. Now positioned as Chapter 3, the essential and high-utility textbook reading/thinking strategies, including highlighting, paraphrasing, outlining, mapping, summarizing and review, are available to students sooner so they can begin using them immediately in all of their college courses.

7. Revised Chapter 10, "Evaluating: Asking Critical Questions." The chapter now includes comprehensive coverage of evaluating Internet sources with material on evaluating the content, accuracy, and timeliness of a Web site.

THE PURPOSE OF THE TEXT

Guide to College Reading, Eleventh Edition, addresses the learning characteristics, attitudes, and skill levels of college students. It is intended to equip them with the skills they need to handle the diverse reading demands of college course work. Specifically, the text guides students in becoming active learners and critical thinkers. Using an encouraging, supportive, nonthreatening voice, the text provides clear instruction and a variety of everyday examples and extensive exercises that encourage students to become involved and apply the skills presented.

The chapters are divided into numerous sections; exercises are frequent but brief and explicit. The language and style are simple and direct; explanations are clear and often presented in step-by-step form. Reading topics and materials have been chosen carefully to relate to students' interests and background, while broadening their range of experience. Many students have compensated for poor reading skills with alternative learning styles; they have become visual and auditory learners. To capitalize on this adaptation, a visual approach to learning is used throughout. The importance of visual literacy in today's world is emphasized by numerous photographs—many with bubble captions designed to provoke thought about how the visuals are used to enhance and add meaning to text—drawings, diagrams, and other visual aids used to illustrate concepts.

CONTENT OVERVIEW

The text is organized into six major sections, following the logical progression of skill development from high-utility, immediately useful skills to vocabulary development to reading paragraphs, articles, essays, and chapters. It also proceeds logically from literal comprehension to critical interpretation and response. An opening chapter focuses on student success strategies, including such topics as attitudes toward college, concentration, learning styles, and comprehension monitoring.

- **Part One presents the basics for success in college reading.** It provides strategies for getting started, presents an overview of the reading process, and includes high-utility skills for organizing and remembering information.

- **Part Two teaches students basic approaches to vocabulary development.** It includes contextual aids, analysis of word parts, pronunciation, and the use of a dictionary and other reference sources.

- **Part Three helps students develop literal comprehension skills.** It emphasizes before-reading techniques that prepare and enable the student to comprehend and recall content. Previewing, activating background knowledge, and using guide questions are emphasized. The unit provides extensive instruction and practice with paragraph comprehension and recognition of thought patterns. An entire chapter is devoted to topics and stated and implied main ideas; another entire chapter focuses on supporting details and transitions.

- **Part Four introduces critical-reading and thinking skills.** It presents skills that enable students to interact with and evaluate written material, including material on the Internet. Topics include making inferences, identifying the author's purpose, recognizing assumptions, and distinguishing between fact and opinion.

- **Part Five, "A Fiction Mini-Reader," offers a brief introduction to reading fiction.** An introductory section discusses the essential elements of a short story, using Chopin's "The Story of an Hour" as an example. Two additional short stories with accompanying apparatus are also included, as well as an introduction to reading novels.

- **Part Six, "A Contemporary Issues Mini-Reader," contains two articles on each of four issues.** The four issues are celebrities and athletes as activists, marketing of human organs, the Internet and technology, and reviving extinct species. Each reading is prefaced by an interest-catching introduction, pre-reading questions, and a vocabulary preview. Literal and critical-thinking questions as well as a words-in-context exercise, vocabulary review, summary exercise, and writing exercises follow each selection. Each issue culminates with an activity, "Analyzing and Synthesizing Ideas," that encourages students to integrate, analyze and synthesize ideas from both readings.

SPECIAL FEATURES

The following features enhance the text's effectiveness and directly contribute to students' success:

- **Reading as thinking.** Reading is approached as a thinking process—a process in which the student interacts with textual material and sorts, evaluates, and reacts to its organization and content. For example, students are shown how to define their purpose for reading, ask questions, identify and use organization and structure as a guide to understanding, make inferences, and interpret and evaluate what they read.

- **Think As You Read feature.** A feature new to this edition expands the reading as thinking emphasis by offering marginal prompts that model the thinking that should occur during reading.

- **Comprehension monitoring.** Comprehension monitoring is also addressed within the text. Through a variety of techniques, students are encouraged to be aware of and to evaluate and control their level of comprehension of the material they read.

- **Skill application.** Chapters 2 through 10 conclude with two full-length reading mastery tests that enable students to apply the skills taught in each chapter and to evaluate their learning.

- **Integration of reading and writing.** The text integrates reading and writing skills. Students respond to exercises by writing sentences and paragraphs. Each reading selection is followed by "Thinking Critically About the Reading" questions, which encourage composition. Writing exercises accompany each reading selection in Part Six.

Text-Specific Ancillary Materials

- **Annotated Instructor's Edition.** The Annotated Instructor's Edition is identical to the student text but includes all answers printed directly on the pages where questions, exercises, or activities occur. (ISBN: 0-13-410527-3)

- **Instructor's Manual.** An Instructor's Manual, including an Answer Key, accompanies the text. The manual describes in detail the basic features of the text and offers suggestions for structuring the course, for teaching non-traditional students, and for approaching each section of the text. Available for download. (ISBN: 0-13-411242-3)

- **Test Bank.** This supplement features two sets of chapter quizzes and a mastery test for each chapter. Available for download. (ISBN: 0-13-410528-1)

- **MyTest.** This electronic test bank includes chapter tests and vocabulary tests in a web-based format. (ISBN: 0-13-411244-X)

- **PowerPoint Presentations.** Classroom presentations for each chapter. Available for download. (ISBN: 0-13-411246-6).

- **Answer Key.** The Answer Key contains the solutions to the exercises in the student edition of the text. Available for download. (0-13-410517-6).

ACKNOWLEDGMENTS

I wish to express my gratitude to my reviewers for their excellent ideas, suggestions, and advice on this and previous editions of this text: Alfradene Armstrong, Tougaloo College; Carla Bell, Henry Ford Community College; Michelle Biferie, Palm Beach Community College; Dorothy Booher, Florida Community College at Jacksonville, Kent Campus; Diane Bosco, Suffolk County Community College; Sharon Cellemme, South Piedmont Community College; Beth Childress, Armstrong Atlantic University; Pam Drell, Oakton Community College, Des Plaines Campus; Donna Duchow, San Diego Mesa College; Adam Floridia, Middlesex Community College; Deborah Paul Fuller, Bunker Hill Community College; Shirley Hall, Middle Georgia College; Pam Hallene, Community College of Rhode Island; Kevin Hayes, Essex County College; Peggy Hopper, Walters State Community College; Deborah House, Dine College; Danica Hubbard, College of DuPage; Suzanne E. Hughes, Florida Community College at Jacksonville; Cathy Hunsicker, Dalton State College; Jana Hutcheson, Bay Mills Community College; Jacqueline Jackson, Art Institute of Philadelphia; Arlene Jellinek, Palm Beach Community College; Mahalia H. Johnson, Greenville Technical College; Barbara Kashi, Cypress College; Jeanne Keefe, Belleville Area College; Patti Levine-Brown, Florida Community College at Jacksonville; Wendy McBride, Kishwaukee Community College; Joan Mooney, Niagara County College; Anne Mueller, Kishwaukee Community College; Mary Myer, Suffolk County Community College; Sharyn Neuwirth, Montgomery College, Tacoma Park Campus; Bernard Ngovo, Pima Community College; Alice Nitta, Leeward Community College; Pauline Noznick, Oakton Community College; Jean Olsen, Oakton Community College; Catherine Packard, Southeastern Illinois College; Elizabeth Parks, Kishwaukee Community College; Kathy Purswell, Frank Phillips College; Regina Rochford, Queensborough Community College, CUNY; Diane Schellack, Burlington County College; Marilyn Schenk, San Diego Mesa College; Jackie Stahlecker, St. Phillips College; Cynthia Taber, Schenectady County Community College, SUNY; Kim Thomas, Polk State College; Marie Ulmen, Harrisburg Area Community College; Pam Walsh, Schenectady County Community College, SUNY; Mary Wolting, Indiana University–Purdue University at Indianapolis; and Nora Yaeger, Cedar Valley College.

I am particularly indebted to Janice Wiggins, Development Editor, and to Gill Cook, Executive Development Editor, for overseeing this project; to Phoebe Mathews for her valuable assistance in developing and producing the manuscript; and to Eric Stano, Editor-in-Chief, VP, English, for his enthusiastic support of this project.

KATHLEEN T. McWHORTER

MyReadingLab™: Improving Reading Through Personalized Learning Experiences

In an ideal world, an instructor would work with each student to help improve reading skills with consistent challenges and rewards. Without that luxury, MyReadingLab offers a way to keep students focused and accelerate their progress using comprehensive pre-assignments and a powerful, adaptive study plan.

Flexible Enough to Fit Every Course Need

MyReadingLab can be set up to fit your specific course needs, whether you seek reading support to complement what you do in class, a way to administer many sections easily, or a self-paced environment for independent study.

Learning in Context

In addition to distinct pre-loaded learning paths for reading/writing skills practice and reading level practice, MyReadingLab incorporates numerous activities for practice and readings from the accompanying textbook. This makes the connection between what's done in and out of the classroom more relevant to students.

NEW! Learning Tools for Student Engagement

Create an Engaging Classroom

Learning Catalytics is an interactive, student-response tool in MyReadingLab that uses students' smartphones, tablets, or laptops, allowing instructors to generate class discussion easily, guide lectures, and promote peer-to-peer learning with real-time analytics.

Build Multimedia Assignments

MediaShare allows students to easily post multimodal assignments for peer review and instructor feedback. In both face-to-face and online courses, MediaShare enriches the student learning experience by enabling contextual feedback to be provided quickly and easily.

Direct Access to MyLab

Users can link from any Learning Management System (LMS) to Pearson's MyReadingLab. Access MyLab assignments, rosters and resources, and synchronize MyLab grades with the LMS gradebook.

Visit www.myreadinglab.com for more information.

CHAPTER
1

Reading and Learning: Getting Started

Focusing on . . . College Success

LEARNING GOALS

This chapter will show you how to

1. Understand what is expected in college

2. Build your concentration

3. Understand and analyze your learning style

4. Improve your comprehension

5. Read and think visually

6. Use writing to learn

7. Learn from and with other students

Your first semester of college is often the most difficult because you don't know what to expect. The classes you have selected are challenging, and your instructors are demanding. This chapter will help you discover how to learn most effectively and help you approach the reading and study demands of your courses successfully.

College is very different from any other type of educational experience. It is different from high school, job training programs, adult education, and technical training programs. New and different types of learning are demanded, and you need new skills and techniques to meet these demands.

UNDERSTAND WHAT IS EXPECTED IN COLLEGE

1 LEARNING GOAL

Understand what is expected in college

Following is a list of statements about college. Treat it like a quiz, if you wish. Decide whether each statement is true or false, and write *T* for true or *F* for false in the space provided. Each statement will make you think about the reading and study demands of college. Check your answers by reading the paragraph following each item. As you work through this quiz, you will find out a little about what is expected of you in college. You will see whether or not you have an accurate picture of what college work involves. You will also see how this text will help you to become a better, more successful student.

_____   1.   For every hour I spend in class, I should spend one hour studying outside of class.

Many students feel that even one hour for each class (or 15 hours per week for students carrying a 15 credit-hour load) is a lot. Actually, the rule of thumb used by many instructors is two hours of study for each class hour. So you can see that you are expected to do a great deal of reading, studying, and learning on your own time. The purpose of this text is to help you read and learn in the easiest and best way for you.

_____   2.   I should expect to read about 80 textbook pages per week in each of my courses.

A survey of freshman courses at one college indicated that the average course assignment was roughly 80 pages per week. This may seem like a lot of reading—and it is. You will need to build your reading skills to handle this task. To help you do this, techniques for understanding and remembering what you read, improving your concentration, and handling difficult reading assignments will be suggested throughout this text.

_____   3.   The more facts I memorize, the higher my exam grades will be.

Learning a large number of facts is no guarantee of a high grade in a course. Some instructors and the exams they give are concerned with your ability to see how facts and ideas fit together, or to evaluate ideas, make comparisons, and recognize trends. Part One of this text will help you to do all these things by showing you how to read textbook chapters and organize and remember information.

_____ 4. There are a lot of words I do not know, but my vocabulary is about as good as it needs to be.

For each college course you take, there will be new words to learn. Some will be everyday words; others will be specialized or technical. Part Two of this text will show you how to develop your vocabulary by learning new words, figuring out words you do not know, and using reference sources.

_____ 5. College instructors will tell me exactly what to learn for each exam.

College instructors seldom tell you exactly what to learn or review. They expect you to decide what is important and to learn that information. In Part Three of this text you will learn how to identify what is important in sentences and paragraphs and how to follow authors' thought patterns.

_____ 6. College instructors expect me to react to, evaluate, and criticize what I read.

Beyond understanding the content of textbooks, articles, and essays, students need to be able to criticize and evaluate ideas. To help you read and think critically, Part Four of this text will show you how to interpret what you read, find the author's purpose, and ask critical questions.

_____ 7. The only assignments that instructors give are readings in the textbook.

Instructors often assign readings in a variety of sources including periodicals, newspapers, reference and library books, and online sources. These readings are intended to add to the information presented in your text and by your instructor. The reading selections contained in Parts Five and Six will give you the opportunity to practice and apply your skills to readings taken from a variety of sources. These selections are similar to the outside readings your instructors will assign.

_____ 8. The best way to read a textbook assignment is to turn to the correct page, start reading, and continue until you reach the end of the assignment.

There are numerous things you can do before you read, while you read, and after you read that can improve your comprehension and retention. These techniques for improving your comprehension and recall are presented throughout this text. For example, later in this chapter you will learn techniques for building your concentration. In Chapter 2 you will be shown how to preview, think about what you will read, use questions to guide your reading, and strengthen comprehension and recall.

_____ 9. Rereading a textbook chapter is the best way to prepare for an exam on that chapter.

Rereading is actually one of the poorest ways to review. Besides, it is often dull and time-consuming. In Chapter 3, you will learn about six more-effective alternatives: *highlighting, marking, paraphrasing, outlining, mapping,* and *summarizing.*

_____ 10. You can never know whether you have understood a textbook reading assignment until you take an exam on the chapter.

As you read, it is possible and important to keep track of and evaluate your level of understanding. You will learn how to keep track of your comprehension, recognize comprehension signals, and strengthen your comprehension.

By analyzing the above statements and the correct responses, you can see that college is a lot of work, much of which you must do on your own. However, college is also a new, exciting experience that will acquaint you with fresh ideas and opportunities.

The opportunity of college lies ahead of you. The skills you are about to learn, along with plenty of hard work, will make your college experience a meaningful and valuable one.

BUILD YOUR CONCENTRATION

2 LEARNING GOAL
Build your concentration

Do you have difficulty concentrating? If so, you are like many other college students who say that lack of concentration is the main reason they cannot read or study effectively. Building concentration involves two steps: (1) controlling your surroundings, and (2) focusing your attention.

Controlling Your Surroundings

Poor concentration is often the result of distractions caused by the time and place you have chosen to study. Here are a few ideas to help you overcome poor concentration:

Controlling Distractions

1. **Choose a place to read where you will not be interrupted.** If people interrupt you at home or in the dormitory, try the campus library.

2. **Find a place that is relatively free of distractions and temptations.** Avoid places with outside noise, friends, a television set, or loud music.

3. **Silence your cell phone and ignore texts.** If left on, these will break your concentration and cost you time.

4. **Read in the same place each day.** Eventually you will get in the habit of reading there, and concentration will become easier, almost automatic.

5. **Do not read where you are too comfortable.** It is easy to lose concentration, become drowsy, or fall asleep when you are too relaxed.

6. **Choose a time of day when you are mentally alert.** Concentration is easier if you are not tired, hungry, or drowsy.

Focusing Your Attention

Even if you follow these suggestions, you may still find it difficult to become organized and stick with your reading. This takes self-discipline, but the following suggestions may help:

Strengthening Your Concentration

1. **Set goals and time limits for yourself.** Before you begin a reading assignment, decide how long it should take, and check to see that you stay on schedule. Before you start an evening of homework, write down what you plan to do and how long each assignment should take. Sample goals for an evening are shown in Figure 1-1.

2. **Choose and reserve blocks of time each day for reading and study.** Write down what you will study in each time block each day or evening. Working at the same time each day establishes a routine and makes focusing your attention a bit easier.

3. **Vary your reading.** For instance, instead of spending an entire evening on one subject, work for one hour on each of three subjects.

4. **Reward yourself for accomplishing things as planned.** Delay entertainment until after you have finished studying. Use such things as

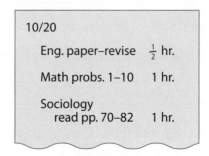

Figure 1-1 Goals and Time Limits

ordering a pizza, texting a friend, or watching a favorite TV program as rewards after you have completed several assignments.

5. **Plan frequent breaks.** Do this at sensible points in your reading—between chapters or after major chapter divisions.

6. **Keep physically as well as mentally active.** Try highlighting, underlining, or making summary notes as you read (see Chapter 3). These activities will focus your attention on the assignment.

EXERCISE   **1-1**   **Analyzing Your Level of Concentration**

Directions: Answer each of the following questions as honestly as you can. They will help you analyze problems with concentration. Discuss your answers with others in your class.

1. Where do you read and study? _____

   What interruptions, if any, occur there? Do you need to find a better place? If so, list a few alternatives.

   _____

   _____

2. How frequently do you respond to text messages? Do you ever turn your phone off while studying? _____

   _____

3. What is the best time of day for you to read? (If you do not know, experiment with different times until you begin to see a pattern.)

   _____

   _____

4. How long do you normally read without a break?

   _____

   _____

5. What type of distraction bothers you the most?

   _____

   _____

6. On average, how many different assignments do you work on in one evening?

   _____

   _____

7. What types of rewards might work for you?

_____

_____

EXERCISE 1-2 **Identifying Distractions**

Directions: As you read your next textbook assignment, either for this course or for another, be alert for distractions. Each time your mind wanders, try to identify the source of the distraction. List in the space provided the cause of each break in your concentration and a way to eliminate each, if possible.

_____

_____

_____

EXERCISE 1-3 **Setting Goals**

Directions: Before you begin your next study session, make a list in the space provided of what you intend to accomplish and how long you should spend on each task.

Assignment	Time
1. _____	_____
2. _____	_____
3. _____	_____

ANALYZE YOUR LEARNING STYLE

3 LEARNING GOAL
Understand and analyze your learning style

Not everyone learns in the same way. In fact, everyone has his or her own individual way of learning, which is called *learning style*. The following section contains a brief learning style questionnaire that will help you analyze how you learn and prepare an action plan for learning what you read.

Learning Style Questionnaire

Directions: Each item presents two choices. Select the alternative that best describes you. In cases in which neither choice suits you, select the one that is closer to your preference. Write the letter of your choice in the space provided.

Part One

_____ 1. I would prefer to follow a set of
   a. oral directions.
   b. print directions.

_____ 2. I would prefer to
   a. attend a lecture given by a famous psychologist.
   b. read an online article written by the psychologist.

_____ 3. When I am introduced to someone, it is easier for me to remember the person's
   a. name.
   b. face.

_____ 4. I find it easier to learn new information using
   a. language (words).
   b. images (pictures).

_____ 5. I prefer classes in which the instructor
   a. lectures and answers questions.
   b. uses PowerPoint illustrations and videos.

_____ 6. To follow current events, I would prefer to
   a. listen to the news on the radio.
   b. read the newspaper.

_____ 7. To learn how to repair a flat tire, I would prefer to
   a. listen to a friend's explanation.
   b. watch a demonstration.

Part Two

_____ 8. I prefer to
   a. work with facts and details.
   b. construct theories and ideas.

_____ 9. I would prefer a job involving
   a. following specific instructions.
   b. reading, writing, and analyzing.

_____ 10. I prefer to
   a. solve math problems using a formula.
   b. discover why the formula works.

_____ 11. I would prefer to write a term paper explaining
   a. how a process works.
   b. a theory.

_____ 12. I prefer tasks that require me to
    a. follow careful, detailed instructions.
    b. use reasoning and critical analysis.

_____ 13. For a criminal justice course, I would prefer to
    a. discover how and when a law can be used.
    b. learn how and why it became law.

_____ 14. To learn more about the operation of a robot, I would prefer to
    a. work with several robots.
    b. understand the principles on which they operate.

Part Three

_____ 15. To solve a math problem, I would prefer to
    a. draw or visualize the problem.
    b. study a sample problem and use it as a model.

_____ 16. To best remember something, I
    a. create a mental picture.
    b. write it down.

_____ 17. Assembling a bicycle from a diagram would be
    a. easy.
    b. challenging.

_____ 18. I prefer classes in which I
    a. handle equipment or work with models.
    b. participate in a class discussion.

_____ 19. To understand and remember how a machine works, I would
    a. draw a diagram.
    b. write notes.

_____ 20. I enjoy
    a. drawing or working with my hands.
    b. speaking, writing, and listening.

_____ 21. If I were trying to locate an office on an unfamiliar campus, I would prefer
    a. a map.
    b. print directions.

Part Four

_____ 22. For a grade in biology lab, I would prefer to
    a. work with a lab partner.
    b. work alone.

_____ 23. When faced with a difficult personal problem, I prefer to
      a. discuss it with others.
      b. resolve it myself.

_____ 24. Many instructors could improve their classes by
      a. including more discussion and group activities.
      b. allowing students to work on their own more frequently.

_____ 25. When listening to a lecturer or speaker, I respond more to the
      a. person presenting the idea.
      b. ideas themselves.

_____ 26. When on a team project, I prefer to
      a. work with several team members.
      b. divide the tasks and complete those assigned to me.

_____ 27. I prefer to shop and do errands
      a. with friends.
      b. by myself.

_____ 28. A job in a busy office is
      a. more appealing than working alone.
      b. less appealing than working alone.

Part Five

_____ 29. To make decisions, I rely on
      a. my experiences and gut feelings.
      b. facts and objective data.

_____ 30. To complete a task, I
      a. can use whatever is available to get the job done.
      b. must have everything I need at hand.

_____ 31. I prefer to express my ideas and feelings through
      a. music, song, or poetry.
      b. direct, concise language.

_____ 32. I prefer instructors who
      a. allow students to be guided by their own interests.
      b. make their expectations clear and explicit.

_____ 33. I tend to
      a. challenge and question what I hear and read.
      b. accept what I hear and read.

_____ 34. I prefer
       a. essay exams.
       b. objective exams.

_____ 35. In completing an assignment, I prefer to
       a. figure out my own approach.
       b. be told exactly what to do.

To score your questionnaire, record the total number of *a*'s you selected and the total number of *b*'s for each part of the questionnaire. Record your totals in the scoring grid on the next page.

    Now, circle your higher score for each part of the questionnaire. The word below the score you circled indicates a strength of your learning style. The next section explains how to interpret your scores.

Interpreting Your Scores

The questionnaire was divided into five parts; each part identifies one aspect of your learning style. Each of these five aspects is explained below.

Part One: Auditory or Visual Learners This score indicates whether you learn better by listening (auditory) or by seeing (visual). If you have a higher auditory than visual score, you tend to be an auditory learner. That is, you tend to learn more easily by hearing than by reading. A higher visual score suggests strengths with visual modes of learning—reading, studying pictures, reading diagrams, and so forth.

Part Two: Applied or Conceptual Learners This score describes the types of learning tasks and learning situations you prefer and find easiest to handle. If you are an applied learner, you prefer tasks that involve real objects and situations. Practical, real-life examples are ideal for you. If you are a conceptual learner, you prefer to work with language and ideas; you do not need practical applications for understanding.

Part Three: Spatial or Verbal (Nonspatial) Learners This score reveals your ability to work with spatial relationships. Spatial learners are able to visualize or mentally see how things work or how they are positioned in space. Their strengths may include drawing, assembling, or repairing things. Verbal learners lack skills in positioning things in space. Instead they rely on verbal or language skills.

Scoring Grid

Parts	Choice A Total	Choice B Total
Part One	_____	_____
	Auditory	Visual
Part Two	_____	_____
	Applied	Conceptual
Part Three	_____	_____
	Spatial	Verbal
Part Four	_____	_____
	Social	Independent
Part Five	_____	_____
	Creative	Pragmatic

Part Four: Social or Independent Learners   This score reveals whether you like to work alone or with others. If you are a social learner, you prefer to work with others—both classmates and instructors—closely and directly. You tend to be people oriented and enjoy personal interaction. If you are an independent learner, you prefer to work alone and study alone. You tend to be self-directed or self-motivated and are often goal oriented.

Part Five: Creative or Pragmatic Learners   This score describes the approach you prefer to take toward learning tasks. Creative learners are imaginative and innovative. They prefer to learn through discovery or experimentation. They are comfortable taking risks and following hunches. Pragmatic learners are practical, logical, and systematic. They seek order and are comfortable following rules.

Evaluating Your Scores

If you disagree with any part of the learning style questionnaire, go with your own instincts rather than the questionnaire results. The questionnaire is just a quick assessment; trust your knowledge of yourself in areas of dispute.

Developing a Learning Action Plan

Now that you know more about *how* you learn, you are ready to develop an action plan for learning what you read. Suppose you discovered that you are an auditory learner. You still have to read your assignments, which is a visual task. However, to learn the assignment you should translate the material into an auditory form.

For example, you could repeat aloud, using your own words, information that you want to remember, or you could record key information and play it back. If you also are a social learner, you could work with a classmate, testing each other out loud, or you might form an online study group with several classmates.

Table 1-1 lists each aspect of learning style and offers suggestions for how to learn from a reading assignment.

TABLE 1-1	Learning Styles and Reading/Learning Strategies
If your learning style is . . .	**Then the reading/learning strategies to use are . . .**
Auditory	• discuss/study with friends • talk aloud when studying • record self-testing questions and answers
Visual	• draw diagrams, charts, tables (Chapter 2) • try to visualize events • use films and videos when available • use computer-assisted instruction or tutorials, if available
Applied	• think of practical situations to which learning applies • associate ideas with their application • use case studies, examples, and applications to cue your learning
Conceptual	• organize materials that lack order • use outlining (Chapter 3) • focus on organizational patterns (Chapter 8)
Spatial	• use mapping (Chapter 3) • use outlining (Chapter 3) • draw diagrams, make charts and sketches (Chapter 2) • use visualization
Verbal (Nonspatial)	• translate diagrams and drawings into language • record steps, processes, procedures in words • write summaries (Chapter 3) • write your interpretation next to textbook drawings, maps, graphics
Social	• form study groups, in person or online • find a study partner, in person or online • interact with your instructor • work with a tutor
Independent	• use computer-assisted instruction and your textbook's online resources • purchase review workbooks or study guides, if available

(Continued)

TABLE 1-1   Learning Styles and Reading/Learning Strategies

If your learning style is . . .	Then the reading/learning strategies to use are . . .
Creative	• ask and answer questions • record your own ideas in margins of textbooks
Pragmatic	• study in an organized environment • write lists of steps, procedures, and processes

To use Table 1-1, do the following:

1. **Circle the five aspects of your learning style in which you received the highest scores.** Disregard the others.
2. **Read through the suggestions that apply to you.**
3. **Place a check mark in front of suggestions that you think will work for you.** Choose at least one from each category.
4. **List the suggestions that you chose in the box labeled Action Plan for Learning below.**

In the Action Plan for Learning you listed five or more suggestions to help you learn what you read. The next step is to experiment with these techniques,

---

Action Plan for Learning

Learning Strategy 1 _____

_____

Learning Strategy 2 _____

_____

Learning Strategy 3 _____

_____

Learning Strategy 4 _____

_____

Learning Strategy 5 _____

_____

Learning Strategy 6 _____

_____

one at a time. (You may need to refer to chapters listed in parentheses in Table 1-1 to learn or review how a certain technique works.) Use one technique for a while, and then move to the next. Continue using the techniques that seem to work; work on revising or modifying those that do not. Do not hesitate to experiment with other techniques listed in the table as well. You may find other techniques that work well for you.

Developing Strategies to Overcome Limitations

You should also work on developing styles in which you are weak. Your learning style is not fixed or unchanging. You can improve areas in which you scored lower. Although you may be weak in auditory learning, for example, many of your professors will lecture and expect you to take notes. If you work on improving your listening and note-taking skills, you can learn to handle lectures effectively. Make a conscious effort to work on improving areas of weakness as well as taking advantage of your strengths.

EXERCISE 1-4   **Evaluating Learning Strategies**

Directions: Write a brief evaluation of each learning strategy you listed in your Action Plan for Learning. Explain which worked; which, if any, did not; and what changes you have noticed in your ability to learn from reading.

EXERCISE 1-5   **Learning Styles I**

Directions: Form several small groups (three to five students), each of which consists of people who are either predominantly visual learners or predominantly auditory learners. Each group should discuss and outline strategies for completing each of the following tasks:

- Task 1: reading a poem for a literature class
- Task 2: revising an essay for a writing class
- Task 3: reviewing an economics textbook chapter that contains numerous tables, charts, and graphs

Groups should report their findings to the class and discuss how visual and auditory learners' strategies differ.

EXERCISE 1-6   **Learning Styles II**

Directions: Form several small groups (three to five students), each of which consists of people who are either predominantly social learners or predominantly independent learners. Each group should discuss and outline strategies for completing each of the following tasks:

- Task 1: reading a sociology textbook chapter that contains end-of-chapter study and review questions

- Task 2: working on sample problems for a math class
- Task 3: reading a case study (a detailed description of a criminal case) for a criminal justice class

Groups should report their findings to the class and discuss how social and independent learners' strategies differ.

IMPROVE YOUR COMPREHENSION

4 LEARNING GOAL

Improve your comprehension

Understanding what you read is the key to success in most college courses. Use the following sections to assess when you are and are not understanding what you read and to take action when you find your comprehension is weak or incomplete.

Paying Attention to Comprehension Signals

Think for a moment about how you feel when you read material you can easily understand. Now compare that with what happens when you read something difficult and complicated. When you read easy material, does it seem that everything "clicks"? That is, do ideas seem to fit together and make sense? Is that "click" noticeably absent in difficult reading?

Read each of the following paragraphs. As you read, be aware of how well you understand each of them.

Paragraph 1

   "Hooking up" is a term used to describe casual sexual activity with no strings attached between heterosexual college students who are strangers or brief acquaintances. When did people start to hook up? Although the term became common in the 1990s, its use with its modern meaning has been documented as early as the mid-1980s. Studies from the early 2000s show that hooking up was already a fairly common practice on U.S. campuses, practiced by as much as 40 percent of female college students. More recent studies have shed some light on the demographic and psychological correlatives of hooking up. In a 2007 study involving 832 college students, it emerged that hooking up is practiced less by African-American than Caucasian students. Hooking up is also associated with the use of alcohol and, interestingly, with higher parental income. Increased financial resources may give teens and young adults more opportunities to socialize and hook up.

—Kunz, *THINK Marriages and Families*, p. 83

Paragraph 2

   Diluted earnings per share (EPS) are calculated under the assumption that all contingent securities that would have dilutive effects are converted and exercised and are therefore common stock. They are found by adjusting basic EPS for the impact of converting all convertibles and exercising all warrants and options that would have dilutive effects on the firm's earnings. This approach treats as common stock all contingent securities. It is calculated by dividing earnings available for common stockholders (adjusted for interest and preferred stock dividends that would not be paid, given assumed conversion of all outstanding contingent securities that would have dilutive effects) by the number of shares of common stock that would be outstanding if all contingent securities that would have dilutive effects were converted and exercised.

—Gitman, *Principles of Managerial Finance*, p. 733

Did you feel comfortable and confident as you read Paragraph 1? Did ideas seem to lead from one to another and make sense? How did you feel while reading Paragraph 2? Most likely you sensed its difficulty and felt confused. Some words were unfamiliar, and you could not follow the flow of ideas.

As you read Paragraph 2, did you know that you were not understanding it? Did you feel lost and confused? Table 1-2 lists and compares some common signals that are useful in monitoring your comprehension. Not all signals

TABLE 1-2 Comprehension Signals	
Positive Signals	**Negative Signals**
Everything seems to fit and make sense; ideas flow logically from one to another.	Some pieces do not seem to belong; the ideas do not fit together or make sense.
You are able to understand what the author is saying.	You feel as if you are struggling to stay with the author.
You can see where the author is leading.	You cannot think ahead or predict what will come next.
You are able to make connections among ideas.	You are unable to see how ideas connect.
You read at a regular, comfortable pace.	You often slow down or lose your place.
You understand why the material was assigned.	You do not know why the material was assigned and cannot explain why it is important.
You can understand the material after reading it once.	You need to reread sentences or paragraphs frequently.
You recognize most words or can figure them out from context.	Many words are unfamiliar.
You can express the key ideas in your own words.	You must reread and use the author's language to explain an idea.
You feel comfortable with the topic; you have some background knowledge.	The topic is unfamiliar; you know nothing about it.

appear at the same time, and not all signals work for everyone. As you study the list, identify those positive signals you sensed as you read Paragraph 1 on hooking up. Then identify those negative signals that you sensed when reading about diluted earnings per share.

Once you are able to recognize negative signals while reading, the next step is to take action to correct the problem. Specific techniques are given on page 20 in the section "Working on Strengthening Your Comprehension."

EXERCISE　**1-7**　## Monitoring Your Comprehension

Directions: Read the following excerpt from a geography textbook about environmental disturbance and disease. It is intended to be difficult, so do not be discouraged. As you read, monitor your comprehension. After reading, answer the questions that follow.

Human alteration of the environment can create breeding grounds for new viruses and increase the number of pathways viruses can take to new populations. As new human settlements put pressure on surrounding habitats, humans come into contact with unfamiliar species that may carry disease capable of jumping to human hosts. Settlers who clear forests often reduce the natural food sources used by forest mammals, which invade the new houses looking to eat. An outbreak of hantavirus occurred in the United States in 1993, when hungry rodents, driven into human settlements by rising waters, left droppings in Arizona kitchens. "Manmade malaria" occurs frequently around irrigation systems that contain large pools of standing water in open fields—ideal mosquito breeding grounds. Even simple deforestation at the edge of a city removes the canopy that normally reduces mosquito activity while leaving behind pockmarked land that fills with water. Dengue fever and Japanese encephalitis also spread through irrigation practices in mosquito habitats. Confined animal breeding, such as pig farms and poultry pens, is under intense scrutiny as the possible cauldron of recent viral outbreaks, including SARS and H1N1. Travel, of course, effectively introduces viruses and fresh hosts who may lack the locals' resistance, shuttling disease around the world. One of the worst scenarios for public health is a highly contagious infection entering the global air transportation network. Humans no longer benefit from relative isolation and the disease barrier of distance.

Large-scale environmental alteration is likely to change the opportunities for old and new diseases to appear. Climate change is increasing the portion of Earth that is hospitable to disease-carrying insects. Mosquitoes are already appearing at previously cooler higher latitudes and higher elevations. These changes may produce more infectious disease such as diarrhea. Climate change may also affect crop production leading to malnutrition, a health problem by itself, which also limits humans' ability to fight off infections. Heart and respiratory diseases may increase due to increased ground-level ozone. Human environmental alteration may, on the other hand, eliminate a pathogen's habitat, eradicate the pathogen, and prevent future epidemics. For example, the completion of Egypt's Aswan Dam in 1971 destroyed the floodwater habitat of the *Aedes aegypti* mosquitoes, carriers of Rift Valley fever virus. By 1980, Rift Valley fever had virtually disappeared from Egypt, although the dam provided an aquatic environment that spread Schistosomiasis.

Because environmental changes are highly localized in their effects, it is impossible to make accurate predictions about what will happen where. Some regions may experience relative relief from some disease burdens but many regions will experience a shift to new, unfamiliar, disease. Vulnerable populations, especially those with weak health systems, will have a difficult time coping with these unanticipated changes.

—Dahlman, Renwick, and Bergman, *Introduction to Geography*, p. 175

1. How would you rate your overall comprehension? What positive signals did you sense? Did you feel any negative signals? _____

2. Test the accuracy of your rating in Question 1 by answering the following questions based on the material read.

   a. Explain how changing human settlements can cause disease. _____
   _____
   _____

   b. How does travel increase disease? _____
   _____

   c. In what ways does climate affect disease? _____
   _____
   _____
   _____

   d. Describe how changes to the environment caused by humans can reduce disease. _____
   _____

3. In which sections was your comprehension strongest? _____

4. Did you feel at any time that you had lost, or were about to lose, comprehension? If so, go back to that paragraph now. What made that paragraph difficult to read?
   _____

5. Underline any difficult words that interfered with your comprehension.
   _____

Working on Strengthening Your Comprehension

When you realize your comprehension is not as strong as needed, be sure to approach the reading task positively and take action right away.

Positive Approaches to Reading

1. **Stick with a reading assignment.** If an assignment is troublesome, experiment with different methods of completing it. Consider highlighting, outlining, testing yourself, preparing vocabulary cards, or drawing diagrams, for example. You will learn these methods in later chapters.

2. **Plan on spending time.** Reading is not something you can rush through. The time you invest will pay off in increased comprehension.

TABLE 1-3   How to Improve Your Comprehension

Problems	Strategies
Your concentration is poor.	1. Take limited breaks. 2. Tackle difficult material when your mind is fresh and alert. 3. Choose an appropriate place to study. 4. Focus your attention.
Words are difficult or unfamiliar.	1. Use context and analyze word parts (see Chapters 4 and 5). 2. Skim through material before reading. Mark and look up meanings of difficult words. Jot meanings in the margin. 3. Refer to the vocabulary preview list, footnotes, or glossary.
Sentences are long or confusing.	1. Read aloud. 2. Locate the key idea(s). 3. Check difficult words. 4. Express each sentence in your own words.
Ideas are hard to understand, complicated.	1. Rephrase or explain each in your own words. 2. Make notes. 3. Locate a more basic text that explains ideas in simpler form. 4. Study with a classmate; discuss difficult ideas.
Ideas are new and unfamiliar; you have little or no knowledge about the topic, and the writer assumes you do.	1. Make sure you didn't miss or skip introductory information. 2. Get background information by referring to a. an earlier section or chapter in the book. b. an encyclopedia. c. a more basic text. d. a reliable online resource
The material seems disorganized or poorly organized.	1. Pay more attention to headings. 2. Read the summary, if available. 3. Try to discover organization by writing an outline or drawing a map as you read (see Chapter 3).
You do not know what is and is not important.	1. Preview. 2. Ask and answer guide questions. 3. Locate and underline topic sentences (see Chapter 6).

3. **Actively search for key ideas as you read.** Try to connect these ideas with what your instructor is discussing in class. Think of reading as a way of sifting and sorting out what you need to learn from the less important information.

4. **Think of reading as a way of unlocking the writer's message to you, the reader.** Look for clues about the writer's personality, attitudes, opinions, and beliefs. This will put you in touch with the writer as a person and help you understand his or her message. Part Four of this text offers valuable suggestions.

Overcoming Incomplete Comprehension   At times, you will realize that your comprehension is poor or incomplete. When this occurs, take immediate action. Identify as specifically as possible the cause of the problem. Do this by answering the question "Why is this not making sense?" Determine whether it is difficult words, complex ideas, organization, or your lack of concentration that is bothering you. Next, make changes in your reading to correct or compensate for the problem. Table 1-3 on the previous page lists common problems and offers strategies to correct them.

EXERCISE **1-8**   **Monitoring Your Comprehension**

Directions: Read each of the following difficult paragraphs, monitoring your comprehension as you do so. After reading each passage, identify and describe any problems you experienced. Then indicate what strategies you would use to correct them.

A.   How are motives identified? How are they measured? How do researchers know which motives are responsible for certain kinds of behavior? These are difficult questions to answer because motives are hypothetical constructs—that is, they cannot be seen or touched, handled, smelled, or otherwise tangibly observed. For this reason, no single measurement method can be considered a reliable index. Instead, researchers usually rely on a combination of research techniques to try to establish the presence and/or the strength of various motives. By combining a variety of research methods—including responses to questionnaires or surveys' data (i.e., self-reports of opinions and behaviors), and insights from focus group sessions and in-depth interviews (i.e., to discover underlying motives)—consumer researchers achieve more valid insights into consumer motivations than they would by using any one technique alone.

—Schiffman, Kanuk, and Wisenblit, *Consumer Behavior*, p. 106

Problem: _____

Strategies: _____

B.   According to the **biological species concept**, a species is defined as a group of individuals that, in nature, can interbreed and produce fertile offspring but cannot reproduce with members of other species. In practice, this definition can be difficult to apply. For example, species that reproduce asexually (such as most bacteria) and species known only via fossils do not easily fit into this species concept. However, the biological species concept does help us understand why species are distinct from each other.

—Belk and Maier, *Biology*, p. 277

Problem: _____

Strategies: _____

C.   A surprising use for elastomers is in paints and other coatings. The substance in a paint that hardens to form a continuous surface coating, often called the *binder*, or resin, is a polymer, usually an elastomer. Paint made with elastomers is resistant to cracking. Various kinds of polymers can be used as binders, depending on the specific qualities desired in the paint. Latex paints, which have polymer particles dispersed in water, and thus avoiding the use of organic solvents, are most common. Brushes and rollers are easily cleaned in soap and water. This replacement of the hazardous organic solvents historically used in paints with water is a good example of green chemistry.

—Hill, McCreary, and Kolb, *Chemistry for Changing Times*, p. 278

Problem: _____

Strategies: _____

LEARNING STYLE TIPS

If you are a(n) . . .	Then improve your comprehension by . . .
Auditory learner	Reading aloud
Visual learner	Visualizing paragraph organization
Applied learner	Thinking of real-life situations that illustrate ideas in the passage
Conceptual learner	Asking questions

EXERCISE **1-9**   **Analyzing Difficult Readings**

Directions: Bring to class a difficult paragraph or brief excerpt. Working in groups, each student should read each piece, and then, together, members should (1) discuss why each piece was difficult and (2) compare the negative and positive signals they received while reading them (refer to Table 1-2). Each student should then select strategies to overcome the difficulties he or she experienced.

READ AND THINK VISUALLY

5 LEARNING GOAL
Read and think visually

Visuals are important in today's world, since Web sites, textbooks, television, and even academic journals contain more graphics than ever before. Visuals include graphics (such as charts, maps, and graphs) and photographs, as well as text that is made more visually appealing by using color, symbols, and design. You will see visuals in every chapter of this text and in most full-length readings. You will learn about visuals in detail in Chapter 2.

The Importance of Visuals

Authors use visuals because they can convey a lot of information in a small amount of space. Visuals are important for you because they are time-savers, allowing you to grasp main ideas, implied main ideas, and details very quickly. Because your brain stores visuals differently, they may be easier to retrieve, as well.

Reading and Analyzing Visuals

When reading any type of visual, be sure to do the following:

- **Read the title or caption.** Often the caption or title identifies its subject.
- **Read any accompanying text.** The corresponding text often explains what the author wants the reader to notice.
- **Identify its main point.** What is the visual trying to explain, show, or illustrate?
- **Identify its purpose.** Determine why it was included.

EXERCISE **1-10**   **Examining a Visual**

Directions: Look at the graphic from a sociology book on the next page, and answer the following questions:

1. What is the first thing you notice when you see this visual?
2. Without reading a single word in the graphic, what do you think it is going to be about?

3. By looking at the graphic, what do you think the textbook chapter in which it was included is about?

4. Carefully examine the graphic. About how many facts do you think are contained in this graphic? Is it more effective to see all of this information in a visual form than to read a long paragraph or textbook section listing all of these facts? Why or why not?

5. This graphic allows you to make numerous comparisons. List as many as you can find.

The Gender Income Gap by Level of Education in 2013

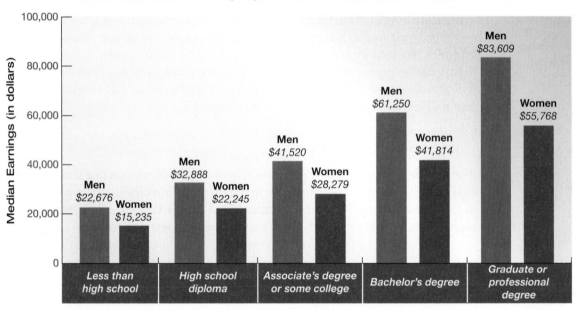

Source: U.S. Census Bureau, 2009–2013 5-Year American Community Survey

USE WRITING TO LEARN

6 LEARNING GOAL

Use writing to learn

Do you read with a pen or pencil in hand? Do you write notes in the margin of your textbook and take notes while your instructors lecture? If so, you have already discovered that writing is one of the best ways to learn. Taking notes as you read makes the process more active. The act of writing out key points and important vocabulary helps cement the information in your brain. It also develops your writing skills, which are valuable in all careers.

Working with Writing Exercises and Assignments

Some students don't like to write because they feel their command of grammar and spelling is not perfect. But grammar is easily learned, and reference tools (such as dictionaries) can help you check your spelling. If you are using a computer program such as Word to write, you can use the program's spell-check and grammar-check features to help you analyze your mistakes and correct them.

Remember that good writing is as much about *ideas* as it is about grammar. Writing exercises and assignments are designed to help you work with information and think deeply about the material.

The following tips can help you approach writing exercises and assignments in the right frame of mind:

Tips for Doing Well on Writing Assignments

1. **Do the reading before working on the writing assignment.** Do not attempt to answer questions until you have completed the reading assignment!

2. **Take notes while reading.** Underline key points and take notes in the margin. Doing so will help you focus on the reading and retain the information. For specific note-taking skills, see Chapter 3, "Organizing and Remembering Information."

3. **Read the writing assignment carefully.** Most writing assignments or questions ask for specific information. If you read the question too quickly, you may not provide the correct answer.

4. **Answer the question with specific information and examples.** The key to good writing is making a point and then supporting it with examples.

5. **Determine the correct length of the answer/response.** Students sometimes write everything they know instead of just the answer to the question. Not all answers require a paragraph or essay; sometimes one sentence is enough.

6. **In writing assignments, "Yes" or "No" is not a complete answer.** Some writing exercises will ask you a "yes or no" or "agree or disagree" question. It is important to include the *reasons* for your answer because the assignment is really asking you how you arrived at your opinion.

7. **Write complete sentences.** On most writing assignments and essay exams, it is important to write in complete sentences. Examine the question to determine when it is acceptable to provide a briefer answer. For example, fill-in-the-blank questions usually require you to write only key words or phrases, not whole sentences.

EXERCISE **1-11**   **Analyzing Exam Questions**

Directions: For each of the essay exam/writing questions that follow, determine whether the best answer would be a single sentence, a paragraph, or a complete essay.

1. Define the term *monopoly* as it is used by economists. _____

2. Compare and contrast the work of William Thackeray and Charles Dickens, making specific reference to at least two books by each novelist. _____

3. Do you agree with the idea of decriminalizing marijuana use in the United States? Why or why not? _____

4. List four of Freud's defense mechanisms, providing a definition of each.

   _____

5. Provide a brief summary of the public reception to Pablo Picasso's famous painting *Guernica.* _____

6. What is the difference between fiction and nonfiction? _____

An Introduction to Summarizing

A **summary** is a brief review of the major idea(s) of something you have read. Its purpose is to record the reading's most important ideas in a condensed form.

Summarizing is an extremely valuable skill because it forces you to identify a reading's key points. It is quite helpful in many college writing situations, such as

- answering essay questions on exams
- reviewing a film
- recording the results of a lab experiment
- summarizing the plot (main events) of a short story

Understanding how to write a good summary requires an understanding of main ideas (Chapter 6) and details (Chapter 7). Complete directions for summary writing are provided in Chapter 3, "Organizing and Remembering Information."

Every chapter in this text includes a summary writing exercise. In early chapters, the summaries are provided in a fill-in-the-blank format that asks you to fill in missing words. In later chapters, you'll be writing complete sentences and more complete summaries.

Here is a reading passage, followed by a sample summary.

On Visiting an Art Museum

It is a mistake to enter a museum with the belief that you should like everything you see—or even that you should see everything that is there. Without selective viewing, the visitor to a large museum is likely to come down with a severe case of museum exhaustion.

It makes sense to approach an art museum the way a seasoned traveler approaches a city for a first visit: Find out what there is to see. In the museum, inquire about the schedule of special shows, then see those exhibitions and out-standing works that interest you.

If you are visiting without a specific exhibition in mind, follow your interests and instincts. Browsing can be highly rewarding. Zero in on what you feel are the high-lights, savoring favorite works and unexpected discoveries.

Don't stay too long. Take breaks. Perhaps there is a garden or café in which you can pause for a rest. The quality of your experience is not measured by the amount of time you spend in the galleries or how many works you see. The most rewarding experiences can come from finding something that "speaks" to you, then sitting and enjoying it in leisurely contemplation.

—adapted from Frank, *Prebles' Artforms*, p. 100

Summary

When you are visiting an art museum, you should practice selective viewing. Find out what the museum has to offer. Decide what special exhibitions and outstanding works appeal to you. Follow your instincts and focus on the highlights. Don't stay too long, and take breaks. Find art that speaks to you and take time to enjoy it.

Note that the summary goes one step beyond recording what the writers say. It pulls together the writers' ideas by condensing and grouping them together.

EXERCISE **1-12** **Writing a Summary**

Directions: Read the passage, and then complete the summary that follows.

What can you do if you have trouble sleeping? Several techniques may help. Restrict your sleeping hours to the same nightly pattern. Avoid sleeping late in the morning, napping longer than an hour, or going to bed earlier than usual, all of which will throw off your schedule, creating even more sleep difficulties. Use your bed only for sleep (don't read or watch TV in bed). Avoid ingesting substances with stimulant properties. Don't smoke cigarettes or drink beverages with alcohol or caffeine in the evening. Alcohol may cause initial drowsiness, but it has a "rebound effect" that leaves many people wide awake in the middle of the night. Don't drink water close to bedtime; getting up to use the bathroom can lead to poor sleep. Consider meditation or progressive muscle relaxation. Either technique can be helpful, if used regularly.

—adapted from Kosslyn and Rosenberg, *Fundamentals of Psychology*, pp. 368–369

Summary

To get a good night's sleep, go to bed at the same _____ every night and get up at the same time every _____. Don't do anything in your bed except _____. Don't smoke or drink beverages with _____ or _____ in the evening, and don't drink _____ before bedtime. Try _____ or progressive muscle relaxation.

LEARN FROM AND WITH OTHER STUDENTS

7 LEARNING GOAL

Learn from and with other students

Many college assignments and activities involve working with a partner or small group of classmates. For example, a sociology professor might divide the class into groups and ask each group to brainstorm solutions to the economic or social problems of recent immigrants. Group presentations may be required in a business course, or groups in your American history class might be asked to research and present a topic.

The Value of Working with Classmates

Group, or **collaborative,** projects are designed to help students learn from one another. Consider the benefits of group projects:

- They help you meet other students.
- They allow you to develop your thinking processes by evaluating the contributions of the group's members.
- They take advantage of your strengths while helping you compensate for your weaknesses. For example, if you are not good with numbers, you can ask one of your group members for help.
- They bring a variety of perspectives to the task. Multiple perspectives provide a deeper, richer understanding of the course content.
- They encourage you to develop interpersonal communication skills that will be valuable in your chosen career.
- They can motivate you to study and stay focused.
- They can lower your workload on a given project.
- They can help you prepare for exams.

In short, group projects are excellent learning opportunities. Throughout this text you will notice that some exercises are labeled "Working Together." These are intended to give you experience working with classmates. Look for this icon:

Tips for Working with Classmates

Some students are reluctant to work in groups. They are shy, or they dislike having their grade depend on the performance of others. Use the following suggestions to help your group function effectively.

How to Work Effectively as a Group

1. **Select alert, energetic classmates** if you are permitted to choose group members.

2. **Create a roster of group members with all contact information** (phone, e-mail, etc.). Get to know your group members. It is always easier to work together when you know something about your collaborators.

3. **Approach each activity seriously.** Save joking and socializing until the group work has been completed.

4. **Be an active, responsible participant.** Accept your share of the work and ask others to do the same.

5. **Choose a leader who will keep the group focused.** The leader should direct the group in analyzing the assignment, organizing a plan of action, distributing the assignments, and establishing deadlines.

6. **Take advantage of individual strengths.** For instance, a person who has strong organizational skills might be assigned the task of recording the group's findings. A person with strong communication skills might be chosen to present group results to the class.

7. **Treat others as you would like to be treated.** Offer praise when it is deserved. Listen to others, but be willing to disagree with them if doing so is in the group's best interests.

8. **If the group is not functioning effectively or if one or more members are not doing their share, take action quickly.** Table 1-4 on the next page lists a few common complaints about working with others in groups and possible solutions for each.

TABLE 1-4   Improving Group Dynamics

If a Group Member . . .	You Might Want to Say . . .
Hasn't begun the work he or she has been assigned	"You've been given a difficult part of the project. How can we help you get started?"
Complains about the workload	"We all seem to have the same amount of work to do. Is there some way we might lessen your workload?"
Seems confused about the assignment	"This is an especially complicated assignment. Would it be useful to summarize each member's job?"
Is uncommunicative and doesn't share information	"Since we are all working from different angles, let's each make an outline of what we've done so far, so we can plan how to proceed from here."
Misses meetings	"To ensure that we all meet regularly, would it be helpful if I texted everyone the night before to confirm the day and time?"
Seems to be making you or other members do all the work	Make up a chart before the meeting with each member's responsibilities. Give each member a copy and ask, "Is there any part of your assignment that you have questions or concerns about? Would anyone like to change his or her completion date?" Be sure to get an answer from each member.

EXERCISE 1-13   Analyzing a Group Project

Working Together

Directions: Imagine that your psychology instructor has assigned a group project on the elderly in America. You must choose two classmates to be part of your group. The project has three components: (1) Read a chapter from the textbook and prepare a brief, written overview of the problems facing the elderly, (2) Interview three people over age 80 and provide transcripts of those interviews, and (3) Prepare a multimedia presentation of photographs, music, and video to accompany your presentation.

1. Which of these three tasks best suits you? Which task suits you least?

2. Take a show of hands. Ask students who are interested in component 1 to raise their hands: then do the same for components 2 and 3. Based on the results, everyone in class should choose two teammates.

3. With your teammates, discuss why you have chosen your specific activity. Did your choice have anything to do with your learning style(s)? Why did you *not* choose the other two activities?

SELF-TEST SUMMARY

1 **What is expected of you in college?**	You are expected to take control of your learning by reading and studying effectively and efficiently.
2 **What can you do to build your concentration?**	Building concentration involves two steps: 1. Control your surroundings by wisely choosing your time and place of study and avoiding distractions. 2. Focus your attention on the assignment by setting goals and rewarding yourself for achieving them by working in planned, small time blocks with frequent breaks, and by getting actively involved in the assignment.
3 **What is learning style and how can knowing your learning style make you a better student?**	Learning style refers to your profile of relative strengths as a learner. Its five components are 1. auditory or visual learner 2. applied or conceptual learner 3. spatial or verbal learner 4. social or independent learner 5. creative or pragmatic learner Discovering what type of learner you are can help you determine what strategies work best for you in reading and studying. It will also help you to recognize your limitations so that you can work on overcoming them.
4 **How can you monitor and strengthen your comprehension?**	Pay attention to whether you sense positive or negative signals while reading. If you sense poor or incomplete comprehension, take immediate action to identify the source of the problem. Determine whether lack of concentration, difficult words, complex ideas, or confusing organization is causing the problem.
5 **What steps should you take when reading a visual?**	First read the title. Next, read any text that accompanies it, which may explain it. Identify the main point of the visual and identify its purpose.

(Continued)

6 What is the purpose of writing a summary when learning new material?	Writing a summary allows you to record the reading's most important ideas in a condensed form, so you will be able to remember them.
7 What are the benefits of working in groups?	Working in groups can • help you meet fellow students • develop your thinking processes by evaluating contributions from the group • bolster your strengths and compensate for your weaknesses. • offer multiple perspectives • develop interpersonal skills • keep you focused • reduce your workload

GOING  ONLINE

1. **Learning Styles Questionnaires**

   Do an Internet search to locate several other learning style questionnaires. Choose one and complete it. Compare your results with those from the assessment in this text. How do online tests differ from those on paper? Which do you prefer? Is your answer a result of your learning style?

2. **Exploring Campus Resources**

   Visit your college's Web site and look for the page titled "Student Life" or "Student Resources." What types of services does your college offer to students? Which of these might help you with your studies and with juggling the demands of school, work, and family?

3. **Managing Your Time**

   Some students like to keep track of their schedules in a paper notebook, while others prefer electronic apps. Conduct a Web search for "time management apps" and download one of your choice. Use it for a week and prepare a report listing its features and benefits. How might it be improved? Would you recommend this app or not? Why? Share your thoughts with the class.

4. **Using Collaborative Online Tools**

   The Web offers many free applications that allow online collaboration. (Some collaboration applications may also be found on the home page of online courses.) Conduct a Web search for applications that can help you collaborate with your classmates. Which of these seem to be the most useful? Share your recommendations with the class.

Assessment Reading Selection

This reading and the questions that follow are intended to help you assess your current level of skill. Read the article and then answer the questions that measure your comprehension. You may refer back to the reading in order to answer them.

The Allure of Disaster

Eric G. Wilson

In this article, which originally appeared in *Psychology Today*, the author discusses why we are drawn to disasters.

> **Vocabulary Preview**
> **unbridgeable** (par. 1) impossible to cross or span
> **unaccountably** (par. 2) without explanation
> **morbid** (par. 6) gruesome
> **sordid** (par. 6) distasteful
> **macabre** (par. 7) suggesting death and decay
> **propensity** (par. 7) tendency, inclination
> **foments** (par. 9) promotes
> **coalesced** (par. 14) began to form

1   STOP STARING. I bet you heard this more than once growing up. This command, after all, marks the unbridgeable gap between the impulsiveness of the child, who gawks at whatever seizes his attention, and the adult's social awareness, based on a fear of giving offense.

2   The auto mechanic has a huge mole on his nose. There's a woman crying unaccountably in the supermarket aisle. The little boy looks and looks, while the mother pulls him away, scolding all the while.

3   Most children eventually get the point and quit their gaping. For good reason: Although we're tempted to gaze at the car wreck on the side of the highway, suffering is involved.

4   But let's be honest. We're running late for work. We hit a traffic jam. We creep angrily ahead, inch by inch, until we finally see the source of the slow-down: an accident. As we near the scene, we realize that the highway's been cleared. The dented cars are on the shoulder. This is just an onlooker delay, rubberneckers braking to stare.

5   We silently judge all those seekers of sick thrills—for making us late, for exploiting the misfortune of others. Surely we won't look, we tell ourselves as we pull beside the crash. Then it comes: the need to stare, like a tickle in the throat before a cough or the awful urge to sneeze. We hold it back until the last minute, then gawk for all we're worth, enjoying the experience all the more because it's frowned upon.

6   Why do we do this? Our list of morbid fascinations is longer than we'd like to admit, including disaster footage on the TV news, documentaries featuring animal attacks, sordid reality shows, funny falls on YouTube, celebrity scandals, violent movies and television shows, gruesome video games, mixed martial arts, *TMZ*, *Gawker*, and the lives of serial killers.

7   Everyone loves a good train wreck. We are enamored of ruin. Our secret and ecstatic wish: Let it all fall down. Why? Does this macabre propensity merely reflect humanity's most lurid tendencies? Or might this grimmer side produce unexpected virtues?

8   In *Killing Monsters: Why Children Need Fantasy, Superheroes and Make-Believe Violence*, Gerard Jones argues that children can benefit from exposure to fictional violence because it makes them feel powerful in a "scary, uncontrollable world." The child's fascination with mayhem has less to do with the fighting and more to do with how the action makes her feel. Children like to feel strong. Those committing violence are strong. By pretending to be these violent figures, children take on their strength and with it negotiate daily dangers.

9   Carl Jung made a similar argument for adults. He maintained that our mental health depends on our shadow, that part of our psyche that harbors our darkest energies, such as murderousness. The more we repress the morbid, the more it foments neuroses or psychoses. To achieve wholeness, we must acknowledge our most demonic inclinations.

10   Yes, I took pleasure in my enemy's tumble from grace. No, I couldn't stop watching 9/11 footage. Once we welcome these unseemly admissions as integral portions of our being, the devils turn into angels. Luke owns the Vader within, offers affection to the actual villain; off comes the scary mask, and there stands a father, loving and in need of love.

11   The gruesome brings out the generous: a strange notion. But think of the empathy that can arise from witnessing death or destruction. This emotion— possibly the grounding of all morals—is rare, but it frequently arises when we are genuinely curious about dreadful occurrences.

12   Renaissance scholars kept skulls on their desks to remind them how precious this life is. John Keats believed that the real rose, because it is dying, exudes more beauty than the porcelain one.

13   In the summer of 2010, I visited the National September 11th Memorial Museum in New York City. Photographs of the tragedy and its aftermath covered the walls. On a portable audio player, I listened to commentaries on each. After an hour of taking in the devastation, raw with sadness and wanting nothing more than to return to my wife and daughter, I stood before a picture of a clergyman praying in an eerie gray haze.

14   The man in the photo was blessing the rescue workers before their day's hellish efforts. They kneeled amidst the fog-covered wreckage, heads bowed. I hit the play button. The commentator spoke. As the search for bodies lengthened and grief and fatigue worsened; as hopes coalesced only to be immediately crushed; as firemen, bonded by their labor, grew close; as those who had lost their children and their parents, their wives and their husbands, realized the depth of their affection—as all of this was transpiring—this horrific terrain had turned into "holy ground."

15   At that moment, I understood the terrible logic of suffering: When we agonize over what has cruelly been taken from us, we love it more, and know it better, than when we were near it. Affliction can reveal what is most sacred in our lives, essential to our joy. Water, Emily Dickinson writes, is "taught by thirst."

16   Staring at macabre occurrences can lead to mere insensitivity—gawking for a cheap thrill—or it can result in stunned trauma, muteness before the horror. But in between these two extremes, morbid curiosity can sometimes inspire us to imagine ways to transform life's necessary darkness into luminous vision. Go ahead. Stare. Take a picture. It will last longer.

Mastery Test Skills Check

Checking Your Comprehension

_____ 1. The main point of this selection is that
   a. terrible events can help make us better people.
   b. children control their emotions better than adults.
   c. clergy can explain disasters to people.
   d. people should not look at car wrecks.

_____ 2. According to the author, adults enjoying gawking because they know
   a. it sets a bad example for children.
   b. they shouldn't.
   c. they will have nightmares.
   d. it distracts the police.

_____ 3. When we come upon a car accident, the author says we
   a. fear for our safety.
   b. look away.
   c. can't help but look.
   d. worry about the people in the crash.

_____ 4. The word *enamored* (par. 7) means
   a. compared.
   b. fascinated.
   c. puzzled.
   d. comforted.

_____ 5. Gerard Jones says children benefit from exposure to fictional violence because it
   a. helps them feel powerful in an uncontrollable world.
   b. teaches them what not to do.
   c. allows them to break the rules.
   d. shows them there are good people nearby.

_____ 6. Carl Jung believed that to achieve wholeness we must
   a. spend years praying.
   b. reject our morbid thoughts.
   c. pretend there is no evil.
   d. acknowledge our dark side.

_____ 7. Renaissance scholars keep skulls on their desks to remind themselves
   a. that the brain is the most important organ.
   b. of how precious life is.
   c. that we are all alike.
   d. of the past.

_____ 8. The photo the author saw at the 9/11 memorial depicted
   a. a clergyman praying.
   b. medics helping people.

   c. what the towers looked like before they fell.
   d. plans for the new tower.

_____ 9. The word *portable* in paragraph 13 means
   a. numbered carefully.
   b. repaired quickly.
   c. carried by hand.
   d. invented long ago.

_____ 10. The main point of paragraph 14 is that
   a. a horrific event changed how people thought and felt.
   b. the rescue workers were successful.
   c. the clergyman had given up hope.
   d. disasters make us lose faith.

For more practice, ask your instructor for an opportunity to work on the mastery tests that appear in the Test Bank.

An Overview of College Textbook Reading

Focusing on . . . College Textbooks

LEARNING GOALS

This chapter will show you how to

1 Use textbooks as learning tools

2 Preview and activate background knowledge before reading

3 Develop questions to guide your reading

4 Read for meaning and test your recall as you read

5 Read to understand graphics and visual aids

6 Review after reading

7 Use the SQ3R system

T he visual shows stacks of textbooks used in an introductory economics course. Most introductory college textbook chapters include a list of learning objectives, a photograph, an introduction to what you will learn in the chapter, and a link to an online study lab. In this chapter you will learn how to get the most out of your textbooks.

College economics texts are filled with detailed information to help students gain a better understanding of the economy around them. If this were your textbook for your economics course, how would you read this chapter? How would you know what to learn? How would you go about learning it all?

This chapter is designed to help you answer these questions. It will show you what features textbook chapters commonly contain to help you learn. It will explain what to do before you read, while you read, and after you read. These before, during, and after strategies lead to a tested and proven reading method—the SQ3R system.

TEXTBOOKS AS LEARNING TOOLS

LEARNING GOAL
Use textbooks as learning tools

While textbooks may seem to be long and impersonal, they are actually carefully crafted teaching and learning systems. They are designed to work with your instructor's lecture to provide you with reliable and accurate information and to help you practice your skills.

Why Buy and Study Textbooks?

Did you know the following?

- **Nearly all textbook authors are college teachers.** They work with students daily and understand students' needs.
- **Along with your instructor, your textbook is the single best source of information for the subject you are studying.**
- **The average textbook costs only about $10–15 a week.** For the price of a movie ticket, you are getting a complete learning system that includes not only a textbook but also a companion Web site, online course management system, and other study materials.
- **Your textbook can be a valuable reference tool in your profession.** For example, many nursing majors keep their textbooks and refer to them often when they begin their career.

Textbooks are an investment in your education and in your future. A textbook is your ally—your partner in learning.

Using Textbook Organization to Your Advantage

Have you ever walked into an unfamiliar supermarket and felt lost? How did you finally find what you needed? Most likely, you looked for the signs hanging over the aisles indicating the types of products shelved in each section. Walking along the aisle, you no doubt found that similar products were grouped together. For example, all the cereal was in one place, all the meat was in another, and so forth.

You can easily feel lost or intimidated when beginning to read a textbook chapter, too. It may seem like a huge collection of unrelated facts, ideas, and numbers that have to be memorized. Actually, a textbook chapter is much like a supermarket. It, too, has signs that identify what is located in each section. These signs are the major **headings** that divide the chapter into topics. Underneath each heading, similar ideas are grouped together, just as similar products are grouped together in a supermarket aisle. In most cases, several paragraphs come under each heading.

Sometimes headings are further divided into **subheadings** (usually set in smaller type than the main heading, indented, or set in a different color). Using headings and subheadings, chapters take a major idea, break it into its important parts, and then break those parts into smaller parts, so you can learn the material one step a time.

A typical textbook chapter might have an organization that looks like the below diagram.

Notice that this diagram shows a chapter divided into four major headings, and the first major heading is divided into four subheadings. The number of major headings and subheadings will vary from chapter to chapter in a book.

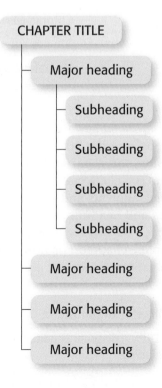

Once you know how a chapter is organized, you will see how ideas are connected. Look at the following partial list of headings and subheadings from a chapter of a sociology textbook.

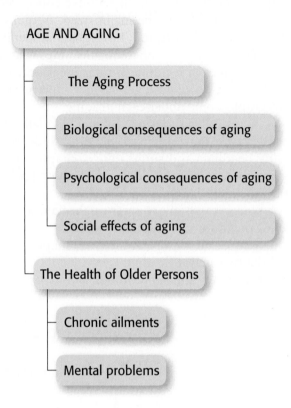

In this chapter on age and aging, "The Aging Process" and "The Health of Older Persons" are the first two major topics. The topic "The Aging Process" is broken into three parts: biological consequences, psychological consequences, and social effects. "The Health of Older Persons" is divided into two parts: chronic ailments and mental problems.

The titles and headings, taken together, form a brief outline of a chapter. In Chapter 3, you will see how these headings can help you create an outline of the complete chapter. For now, think of headings as guides that direct you through a chapter one step at a time.

EXERCISE **2-1**   **Analyzing Chapter Organization**

Directions: Draw a diagram of headings and subheadings for this chapter of *Guide to College Reading*.

EXERCISE 2-2   Drawing an Organizational Diagram

Directions: Choose a textbook that you are using for another course. Select a chapter you have already read. On a separate sheet of paper, draw an organizational diagram of its contents. Use the diagram on page 39 as a guide.

Textbook Learning Aids and How to Use Them

Textbooks contain numerous features to help you learn. Features vary from book to book and from discipline to discipline, but most textbooks contain the following:

Preface   The preface is the author's introduction to the text. It presents information you should know before you begin reading Chapter 1. It may contain such information as

- why and for whom the author wrote the text
- how the text is organized
- the purpose of the text
- references and authorities consulted
- major points of emphasis
- learning aids included and how to use them
- special features of the text
- new materials included since the book's last update

The last point is particularly important. Knowledge is not static; it is ever-changing. Textbooks must include this new information, as well as new *perspectives*, or ways of looking at the subject. As an example, for many years most of the art shown in art history textbooks was created by male artists. In the last couple of decades, however, art history textbooks have included more works by female artists.

To the Student   Some textbooks contain a section titled "To the Student." This section is written specifically for you. It contains practical information about the text. It may, for example, explain textbook features and how to use them, or it may offer suggestions for learning and studying the text.

EXERCISE 2-3   Analyzing a Preface

Directions: Use the preface to *Guide to College Reading* to answer the following questions.

1. Look at the book's content overview (p. v). In what part of the book are vocabulary skills discussed? _____ Which part of the book is devoted to developing your critical reading skills? _____

2. Name three special features of *Guide to College Reading* that are designed to enhance the text's effectiveness. (*Hint:* Look for the heading titled "Special Features.")

   _____

   _____

EXERCISE   2-4   **Analyzing "To the Student"**

Directions: Read the "To the Student" section in a textbook from one of your other courses and answer the following questions.

1. What is the purpose of the text?

   _____

   _____

2. How is the textbook organized?

   _____

   _____

3. What learning aids does the book contain? How useful have you found them?

   _____

   _____

Table of Contents   The **table of contents** is an outline of a text found at the beginning of the book. It lists all the important topics and subtopics covered. Glancing through a table of contents will give you an overview of a text and suggest its organization.

Before beginning to read a chapter, refer to the table of contents. Although chapters are intended to be separate parts of a book, it is important to see how they fit together as parts of the whole—the textbook itself.

The table of contents can be a useful study aid when preparing for exams. To review the material on which you will be tested, read through the table of contents listings for chapters covered on the exam. This review will give you a sense of which topics you are already familiar with and which topics you have yet to learn about.

EXERCISE **2-5** **Analyzing the Table of Contents**

Directions: Use the table of contents for this text to answer the following questions.

1. This text includes not only a *detailed* table of contents (p. vii) but also a *brief* table of contents (p. v). What is the difference between the two?

   _____

   _____

2. What value do you see in the brief table of contents?

   _____

   _____

3. In which chapter will you learn about topics and main ideas?

   _____

4. Name two of the writers whose work is represented in the Contemporary Issues Mini-Reader.

   _____

Opening Chapter   The first chapter of a textbook sets the stage for what is to follow. More important, it defines the discipline, explains basic principles, and introduces terminology that will be used throughout the text.

Typically, you can expect to find as many as 20 to 50 new words introduced and defined in the first chapter. These words are the language of the course, so to speak. To be successful in any new subject area, you must learn to read and speak its language. (Chapters 4 and 5 of this text will help you develop your vocabulary skills.)

EXERCISE **2-6** **Analyzing Chapter 1**

Directions: Refer to Chapter 1 of *Guide to College Reading.* List at least two techniques or features the author uses to get students involved with and interested in the material.

   _____

   _____

   _____

Typographical AIDS   Textbooks contain various **typographical aids** (arrangements or types of print) that make it easy to pick out what is important to learn and remember. These include the following:

1. **Different types of font.** Italic type (*slanted print*) and boldfaced type (**dark print**) are often used to call attention to a particular word or phrase.

> The term *drive* is used to refer to internal conditions that force an individual to work toward some goal.

   Note: **Colored print** is sometimes used to emphasize important ideas or definitions.

2. **Enumeration. Enumeration** refers to the numbering or lettering of facts and ideas within a paragraph. It is used to emphasize key ideas and make them easy to locate.

> Consumer behavior and the buying process involve five mental states: (1) awareness of the product, (2) interest in acquiring it, (3) desire or perceived need, (4) action, and (5) reaction or evaluation of the product.

3. **Listing. Bulleted lists** and **numbered lists** provide important information in a list format. (A bullet looks like this: •). These lists are typically indented, which makes them easy to find as you read and review the chapter.

> Sigmund Freud defined three parts of the human psyche:
>   1. Id
>   2. Ego
>   3. Superego

> The U.S. criminal justice system offers four alternatives to traditional bail:
>   • Release on recognizance
>   • Unsecured bond
>   • Signature bond
>   • Conditional release

EXERCISE 2-7   **Evaluating Typographical Aids**

Directions: Bring a textbook from one of your other courses to class. With a partner or in a small group, point out the typographical aids used in the book. Discuss how each can help you learn.

Chapter Exercises and Questions   Exercises and questions fall into several categories.

1. *Review questions* cover the factual content of the chapter.
   - **In-chapter review questions appear at the end of a major section.** They allow you to test your mastery of the material before you move on to the next section.
   - **End-of-chapter review questions appear at the end of the chapter.** They test your comprehension of the entire chapter.

   Here is an example of a review question from a marketing textbook:

   > - List some product characteristics that are of concern to marketers.

2. *Discussion questions* deal with interpretations of content. These are often meant to be jumping-off points for discussion in the classroom or with other students. Here is an example of a discussion question from a marketing textbook:

   > - What do you think is the future of generic products?

3. *Application questions* ask you to apply your knowledge to the world around you or to a real-life situation. Many students like these questions because they help prepare them for their chosen career. Here is a sample application question:

   > - How would you go about developing a brand name for a new type of soft drink?

4. *Critical-thinking questions* ask you to think deeply about a topic or issue. These questions require close attention and are often asked on exams. Here is a sample critical-thinking question:

   > - How is advertising good for society? How is it bad for society?

5. *Problem questions* **are usually mathematical in nature.** You are given an equation to solve, or you are given a problem in words and asked to use mathematical concepts to find the solution. Working with problems is one of the most important parts of any math, science, or technical course. Here is a sample problem:

> • If a microwave oven costs the retailer $325 and the markup is 35%, find the selling price of the microwave.

Boxes and Case Studies   Many textbooks include boxed inserts or case studies that are set off from the text. Generally, these "boxes" contain interesting information or extended examples to illustrate text concepts. Boxes are sometimes a key to what the author considers important. For example, a business textbook may contain boxes in each chapter about green (environmentally friendly) business practices. From the presence of these boxes, you can assume that the author is interested in how business practices can be changed to help preserve the environment.

Case studies usually follow the life history of a person, or the business practices of a particular company. These are valuable applications of the textbook concepts to the real world.

Vocabulary Lists   Textbooks usually contain a list of new terms introduced in each chapter. This list may appear at the beginning or end of the chapter. Sometimes they include page numbers that identify where the term is defined.

Regardless of where they appear, vocabulary lists are a valuable study aid. Here is a sample vocabulary list (sometimes called a **key terms list**) from a financial management textbook:

Key Terms

assets	liabilities
budget	money market fund

Notice that the author identifies the terms but does not define them. In such cases, mark the new terms as you come across them in the chapter. (The key terms are often printed in boldfaced type, so pay close attention whenever you see boldface.) After you have finished the chapter, review each marked item and its definition. To learn the terms, use the index card system suggested in Chapter 5 ("Resources for Learning New Words," p. 177).

EXERCISE 2-8 **Creating a List of Key Terms**

Directions: If a textbook does not contain a key terms list, you should make one of your own for each chapter. Using boldfaced terms as your guide, create a key terms list for this chapter of *Guide to College Reading*.

Chapter Summary In most textbooks, each chapter ends with a **chapter summary** that reviews all the chapter's key points. While the summary is sometimes in paragraph form, it is more often formatted as a numbered list. If you are having difficulty extracting the main points from the chapter, the summary is an excellent resource.

This text features a "Self-Test Summary" at the end of each chapter. For an example, see page 64. Note how the summary is provided in a question-and-answer format to help you quiz yourself on the concepts (which correspond to the learning goals at the start of the chapter).

Glossary Usually found at the end of the book, a **glossary** is a mini-dictionary that lists alphabetically the important vocabulary used in the book. It does not list all the common meanings of a word, as a dictionary does, but instead gives only the meaning used in the text.

Here is an excerpt from the glossary of a health textbook:

> **latent functions** unintended beneficial consequences of people's actions
>
> **leadership styles** ways in which people express their leadership
>
> —Henslin, *Sociology*, p. G4

In some textbooks, a key term is defined in the text, and the term and its definition are repeated in the margin. Many students say that a **marginal glossary** is one of the most useful textbook features.

Index Suppose you are studying for a final exam and want to review a key concept, but you can't remember where it's located in your textbook. The book's **index**, found at the end of the book, is an alphabetical listing of all the topics in the book. It includes not only key terms and concepts, but also topics, names of authors, and titles of texts or readings. Next to each entry you will find the page number(s) on which the topic is discussed.

Online Learning Aids Many textbooks contain icons that point the reader to additional online resources, such as electronic flash cards, graded chapter quizzes, videos, simulations, worked problems, and tutorials.

EXERCISE   2-9   **Evaluating Textbook Learning Aids**

Directions: With a partner or in a small group, choose a textbook from one of your other courses. Each person in the group should take turns answering the following questions and showing examples.

1. What learning aids does the book contain? Does it contain any special features not listed in this section? If so, what are they and what is their function? Which of these features do you expect to use most often?

   _____

   _____

2. Explain how you will use each learning aid to study.

   _____

   _____

3. How is the information given in the preface important?

   _____

   _____

4. Look at the opening chapter. What is its function?

   _____

   _____

5. Review the table of contents. What are its major parts?

   _____

   _____

6. What electronic learning aids accompany the text? Which do you find most useful?

   _____

   _____

BEFORE READING: PREVIEW AND ACTIVATE BACKGROUND KNOWLEDGE

2 LEARNING GOAL

Preview and activate background knowledge before reading

Would you cross a city street without checking for traffic first? Would you pay to see a movie you had never heard of and knew nothing about? Would you buy a car without test-driving it or checking its mechanical condition?

Most likely you answered "no" to these questions. Now answer a related question, one that applies to reading: Should you read an article or textbook chapter without knowing what it is about or how it is organized? You can probably guess that the answer is "no." This section explains a technique called previewing.

Previewing is a way of quickly familiarizing yourself with the organization and content of written material *before* beginning to read it. It is an easy method to use and will make a dramatic difference in how effectively you read.

How to Preview

When you preview, you try to (1) find only the most important ideas in the material, and (2) note how these ideas are organized. To preview effectively, look only at the parts that state these important ideas, and skip the rest. Previewing is a fairly rapid technique. You should take only a few minutes to preview a 15- to 20-page textbook chapter. The parts to look at in previewing a textbook chapter are listed here:

How to Preview Textbook Chapters

1. **The title and subtitle** The title is a label that tells what the chapter is about. The subtitle, if there is one, suggests how the author approaches the subject. For example, an article titled "Brazil" might be subtitled "The World's Next Superpower." In this instance, the subtitle tells which aspects of Brazil the article discusses.

2. **Chapter introduction** If it is brief, read the entire introduction to the chapter. If it is lengthy, read only the first few paragraphs.

3. **The first paragraph** The first paragraph of, or introduction to, each section of the chapter may provide an overview of the section and/or offer clues about its organization.

4. **Boldfaced headings** Headings, like titles, serve as labels and identify the topic of the material. By reading each heading, you will be reading a list of the important topics the chapter covers. Together, the headings form a mini-outline of the chapter.

5. **The first sentence under each heading** The first sentence following the heading often further explains the heading. It may also state the central thought of the entire selection. If the first sentence is purely introductory, read the second sentence, too.

(Continued)

6. **Typographical aids** Typographical aids help to highlight and organize information. These include *italics*, **boldfaced type**, marginal notes, colored ink, underlining, and enumeration (listing). A writer frequently uses typographical aids to call attention to important key words, definitions, and facts.

7. **Graphs, charts, and pictures** Graphs, charts, and pictures will point you toward the most important information. Glance at these to determine quickly what information is being emphasized or clarified.

8. **The final paragraph or summary** The final paragraph or summary will give a condensed view of the chapter and help you identify key ideas. Often, a summary outlines the chapter's key points.

9. **End-of-chapter material** Glance through any study or discussion questions, vocabulary lists, or outlines that appear at the end of the chapter. These will help you decide what in the chapter is important.

Demonstration of Previewing

The article below originally appeared in a chapter in a communications textbook. It discusses lying, how people lie, and the behavior of liars. The reading also contains a visual aid and a box. Everything that you should look at or read has been shaded. Preview this excerpt now, reading only the shaded portions.

The Process and Ethics of Lying

It comes as no surprise that some messages are truthful and some are deceptive. Although we operate in interpersonal communication on the assumption that people tell the truth, some people do lie. In fact, many view lying as common, whether in politics, business, or interpersonal relationships. Lying also begets lying; when one person lies, the likelihood of the other person lying increases. Furthermore, people like people who tell the truth more than they like people who lie. So, lying needs to be given some attention in any consideration of interpersonal communication.

Lying refers to the act of (1) sending messages (2) with the intention of giving another person information you believe to be false. (1) Lying involves sending some kind of verbal and/ or nonverbal message (and remember the absence of facial expression or the absence of verbal comment communicates); it also requires reception by another person. (2) The message must be sent to intentionally deceive. If you give false information to someone but you believe it to be true, then you haven't lied. You do lie when you send information that you believe to be untrue and you intend to mislead the other person.

VIEWPOINTS Most often people lie to gain some benefit or reward (for example, to increase desirable relationships, to protect their self-esteem, or to obtain money) or to avoid punishment. In an analysis of 322 lies, researchers found that 75.8 percent benefited the liar, 21.7 percent benefited the person who was told the lie, and 2.5 percent benefited a third party. Are lies told to benefit others less unethical than lies told to benefit yourself?

Not surprisingly, cultural differences exist with lying—in the way lying is defined and in the way lying is treated. For example, as children get older, Chinese and Taiwanese (but not Canadians) see lying about the good deeds that they do as positive (as we'd expect for cultures that emphasize modesty), but taking credit for these same good deeds is seen negatively. Some cultures consider lying to be more important than others—in one study, for example, European Americans considered lies less negatively than did Ecuadorians. Both, however, felt that lying to an out-group member was more acceptable than lying to an in-group member.

How People Lie

As you can imagine people lie in various ways:

- **Exaggeration.** Here you lead people to believe that, for example, you earn more money than you do or that your grades are better than they are, or that your relationship is more satisfying than it really is.
- **Minimization.** Instead of exaggerating the facts, here you minimize them. You can minimize your lack of money (we have more than enough), the importance of poor grades, or your relationship dissatisfaction.
- **Substitution.** In this method you exchange the truth for a lie—for example, *I wasn't at the bar, I stopped in at Starbucks for coffee.*
- **Equivocation.** When you equivocate, your message is sufficiently ambiguous to lead people to think something different from your intention. *That outfit really is something, very interesting* instead of *Ugh!*

- **Omission.** And of course you can lie by not sending certain messages. So, when your romantic partner asks where you were last night, you might omit those things your partner would frown on and just include the positives.

The Behavior of Liars

One of the more interesting questions about lying is how do liars act. Do they act differently from those telling the truth? And, if they do act differently, how can we tell when someone is lying to us? These questions are not easy to answer and we are far from having complete answers to such questions. But, we have learned a great deal.

For example, after an examination of 120 research studies, the following behaviors were found to most often accompany lying:

- **Liars hold back.** They speak more slowly (perhaps to monitor what they're saying), take longer to respond to questions (again, perhaps monitoring their messages), and generally give less information and elaboration.
- **Liars make less sense.** Liars' messages contain more discrepancies; more inconsistencies.
- **Liars give a more negative impression.** Generally, liars are seen as less willing to be cooperative, smile less than truth-tellers, and are more defensive.
- **Liars are tense.** The tension may be revealed by their higher pitched voices and excessive body movements.

It's very difficult to detect when a person is lying and when telling the truth. The hundreds of research studies conducted on this topic find that in most instances people judge lying accurately in less than 60 percent of the cases—only slightly better than chance. And there is some evidence to show that lie detection is even more difficult (that is, less accurate) in long-standing romantic relationships—the very relationships in which the most significant lying occurs.

Ethics in Interpersonal Communication

LYING

Not surprisingly, lies have ethical implications. In fact, one of the earliest cultural rules children are taught is that lying is wrong. At the same time, children also learn that in some cases lying is effective—in gaining some reward or in avoiding some punishment.

Some lies are considered ethical (for example, publicly agreeing with someone you really disagree with to enable the person to save face, saying that someone will get well despite medical evidence to the contrary, or simply bragging about your accomplishments). Some lies are considered not only ethical but required (for example, lying to protect someone from harm or telling the proud parents that their child is beautiful). Other lies (largely those in the anti-social category) are considered unethical (for example, lying to defraud investors or to falsely accuse someone).

However, a large group of lies are not that easy to classify as ethical or unethical, as you'll see in the Ethical Choice Points.

Ethical Choice Points

Is it ethical to lie to get what you deserved but couldn't get any other way? For example, would you lie to get a well-earned promotion or raise? Would it matter if you hurt a colleague's chances of advancement in the process?

Is it ethical to lie to your relationship partner to avoid a conflict and perhaps splitting up? In this situation, would it be ethical to lie if the issue was a minor one (you were late for an appointment because you wanted to see the end of the football game) or a major one (say, continued infidelity)?

Is it ethical to lie to get yourself out of an unpleasant situation? For example, would you lie to get out of an unwanted date, an extra office chore, or a boring conversation?

Lie detection is so difficult in close relationships because the liar knows how to lie largely because he or she knows how you think and can therefore tailor lies that you'll fall for. And, of course, the liar often has considerable time to rehearse the lie, which generally makes lying more effective (that is, less easy to detect).

Nevertheless, there are some communication factors that seem to be more often associated with lying. None of these, taken alone or in a group, is proof that a person is lying. Liars can be especially adept at learning to hide any signs that they might be lying. Nor is an absence of these features proof that the person is telling the truth. Generally, however, liars exhibit:

- greater pupil dilation and more eye blinks; more gaze aversion.
- higher vocal pitch; voices sound as if they were under stress.
- more errors and hesitations in their speech; they pause more and for longer periods of time.
- more hand, leg, and foot movements.
- more self-touching movements—for example, touching their face or hair—and more object touching—for example, playing with a coffee cup or pen.

In detecting lying, be especially careful that you formulate any conclusions with a clear understanding that you can be wrong, and that accusations of lying (especially when untrue but even when true) can often damage a relationship to the point where it's beyond repair. In addition, keep in mind all the cautions and potential errors in perception discussed earlier; after all, lie detection is a part of person perception.

—DeVito, *The Interpersonal Communication Book*, pp. 114–118

Although you may not realize it, you have gained a substantial amount of information from the minute or so that you spent previewing. You have become familiar with the key ideas in this section. To demonstrate, read each of the following statements and mark them *T* for true or *F* for false based on what you learned by previewing.

_____ 1. Some messages are deceptive, while others are truthful.

_____ 2. A main reason that people lie is to gain a benefit or reward.

_____ 3. An exaggeration is not considered a lie.

_____ 4. Liars are tense and hold back.

_____ 5. False accusations of lying can damage a relationship.

This quiz tested your recall of some of the more important ideas in the article. Check your answers by referring back to the article. Did you get most or all of the above items correct? You can see, then, that previewing acquaints you with the major ideas contained in the material before you read it.

EXERCISE 2-10   **Practicing Previewing**

Directions: Preview Chapter 6 in this text. After you have previewed it, complete the items below.

1. What is the subject of Chapter 6? _____

2. List three major topics Chapter 6 covers.
   a. _____
   b. _____
   c. _____

EXERCISE 2-11   **Previewing Your Textbooks**

Directions: Preview a chapter from one of your other textbooks. After you have previewed it, complete the items below.

1. What is the chapter title?

   _____

   _____

2. What subject does the chapter cover?

   _____

   _____

3. List some of the major topics covered.

_____

_____

Previewing Articles and Essays

Previewing works on articles and essays, as well as textbook chapters. However, you may have to make a few changes in the steps listed on pages 49–50. Here are some guidelines:

How to Preview Articles and Essays

1. **Check the author's name.** If you recognize the author's name, you may have an idea of what to expect in the article or essay. For example, you would expect humor from an article by Dave Barry but more serious material from an article written by the governor of your state.

2. **Check the source of the article.** Where was it originally published? The source may suggest something about the content or slant of the article. (For more about sources, see Chapter 10.)

3. **If there are no headings, read the first sentence of a few paragraphs throughout the essay.** These sentences will usually give you a sense of what each paragraph is about.

EXERCISE 2-12   **Previewing a Reading Selection**

Directions: Preview the reading selection that appears in Mastery Test 1 at the end of this chapter, "Looking for Love" (p. 66). Then answer the following questions.

1. What is the purpose of the article?

_____

2. Which types of dating can you recall?

_____

Discovering What You Already Know

After you have previewed an assignment, take a moment to discover what you already know about the topic. Regardless of the topic, you probably know *something* about it. We will call this your **background knowledge**. Here is an example.

A student was about to read an article titled "Growing Urban Problems" for a sociology class. At first she thought she knew very little about urban problems, since she lived in a small town. Then she began thinking about her recent trip to a nearby city. She remembered seeing homeless people and overcrowded housing. Then she recalled reading about drug problems, drive-by shootings, and muggings.

Now let us take a sample chapter from a business textbook titled *Small Business Management*. The headings are listed below. Spend a moment thinking about each one; then make a list of things you already know about each.

- Characteristics of Small Businesses
- Small-Business Administration
- Advantages and Disadvantages of Small Businesses
- Problems of Small Businesses

Discovering what you already know is useful for three important reasons. First, it makes reading easier because you have already thought about the topic. Second, the material is easier to remember because you can connect the new information with what you already know. Third, topics become more interesting if you can link them to your own experiences. You can discover what you know by using one or more of the following techniques:

How to Activate Your Background Knowledge

1. **Ask questions and try to answer them.** For the above business textbook headings, you might ask and try to answer questions such as: Would I want to own a small business or not? What problems could I expect?

2. **Draw upon your own experience.** For example, if a chapter in your business textbook is titled "Advertising: Its Purpose and Design," you might think of several ads you have seen on television, in magazines, and on the Web, analyzing the purpose of each and how it was constructed.

3. **Brainstorm.** On a scratch sheet of paper, jot down everything that comes to mind about the topic. For example, suppose you are about to read a chapter on domestic violence in your sociology textbook. You might list types of violence—child abuse, rape, and so on. You could write questions such as: "What causes child abuse?" or "How can it be prevented?" Or you might list incidents of domestic violence you have heard or read about. Any of these approaches will help to make the topic interesting or relevant.

EXERCISE **2-13** **Discovering What You Already Know**

Directions: Assume you have just previewed a chapter in your American government text on freedom of speech. Discover what you already know about freedom of speech by using each of the techniques suggested above and on page 56. Then answer the questions below.

1. Did you discover you knew more about freedom of speech than you initially thought?

   _____

2. Which technique worked best? Why?

   _____

   _____

EXERCISE **2-14** **Discovering What You Already Know**

Directions: Preview the essay "Looking for Love" in Mastery Test 1 at the end of the chapter, and discover what you already know about types of dating by using one of three techniques described in this section.

LEARNING STYLE TIPS

If you tend to be a(n) . . .	Then strengthen your previewing skills by . . .
Auditory learner	Asking and answering guide questions aloud or recording them
Visual learner	Writing guide questions and their answers

DEVELOP QUESTIONS TO GUIDE YOUR READING

3 LEARNING GOAL

Develop questions to guide your reading

Did you ever read an entire page or more and not remember anything you read? Have you found yourself going from paragraph to paragraph without really thinking about what the writer is saying? Most likely you are not looking for anything in particular as you read. As a result, you do not notice or remember anything specific, either. The solution is a relatively simple technique that takes just a few seconds: develop questions that will guide your reading and hold your attention.

Asking Guide Questions

Here are a few useful suggestions to help you form questions to guide your reading:

How to Ask Guide Questions

1. **Preview before you try to ask questions.** Previewing will give you an idea of what is important and indicate which questions you should ask.
2. **Turn each major heading into a series of questions.** The questions should ask something that you feel is important to know.
3. **As you read the section, look for the answers to your questions.** Highlight the answers as you find them.
4. **When you finish reading a section, stop and check to see whether you can recall the answers.** Place check marks by those you cannot recall.
5. **Avoid asking questions that have one-word answers.** Questions that begin with *what*, *why*, or *how* are more useful.

Here are a few headings from the reading "The Process and Ethics of Lying" on page 50 and some examples of questions you could ask:

Heading	Questions
1. The Process and Ethics of Lying	1. How is lying a process?
2. How People Lie	2. How and why do people lie?
3. The Behavior of Liars	3. How do liars behave? How can I tell if someone is lying?

EXERCISE 2-15 **Writing Guide Questions**

Directions: Write at least one question for each of the following headings.

Heading	Questions
1. World War II and Black Protest	1. _____
	_____
2. Foreign Policy Under President Obama	2. _____
	_____
3. The Increase in Single-Parent Families	3. _____
	_____
4. Changes in Optical Telescopes	4. _____
	_____
5. Causes of Violent Behavior	5. _____
	_____

EXERCISE 2-16 **Writing Guide Questions**

Directions: Preview Chapter 8 of this text. Then write a question for each major heading.

1. _____

2. _____

3. _____

4. _____

5. _____

6. _____

EXERCISE 2-17 **Writing and Answering Guide Questions**

Directions: Turn to the reading titled "Looking for Love" in Mastery Test 1 (p. 66). You have already previewed it. Without reading the article, write four important questions to be answered after finishing it. Then read the article and answer your questions.

1. _____

2. _____

3. _____

4. _____

EXERCISE 2-18   Previewing and Writing Guide Questions

Directions: Select a textbook from one of your other courses. Preview a five-page portion of a chapter that you have not yet read. Then write questions for each heading.

_____

_____

_____

EXERCISE 2-19   Previewing and Writing Guide Questions

Directions: Bring two brief magazines, newspapers, or Web articles or two 2-page textbook excerpts on interesting subjects to class. You should preview and then read both articles before class. Working with another student, exchange and preview each other's articles. Take turns predicting each article's content and organization. The student who has read the article verifies or rejects the predictions. Alternatively, the "reader" may ask the "previewer" about the article's content or organization. Then work together to generate a list of guide questions that could be used when reading the material.

DURING READING: READ FOR MEANING AND TEST YOUR RECALL AS YOU READ

4 LEARNING GOAL

Read for meaning and test your recall as you read

Once you have previewed an assignment and written guide questions to focus your attention, you are ready to begin reading. Read to answer your guide questions. Each time you find an answer to one of your guide questions, highlight it. Also, highlight what is important in each paragraph. In Chapter 6 you will learn more about how to discover what is important in a paragraph; in Chapter 3 you will learn specific strategies for highlighting.

Many students read an assignment from beginning to end without stopping. Usually, this is a mistake. Instead, it is best to stop frequently to test yourself to see if you are remembering what you are reading. You can do this easily by using your guide questions. If you write guide questions in the textbook margin next to the section to which they correspond, you can easily use them as test questions after you have read the section. Cover the textbook section and try to recall the answer. If you cannot, reread the section. You have not yet learned the material. Depending on your learning style, you might either repeat the answer aloud (auditory style) or write it (verbal style).

READ TO UNDERSTAND GRAPHICS AND VISUAL AIDS

5 LEARNING GOAL
Read to understand graphics and visual aids

Graphics and visual aids are common in all types of reading material, not just textbooks. Because they usually contain important information, you should pay close attention to them as you read. Do not simply skip visual aids. Rather, use text cues to read the visual aids when the author directs you to do so. Look for references that say something like "See Figure 1" or "As Table 4 shows."

Table 2-1 below lists some common types of graphics and suggestions for reading them effectively.

TABLE 2-1   How to Read Graphics and Visual Aids

Type of Graphic	Purpose	Sample Graphic	Tips for Reading and Understanding
Diagrams	To explain the relationship between parts or how a process works		1. Switch back and forth between the diagram and the text paragraphs that describe it. 2. Be sure you understand all the vocabulary used in the diagram. 3. Test your understanding by explaining the relationship or the parts of the process in your own words.
Graphs	To show how two ideas or types of information are related		1. Understand the types of information that are being shown and related. 2. Read any notes that accompany the graph. 3. Use colors and the legend (key) to help you understand the content of the graph.
Maps	To provide information about location, direction, or regional data		1. Use the legend or key to identify the symbols or codes used. 2. Look for trends or comparisons in the map. 3. Describe the map's main points in your own words.
Photos	To provide information, to grab the reader's attention		1. Examine the photograph and understand what is showing. Ask yourself why the author chose to include it. 2. Determine your first impression of the photograph. 3. Understand your reaction to the photograph.

(Continued)

TABLE 2-1   How to Read Graphics and Visual Aids

Type of Graphic	Purpose	Sample Graphic	Tips for Reading and Understanding
Pie Charts	To show the relationship between parts and the whole	78 % Nitrogen / 1 % Carbon dioxide, Argon, Water vapour and other gases / 21 % Oxygen	1. Identify what is being divided into parts. 2. Understand what each slice of the pie represents. 3. Look for trends, patterns, or realistic conclusions.
Tables	To summarize large amounts of data	Calories Used During Activities	1. Determine how the data are classified or divided. 2. Make comparisons and look for trends. 3. Write a note that summarizes trends or conclusions.

EXERCISE **2-20**   **Reading and Understanding a Visual Aid**

Directions: Turn to the visual aid titled "Relationship Escalation Model," which appears in the "Looking for Love" reading in Mastery Test 1 (p. 67). Answer the following questions.

1. What are the five stages of relationship escalation?

   _____

2. In which stage do outsiders begin to see two people as a couple?

   _____

3. Which stage is marked by a state of interdependence between two people?

   _____

AFTER READING: REVIEW AFTER YOU READ

6 LEARNING GOAL

Review after reading

Once you have finished reading, it is tempting to close the book, take a break, and move on to your next assignment. If you want to be sure that you remember what you have just read, take a few moments to go back through the material, looking things over one more time.

You can review using some or all of the same steps you followed to preview (see pp. 49–50). Instead of viewing the assignment *before* reading, you are viewing it again *after* reading. Think of it as a "re-view." Review will help you pull ideas together as well as help you retain them for later use on a quiz or exam.

EXERCISE **2-21** **Reviewing After Reading**

Directions: Work with a partner to choose a mastery test at the end of this chapter. Preview and then read the selection. Next, each student should write five questions on the reading. Test each other's recall of the reading's content by taking turns asking and answering your questions.

BUILD A READING-STUDY SYSTEM: SQ3R

7 LEARNING GOAL

Use the SQ3R system

Each of the techniques presented in this chapter—(1) previewing, (2) asking guide questions, (3) reading for meaning, (4) testing yourself, and (5) reviewing—will make a difference in how well you comprehend and remember what you read. While each of these makes a difference by itself, when you use all five together you will discover a much bigger difference. Because these five techniques work together, numerous researchers and psychologists have put them together into a reading–learning system. One of the most popular systems is called SQ3R. The steps in the system are listed below. You will see that the steps are just other names for what you have already learned in this chapter.

SQ3R

S	Survey	(Preview)
Q	Question	(Ask Guide Questions)
R	Read	(Read for Meaning)
R	Recite	(Test Your Recall)
R	Review	(Review After You Read)

Be sure to use SQ3R on all your textbook assignments. You will find that it makes an important difference in the amount of information you can learn and remember.

EXERCISE **2-22** **Using SQ3R**

Directions: Choose one of the Mastery Test Readings at the end of this chapter, or use one assigned by your instructor. Complete each of the following steps.

1. Preview the chapter excerpt. Write a sentence describing what the chapter excerpt will be about.

   _____

   _____

2. Form several questions that you want to answer as you read. Write them in the space provided.

_____

_____

3. Read the first section (major heading) of the chapter excerpt, and highlight the important information.

4. Review the section immediately after you finish reading and highlighting.

5. On a separate sheet of paper, write a brief outline or draw a map of the major ideas in the section of the chapter that you read.

6. Evaluate how effectively SQ3R worked for you. Explain how it helped you or what you would change to make it work better for you.

EXERCISE **2-23**　**Using SQ3R**

Directions: Choose a chapter from one of your textbooks, or use a later chapter in this text. Complete each of the steps listed in Exercise 2-22 on page 63.

SELF-TEST SUMMARY

1	**How can you use textbooks as learning tools?**	Use headings and subheadings to understand chapter organization. Use the preface, to the student, table of contents, opening chapter, typographical aids, chapter exercises and questions, boxes and case studies, vocabulary lists, chapter summary, glossary, index, and electronic learning aids.
2	**What is previewing? How is it related to discovering what you already know?**	Previewing is a method of becoming familiar with the content and organization of written material before reading. After previewing, take a moment to discover what you already know about the topic by activating your background knowledge.

3 What are guide questions?	Guide questions are often based on headings. They focus your attention on what you need to learn and remember.
4 How can you read for meaning and test your recall as you read?	Highlight answers to your guide questions. Also, highlight important information in each paragraph. Cover the text and try to recall answers to each of your guide questions.
5 How can you increase your under-standing of graphics and visual aids?	Use the suggestions in Table 2-1(pages 61–62) to help you understand the content of diagrams, graphs, maps, photos, pie charts, and tables.
6 How can you review after you read?	Use the steps you followed to preview the assignment.
7 What is the SQ3R system?	SQ3R (Survey, Question, Read, Recite, and Review) is a system that enables you to learn as you read.

GOING ONLINE

1. **Exploring Online Textbook Learning Aids**

   Most of your college textbooks offer a companion Web site. These sites often offer a variety of helpful study resources. Choose a textbook from one of your other courses and visit its Web site. Make a list of the resources provided. Which of these would you find most helpful and useful? Why?

Looking for Love

Jenifer Kunz

Before Reading

This selection, taken from the sociology textbook *THINK Marriages and Families*, explores the dating ritual.

Previewing the Reading

Using the steps listed on pages 49–50, preview the reading selection. When you have finished, indicate whether each statement is true (T) or false (F).

_____ 1. Dating has changed, but many aspects of it have remained the same.

_____ 2. The selection will discuss speed dating but not online dating.

_____ 3. The selection will define the terms "going steady" and "pack dating."

Predicting and Connecting

1. If you are in a relationship, where and how did you meet your romantic partner? If you are single and interested in dating, how do you typically try to meet people?

2. Use typographical aids to identify five key terms that the reading will define.

> **Vocabulary Preview**
>
> **primping** (par. 1) carefully grooming
>
> **intimacy** (par. 2) closeness
>
> **conformity** (par. 4) fitting in with others
>
> **compatibility** (par. 8) ability to get along with each other
>
> **accelerated** (par. 13) faster

1   Dating has changed, but many aspects of it remain the same. Visit the home of a single man or woman on a typical Saturday night and you will likely witness a familiar routine: the primping and preening in front of the mirror, the nervous glancing at the watch, the hopeful conversations with friends and family members about tonight's date. But apart from the excitement of a night out, what do people get out of dating?

Reasons for Dating

2   Dating fulfills a number of important functions in people's lives. It is a form of recreation that enables couples to socialize together and have fun. It provides companionship and intimacy. Dating also helps individuals learn social skills,

gain self-confidence, and develop one-on-one communication skills. Through their relationships with other people, adolescents in particular develop a sense of their own identity, increasing their feelings of self-worth. Finally, dating is a possible opportunity to meet a future martial partner through the process of mate selection.

3   Researchers describe the dating process as a **marriage market**. Just as employers in a labor market attempt to hire the best possible employees for the

Relationship Escalation Model

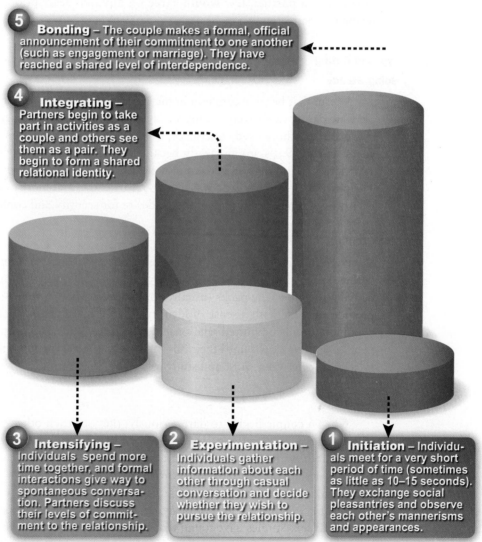

5 Bonding – The couple makes a formal, official announcement of their commitment to one another (such as engagement or marriage). They have reached a shared level of interdependence.

4 Integrating – Partners begin to take part in activities as a couple and others see them as a pair. They begin to form a shared relational identity.

3 Intensifying – Individuals spend more time together, and formal interactions give way to spontaneous conversation. Partners discuss their levels of commitment to the relationship.

2 Experimentation – Individuals gather information about each other through casual conversation and decide whether they wish to pursue the relationship.

1 Initiation – Individuals meet for a very short period of time (sometimes as little as 10–15 seconds). They exchange social pleasantries and observe each other's mannerisms and appearances.

Source: Knapp, Mark, *Interpersonal Communication and Human Relationships* (Boston: Allyn & Bacon, 1984).

lowest possible wage, potential spouses in the marriage market look for a partner with the highest number of desired characteristics and the fewest flaws. The three components to the marriage market include the *supply* of men and women who are looking for partners, the *preferences* of these men and women for particular physical characteristics and personal attributes in their partners, and the *resources* that the men and women can offer potential partners themselves (attributes that other people are likely to find attractive). Unlike the labor market, which tends to value the same characteristics in all potential employees—for example, punctuality, reliability, and efficiency—the marriage market is extremely varied. Although most people value qualities such as honesty and integrity in a partner, few would agree on any one description of the perfect woman or perfect man.

Types of Dating

Going Steady

4   A term that became common in the 1930s, **going steady** meant that two people were dating exclusively. Going steady sometimes led to engagement, although it was often a short-lived experience, lasting anywhere from a few days to a few years. In the 1950s, going steady became the dominant form of dating, and a 1958 study found that 68 percent of college coeds had gone steady at least once. The practice of going steady was less about true love and more about status and peer pressure, representing the teenage desire for security and conformity.

Pack Dating

5   Popular among undergraduates, **pack dating** is a less pressurized form of dating, in which small groups of students go to dinner, watch movies, or go out dancing together. The packs (usually consisting of about five or six individuals) provide students with a sense of identity and self-assurance, but enable them to avoid long-term committed relationships. This may appeal to people who do not plan on settling down until their 30s or who have little free time to commit to a relationship between work and study responsibilities.

Serious Dating

6   When a couple begins to date seriously, they see each other exclusively and usually spend most of their leisure time together. They may discuss marriage or the possibility of living together and begin to talk about the future as a couple, rather than as two individuals with independent life goals. Many couples are sexually intimate by this point, although the practice of premarital sex often depends on whether one or both partners have strong religious beliefs opposing premarital sex. Studies have found that religious commitment is inversely related to the age at first sexual intercourse and the number of lifetime sexual partners.

Engagement

7   **Engagement** is a public commitment made by a couple when they announce their intention to marry. During the engagement period, couples plan their wedding and discuss issues such as where they will live, whether they will have children, and what they hope to accomplish together in the future.

8   An engagement is also a chance for couples to test their compatibility and may be a time of high stress and conflict. If one partner is considerably wealthier than the other, he or she may wish to draw up a **prenuptial agreement**, which stipulates what should happen financially in the event of a divorce. Researchers have discovered that prenuptial agreements are almost always sought by the economically stronger party in a relationship, usually masking underlying issues of power, trust, and sharing. When prenuptial agreements are used to legally reinforce unequal power in a relationship, they may negatively affect the couple's chance of a healthy marriage.

How People in Married or Long-term Relationships Met Their Current Partner

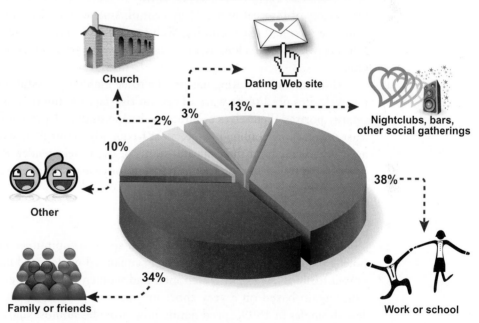

Church   Dating Web site

2% 3% 13%   Nightclubs, bars, other social gatherings

10%

Other   38%

34%   Work or school

Family or friends

9   The trend toward longer periods of engagement provides couples with more than enough time to question whether the relationship is truly right. This, coupled with high levels of stress, has led to an increasing number of **disengagements**— calling off the engagement to avoid a later divorce. Authors Rachel Safier and Wendy Roberts estimate that about 15 percent of all engagements are called

off each year. Some couples realize that they are incompatible before the big day, others are unable to work through the stresses that accompany marriage preparation, and many fear that the issues raised during the stressful planning period may soon escalate into divorce if they proceed with the wedding.

Meeting Potential Partners

10   "How did you two meet?" is a common question asked of new couples. Although traditional responses such as "through a friend" or "at work" are still the most popular answers, matchmaking is becoming an increasingly creative business. In addition, people can now meet potential partners on a singles cruise, during singles nights at their local supermarket, or even by placing a flirtatious bumper sticker on their car to let other drivers know that they are available. Other avenues include online dating and speed dating.

Online Dating

11   Once dismissed as the last resort, **online dating**—the use of specialist dating Web sites—has become an acceptable way to meet a potential partner. In a 2006 Pew survey of Internet users, 31 percent of American adults said that they knew someone who had used a dating Web site, and 15 percent said that they knew someone who was in a long-term relationship with a person that he or she had met online.

12   Although online dating has proven to be highly successful, members of dating Web sites need to be wary of certain risk factors. Internet users do not necessarily portray themselves accurately—in one study, 81 percent of daters lied at least once or their online profile, most frequently about their weight, height, or age. Others lie about their marital status or even their gender. Researchers also point to the use of the Internet as a forum for casual sexual encounters, increasing the potential risk of sexually transmitted diseases.

Speed Dating

13   No time to socialize? Surely you can spare six minutes. That's how long potential couples usually spend getting acquainted while **speed dating**—an accelerated form of dating in which men and women choose whether to see each other again based on a very short interaction. Originally created for young Jewish singles in 1999, speed dating now provides homosexuals, heterosexuals, and a number of religious and ethnic groups with an opportunity to participate in quick, one-on-one dates with like-minded singles. Individuals spend six minutes talking to each date. If both individuals are interested, they are provided with each other's e-mail addresses.

14   Although a fun dating strategy, speed dating is superficial by nature. Researchers have noted that speed-daters usually focus on physical attractiveness and rarely ask pertinent questions about characteristics such as education

and religion. When it comes to speed dating, social scientists Michéle Belot and Marco Francesconi note that women prefer men who are young and tall, and men prefer women who are young and thin. Both sexes prefer partners of a similar age, height, and education, and select partners according to physical attributes that might predict socioeconomic status (such as age, height, and weight).

—Kunz, *THINK Marriages and Families*, pp. 118–120

After Reading

Checking Your Comprehension

_____ 1. The purpose of this selection is to
   a. offer dating advice.
   a. discuss why and how people date.
   b. explore cultural differences in dating.
   c. compare old and new dating styles.

_____ 2. According to the author, dating fulfills all of the following functions *except*
   a. it helps people improve their social status.
   b. it helps people learn social skills.
   c. it creates opportunities to meet a future spouse.
   d. it allows people to socialize and have fun.

_____ 3. The type of dating in which small groups of people go out together is called
   a. going steady.
   b. initiation.
   c. disengagement.
   d. pack dating.

_____ 4. The marriage market includes all of the following components *except*
   a. the supply of men and women who are looking for partners.
   b. people's preferences for certain attributes in their partners.
   c. financial arrangements agreed upon by prospective partners.
   d. the resources that people can offer potential partners themselves.

_____ 5. The main point of paragraph 11 is that online dating
   a. is more effective than speed dating.
   b. offers the most potential mates.
   c. will most likely lead to a long-term relationship.
   d. has become popular and accepted.

Applying Your Skills: College Textbook Reading

_____ 6. All of the following terms would most likely be included on a key terms list for this selection *except*
   a. marriage market.
   b. disengagement.
   c. labor market.
   d. speed dating.

_____ 7. The purpose of the Relationship Escalation Model on page 67 is to
   a. demonstrate how dating has changed over time.
   b. explain the stages relationships go through.
   c. illustrate the various ways to meet potential partners.
   d. describe how the Internet has influenced dating.

_____ 8. According to the pie chart on page 69, the most common way to meet a partner is
   a. through work or school.
   b. at nightclubs, bars, or other social gatherings.
   c. through family or friends.
   d. on a dating Web site.

_____ 9. The best glossary entry for the term **prenuptial agreement** is
   a. a public announcement of a couple's decision to marry.
   b. a system in which prospective partners evaluate potential spouses.
   c. the breakdown of a relationship or engagement.
   d. a legal document stipulating financial arrangements in the event of divorce.

_____ 10. The explanation of speed dating is found under the heading
   a. Reasons for Dating.
   b. Types of Dating.
   c. Pack Dating.
   d. Meeting Potential Partners.
   e. Studying Words

Studying Words

_____ 11. The word *punctuality* (par. 3) means
   a. exclusivity.
   b. cooperation.
   c. promptness.
   d. uncertainty.

_____ 12. The word *inversely* (par. 6) means
   a. having the opposite effect.
   b. making a comparison.
   c. at the same time.
   d. having no effect.

_____ 13. The word *escalate* (par. 9) means
   a. increase.
   b. improve.
   c. remove.
   d. hide.

_____ 14. The word *wary* (par. 12) means
   a. angry.
   b. joyful.
   c. accepting.
   d. guarded.

_____ 15. The word *superficial* (par. 14) means
   a. expensive.
   b. shallow.
   c. spontaneous.
   d. lengthy.

For more practice, ask your instructor for an opportunity to work on the mastery tests that appear in the Test Bank.

Thinking Visually

1. According to the Relationship Escalation Model (p. 67), how do relationships begin?

_____

_____

2. How are the stages in the Relationship Escalation Model (p. 67) similar to the types of dating discussed in the selection?

    _____

    _____

3. What is the purpose of the pie chart on page 69?

    _____

Thinking Critically About the Reading

1. Make a connection between your own dating life and the Relationship Escalation Model graphic on page 67. How many stages have you experienced? Why is it important for a relationship to progress through these stages?

2. What do you think is the most effective way to meet people to date? What has worked for you in the past? What might you be willing to try?

Academic Application: Summarizing the Reading

Directions: Assume your instructor has asked you to write a one-paragraph summary of the reading. Complete the following summary by filling in the blanks.

Dating fulfills _____ in people's lives. The dating process is described as a

_____, which includes the components of supply, _____, and resources.

Types of _____ include going steady, pack dating, serious dating, and _____

People meet potential partners in many ways, but _____ and _____

have recently become popular methods.

MASTERY TEST 2 Reading Selection

Saving Species

Colleen Belk and Virginia Borden Maier

Before Reading

This selection appeared in an introductory biology textbook in a chapter titled "Conserving Biodiversity." *Biodiversity* means "the diversity of life."

Previewing the Reading

Using the steps listed on pages 49–50, preview the reading selection. When you have finished, complete the following items.

1. What is the topic of the selection? _____

2. The most effective way to prevent species loss is to preserve as many _____

3. as possible.

4. Indicate whether each statement is true (T) or false (F).

   _____ a. Some endangered species require more than the simple preservation of habitats.

   _____ b. Preserving habitat is the sole responsibility of national governments.

   _____ c. Financial aid to poor countries may help preserve natural habitats.

Predicting and Connecting

1. How much do you know about the topic of endangered species? How do you think the destruction of natural environments (such as forests and fields) might contribute to a species going extinct?

2. Do you expect the reading to be fairly easy to understand, of moderate difficulty, or challenging? Why?

> **Vocabulary Preview**
>
> **amphibian** (par. 3) family of animals that includes frogs and toads
>
> **ESA** (par. 6) Ecological Society of America
>
> **developing countries** (par. 9) poor countries

During Reading

Think as You Read
Read • Respond

As you read the selection, complete each of the following. When highlighting, use a different color highlighter for each task.

a. Highlight the topic sentence of each paragraph. If the main idea is unstated, write a sentence that states it.

b. Highlight the most important details in each paragraph.

c. Highlight useful transitional words and phrases that help you understand and connect the author's ideas.

d. Read and respond to the questions in the margin.

Saving Species

1   We have established the possibility of a modern mass extinction occurring, and we have described the potentially serious costs of this loss of biodiversity to human populations. Because the sixth extinction is largely a result of human activity, reversing the trend of species loss requires political and economic, rather than scientific, decisions. But what can science tell us about how to stop the rapid erosion of biodiversity?

> What question will this reading answer?

Protecting Habitat

2   Without knowing exactly which species are closest to extinction and where they are located, the most effective way to prevent loss of species is to preserve as many habitats as possible. In theory we can lose 50% of a habitat but still retain 90% of its species. This estimate is optimistic because habitat destruction is not the only threat to biodiversity, but if the rate of habitat destruction is slowed or stopped, extinction rates will slow as well.

3   **Protecting the Greatest Number of Species.** Given the growing human population, it is difficult to imagine a complete halt to habitat destruction. However, biologist Norman Myers and his collaborators have concluded that 25 biodiversity "hot spots," making up less than 2% of Earth's surface, contain up to 50% of all mammal, bird, reptile, amphibian, and plant species (Figure 1). Hot spots occur in areas of the globe where favorable climate conditions lead to high levels of plant production, such as rain forests, and where geological factors have resulted in the isolation of species groups, allowing them to diversify.

4   Stopping habitat destruction in biodiversity hot spots could greatly reduce the global extinction rate. By focusing conservation efforts on hot spot areas at the greatest risk, humans can very quickly prevent the loss of a large number of species. Of course, even with habitat protection, many species in these hot spots will likely become extinct anyway for other human-mediated reasons.

> What are the authors implying about the role of humans in species extinction?

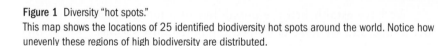

Why did the authors include this figure?

Figure 1 Diversity "hot spots."
This map shows the locations of 25 identified biodiversity hot spots around the world. Notice how unevenly these regions of high biodiversity are distributed.

Why do the authors mention ecotourism?

5   In the long term, we must find ways to preserve biodiversity while including human activity in the landscape. One option is **ecotourism**, which encourages travel to natural areas in ways that conserve the environment and improve the well-being of local people. Some hot spot countries, such as Costa Rica and Kenya, have used ecotourism to preserve natural areas and provide much-needed jobs; other countries have been less successful.

Underline the sentence showing that the authors are moving from one topic to another.

6   **Protecting Habitat for Critically Endangered Species.** Although preserving a variety of habitats ensures fewer extinctions, already-endangered species require a more individualized approach. The ESA requires the U.S. Department of the Interior to designate critical habitats for endangered species—that is, areas in need of protection for the survival of the species. The amount of critical habitat that becomes designated depends on political as well as biological factors.

7   The biological part of a critical habitat designation includes conducting a study of habitat requirements for the endangered species and setting a population goal for it. The U.S. Department of the Interior's critical habitat designation has to include enough area to support the recovery population. However, federal designation of a critical habitat results in the restriction of human activities that can take place there. The U.S. Department of Interior has the ability to exclude some habitats from protection if there are "sufficient economic benefits" for doing so—a decision that is political in nature.

What are the authors implying about the role of politics in species conservation?

8   **Decreasing the Rate of Habitat Destruction.** Preserving habitat is not simply the job of national governments that designate protected areas or of private conservation organizations that purchase at-risk habitats. All of

us can take actions to reduce habitat destruction and stem the rate of species extinction. Conversion of land to agricultural production is a major cause of habitat destruction, so eating lower on the food chain and reducing your consumption of meat and dairy products from grain-fed animals is one of the most effective actions you can take. Reducing your use of wood and paper products and limiting your consumption of these products to those harvested sustainably (that is, in a manner that preserves the long-term health of the forest) can help slow the loss of forested land.

> Why do the authors close by talking about the individual's role in preserving habitats in the last two paragraphs?

9   Other measures to decrease the rate of habitat destruction require group effort. For instance, increased financial aid to developing countries may help slow the rate of habitat destruction. This would allow poor countries to invest money in technologies that decrease their use of natural resources, for example, cooking technologies that reduce the need to harvest large amounts of woody plants for fuel. Strategies that slow the rate of human population growth offer more ways to avoid mass extinction. You can participate in group conservation efforts by joining nonprofit organizations focused on these issues, writing to politicians, and educating others.

—Belk and Borden Maier, *Biology*, pp. 376–377

After Reading

Checking Your Comprehension

_____ 1. The most effective way to prevent the extinction of a species is to
   a. forbid hunting and imprison hunters.
   b. prevent the sale of items made from that species.
   c. keep breeding pairs of the species in captivity.
   d. preserve as many habitats as possible.

_____ 2. In theory, we can lose _____ of a habitat but retain _____ of its species.
   a. a quarter, half.
   b. a third, a quarter.
   c. half, 90%.
   d. 40%, 85%.

_____ 3. What percentage of Earth's surface is home to up to half of all plant, amphibian, bird, mammal, and reptile species?
   a. 2%.
   b. 10%.
   c. 38%.
   d. 44%.

_____ 4. Which term is used to describe travel that conserves the environment and promotes the well-being of local people?
   a. biotravel.
   b. ecotourism.
   c. speciation.
   d. biodiversity.

_____ 5. All of the following are ways that you can prevent species extinction *except*
  a. reducing your consumption of meat and dairy products.
  b. decreasing your use of wood and paper products.
  c. living in an urban rather than rural environment.
  d. joining nonprofit groups dedicated to conservation efforts.

Applying Your Skills: College Textbook Reading

_____ 6. This reading makes use of a major heading and three subheadings. Which of the following is *not* a subheading?
  a. Protecting Habitat.
  b. Protecting the Greatest Number of Species.
  c. Protecting Habitat for Critically Endangered Species.
  d. Decreasing the Rate of Habitat Destruction.

_____ 7. Which type of typographical aid calls attention to the term *ecotourism* as a key term that you should learn?
  a. italics.
  b. colored type.
  c. bullets.
  d. boldface.

_____ 8. Suppose that you are reading paragraph 1 and you encounter a word you do not understand: *biodiversity*. Where in the textbook are you likely to easily find a definition of this word?
  a. the preface.
  b. the glossary.
  c. the index.
  d. to the student.

_____ 9. Which of the following would you *not* read as part of your preview of this selection?
  a. the first paragraph of the selection.
  b. the last paragraph of the selection.
  c. the headings and the first sentence after each heading.
  d. the last sentence of each paragraph.

_____ 10. Which of the following would *not* be an effective guide question for you to ask and answer as you read the selection?
  a. What is involved in protecting habitat?
  b. How does the Department of the Interior determine economic benefits?
  c. How do we decrease the rate of habitat destruction?
  d. How can we protect the greatest number of species?

Studying Words

Using context or a dictionary, define each of the following words as it is used in the reading.

11. erosion (par. 1) _____

12. halt (par. 3) _____

13. geological (par. 3) _____

14. critical (par. 6) _____

15. stem (par. 8) _____

Thinking Visually

1. What key concept discussed in the selection does Figure 1 illustrate?

   _____

2. Closely examine Figure 1. Which of the following is not an area with a high level of biodiversity: Southwest Australia, Scandinavia, the Tropical Andes, Madagascar, or the Caucasus? _____

3. What other types of photos, charts, or visual aids might be useful with this selection? _____

Thinking Critically About the Reading

1. How would you describe the authors' attitude toward the role of humanity in species extinction?

2. This selection comes from a science textbook, and science textbooks often require you to read more slowly. What other strategies would you use to read and learn this selection?

3. What other types of information would you like to have seen included in the reading? How would this additional information have increased your enjoyment and/or understanding of the reading?

4. Summarize how you could use the SQ3R method to read and study this selection.

Academic Application: Summarizing the Reading

Directions: You walk into class and your instructor announces that there will be a pop quiz on the reading. She says, "If you read the article, you'll have no trouble getting an A on this fill-in-the-blank quiz." Complete the following summary by filling in the blanks.

Belk and Borden Maier are concerned with preserving biodiversity. The best way to prevent _____ is by preserving habitats. By saving _____ % of a habitat, we can in theory save 90% of its species. It is particularly important to preserve global _____ spots. We must also be aware that preserving habitats is not just biological but also _____—that is, governments play a role in designating habitats for preservation. Fortunately, individuals can aid conservation efforts by lowering their consumption of meat and _____ products and by using products that have been harvested sustainably.

Organizing and Remembering Information

LEARNING GOALS

This chapter will show you how to

1 Highlight and mark important information in textbook chapters

2 Paraphrase to record and remember information

3 Outline information to show its organization

4 Draw maps to organize information

5 Summarize ideas for review purposes

6 Review for maximum retention

Focusing on . . . Organizing and Remembering Information

The blueprint above, created by an architect, is used by the contractor to build the building to specifications. The blueprint organizes all the details about the building, such as the size of rooms and the location of windows, electrical outlets, and appliances. Can you imagine how difficult it would be to keep track of all the details involved in a construction project without a blueprint? Textbook chapters are also filled with details, and you need a system to keep track of them all. This chapter shows you six ways to create a "blueprint" or learning guide of a textbook chapter.

Suppose you are planning a cross-country trip next summer. To get ready, you begin to collect all kinds of information: maps, Web articles on various cities, places to visit, names of friends' friends, and so forth. After a while, you find that you have a great deal of information and that it is difficult to locate any one item. You begin to realize that the information you have collected will be of little or no use unless you organize it in some way. You decide to buy large envelopes and put different kinds of information into separate envelopes, such as information on individual states.

In this case, you found a practical, common-sense solution to a problem. The rule or principle that you applied was this: when something gets confusing, organize it.

This rule also works well when applied to college textbooks. Each text contains thousands of pieces of information—facts, names, dates, theories, principles. This information quickly becomes confusing unless it is organized. Once you have organized it, you will be able to find and remember what you need more easily.

Organizing information requires sifting, sorting, and in some cases rearranging important facts and ideas. There are six common methods of organizing textbook materials:

- highlighting
- marking
- paraphrasing
- outlining
- mapping
- summarizing

In this chapter you will learn techniques for doing each. You will also see how to study and review more effectively.

HIGHLIGHTING AND MARKING

1 LEARNING GOAL
Highlight and mark important information in textbook chapters

Highlighting and **marking** important facts and ideas as you read are effective methods of identifying and organizing information. They are also the biggest time-savers known to college students. Suppose it took you four hours to read an assigned chapter in sociology. One month later you need to review that chapter to prepare for an exam. If you did not highlight or mark as you read the first time, then, in order to review the chapter once, you would have to spend another four hours rereading it. However, if you had highlighted and marked as you read, you could review the chapter in an hour or less—a savings of 75 percent. This means you can save many hours each semester. More important, the less time you spend identifying what to learn, the more thoroughly you can learn the necessary information. This strategy can help improve your grades.

Highlighting Effectively

Here are a few basic suggestions for highlighting effectively:

How to Highlight

1. **Read a paragraph or section first.** Then go back and highlight what is important.
2. **Highlight important portions of the topic sentence.** Also highlight any supporting details you want to remember (see Chapter 7).
3. **Be accurate.** Make sure your highlighting reflects the content of the passage. Incomplete or hasty highlighting can mislead you as you review the passage and may cause you to miss the main point.
4. **Use a system for highlighting.** There are several from which to choose: for instance, using two or more different colors of highlighters to distinguish between main ideas and details, or placing a bracket around the main idea and using a highlighter to mark important details. No one system is more effective than another. Develop a system that works well for you.
5. **Highlight as few words as possible in a sentence.** Seldom should you highlight an entire sentence. Usually highlighting the key idea along with an additional phrase or two is sufficient. Read the following paragraph. Notice that you can understand its meaning from the highlighted parts alone.

   Police are primarily a reactive force. In the vast majority of cases, police are informed of an incident *after* it occurs by a complaining victim, a witness, or an alarm. (A study of police response time found that only about 6 percent of callers reported crimes while they were in progress.) In addition, the National Crime Victimization Survey (NCVS) reveals that only about a third of serious crime is reported to police. It is difficult to hold police responsible for increases in the crime rate when they are not called for most crimes or are called after the incident has ended. Several other factors may cause the crime rate to rise, such as an increase in the proportion of young people in the population, higher rates of long-term unemployment, and the criminalization of drug use. Police have no control over these conditions. Thus, the crime rate is really not a useful indictor of police effectiveness.

6. **Use headings to guide your highlighting.** Use the headings to form questions that you expect to be answered in the section (see Chapter 2). Then highlight the answer to each question.

Highlighting the Right Amount

If you highlight either too much or too little, you defeat the purpose. By highlighting too little, you miss valuable information, and your review and study of the material will be incomplete. On the other hand, if you highlight too much, you are not identifying the most important ideas and eliminating less-important facts. The more you highlight, the more you will have to reread when studying and the less of a time-saver the procedure will prove to be. As a general rule of thumb, highlight no more than 20 to 30 percent of the material.

Here is a paragraph highlighted in three different ways. First read the paragraph that has not been highlighted; then look at each highlighted version. Try to decide which version would be most useful if you were rereading it for study purposes.

The Maglevs are coming. Not aliens from outer space, but superfast trains suspended in the air and propelled by magnetic force. Maglevs can travel at speeds of more than 300 miles per hour, lifted off the ground on a cushion formed by magnetic forces and pulled forward by magnets. They run more quietly and smoothly and can climb steeper grades than conventional trains can. Maglevs are more energy efficient, have lower maintenance costs, and require fewer staff than does comparable transportation. However, given the high cost of construction, the concept may not prove viable.

—adapted from Walker, *Introduction to Hospitality Management*, p. 45

Example 1

The Maglevs are coming. Not aliens from outer space, but superfast trains suspended in the air and propelled by magnetic force. Maglevs can travel at speeds of more than 300 miles per hour, lifted off the ground on a cushion formed by magnetic forces and pulled forward by magnets. They run more quietly and smoothly and can climb steeper grades than conventional trains can. Maglevs are more energy efficient, have lower maintenance costs, and require fewer staff than does comparable transportation. However, given the high cost of construction, the concept may not prove viable.

Example 2

The Maglevs are coming. Not aliens from outer space, but superfast trains suspended in the air and propelled by magnetic force. Maglevs can travel at speeds of more than 300 miles per hour, lifted off the ground on a cushion formed by magnetic forces and pulled forward by magnets. They run more quietly and smoothly and can climb steeper grades than conventional trains can. Maglevs are more energy efficient, have lower maintenance costs, and require fewer staff than does comparable transportation. However, given the high cost of construction, the concept may not prove viable.

Example 3

The Maglevs are coming. Not aliens from outer space, but superfast trains suspended in the air and propelled by magnetic force. Maglevs can travel at speeds of more than 300 miles per hour, lifted off the ground on a cushion formed by magnetic forces and pulled forward by magnets. They run more quietly and smoothly and can climb steeper grades than conventional trains can. Maglevs are more energy efficient, have lower maintenance costs, and require fewer staff than does comparable transportation. However, given the high cost of construction, the concept may not prove viable.

The last example is the best example of effective highlighting. Only the most important information has been highlighted. In the first example, too little of the important information has been highlighted, while what *has* been highlighted is either unnecessary or incomplete. The second example has too much highlighting to be useful for review.

EXERCISE 3-1   Practicing Highlighting

Directions: Read and highlight the following passage using the guidelines presented in this section.

Generic Names

When filing for a trademark, if a word, name, or slogan is too generic, it cannot be registered as a trademark. If it is not generic, it can be trademarked. For example, the word "apple" cannot be trademarked because it is a generic name. However, the brand name "Apple Computer" is permitted to be trademarked because it is not a generic name. Similarly, the word "secret" cannot be trademarked because it is a generic name, but the brand name "Victoria's Secret" is permitted to be trademarked because it is not a generic name.

Once a company has been granted a trademark, the company usually uses the mark as a brand name to promote its goods or services. However, sometimes a company may be *too* successful in promoting a mark and at some point the public begins to use the brand name as a common name for the product or service being sold, rather than as the trademark of the individual seller. A trademark that becomes a common term for a product line or type of service is called a generic name. Once a trademark becomes a generic name, the term loses its protection under federal trademark law. To illustrate, sailboards are surfboards that have sails mounted on them and are used by one person to glide on oceans and

lakes. There were many manufacturers and sellers of sailboards. The most successful brand was "Windsurfer." However, the word "windsurfing" was used so often by
the public for all brands of sailboards that the trademarked name "Windsurfer" was
found to be a generic name and its trademark was canceled.

—adapted from Goldman and Cheeseman, *The Paralegal Professional*, p. 745

EXERCISE 3-2   Highlighting Chapter 2

Directions: Read or reread and highlight Chapter 2 in this text. Follow the guidelines
suggested in this chapter.

Testing Your Highlighting

As you highlight, check to be certain your highlighting is effective and will
be helpful for review purposes. To test the effectiveness of your highlighting,
take any passage and reread only the highlighted portions. Then ask yourself
the following questions:

> ## Testing Your Highlighting
>
> - Does the highlighting tell what the passage is about?
> - Does it make sense?
> - Does it indicate the most important idea in the passage?

EXERCISE 3-3   Evaluating Your Highlighting

Directions: Test the effectiveness of your highlighting for the material you highlighted
in Exercises 3-1 and 3-2. Make changes, if necessary.

Marking

Highlighting alone will not clearly identify and organize information in many
textbooks. Also, highlighting does not allow you to react to or sort ideas. Try
making notes in the margin in addition to highlighting. Notice how the marginal notes in the following passage organize the information in a way that
highlighting cannot.

Seasonal Affective Disorder (SAD)

Some people only get depressed at certain times of the year. In particular, depression seems to set in during the winter months and goes away with the coming of spring and summer. If this describes someone you know, it could be seasonal affective disorder (SAD). SAD is a mood disorder caused by the body's reaction to low levels of light present in the winter months.

def. of SAD

SAD can cause feelings of tiredness, lack of energy, and daytime sleepiness that the mind interprets as depression. Other symptoms include excessive eating, a craving for sugary and starchy foods, excessive sleeping, and weight gain. The worst months for SAD are January and February, and true SAD disappears in the spring and summer.

symptoms

Treatment of SAD can include antidepressant drugs, but one of the most effective treatments is **phototherapy**, or daily exposure to bright light. Lamps are used to create an "artificial daylight" for a certain number of hours during each day, and the person with SAD sits under that light. Milder symptoms can be controlled with more time spent outdoors when the sun is shining and increasing the amount of sunlight that comes into the workplace or home.

treatment

—adapted from Ciccarelli and White, *Psychology*, p. 454

Here are a few examples of useful types of marking:

1. **Circle words you do not know.**

   Sulfur is a yellow, solid substance that has several (allotropic) forms.

2. **Mark definitions with an asterisk.**

   * *Chemical reactivity* is the tendency of an element to participate in chemical reactions.

3. **Write summary words or phrases in the margin.**

   Reaction w/ air

   Some elements, such as aluminum (Al) or Copper (Cu), tarnish just from sitting around in the air. They react with oxygen (O_2) in the air.

4. **Number lists of ideas, causes, and reasons.**

   ①   ②   ③

   Metallic properties include conductivity, luster, and ductility.

5. **Place brackets around important passages.**

   In Group IVA, carbon (C) is a nonmetal, silicon (Si) and germanium (Ge) are metalloids, and tin (Sn) and lead (Pb) are metals.

6. **Draw arrows or diagrams to show relationships or to clarify information.**

graphite

> Graphite is made up of a lot of carbon layers stacked on top of one another, like sheets of paper. The layers slide over one another, which makes it a good lubricant.

7. **Make notes to yourself, such as "good test question," "reread," or "ask instructor."**

Test!

> Carbon is most important to us because it is a basic element in all plant and animal structures.

8. **Put question marks next to confusing passages or when you want more information.**

why?

> Sometimes an element reacts so violently with air, water, or other substances that an explosion occurs.

Try to develop your own code or set of abbreviations. Here are a few examples:

Types of Marking	Examples
ex	example
T	good test question
sum	good summary
def	important definition
RR	reread later

EXERCISE 3-4   Practicing Highlighting and Marking

Directions: Read each of the following passages and then highlight and mark each. Try various ways of highlighting and marking.

Passage A

National and Regional Presidential Primary Proposals

1   The idea of holding a **national primary** to select party nominees has been discussed virtually ever since state primaries were introduced. In 1913, President Woodrow Wilson proposed it in his first message to Congress. Since then, over 250 proposals for a national presidential primary have been introduced in Congress.

These proposals do not lack public support; opinion polls have consistently shown that a substantial majority of Democrats, Republicans, and Independents alike favor such reform.

2   According to its proponents, a national primary would bring directness and simplicity to the process for the voters as well as the candidates. The length of the campaign would be shortened, and no longer would votes in one state have more political impact than votes in another. The concentration of media coverage on this one event, say its advocates, would increase not only political interest in the nomination decision but also public understanding of the issues involved.

3   A national primary would not be so simple, respond the critics. Because Americans would not want a candidate nominated with 25 percent of the vote from among a field of six candidates, in most primaries a runoff election between the top two finishers in each party would have to be held. So much for making the campaign simpler, national primary critics note. Each voter would have to vote three times for president—twice in the primaries and once in November.

4   Perhaps more feasible than a national primary is holding a series of **regional primaries** in which, say, states in the eastern time zone would vote one week, those in the central time zone the next, and so on. This would impose a more rational structure and cut down on candidate travel. A regional primary system would also put an end to the jockeying between states for an advantageous position in the primary season.

5   The major problem with the regional primary proposal, however, is the advantage gained by whichever region goes first. For example, if the Western states were the first to vote, any candidate from California would have a clear edge in building momentum. Although most of the proposed plans call for the order of the regions to be determined by lottery, this would not erase the fact that regional advantages would surely be created from year to year.

—adapted from Edwards et al., *Government in America*, p. 285

Passage B

Predators

1   Predation is the process by which animals capture, kill, and consume animals of another species, their prey. Predators employ two basic feeding strategies—filter feeding and hunting.

2   Filter-feeding predators use webs or netlike structures to catch their prey. Spiders use webs to "filter" organisms from their environment. As marine shrimp swim through the water, they trap small organisms in the hairlike setae on their legs and transfer them to their mouths. Blue whales, Earth's largest living animals, are filter feeders. Blue whales and their baleen whale relatives use their comblike "teeth" to filter plankton from the water.

3   Hunting predators actively stalk and capture their prey. Natural selection has favored predators with keen senses of sight and smell as well as structures such as talons, claws, and sharp teeth that allow predators to seize and kill their prey.

Coevolution has played a significant role in predator-prey relationships, and prey organisms have evolved a variety of defenses against capture.

4   Populations of predators are often limited by the availability of prey. Likewise, populations of prey are often limited by their predators. Where predators are dependent on a single species of prey, interactions between the two species may result in synchronized cycles of population growth and decline.

—Christensen, *The Environment and You*, p. 153

EXERCISE 3-5   Comparing Highlighting and Marking

Working Together

Directions: Read, highlight, and mark a reading selection from Part Six assigned by your instructor. Then, working with a partner, review each other's highlighting, discuss similarities and differences, and settle upon an acceptable version.

PARAPHRASING SENTENCES AND PARAGRAPHS

2 LEARNING GOAL

Paraphrase to record and remember information

Paraphrasing is a useful technique for recording and remembering information in a sentence or paragraph. When you **paraphrase**, you rewrite the author's material in your own words. Writing a paraphrase involves two steps:

1. substituting synonyms
2. maintaining the order of ideas

By taking a sentence apart word by word, or by taking a paragraph apart sentence by sentence, you are forced to understand the meaning of each sentence and see how ideas relate to one another. To paraphrase a sentence, simply use words different from the author's while using the same order and expressing the same idea. You may not find a substitute for *every* word in the paragraph, but you should be able to find substitutes for *many* or *most* of the words. Here is an example:

ORIGINAL: Rescuing a homeless animal companion from a shelter is one of the most selfless acts you can perform.

PARAPHRASE: Adopting a pet from the local animal shelter is generous and noble.

Here are some guidelines for paraphrasing paragraphs.

1. Concentrate on maintaining the author's focus and emphasis. Ideas that seem most important in the paragraph should appear as most important in your paraphrase.
2. Work sentence by sentence, paraphrasing the ideas in the order in which they appear in the paragraph.

Here are two sample paraphrases of a paragraph. One is a good paraphrase; the other is poor and unacceptable.

Paragraph

Even if you're not among the 6 million Americans currently practicing yoga, you probably have a friend or relative who is. Virtually unknown in the United States 50 years ago, yoga has grown steadily in popularity. Although many styles of yoga are practiced in the United States today, all teach students basic postures called *asanas*. In a yoga session of 60 to 90 minutes, the full body is stretched. In addition, several postures can be linked together in one seamless sequence of dynamic stretching, such as the Sun Salutation. Throughout the yoga session, students practice controlled breathing, coordinating their inhalations and exhalations with their movements.

—adapted from Blake, *Nutrition & You*, p. 24/7

Good Paraphrase

Yoga has become more popular over the last 50 years and now 6 million Americans practice it. Many styles are practiced but all include asanas, basic postures. The entire body is stretched in a yoga session. Postures can be linked together into dynamic stretching sequences, like Sun Salutations. Controlled breathing is used to coordinate breath with movement.

Poor and Unacceptable Paraphrase

Americans are getting crazy about yoga. All types of yoga require you to contort yourself into all sorts of positions called asanas. A yoga session takes at least an hour. One of the nuttiest things in yoga is the Sun Salutation, which stretches the whole body. People who practice yoga also have to hold their breath.

The second paraphrase is unacceptable because it is inaccurate and incomplete. It does not stay true to the original author's intentions, and it does not contain all the information in the original paragraph.

EXERCISE **3-6**   **Writing a Paraphrase**

Directions: Turn to Mastery Test 1 at the end of this chapter, "Applying Psychology to Everyday Life: Are You Sleep Deprived?" (p. 104). Paraphrase paragraphs 5 and 6.

OUTLINING

3 **LEARNING GOAL**

Outline information to show its organization

Outlining is a good way to create a visual picture of what you have read. In making an **outline**, you record the writer's organization and show the relative importance of and connection between ideas.

Outlining has a number of advantages:

- It gives an overview of the topic and enables you to see how various subtopics relate to one another.

- Recording the information in your own words tests your understanding of what you read.

- It is an effective way to record needed information from reference books you do not own.

How to Outline

Generally, an outline follows a format like the one below.

> I. First major idea
>   A. First supporting detail
>   1. Detail
>   2. Detail
>   B. Second supporting detail
>   1. Detail
>   a. Minor detail or example
>   b. Minor detail or example
> II. Second major idea
>   A. First supporting detail

Notice that the most important ideas are closer to the left margin. Less important ideas are indented toward the middle of the page. A quick glance at an outline shows what is most important, what is less important, and how ideas support or explain one another.

Using the Outline Format

1. **Do not be overly concerned with following the outline format exactly.** As long as your outline shows an organization of ideas, it will work for you.
2. **Write words and phrases rather than complete sentences.**

3. **Use your own words.** Do not lift words from the text.

4. **Do not write too much.** If you need to record numerous facts and details, underlining rather than outlining might be more effective.

5. **Pay attention to headings.** Be sure that all the information you place underneath a heading explains or supports that heading. Every heading indented the same amount on the page should be of equal importance.

Now read the following passage on sleep apnea and then study the outline of it.

What key point does this photograph illustrate?

From insomnia to sleepwalking to narcolepsy, sleep disorders are more common than you might think. There are more than 80 different clinical sleep disorders, and it is estimated that between 50 and 70 million Americans—children and adults—suffer from one. Many aren't even aware of their disorder, and many others never seek treatment.

Sleep Apnea

Sleep apnea is a disorder in which breathing is briefly and repeatedly interrupted during sleep. *Apnea* refers to a breathing pause that lasts at least 10 seconds. During that time, the chest may rise and fall, but little or no air may be exchanged, or the person may actually not breathe until the brain triggers a gasping inhalation. Sleep apnea affects more than 18 million Americans, or 1 in every 15 people.

There are two major types of sleep apnea: central and obstructive. *Central sleep apnea* occurs when the brain fails to tell the respiratory muscles to initiate breathing. Consumption of alcohol, certain illegal drugs, and certain medications can contribute to this condition. *Obstructive sleep apnea (OSA)*, which is the more common form, occurs when air cannot move in and out of a person's nose or mouth, even though the body tries to breathe.

Typically, OSA occurs when a person's throat muscles and tongue relax during sleep and block the airways. People who are overweight or obese often have more tissue that flaps or sags, which puts them at higher risk for sleep apnea. People with OSA are prone to heavy snoring, snorting, and gasping. These sounds occur because, as oxygen saturation levels in the blood fall, the body's autonomic nervous system is stimulated to trigger inhalation, often via a sudden gasp of breath. This response may wake the person, preventing deep sleep and causing the person to wake up in the morning feeling tired and unwell. More serious risks of OSA include chronic high blood pressure, irregular heartbeats, heart attack, and stroke. Apnea-associated sleeplessness may be a factor in an increased risk of type 2 diabetes, immune system deficiencies, and a host of other problems.

—Donatelle, *Health*, pp. 94 and 96

Sleep Apnea

I. Disorder with brief, repeated interruptions in breathing
   A. Pause in breathing for at least 10 seconds
   B. Over 18 million Americans (1 in 15) affected
II. Two major types
   A. Central sleep apnea
      1. Occurs when brain fails to initiate breathing
      2. Associated with alcohol, drugs, medications
   B. Obstructive sleep apnea (OSA)
      1. Occurs when air can't move in and out despite body's efforts
         a. Throat muscles and tongue relax in sleep and block airways
      2. Overweight or obese people at higher risk
      3. Low levels of oxygen trigger snoring, gasping
      4. Many health effects/risks
         a. Feeling tired, unwell from lack of deep sleep
         b. High blood pressure, irregular heartbeats, heart attack, stroke
         c. Increased risk of type 2 diabetes, immune system deficiencies

---

EXERCISE 3-7   Completing an Outline

Directions: Read the following passage and the incomplete outline that follows. Fill in the missing information in the outline.

The Victims' Rights Movement
Several events were key to the emergence of the **victims' rights movement**. First, the 1960s brought general concern about individual rights in many arenas, including civil rights, women's rights, inmates' rights, gay rights, and students' rights. The women's rights movement was a particularly strong supporter of victims' rights because its agenda included addressing the harms caused by the way in which the criminal justice system processed rape cases and domestic violence cases. Second, several government initiatives increased awareness and provided financial support

for victim-assistance programs. Results from national surveys helped raise awareness of the harms caused by crime and documented the large number of victims who do not report their victimization to the police. The Law Enforcement Assistance Administration (LEAA) provided funds to assist in the professionalization of law enforcement. The LEAA also provided funds for the support of innovative programs to reduce crime and research to evaluate the impact of these programs. Third, the number of victims' rights organizations increased dramatically, and national coordinating bodies such as the **National Organization for Victim Assistance (NOVA)** were founded.

—Fagin, *CJ*, p. 31

I. Key events in emergence of victims' rights movement

    A. 1960s general concern about individual rights

        1. civil rights

        2. women's rights: strong supporter of victims' rights, including rape and domestic violence

        3. inmates' rights

        4. _____

        5. _____

    B. _____

      _____

        1. _____

        2. _____

    C. _____

        1. _____

MAPPING

4 LEARNING GOAL

Draw maps to organize information

Mapping is a visual method of organizing information. It involves drawing diagrams to show how ideas in an article or chapter are related. Some students prefer mapping to outlining because they feel it is freer and less tightly structured.

Maps can take numerous forms. You can draw them in any way that shows the relationships of ideas. Figure 3-1 below shows two sample maps. Each was drawn to show the overall organization of Chapter 6 in this text.

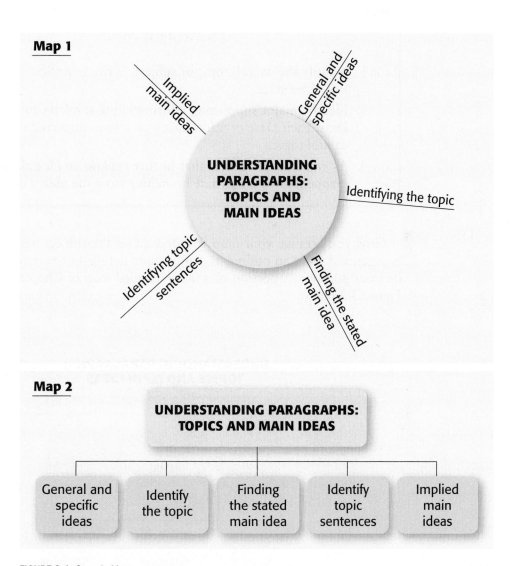

Map 1

Implied main ideas

General and specific ideas

UNDERSTANDING PARAGRAPHS: TOPICS AND MAIN IDEAS

Identifying the topic

Identifying topic sentences

Finding the stated main idea

Map 2

UNDERSTANDING PARAGRAPHS: TOPICS AND MAIN IDEAS

| General and specific ideas | Identify the topic | Finding the stated main idea | Identify topic sentences | Implied main ideas |

FIGURE 3-1 Sample Maps

How to Draw Maps

Think of a map as a picture or diagram that shows how ideas are connected.

Drawing a Map

1. **Identify the overall topic or subject.** Write it in the center or at the top of the page.
2. **Identify major supporting information that relates to the topic.** Draw each piece of information on a line connected to the central topic.
3. **As you discover details that further explain an idea already mapped, draw a new line branching from the idea it explains.**

How you arrange your map will depend on the subject matter and how it is organized. Like an outline, it can be quite detailed or very brief, depending on your purpose. A portion of a more detailed map of Chapter 6 is shown in Figure 3-2 below.

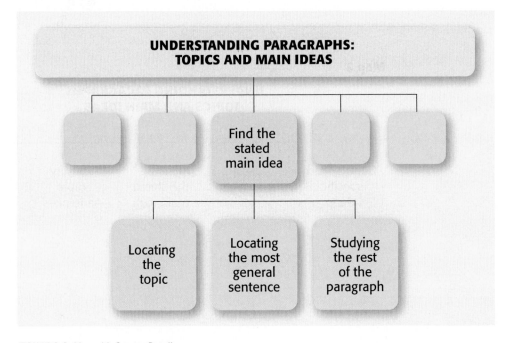

FIGURE 3-2 Map with Greater Detail

Once you are skilled at drawing maps, you can become more creative, drawing different types of maps to fit what you are reading. For example, you can draw a time line (see Figure 3-3) that shows historical events, or a process diagram to show processes and procedures (see Figure 3-4).

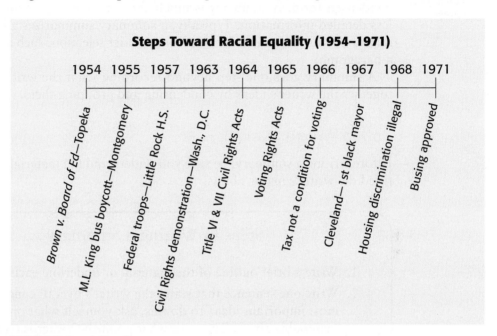

FIGURE 3-3 Sample Time Line

FIGURE 3-4 Sample Process Diagram

EXERCISE 3-8 | **Drawing a Map**

Directions: Draw a map of the excerpt "Generic Names" on page 84.

EXERCISE 3-9 | **Drawing a Map**

Directions: Draw a map of Chapter 7 of this text.

SUMMARIZING

5 LEARNING GOAL

Summarize ideas for review purposes

A **summary** is a brief statement that reviews the major idea of something you have read. Its purpose is to make a record of the most important ideas in condensed form. A summary is much shorter than an outline and contains less detailed information. Typically, a summary summarizes a longer reading selection, while a paraphrase condenses a brief selection, such as a sentence or a paragraph.

A summary goes one step beyond recording what the writer says. It pulls together the writer's ideas by condensing and grouping them.

How to Write a Summary

Before writing a summary, be sure you understand the material and have identified the writer's major points.

Steps in Writing a Summary

1. **Write a brief outline of the material or underline each major idea.**

2. **Write one sentence that states the writer's overall concern or most important idea.** To do this, ask yourself what one topic the material is about. Then ask what point the writer is trying to make about that topic. This sentence will be the topic sentence of your summary.

3. **Be sure to use your own words rather than those of the author.**

4. **Review the major supporting information that the author gives to explain the major ideas.** See Chapter 7 for further information.

5. **Decide on the level of detail you need.** The amount of detail you include, if any, will depend on your purpose for writing the summary.

6. **Normally, present ideas in the summary in the same order in which they appear in the original material.**

7. **For other than textbook material, if the writer presents a clear opinion or expresses an attitude toward the subject matter, include it in your summary.**

8. **Do not concentrate on correctness when writing summaries for your own use.** Some students prefer to write summaries using words and phrases rather than complete sentences.

Read the following summary of "The Victims' Rights Movement," which appeared on pages 93–94.

Notice that this summary contains only the broadest, most important ideas. Details are not included.

Sample Summary

> *Three events were important in the growth of the victims' rights movement. In the 1960s there was concern about individual rights, including women's rights, and the women's rights movement was supportive of victims' rights because the victims were often female. Government programs and surveys raised awareness of victims' rights and created funding for victims' programs and research, as well as for training law enforcement. The number of victims' rights organizations increased and national coordinating bodies were formed.*

EXERCISE 3-10   Writing a Summary

Working Together

Directions: Form teams of three or four students. Each team should choose and agree to watch a particular television show that airs before the next class. During the next class meeting, collaborate to write a summary of the show. Summaries may be presented to the class for discussion and evaluation.

EXERCISE 3-11   Writing a Summary

Directions: On a separate sheet of paper, write a summary of one of the reading selections in Part Six of this text.

EXERCISE 3-12   Writing a Summary

Directions: Write a summary of the article "Sleep Apnea" on pages 92–93. When you have finished, compare it with the sample summary shown in Figure 3-5 on the next page. Then answer the following questions.

1. How does your summary differ from the sample?

2. Does your summary begin with a topic sentence? How does it compare with the one in the sample?

3. Does your summary include ideas in the order in which they were given in the article?

Sleep apnea is a disorder in which breathing is repeatedly interrupted during sleep, with pauses lasting at least 10 seconds. The two major types are central sleep apnea, in which the brain fails to initiate breathing, and obstructive sleep apnea (OSA), in which air is unable to move in and out of a person's nose or mouth, typically because airways are blocked. Falling oxygen saturation levels in the blood trigger sudden inhalation, which may prevent deep sleep. People with OSA may feel tired or unwell from sleep interruptions or they may face much more serious health problems.

FIGURE 3-5 Sample Summary: "Sleep Apnea"

EXERCISE 3-13   **Comparing Methods of Organization**

Directions: Your instructor will choose a reading from Part Six and will then divide the class into three groups. Members of one group should outline the material, another group should draw maps, and the third should write summaries. When the groups have completed their tasks, the class members should review each other's work. Several students can read their summaries, draw maps, and write outlines on the chalkboard. Discuss which of the three methods seemed most effective for the material and how well prepared each group feels for (1) an essay exam, (2) a multiple-choice exam, and (3) a class discussion.

IMMEDIATE AND PERIODIC REVIEW

6 LEARNING GOAL

Review for maximum retention

Once you have read and organized information, the last step is to learn it. Fortunately, this is not a difficult task if you have organized the information effectively. In fact, through underlining, outlining, and/or summarizing, you have already learned a large portion of the material. **Review**, then, is a way to fix, or store, information in your memory for later recall. There are two types of review, *immediate* and *periodic*.

How Immediate Review Works

Immediate review is done right after you have finished reading an assignment or writing an outline or summary. When you finish any of these, you may feel like breathing a sigh of relief and taking a break. However, it is worth the time and effort to spend another five minutes reviewing what you just read and refreshing your memory. The best way to do this is to go back through the chapter and reread the headings, graphic material, introduction, summary, and any underlining or marginal notes.

Immediate review works because it consolidates, or draws together, the material just read. It also gives a final, lasting impression of the content. Considerable research has been done on the effectiveness of immediate review. Results indicate that review done immediately rather than delayed until a later time makes a large difference in the amount remembered.

How Periodic Review Works

Although immediate review will increase your recall of information, it will not help you retain information for long periods of time. To remember information over time, periodically refresh your memory. This is known as **periodic review**. Go back over the material on a regular basis. Do this by looking again at those sections that carry the basic meaning and reviewing your underlining, outlining, and/or summaries. Below is an example of a schedule one student set up to periodically review assigned chapters in a psychology textbook. You can see that this student reviewed each chapter the week after reading it and again two weeks later. This schedule is only an example. You will need to make a schedule for each course that fits the course requirements. For math and science courses, for example, you may need to include a review of previous homework assignments and laboratory work. In other courses, less or more frequent review of previous material may be needed.

Week 1	Read ch. 1
Week 2	Review ch. 1
	Read ch. 2
Week 3	Review ch. 2
	Read ch. 3
Week 4	Review ch. 3
	Review ch. 1
	Read ch. 4
Week 5	Review ch. 4
	Review ch. 2
	Read ch. 5

EXERCISE 3-14   Planning a Review Schedule

Directions: Choose one of your courses that involves regular textbook reading assignments. Plan a reading and periodic review schedule for the next three weeks. Assume that new chapters will be assigned as frequently as in previous weeks and that you want to review whatever has been covered over the past three weeks.

LEARNING STYLE TIPS

If you tend to be a . . .	Then strengthen your review strategies by . . .
Creative learner	Brainstorming before and after each assignment to discover new ways to tie the material together
Pragmatic learner	Creating, writing, and answering review questions; preparing and taking self-tests

SELF-TEST SUMMARY

1 What are high-lighting and marking and how are they used?

Highlighting is a way of sorting important information from less important information. It eliminates the need to reread entire textbook chapters in order to review the key content. It also has the advantage of helping you stay active and involved with what you are reading.

Marking is a system that involves using signs, symbols, and marginal notes to react to, summarize, or comment on the material.

2 What two steps are involved in paraphrasing?

To paraphrase effectively, (1) substitute synonyms while (2) maintaining the original order of ideas. Your paraphrase should maintain the author's focus and emphasis.

3 What is outlining and how is it used?

Outlining is a method of recording the most important information and showing the organization and relative importance of ideas. It is particularly useful when you need to see how ideas relate to one another or when you want to get an overview of a subject.

4 What is mapping and how is it used?

Mapping is a visual method of organizing information. It involves drawing diagrams to show how ideas are related.

5 **What is summarizing and how is it used?**	Summarizing is a way to pull together the most important ideas in condensed form. It provides a quick review of the material and forces you to explain the writer's ideas in your own words.
6 **What are two types of review and how do they increase retention?**	Immediate review is done right after finishing an assignment. It consolidates the material and makes it stick in your memory. Periodic review is done regularly, at specified intervals. It keeps information fresh in your mind.

GOING ◯ ONLINE

1. **Highlighting Text Electronically**

   Most word-processing programs (including Microsoft Word) offer highlighting capabilities. Go to a Web site of your choice, and cut and paste three paragraphs into a Word document. (Be sure to provide complete source information at the end of your document.) Read the paragraphs and then highlight the document on screen. How is this process similar to highlighting a printed document? How is it different?

2. **Exploring Your Web Browser**

   While most students surf the Web every day, many are not aware of all of their Web browser's capabilities. Take 15 minutes to explore the menu options on your Web browser. Name two or three features that might be helpful as you read online. Share your findings with the class. Specify which browser you have evaluated (such as Chrome, Firefox, or Safari).

3. **Paraphrasing Online Sources**

   Given the amount of online research you will likely conduct during your college studies, it can be helpful to paraphrase online sources. Select a Web site and paraphrase the contents of its home page.

Applying Psychology to Everyday Life: Are You Sleep Deprived?

Saundra K. Ciccarelli and J. Noland White

Before Reading

This selection, taken from a psychology textbook, explores the causes and hazards of sleep deprivation.

Previewing the Reading

Using the steps listed on pages 49–50, preview the reading selection. When you have finished, complete the following items.

1. What two key questions do you expect this reading selection to answer?

   a. _____

   b. _____

2. Indicate whether each statement is true (T) or false (F).

   _____ a. Sleep deprivation is a problem mostly among the elderly.

   _____ b. The Internet is a good source of quizzes to help you determine if you have a sleep disorder.

   _____ c. Sleep disorders can cause sleep deprivation.

Predicting and Connecting

1. Do you get enough sleep? Would you like to get more?

2. How can you use the headings included with this reading to help you study?

> **Vocabulary Preview**
>
> **insomnia** (par. 4) the inability to fall asleep, stay asleep, or get enough sleep
>
> **narcolepsy** (par. 5) a disorder in which a person falls suddenly into a deep sleep

How Serious Is the Problem of Sleep Deprivation?

1   Sleep deprivation has long been considered a fact of life for many people, especially college students. Dr. William Dement, one of the most renowned sleep experts in the field, believes that people are ignorant of the detrimental effects of sleep deprivation. Here are some of the facts he points out concerning the widespread nature of sleep deprivation:

- 55 percent of drowsy driving fatalities occur under the age of 25.
- 56 percent of the adult population reports that daytime drowsiness is a problem.

- In a study of 1,000 people who reported no daytime drowsiness, 34 percent were actually found to be dangerously sleepy.
- In samples of undergraduates, nurses, and medical students, 80 percent were dangerously sleep deprived.

The student in the background is unable to stay awake during his class, indicating that he is seriously sleep deprived. Has this happened to you?

2   Dr. Dement cautions that drowsiness should be considered a red alert. Contrary to many people's belief that drowsiness indicates the first step in failing asleep, he states that drowsiness is the last step—if you are drowsy, you are seconds away from sleep.

3   In an article published by CNN on its interactive Web site, the National Commission on Sleep Disorders estimates that "sleep deprivation costs $150 billion a year in higher stress and reduced workplace productivity." Sleep deprivation was one of the factors indicated in such disasters as the explosion of the *Challenger*, the Exxon *Valdez* oil spill, and the Chernobyl disaster.

More disturbing facts:

- 30 to 40 percent of all heavy truck accidents can be attributed to driver fatigue.
- Drivers who are awake for 17 to 19 hours were more dangerous than drivers with a blood alcohol level of .05.
- 16 to 60 percent of road accidents involve sleep deprivation (the wide variation is due to the inability to confirm the cause of accidents, as the drivers are often killed).
- Sleep deprivation is linked to higher levels of stress, anxiety, depression, and unnecessary risk taking.

4   Clearly, sleep deprivation is a serious and all-too-common problem. In today's 24-hour-a-day society, stores are always open, services such as banking and transportation are always available, and many professionals (such as nurses, doctors, and firefighters) must work varying shifts around the clock. As stated earlier, shift work can seriously disrupt the normal sleep–wake cycle, often causing insomnia.

Causes of Sleep Deprivation

5   Many of the sleep disorders that were discussed in this chapter are themselves causes of sleep deprivation. Sleep apnea, narcolepsy, sleepwalking, night terrors, and a condition called "restless leg syndrome," in which a person constantly moves his or her legs that are tingly or have crawling sensations, are all causes. Yet these problems are not the sole, or most common, cause of sleep deprivation.

6   The most obvious cause is the refusal of many people to go to sleep at a reasonable time, so that they can get the 8 hours of sleep that most adults need in order to function well. People want to watch that last bit of news or get a little more work done or party into the wee hours. Another reason for sleep loss is worry. People live in stressful times, and many people worry about a variety of concerns: debts, the stock market, relationships, war, rising crime, and so on. Finally, some medications that people take, both prescription and over-the-counter drugs, interfere with the sleep–wake cycle. For example, decongestants that some people take to relieve sinus congestion may cause a racing heartbeat, preventing them from relaxing enough to sleep.

How Can You Tell if You Are Sleep Deprived?

7   You may be sleep deprived if you:

- actually need your alarm clock to wake up.
- find getting out of bed in the morning is a struggle.
- feel tired, irritable, or stressed out for much of the day.
- have trouble concentrating or remembering.
- fall asleep watching TV, in meetings, lectures, or warm rooms.
- fall asleep after heavy meals or after a low dose of alcohol.
- fall asleep within 5 minutes of getting into bed. (A well-rested person actually takes 15 to 20 minutes to fall asleep.)

8   If you are interested in learning more about sleep deprivation and sleep disorders that can cause it, try searching the Internet. There are some excellent sites about sleep and sleep disorders, including many with online tests that can help people decide whether or not they have a sleep disorder.

—Ciccarelli and White, *Psychology*, pp. 169–171

After Reading

Checking Your Comprehension

_____ 1. The focus of this selection is on
   a. the sleep–wake cycle.
   b. brain activity during sleep.
   c. sleep deprivation.
   d. common sleep disorders.

_____ 2. The main idea of paragraph 1 is that
   a. sleep deprivation is a fact of life for college students.
   b. sleep deprivation is widespread and harmful.
   c. Dr. William Dement is an authority on sleep deprivation.
   d. drowsiness is actually a sign of being dangerously sleepy.

_____ 3. Of the following signs, the only one that does *not* indicate you may be sleep deprived is
  a. you actually need your alarm clock to wake up.
  b. you fall asleep after heavy meals.
  c. it takes you 15 to 20 minutes to fall asleep after going to bed.
  d. it is a struggle to get out of bed in the morning.

_____ 4. According to the selection, the most obvious cause of sleep deprivation is
  a. restless leg syndrome.
  b. narcolepsy.
  c. sleep apnea.
  d. the failure to go to bed at a reasonable time.

_____ 5. The authors use all of the following types of supporting details in this selection *except*
  a. examples.
  b. facts.
  c. statistics.
  d. procedures.

Applying Your Skills: Organizing and Remembering Information

_____ 6. The most important words to highlight in the last sentence of paragraph 2 are
  a. drowsiness sleep.
  b. drowsiness last step from sleep.
  c. many people's belief drowsiness first step falling asleep last step drowsy away from sleep.
  d. Contrary many people's belief drowsiness indicates first step falling asleep drowsiness is last step you are drowsy seconds away from sleep.

_____ 7. The most important words to highlight in the last sentence of paragraph 4 are
  a. shift work seriously normal.
  b. work can disrupt normal cycle often.
  c. shift work disrupt sleep–wake cycle insomnia.
  d. shift work seriously disrupt normal sleep–wake cycle often insomnia.

Use the following outline of paragraphs 5 and 6 to answer questions 8–10.

Causes of Sleep Deprivation
  I. Sleep disorders
    A. Sleep apnea
    B. Narcolepsy
    C. _____
    D. Night terrors
    E. _____
      1. Tingly/crawling sensations cause legs to move
  II. Refusal to go to bed on time
  III. Worry
  IV. _____
    A. Prescription and over-the-counter
    B. Interfere with sleep–wake cycle

_____ 8. The phrase that belongs next to [C] in the outline is
  a. Sleep deprivation.
  b. Sleepwalking.
  c. Sleep–wake cycle.
  d. Sleep disorder.

_____ 9. The phrase that belongs next to [E] in the outline is
  a. Shift work.
  b. Common cause.
  c. Restless leg syndrome.
  d. Sleepwalking.

_____ 10. The word or words that belong next to [IV] in the outline are
  a. Some medications.
  b. Illegal drugs.
  c. Decongestants.
  d. Racing heartbeat.

Studying Words

_____11. The word *renowned* (par. 1) means
   a. unpopular.
   b. famous.
   c. unfamiliar.
   d. local.

_____12. The word *detrimental* (par. 1) means
   a. harmful.
   b. emotional.
   c. pleasant.
   d. skillful.

_____13. The word *cautions* (par. 2) means
   a. reminds.
   b. guesses.
   c. warns.
   d. allows.

_____14. The prefix of the word *interactive* (par. 3) means
   a. away.
   b. between.
   c. over.
   d. without.

_____15. The word *disrupt* (par. 4) means
   a. assist.
   b. surround.
   c. maintain.
   d. disturb.

For more practice, ask your instructor for an opportunity to work on the mastery tests that appear in the Test Bank.

Thinking Visually

1. What does the photograph contribute to the reading overall? What details do you notice that are relevant to the reading?

2. What is the purpose of the box included with the reading? How might the information in the box be helpful to the author's audience?

3. If you can, take an online test for sleep disorders, as mentioned in paragraph 8. Did you identify a sleep problem?

Thinking Critically About the Reading

1. What is the authors' approach to their topic? Would you consider them sympathetic to those who are suffering from a lack of sleep?

2. Do you consider yourself sleep deprived? Were you aware of any of the serious effects before you read this selection?

3. How does our "24-hour-a-day society" contribute to the problem of sleep deprivation?

4. If you knew someone suffering from sleep deprivation, what advice would you give him or her?

Academic Application: Summarizing the Reading

Directions: Suppose you are studying for an exam on this reading selection. Complete the following summary of the reading by filling in the blanks.

Sleep deprivation is _____. The National

Commission on _____ estimates _____

_____ Sleep deprivation

was a factor _____ and is linked to _____

_____.

Sleep deprivation may be caused by _____

_____.

MASTERY TEST 2 Reading Selection

Corporate Social Responsibility

Michael R. Solomon, Mary Anne Poatsy, and Kendall Martin

Before Reading

This selection originally appeared in an introductory business textbook. It is an excerpt from a chapter titled "Ethics in Business."

Previewing the Reading

Using the steps listed on pages 49–50, preview the reading selection. When you have finished, complete the following items.

1. _____ is defined as a company's obligation to conduct its activities with the aim of achieving social, environmental, and economic development.

2. Place an X next to the topics that you expect will be discussed in the selection.

   _____ a. Marketing and consumer issues

   _____ b. Expanding product lines into new markets

   _____ c. Community and good neighbor policies

   _____ d. Ethical sourcing and procurement

   _____ e. Selecting the best office machinery

Predicting and Connecting

1. What responsibilities do employers have with regard to their employees and communities?

2. Do you expect the reading to be fairly easy to understand, of moderate difficulty, or challenging? Why?

> **Vocabulary Preview**
>
> **sourcing and procurement** (par. 3) purchase of resources used by a business
>
> **size-zero** (par. 5) extremely thin

During Reading

As you read the selection, complete each of the following. When highlighting, use a different color highlighter for each task.

a. Highlight the topic sentence of each paragraph. If the main idea is unstated, write a sentence that states it.

b. Highlight the most important details in each paragraph.

c. Highlight useful transitional words and phrases that help you understand and connect the author's ideas.

d. Read and respond to the questions in the margin.

---

1 Corporate social responsibility (CSR) is defined as a company's obligation to conduct its activities with the aim of achieving social, environmental, and economic development. All business organizations, regardless of their size, have a corporate responsibility. By being socially responsible, a company makes decisions in five major areas:

  1. Human rights and employment standards in the workplace
  2. Ethical sourcing and procurement
  3. Marketing and consumer issues
  4. Environmental, health, and safety concerns
  5. Community and good neighbor policies

> Why do the authors provide this numbered list?

Let's look at each of these areas.

Human Rights and Employment Standards in the Workplace

2 CSR concerns affect the world outside the office in both local and global communities. For example, employment standards—how a company respects and cares for its employees—are reflected locally in the policies a company sets and the impact a company has on the community. As a business interacts more with the global marketplace, a company will have to make decisions about ethical standards on tough issues such as child labor, pollution, fair wages, and human rights. Consider the case of the Vadanta Resources, a mining and aluminum refining company based in the United Kingdom. When Vadanta came into the Indian community of Orissa, it promised great gains in the quality of life for its employees and the entire region. Such gains have not appeared, however, and, because of the refining company's practices, the air is hard to breathe. Meanwhile, the river, the main source of drinking water, is so polluted that bathing in it causes rashes and blisters. What responsibility does Vadanta have to its employees, the people of the area, and company stockholders?

> Why do the authors provide this specific example?

Ethical Sourcing and Procurement

3   Finding a source for raw materials and making agreements with suppliers is an aspect of many businesses. In today's global marketplace, many companies find themselves working with international suppliers. Once a business considers purchasing materials from a supplier in a different country or even a different region of their home country, the company is tied to environmental and social concerns in that area. Consider a company that has an assembly plant in a different country. That company is now tied to the social conditions there. To keep its supplier operating or keep an assembly plant running smoothly, the company has a vested interest in the quality of the schools in that area so that the local workforce is educated.

4   Many people have purchased the Apple iPhone but few were aware of the working conditions of Apple suppliers. Apple was forced to take a serious look at ethical sourcing with increased production of the iPhone, iPad, and iTouch. An audit of supplier factories in China revealed the use of underage workers, environmental violations, and unsafe worker conditions sometimes so severe that there were suicide attempts by workers. Apple disclosed the results of this audit publicly in their Apple Supplier Responsibility Progress Report, but it is not clear how the company will move to correct conditions.

Marketing and Consumer Issues

What are the authors implying?

Why does the paragraph close with these questions?

5   Marketing can often present ethical challenges. In addition to issues regarding truth in advertising, marketers must consider messages that may be manipulative even if they are not outright lies. For example, several major fashion labels like Prada, Versace, and Armani have agreed to ban size-zero models from their fashion shows. As more medical authorities have linked the viewing of these images with an increase in eating disorders, the fashion industry is faced with a decision. There are many marketing and consumer issues that companies must consider if they are to behave in a socially responsible way. What do you think? Is the use of size-zero professional models socially irresponsible? How do we judge when responsible behavior turns into irresponsible behavior?

Environmental, Health, and Safety Concerns

6   Many industries, even small companies, make decisions every day that affect the environment and the safety of their workers or neighbors. From multinational manufacturing giants to the local auto body shop,

any industry involved with processes that produce toxic waste must make decisions that directly affect the environment. Meanwhile, the production of toxic materials is moving at a far faster pace than the growth of proper storage and disposal facilities and techniques, so disposal becomes more and more expensive. One of the most infamous cases was documented in the award-winning book *A Civil Action* (Vintage, 1996). A high incidence of childhood leukemia appeared in a small Massachusetts town. A civil action lawsuit filed by one boy's mother ultimately found that the town water supply had been poisoned by trichloroethylene dumped by two local businesses. What are the short- and long-term costs of ignoring these concerns? Companies that have a CSR focus concentrate on ways to make such decisions in a socially sound way.

What feeling does this photograph create?

Community and "Good Neighbor" Policies

7   Finally, CSR is concerned with how a company affects the community, particularly the surrounding neighborhood. This issue has been a challenge for Walmart for years. In the documentary *Wal-Mart: The High Cost of Low Price*, film director Robert Greenwald argues that Walmart pays its associates so little that the arrival of a Walmart outlet in a community actually costs the community. Because workers are paid poorly and are not offered medical benefits to cover their children, Medicaid expenditures increase. In addition, Greenwald argues that many local and smaller businesses cannot compete with the giant and are forced to close. Adding insult to injury, often a community has given Walmart subsidies to attract them to the area. Finding a way to be a good corporate neighbor is important to avoid the tensions and bad publicity that Walmart has struggled against.

What does the phrase "add insult to injury" mean?

—Solomon et al., *Better Business*, pp. 64–66

After Reading

Checking Your Comprehension

_____ 1. Which company, mentioned in the reading, was responsible for polluting a major source of drinking water in India?
  a. Apple.
  b. Vedanta.
  c. Walmart.
  d. Prada.

_____ 2. A company that behaves in a way that reflects a good sense of corporate social responsibility would concern itself with all of the following *except*
  a. contributing to local political campaigns.
  b. paying fair wages.
  c. protecting the environment.
  d. advertising fairly.

_____ 3. Why have some fashion companies decided not to use size-zero models in fashion shows?
  a. The requirement for a size zero discriminates against males.
  b. Clothing designers find it difficult to create fashions for such thin people.
  c. The fabrics used to make size-zero clothing are not durable or attractive.
  d. Viewing thin models has been linked to eating disorders.

_____ 4. The book *A Civil Action* focused on the high number of cases of _____ in a Massachusetts town.
  a. cancer.
  b. leukemia.
  c. lupus.
  d. diabetes.

_____ 5. Which of the following is *not* one of the common effects of a Walmart moving into town?
  a. The Walmart costs the town more than the store contributes to the town.
  b. Medicaid expenditures increase because Walmart does not give its employees medical benefits.
  c. Smaller businesses cannot compete with Walmart and end up going out of business.
  d. The high-school graduation rate drops as students leave school to work for Walmart.

Applying Your Skills: Organizing and Remembering Information

_____ 6. By highlighting the five subheadings in this reading, you could easily create _____ of the reading.
  a. a paraphrase.
  b. an outline.
  c. a summary.
  d. a critique.

_____ 7. Which of the following would be the best way to mark or annotate paragraph 7?
  a. history of Walmart.
  b. Robt. Greenwald, director.
  c. good corporate neighbor qualities.
  d. Walmart: costs imposed on community.

Use the following outline to answer questions 8 and 9.

Corporate Social Responsibility
1. Human rights and employment standards in the workplace
   ex. Vedanta, polluted river in India.
2. Ethical sourcing and procurement.
   ex. Apple found human rights violations in China.
3. (question 8 _____)
   ex. Fashion industry bans size-zero models.
4. Environmental, health, and safety concerns
   ex. A Civil Action: story of pollution in Mass.
5. Community and good neighbor policies
   (question 9_____)

_____ 8 Which phrase should appear on the line marked (question 8)?
   a. Truth and lies.
   b. Social responsibility and the media.
   c. Marketing and consumer issues.
   d. Prada, Versace, and Armani.

_____ 9 Which phrase should appear on the line marked (question 9)?
   a. ex. Walmart.
   b. The high cost of a low price.
   c. ex. Employee benefits and Medicare.
   d. Avoiding tensions and bad publicity.

_____ 10 Which words complete the following paraphrase of paragraph 4?

   Those who buy Apple products may not be aware of the working conditions at foreign companies that supply Apple with raw materials and other products. When Apple looked closely at its _____ suppliers, it found underage _____, dangerous working conditions, and even cases of employees who tried to kill themselves. Apple made all of this information public, but it does not seem that Apple has done anything to address the problems yet.
   a. global, girls.
   b. Indian, drinking.
   c. product, drug abuse.
   d. Chinese, employees.

Studying Words

Using context or a dictionary, define each of the following words as it is used in the reading.

11. vested (par. 3) _____

12. audit (par. 4) _____

13. outright (par. 5) _____

14. toxic (par. 6) _____

15. subsidies (par. 7) _____

Thinking Visually

1. How does the photo on page 113 illustrate the content of the selection?

2. Create a map of the reading, following the directions on page 96.

3. What other types of photos or visual aids would be useful with this reading? Explain.

Thinking Critically About the Reading

1. How would you describe the authors' approach to corporate social responsibility?

2. The reading summarizes several good pieces of advice for companies that want to behave in a socially responsible way. List at least five ways companies should *not* behave.

3. Paragraph 5 lists one way that the fashion industry is behaving in a socially responsible fashion. What other advice would you give to the fashion industry?

4. The authors talk about the problems that a Walmart can bring to a community (par. 7). Can you think of any benefits a Walmart brings to a town?

5. What would be the best way to study this reading for an upcoming quiz or exam?

Academic Application: Writing a Paraphrase

Directions: You are working in a group setting, and each group member must paraphrase one paragraph from the reading. Your assignment is to paraphrase paragraph 5. Fill in the blanks in the following paraphrase with the appropriate words or phrases.

Companies that engage in marketing must be concerned with _____. They must be sure their advertising does not _____ or even twist the truth, while also making sure it is not misleading. Several designers, including Armani, _____, and Versace, have promised not to use extremely thin models in fashion shows, because research shows that people who view these models may develop an _____. Companies must also be aware when they cross the line from acceptable marketing into _____ marketing.

CHAPTER

4

Using Context Clues

Focusing on . . . Context Clues

LEARNING GOALS

This chapter will show you how to

1 Understand context clues

2 Use five types of context clues

3 Understand the limitations of context clues

Suppose you saw this photograph in a psychology textbook. Why is the photo confusing? The top half of the photo does not fit with the bottom half. No doubt you would have trouble understanding and explaining the photograph. What is missing is its context—the information surrounding the image shown in the photo. However, if you read the chapter opener and learned that the chapter is about the aging process, then you would be able to grasp its meaning and purpose.

WHAT IS CONTEXT?

LEARNING GOAL

Understand context clues

Try to figure out what is missing in the following brief paragraph. Write the missing words in the blanks.

> Most Americans can speak only one _____. Europeans, however, _____ several. As a result, Europeans think _____ are unfriendly and unwilling to communicate with them.

Did you insert the word *language* in the first blank, *speak* or *know* in the second blank, and *Americans* in the third blank? Most likely, you correctly identified all three missing words. You could tell from the sentence which word to put in. The words around the missing words—the sentence context— gave you clues as to which word would fit and make sense. Such clues are called **context clues**.

While you probably will not find missing words on a printed page, you will often find words that you do not know. Context clues can help you figure out the meanings of unfamiliar words.

Example

Phobias, such as fear of heights, water, or confined spaces, are difficult to eliminate.

From the sentence, you can tell that *phobia* means "fear of specific objects or situations."

Here is another example:

> The couple finally **secured** a table at the popular, crowded restaurant.

You can figure out that *secured* means "got" or "took ownership of" the table.

TYPES OF CONTEXT CLUES

LEARNING GOAL

Use five types of context clues

There are five types of context clues to look for: (1) definition, (2) synonym, (3) example, (4) contrast, and (5) inference.

Definition Clues

Many times a writer defines a word immediately following its use. The writer may directly define a word by giving a brief **definition** or a synonym (a word that has the same meaning). Such words and phrases as *means, is, refers to,* and *can be defined as* are often used. Here are some examples:

> **Corona** refers to the outermost part of the sun's atmosphere.
>
> A **soliloquy** is a speech made by a character in a play that reveals his or her thoughts to the audience.

Sometimes, rather than formally define the word, a writer may provide clues or synonyms. Punctuation is often used to signal that a definition clue to a word's meaning is to follow. Punctuation also separates the meaning clue from the rest of the sentence. Three types of punctuation are used in this way. In the examples below, notice that the meaning clue is separated from the rest of the sentence by punctuation.

1. Commas

    > An **oligopoly**, *control of a product by a small number of companies,* exists in the long-distance phone market.
    >
    > **Equity**, *general principles of fairness and justice,* is used in law when existing laws do not apply or are inadequate.

2. Parentheses

    > A leading cause of heart disease is a diet with too much **cholesterol** (*a fatty substance made of carbon, hydrogen, and oxygen*).

3. Dashes

    > Ancient Egyptians wrote in **hieroglyphics**—*pictures used to represent words.*
    >
    > **Facets**—*small flat surfaces at different angles*—bring out the beauty of a diamond.

EXERCISE 4-1   Using Definition Context Clues

Directions: Read each sentence and write a definition or synonym for each boldfaced word or phrase. Use the definition context clue to help you determine word meaning.

1. **Glog**, a Swedish hot punch, is often served at holiday parties.

---

2. The judge's **candor**—his sharp, open frankness—shocked the jury.

_____

3. A **chemical bond** is a strong attractive force that holds two or more atoms together.

_____

4. **Lithium** (an alkali metal) is so soft it can be cut with a knife.

_____

5. Hearing, technically known as **audition**, begins when a sound wave reaches the outer ear.

_____

6. Five-line rhyming poems, or **limericks**, are among the simplest forms of poetry.

_____

7. Our country's **gross national product**—the total market value of its national output of goods and services—is increasing steadily.

_____

8. A **species** is a group of animals or plants that share similar characteristics and are able to interbreed.

_____

9. Broad, flat noodles that are served covered with sauce or butter are called **fettuccine**.

_____

10. Many diseases have **latent periods**, periods of time between the infection and the first appearance of a symptom.

_____

Synonym Clues

Rather than formally define the word, a writer may provide a **synonym**—a word or brief phrase that is close in meaning. The synonym may appear in the same sentence as the unknown word.

> The author purposely left the ending of his novel **ambiguous,** or *unclear,* so readers would have to decide for themselves what happened.

Other times, the synonym may appear anywhere in the passage, in an earlier or later sentence.

> After the soccer match, a **melee** broke out in the parking lot. Three people were injured in the *brawl,* and several others were arrested.

EXERCISE 4-2   **Using Synonym Context Clues**

Directions: Read each sentence and write a definition or synonym for each boldfaced word or phrase. Use the synonym context clue to help you determine word meaning.

1. The mayor's assistant was accused of **malfeasance**, although he denied any wrongdoing. _____

2. The words of the president seemed to excite and **galvanize** the American troops, who cheered enthusiastically throughout the speech. _____

3. Venus and Serena Williams's superior ability and **prowess** on the tennis court have inspired many girls to become athletes. _____

4. Many gardeners improve the quality of their soil by **amending** it with organic compost. _____

5. Eliminating salt from the diet is a **prudent**, sensible decision for people with high blood pressure. _____

6. The **cadence**, or rhythm, of the Dixieland band had many people tapping their feet along with the music. _____

7. Edgar Allan Poe is best known for his **macabre** short stories and poems. His eerie tale "The Fall of the House of Usher" was later made into a horror movie starring Vincent Price. _____

8. While she was out of the country, Greta authorized me to act as her **proxy**, or agent, in matters having to do with her business and her personal bank accounts.

_____

9. The **arsenal** of a baseball pitcher ideally includes several different kinds of pitches. From this supply of pitches, he or she needs to have at least one that can fool the batter. _____

10. A **coalition** of neighborhood representatives formed to fight a proposed highway through the area. The group also had the support of several local businesses.

_____

Example Clues

Writers often include **examples** that help to explain or clarify a word. Suppose you do not know the meaning of the word *toxic*, and you find it used in the following sentence:

> **Toxic** materials, such as arsenic, asbestos, pesticides, and lead, can cause bodily damage.

This sentence gives four examples of toxic materials. From the examples given, which are all poisonous substances, you could conclude that *toxic* means "poisonous."

Examples

Forest floors are frequently covered with **fungi**—molds, mushrooms, and mildews.

Legumes, such as peas and beans, produce pods.

Arachnids, including tarantulas, black widow spiders, and ticks, often have segmented bodies.

EXERCISE 4-3   Using Example Context Clues

Directions: Read each sentence and write a definition or synonym for each boldfaced word or phrase. Use the example context clue to help you determine meaning.

1. Many **pharmaceuticals**, including morphine and penicillin, are not readily available in some countries. _____

2. The child was **reticent** in every respect; she would not speak, refused to answer questions, and avoided looking at anyone. _____

3. Most **condiments**, such as pepper, mustard, and catsup, are used to improve the flavor of foods. _____

4. Instructors provide their students with **feedback** through test grades and comments on papers. _____

5. **Physiological needs**—hunger, thirst, and sex—promote survival of the human species. _____

6. Clothing is available in a variety of **fabrics**, including cotton, wool, polyester, and linen. _____

7. In the past month, we have had almost every type of **precipitation**—rain, snow, sleet, and hail. _____

8. **Involuntary reflexes**, like breathing and beating of the heart, are easily measured. _____

9. The student had a difficult time distinguishing between **homonyms**—words such as *see* and *sea, wore* and *war,* and *deer* and *dear.*

   _____

10. Abstract paintings often include such **geometrics** as squares, cubes, and triangles. _____

Contrast Clues

It is sometimes possible to determine the meaning of an unknown word from a word or phrase in the context that has an opposite meaning. If a single word provides a clue, it is often an **antonym**—a word opposite in meaning to the unknown word. Notice, in the following sentence, how a word opposite in meaning to the boldfaced word provides a clue to its meaning:

> One of the dinner guests **succumbed** to the temptation to have a second piece of cake, but the others resisted.

Although you may not know the meaning of *succumbed*, you know that the one guest who succumbed was different from the others who resisted. The word *but* suggests this. Since the others resisted a second dessert, you can tell that one guest gave in and had a piece. Thus, *succumbed* means the opposite of *resist*; that is, "to give in to."

Examples

The professor **advocates** testing on animals, *but* many of her students feel it is cruel.

Most of the graduates were **elated**, *though* a few felt sad and depressed.

The old man acted **morosely**, *whereas* his grandson was very lively.

The gentleman was quite **portly**, *but* his wife was thin.

EXERCISE 4-4   **Using Contrast Context Clues**

Directions: Read each sentence and write a definition or synonym for each boldfaced word. Use the contrast clue to help you determine meaning.

1. Some city dwellers are **affluent**; others live in or near poverty.

   _____

2. I am certain that the hotel will hold our reservation; however, if you are **dubious**, call to make sure. _____

3. Although most experts **concurred** with the research findings, several strongly disagreed. _____

4. The speaker **denounced** certain legal changes while praising other reforms.

   _____

5. The woman's parents **thwarted** her marriage plans though they liked her fiancé.

   _____

6. In medieval Europe, **peasants** led difficult lives, whereas the wealthy landowners lived in luxury. _____

7. When the couple moved into their new home they **revamped** the kitchen and bathroom but did not change the rest of the rooms. _____

8. The young nurse was **bewildered** by the patient's symptoms, but the doctor realized she was suffering from a rare form of leukemia. _____

9. Despite my husband's **pessimism** about my chances of winning the lottery, I was certain I would win. _____

_____

10. The mayoral candidate praised the town council, while the mayor **deprecated** it.

_____

Inference Clues

Many times you can figure out the meaning of an unknown word by using logic and reasoning skills. For instance, look at the following sentence:

> Bob is quite **versatile**; he is a good student, a top athlete, an excellent car mechanic, and a gourmet cook.

You can see that Bob is successful at many different types of activities, and you could reason (**infer**) that *versatile* means "capable of doing many things competently."

Examples

When the customer tried to pay with Mexican **pesos**, the clerk explained that the store accepted only U.S. dollars.

The potato salad looked so plain that I decided to **garnish** it with parsley and paprika to give it some color.

We had to leave the car and walk up because the **incline** was too steep to drive.

Since Reginald was nervous, he brought his rabbit's foot **talisman** with him to the exam.

EXERCISE **4-5**   **Using Inference Context Clues**

Directions: Read each sentence and write a definition or synonym for each bold-faced word. Try to reason out the meaning of each word using information provided in the context.

1. The **wallabies** at the zoo looked like kangaroos. _____

2. The foreign students quickly **assimilated** many aspects of American culture.

_____

3. On hot, humid summer afternoons, I often feel **languid**.

   _____

4. Some physical fitness experts recommend jogging or weight lifting to overcome the effects of a **sedentary** job. _____

5. The legal aid clinic was **subsidized** by city and county funds. _____

6. When the bank robber reached his **haven**, he breathed a sigh of relief and began to count his money. _____

7. The teenager was **intimidated** by the presence of a police officer walking the beat and decided not to spray-paint the school wall. _____

8. The vase must have been **jostled** in shipment because it arrived with several chips in it. _____

9. Although she had visited the fortune-teller several times, she was not sure she believed in the **occult**. _____

10. If the plan did not work, the colonel had a **contingency** plan ready.

   _____

EXERCISE **4-6**   **Using Context Clues**

Directions: Read each sentence and write a definition or synonym for each boldfaced word. Use the context clue to help you determine meaning.

1. The economy was in a state of continual **flux**; inflation increased one month and decreased the next. _____

2. The grand jury **exonerated** the police officer of any possible misconduct or involvement in illegal activity. _____

3. Art is always talkative, but Ed is usually **taciturn**. _____

4. Many **debilities** of old age, including poor eyesight and loss of hearing, can be treated medically. _____

5. Police **interrogation**, or questioning, can be a frightening experience.

   _____

6. The soap opera contained numerous **morbid** events: the death of a young child, the suicide of her father, and the murder of his older brother.

   _____

7. After long hours of practice, Xavier finally learned to type; Riley's efforts, however, were **futile**. _____

8. Although the farm appeared **derelict**, we discovered that an elderly man lived there.

   _____

9. The newspaper's error was **inadvertent**; the editor did not intend to include the victim's name. _____

10. To save money, we have decided to **curtail** the number of DVDs we buy each month. _____

11. Steam from the hot radiator **scalded** the mechanic's hand. _____

12. The businesswoman's **itinerary** outlined her trip and listed Cleveland as her next stop. _____

13. **Theologies**, such as Catholicism, Buddhism, and Hinduism, are discussed at great length in the class. _____

14. Sven had a very good **rapport** with his father but was unable to get along well with his mother. _____

15. The duchess had a way of **flaunting** her jewels so that everyone could see and envy them. _____

EXERCISE **4-7**   **Using Context Clues**

Directions: Read each of the following passages and use context clues to figure out the meaning of each boldfaced word or phrase. Write a synonym or brief definition for each in the space provided.

A.   Some **visionaries** say that we can **transform** nursing homes into warm, inviting places. They started with a clean piece of paper and asked how we could redesign nursing homes so they **enhance** or maintain people's quality of life. The model they came up with doesn't look or even feel like a nursing home. In Green Houses, as they are called, elderly people live in a homelike setting. Instead of a **sterile** hallway lined with rooms, 10 to 12 residents live in a carpeted ranch-style house. They receive medical care suited to their personal needs, share meals at a **communal** dining table, and, if they want to, they can cook together in an open kitchen. They can even play **virtual** sports on plasma televisions. This home-like setting **fosters** a sense of community among residents and staff.

—adapted from Henslin, *Sociology*, p. 386

> This photograph is a visual context clue for one of the terms used in the paragraph. Find the term and circle it.

1. visionaries _____

2. transform _____

3. enhance _____

4. sterile _____

5. communal _____

6. virtual _____

7. fosters _____

B.   Marketers and consumers **coexist** in a complicated, two-way relationship. It's often hard to tell where marketing efforts leave off and "the real world" begins. One result of these **blurred** boundaries is that we are no longer sure (and perhaps we don't care) where the line separating this **fabricated** world from reality begins and ends. Sometimes, we **gleefully** join in the illusion. A story line in a Wonder Woman comic book featured the usual out-of-this-world **exploits** of a **vivacious** superhero. But it also included the real-world proposal of the owner of a chain of comic book stores, who persuaded DC Comics to let him **woo** his beloved in the issue.

—Solomon, *Consumer Behavior*, p. 19

8. coexist _____

9. blurred _____

10. fabricated _____

11. gleefully _____

12. exploits _____

13. vivacious _____

14. woo _____

C.   Rising tuition; roommates who bug you; social life drama; too much noise; no privacy; long lines at the bookstore; pressure to get good grades; never enough money; worries about the economy, terrorism, and natural disaster all add up to: STRESS! You can't run from it, you can't hide from it, and it can affect you in **insidious** ways that you aren't even aware of. When we try to sleep, it **encroaches** on our **psyche** through outside noise or internal worries over all the things that need to be done. While we work at the computer, stress may interfere in the form of noise from next door, strain on our eyes, and **tension** in our back. Even when we are out socializing with friends, we feel guilty, because there is just not enough time to do what needs to be accomplished. The **precise** toll that stress exacts from us over a lifetime is unknown, but increasingly, stress is recognized as a major threat to our health.

—Donatelle, *Health*, p. 57

15. insidious _____

16. encroaches _____   18. tension _____

17. psyche _____   19. precise _____

EXERCISE **4-8**   **Working with Context Clues**

Directions: Bring a brief textbook excerpt, editorial, or magazine article that contains difficult vocabulary to class. Working with another student, locate and underline at least three words in the article that your partner can define by using context clues. Work together in reasoning out each word, checking a dictionary to verify meanings.

EXERCISE **4-9**   **Using Context Clues**

Directions: Bring to class three sentences, each containing a word whose meaning is suggested by the context of the sentence. The sentences can come from textbooks, Web sites, or other sources, or you can write them yourself. Write each sentence on a separate index card, underlining the word to be figured out.

Form groups of three to five students. Each student should create a definition sheet to record meanings.

Pass the index cards around the group. For each card, each student should list the underlined word and write its meaning on the definition sheet. When everyone has read each card, compare meanings.

EXERCISE 4-10   A Nonsense Words Activity

Directions: Each student should write five sentences, each containing a nonsense word whose meaning is suggested by the context of the sentence. Here is an example:

> Before I went out to pick up a pizza, I put on my purplut. I buttoned up my purplut and went outside, glad that it was filled with down.
>
> (Can you figure out the meaning of a purplut?)

Form groups of three to five students. Students should take turns reading aloud their sentences as group members guess the meanings of the nonsense words.

THE LIMITATIONS OF CONTEXT CLUES

3 LEARNING GOAL

Understand the limitations of context clues

There are two limitations to the use of context clues. First, context clues seldom lead to a complete definition. Second, sometimes a sentence does not contain clues to a word's meaning. In these cases you will need to draw on other vocabulary skills. Chapter 5 will help you with these skills.

LEARNING STYLE TIPS

If you tend to be a(n) . . .	Then use context by . . .
Auditory learner	Reading the context aloud
Visual learner	Visualizing the context

SELF-TEST SUMMARY

1	**What are context clues used for?**	They are used to figure out the meaning of an unknown word used in a sentence or paragraph.
2	**What are the five types of context clues?**	The five types of context clues are • **Definition**—a brief definition of or synonym for a word • **Synonym**—a word or phrase that is similar in meaning to the unknown word • **Example**—specific instances or examples that clarify a word's meaning • **Contrast**—a word or phrase of opposite meaning • **Inference**—the use of reasoning skills to figure out word meanings
3	**What are the limitations of context clues?**	Context clues usually do not offer a complete definition. Context clues are not always provided.

GOING ⊙ ONLINE

1. **Synonyms**

   The Web is home to many free dictionaries and thesauruses, most of which offer a synonym search function. Using an online dictionary, thesaurus, or synonym finder, list five synonyms for each of the following words: *apathetic, belligerent, eschew, vice, wrest*.

2. **Antonyms (Contrast Clues)**

   Using an online dictionary or thesaurus, list five antonyms for each of the following words: *meager, overt, futile, ennui, torrid*. Compile a list of all student responses and discuss some of the most popular antonyms for each word. What other shades of meaning (called *connotations*) does each of these words have?

MASTERY TEST 1 Reading Selection

Compulsive or Pathological Gambling

Rebecca J. Donatelle

Before Reading

This selection from the health textbook *Access to Health, Green Edition,* describes the characteristics and consequences of the disorder known as compulsive gambling.

Previewing the Reading

Using the steps listed on pages 49–50, preview the reading selection. When you have finished, complete the following items.

1. Complete the following statement: Gambling is a form of _____ and _____ for millions of Americans.

2. What is the topic of the boxed feature that accompanies the reading? (see page 134)

   _____

3. Indicate whether each statement is true (T) or false (F).
   _____ a. Compulsive gamblers can stop gambling any time they wish.
   _____ b. Compulsive gambling can have a negative effect on the gambler's health.
   _____ c. Frequent talk about gambling can be a warning sign of a gambling problem.

Predicting and Connecting

1. How would you define the term *gambling*?

2. The box beginning with paragraph 9 is labeled "Health Headlines." What does this label imply about the content of the feature?

Vocabulary Preview

pathological (par. 2) caused by or related to a disease

1   Gambling is a form of recreation and entertainment for millions of Americans. Most people who gamble do so casually and moderately to experience the excitement of anticipating a win.

2   However, over 2 million Americans are **compulsive (pathological) gamblers**, and 6 million more are considered at risk for developing a gambling addiction. The American Psychiatric Association (APA) recognizes pathological gambling as a mental disorder and lists ten characteristic behaviors, including preoccupation with gambling, unsuccessful efforts to cut back or quit, using gambling to

_____12. In the sentence "Men dominated the gambling scene" (par. 5), the word *dominated* means
   a. took command.
   b. were powerful.
   c. were larger in number.
   d. looked down on.

_____13. The word *advent* (par. 6) means
   a. arrival.
   b. average.
   c. ending.
   d. advertisement.

_____14. The word *nonacademic* (par. 7) means
   a. published.
   b. studious.
   c. not harmful.
   d. not educational.

_____15. The word *epitome* (par. 9 in the Health Headlines box) means
   a. opponent.
   b. model.
   c. message.
   d. delivery.

For more practice, ask your instructor for an opportunity to work on the mastery tests that appear in the Test Bank.

Thinking Visually

1. What concept does the "Did You Know?" illustration on page 133 illustrate or correspond to in the reading?

_____

2. What is your overall impression of the photograph in the Health Headlines box on page 134? How does the photograph contrast with the information that is discussed in the box?

_____

_____

_____

Thinking Critically About the Reading

1. How big a problem do you think gambling is at your school or among the people you know? Were the statistics in the selection surprising to you?

2. Reread the warning signs of problem gambling in the Health Headlines box. Could those warning signs apply to any of your own habits or behaviors? Try replacing the word *gambling* with another word or phrase such as *shopping*, *texting*, or *video gaming*.

3. Why did the author include the story about John (par. 9, in the Health Headlines box)? What does his story contribute to the selection?

Academic Application: Summarizing the Reading

Directions: You are writing a research paper about compulsive gamblers and want to summarize this reading for your notes. Complete the following summary by filling in the blanks. Note that you will write the entire last sentence.

Over 2 million Americans are _____ or pathological gamblers, and 6 million more may develop a gambling _____. The American _____Association recognizes pathological gambling as a _____ with ten characteristic behaviors. Compulsive gambling is similar to _____. Gambling problems are more _____ among men, and gambling rates are higher among several groups. Gambling is increasing among _____, a trend related to students' easy access to gambling opportunities and especially to the revival of _____. _____

_____

_____.

CHAPTER 4

MASTERY TEST 2 Reading Selection

Paying It Forward

Teresa Audesirk, Gerald Audesirk, and Bruce E. Byers

Before Reading

This selection originally appeared as a case study in an introductory biology textbook. What does the term "pay it forward" mean to you?

Previewing the Reading

Using the steps listed on pages 49–50, preview the reading selection. As part of your preview, read the first sentence of each paragraph. When you have finished, complete the following items.

1. Which organ of the human body is discussed in this reading? _____

2. Paying forward means _____.

Predicting and Connecting

1. Are you willing to donate any organs upon your death or even while you are alive? Why or why not?

2. Do you expect the reading to be fairly easy to understand, of moderate difficulty, or challenging? Why?

> **Vocabulary Preview**
>
> nebulous (par. 1) unclear or vague
>
> cadaver (par. 5) a dead body

Think As You Read
Read • Respond ▶ ## During Reading

As you read the selection, complete each of the following. When highlighting, use a different color highlighter for each task.

a. Highlight the topic sentence of each paragraph. If the main idea is unstated, write a sentence that states it.

b. Highlight the most important details in each paragraph.

c. Highlight useful transitional words and phrases that help you understand and connect the author's ideas.

d. Read and respond to the questions in the margin.

Paying It Forward

How do you react to the first sentence of the reading?

1   Anthony DeGiulio had a dream—he wanted to save someone's life. At first, it was a nebulous ambition, but it started to take shape as he watched a segment of the TV show *60 Minutes* that highlighted living kidney donation. DeGiulio, who hadn't realized that a live person could donate a kidney, immediately saw this as a way to achieve his ambition. "I want to do this," he told his wife.

What feeling does this photograph create?

2   DeGiulio called New York-Presbyterian Hospital, and set in motion a series of events described as an "altruistic chain" that gave new life

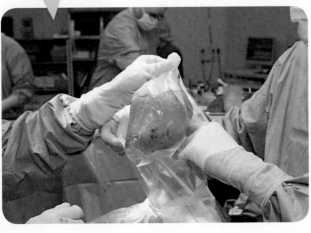

not to one person, but to four. The chain of events was possible because three people in the area needed kidneys, and each had a family member eager to donate, but were prevented from doing so because of incompatibility between their tissue types. Barbara Asofsky, a nursery school teacher, had known for 5 years that she would need a kidney transplant. When DeGiulio's kidney was found to be a good match for Asofsky, her husband, Douglas, was happy to donate the kidney he had hoped to give to his wife—but couldn't because of incompatibility—to a stranger instead. The fortunate stranger was Alina Binder, a student at Brooklyn College. Alina's father, Michael, was a good match for Andrew Novak, a telecommunications technician. Finally, Andrew's sister, Laura Nicholson, donated her kidney to Luther Johnson, a hotel kitchen steward.

Why do the authors list the donors' and recipients' names?

3   Do kidney transplant recipients lead completely normal lives? How is a donor kidney removed, and what are the risks to the donor? For people with kidney failure, are there alternatives to a kidney transplant? Why are kidneys so important, and how do they work?

How does this paragraph serve as a preview of the remainder of the reading?

4   When a person's kidneys fail, wastes accumulate in the blood, and imbalances in ion concentrations occur. Most people awaiting kidney transplants are kept alive using hemodialysis, a treatment in which wastes and excess water are filtered from the blood by an elaborate machine. Although people may remain on hemodialysis for many years, the treatment is far from ideal. Whereas healthy kidneys work nonstop, hemodialysis treatments are performed only about three times weekly. Patients

Explain how hemodialysis works.

must carefully monitor their diets between sessions, and those whose kidneys cannot produce urine must also carefully limit fluid intake to minimize the accumulation of water in their blood.

5   Since the 1950s, when living kidney donation was first recognized as a viable alternative to cadaver organ donors, family and friends have come forward to offer a kidney to a victim of kidney failure. Ideally, in addition to blood type, several important glycoproteins of the donor such as major histocompatibility complex (MHC) proteins, which identify cells as belonging to a particular individual, should match those of the recipient. This reduces the chances that the recipient's immune system will attack the donated kidney as if it were a foreign invader. But, with the exception of identical twins, no two people have perfectly matching tissues. This means that people with kidney transplants must take immune-suppressing drugs for the remainder of their lives, making them vulnerable to infections and some types of cancer. Despite this drawback, a transplanted kidney is by far the best option for those lucky enough to receive one.

> Circle the function of MHC proteins.

6   To remove a kidney from the donor, surgeons generally use a technique called laparoscopic surgery, where they make three or four incisions about one-half inch long through which they insert surgical tools, including a tiny video camera. The kidney is removed through an incision about 2½ inches long, put on ice, and rushed to its recipient. The operation takes 3 to 4 hours; donors remain in the hospital for about 3 days and return to work in about 3 weeks. Donating a kidney requires major surgery, with its associated risks. Kidney donors will also lack a back-up kidney in the unlikely event that their remaining kidney fails. But a recent study of deaths among 80,000 kidney donors during a 15-year period found no greater mortality among this group (once they had recovered from their surgery) than among non-donors.

7   Since 2008, when DeGiulio's donated kidney started a chain that saved four lives (Fig. 1), such "domino donation chains" have become longer and more frequent. For example, during a 4-month period in 2011, 17 hospitals in 11 states from California to New Jersey matched 30 people—who might otherwise have died—with kidneys from 30 donors they had never met. This heroic enterprise was started by Good Samaritan Rick Ruzzamenti, who got the idea from the desk clerk at his yoga studio, who had mentioned to him that she had donated a kidney to a friend. Of the 13,000 to 14,000 kidney transplants that are performed annually in the United States, about 6,000 are from living donors who are usually relatives or close friends of the recipients. The approximately 60,000 eligible individuals awaiting a kidney transplant who haven't found compatible donors ardently hope that domino donation chains continue to be forged.

> Why do the authors include this sentence?

LIFESAVER TIMES 4

DONORS

Anthony DeGiulio
Good Samaritan
Blood Group B

DONATED KIDNEY TO

Douglas Asofsky
Husband
Blood Group O

INCOMPATIBLE

DONATED KIDNEY TO

Michael Binder
Father
Blood Group A

INCOMPATIBLE

DONATED KIDNEY TO

Laura Nicholson
Sister
Blood Group B

INCOMPATIBLE

DONATED KIDNEY TO

RECIPIENTS

Barbara Asofsky
Wife
Blood Group B

Alina Binder
Daughter
Blood Group O

Andrew Novak
Brother
Blood Group A

Luther Johnson
Waiting List
Blood Group B

Donors, recipients and kidney transplant team gather at New York-Presbyterian Hospital Columbia yesterday. Anthony DeGiulio gets hug (c.) from recipient Barbara Asofsky while recipient Andrew Novak (below, l.) gives donor Michael Binder pat on back. Photos by Susan Watts/Daily News

Kidney offer leads to multiple swap

EXCLUSIVE

BY JORDAN LITE
DAILY NEWS STAFF WRITER

ONE GOOD Samaritan determined to donate a kidney to anyone who needed it set off a chain reaction that let four patients without a compatible organ donor get transplants.

The four-way kidney swap at New York-Presbyterian Hospital Columbia is believed to be the largest performed in the city. The July 24, all-day endeavor involved nearly 50 clinicians working in eight operating rooms.

"It's easily the greatest thing I've ever done in my life, and also the easiest decision I ever made," said Anthony DeGiulio, 32, the altruistic donor who got the idea from a TV program.

"It was a dream of mine to save someone's life, and this is the only way I could come up with to do it," explained DeGiulio, a securities trader from the Dutchess County town of Red Hook.

Here's how it worked: Three area patients with kidney disease had family members who wanted to donate an organ to them but couldn't because their blood types didn't match.

DeGiulio was a match for one of those patients, Barbara Asofsky, a 57-year-old nursery school teacher from Wantagh, L.I. She got his kidney.

Asofsky's husband, Douglas, 56, was a match for Alina Binder, a 22-year-old Brooklyn College student.

Binder's dad, Michael, 46, was compatible with Andrew Novak, a 42-year-old telecommunications field technician from Poughkeepsie.

And Novak's sister, Laura Nicholson, 40, was a suitable donor for a patient on the waiting list, Luther Johnson, 31, a hotel kitchen steward from Harlem.

None of them knew who their donor or recipient would be before the surgeries, but the donors didn't have to think long about whether they'd give their kidney to a stranger. "I didn't care who it would go to; I knew it would save a life — and save Barbara's life," said Douglas Asofsky, a bank veep.

Kidney swaps are becoming an increasingly important option for patients facing a years-long wait for a donor organ, said Dr. Lloyd Ratner, director of renal transplantation at the hospital. There are 76,650 people in the U.S. waiting for donor kidneys with 6,673 in New York, officials said.

The swaps, also known as paired exchanges, have been responsible for 373 kidney transplants in the U.S., the United Network for Organ Sharing said.

Doctors at Johns Hopkins University performed a six-way exchange in April. They believe that a national registry of living kidney donors — including those willing to donate to strangers — could result in 6,000 transplants a year.

Some of his friends and family thought DeGiulio was "nuts" to donate his kidney, he said. "I wish it was more common," he noted. "I sacrificed three days of my life, and this woman gets her life back. If I could feel like this every day, I'd do it any day of the week."

jlite@nydailynews.com

nydailynews.com DAILY NEWS Tuesday, August 5, 2008

Figure 1 The domino chain of kidney donations

8   When DeGiulio shared his plans to donate a kidney with his friends and family members, some of them told him he was "nuts." DeGiulio disagrees. "It's easily the greatest thing I've ever done in my life, and also the easiest decision I ever made," said the 32-year-old donor. Ruzzamenti had a similar reaction. "People think it's so odd that I'm donating a kidney," he told the transplant coordinator at his hospital, but "I think it's so odd that they think it's so odd . . . . It causes a shift in the world."

Why do the authors end the reading by quoting two organ donors?

—Audesirk, Audesirk, and Byers, *Biology*, pp. 673, 677, 685–686

After Reading

Checking Your Comprehension

_____ 1. Which organ did Anthony DeGiulio, Laura Nicholson, and Douglas Asofsky donate while they were still alive?
  a. kidney.
  b. lung.
  c. pancreas.
  d. liver.

_____ 2. The "altruistic chain" of donating an organ occurs when
  a. TV shows like *60 Minutes* report on organ donations.
  b. family members donate an organ to a spouse or child.
  c. more people sign up to donate their organs upon their death.
  d. a single organ donation leads to multiple lives being saved.

_____ 3. When a kidney fails, waste accumulates in the
  a. colon.
  b. stomach.
  c. blood.
  d. large intestine.

_____ 4. Hemodialysis is essentially a(n) _____ system; it is typically performed _____ times a week on patients who are suffering from kidney failure.
  a. monitoring; five.
  b. filtration; three.
  c. disposal; two.
  d. evaporation; four.

_____ 5. The only people who have perfectly matching kidneys are
  a. mothers and daughters.
  b. identical twins.
  c. fathers and sons.
  d. two brothers from the same set of parents.

Applying Your Skills: Using Context Clues

Following are five sentences from the reading. Identify the type of context clue that helps you determine the meaning of the boldfaced term.
  a. definition.
  b. synonym.
  c. example.
  d. contrast.
  e. inference.

_____ 6. "At first, it was a **nebulous** ambition, but it started to take shape as he watched a segment of the TV show *60 Minutes* that highlighted living kidney donation." (par. 1)

_____ 7. "DeGiulio called New York-Presbyterian Hospital, and set in motion a series of events described as an '**altruistic chain**' that gave new life not to one person, but to four." (par. 2)

_____ 8. "Most people awaiting kidney transplants are kept alive using **hemodialysis**, a treatment in which wastes and excess water are filtered from the blood by an elaborate machine." (par. 4)

_____ 9. "Since the 1950s, when living kidney donation was first recognized as a viable alternative to **cadaver** organ donors, family and friends have come forward to offer a kidney to a victim of kidney failure." (par. 5)

_____ 10. "To remove a kidney from the donor, surgeons generally use a technique called **laparoscopic surgery**, where they make three or four incisions about one-half inch long through which they insert surgical tools, including a tiny video camera." (par. 6)

Studying Words

Using context or a dictionary, define each of the following words as it is used in the reading.

11. altruistic (par. 2) _____

12. elaborate (par. 4) _____

13. incisions (par. 6) _____

14. mortality (par. 6) _____

15. ardently (par. 7) _____

Thinking Visually

1. How do the photos on page 142 illustrate the content of the selection?

2. Name two processes, described in the reading, that would benefit from a visual aid showing how those processes work.

Thinking Critically About the Reading

1. Are the two quotations in paragraph 8 facts or opinions? Explain.

2. How would you describe the author's attitude toward living organ donations?

3. The reading contains some complicated medical explanations. How does the author capture and maintain your interest?

4. Which words/phrases in paragraph 7 summarize the author's feelings about those who donate organs while they are alive? Did the authors convince you to share their opinion?

Academic Application: Writing a Paraphrase

Directions: To get a good grade in your biology class, it is essential that you be able to explain in your own words what happens when kidneys fail and how hemodialysis can keep a person alive. Check your paraphrasing skills by filling in the missing words or phrases in the following paraphrase of paragraph 4.

_____collect in the blood stream when someone's kidney fails, and the _____balance becomes disrupted. Hemodialysis, although not the perfect solution, is used to treat people who are waiting for a kidney _____. In this process, a _____removes waste and excessive _____from the blood. Patients usually receive hemodialysis _____times a week (in contrast, real kidneys work all day, every day). People on hemodialysis must be careful about what they _____, and people who cannot _____must be cautious about drinking too many fluids.

CHAPTER 5

Using Word Parts and Learning New Words

LEARNING GOALS

This chapter will show you how to

1 Use prefixes, roots, and suffixes

2 Learn new words

3 Use a dictionary and thesaurus effectively

4 Pronounce unfamiliar words

5 Develop a system for learning new words

Focusing on ... Word Parts

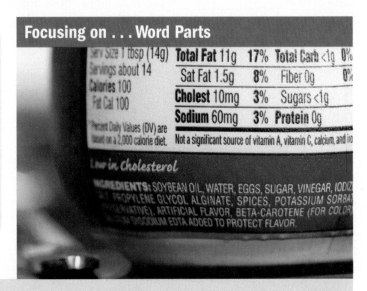

Serv Size 1 tbsp (14g)	**Total Fat** 11g	17%	Total Carb <1g	0%
Servings about 14	Sat Fat 1.5g	8%	Fiber 0g	0%
Calories 100	**Cholest** 10mg	3%	Sugars <1g	
Fat Cal 100	**Sodium** 60mg	3%	**Protein** 0g	

Percent Daily Values (DV) are based on a 2,000 calorie diet. Not a significant source of vitamin A, vitamin C, calcium, and iron

Low in Cholesterol

INGREDIENTS: SOYBEAN OIL, WATER, EGGS, SUGAR, VINEGAR, IODIZ... PROPYLENE GLYCOL ALGINATE, SPICES, POTASSIUM SORBA... ...ATIVE), ARTIFICIAL FLAVOR, BETA-CAROTENE (FOR COLOR)... ...DISODIUM EDTA ADDED TO PROTECT FLAVOR.

This ingredients label is taken from a jar of mayonnaise. How many of the ingredients and terms are familiar? Do you know what propylene glycol alginate and beta-carotene are? If not, how could you figure out the meanings?

This chapter shows you how to use your knowledge of word parts to figure out the meanings of words you do not know, how to use a dictionary and thesaurus, and how to use a flash card system to learn and remember new words.

LEARN PREFIXES, ROOTS, AND SUFFIXES

1 LEARNING GOAL

Use prefixes, roots, and suffixes

Many students build their vocabulary word by word: if they study ten new words, then they have learned ten new words. If they study 30 words, they can recall 30 meanings. Would you like a better and faster way to build your vocabulary?

By learning the meanings of the parts that make up a word, you will be able to figure out the meanings of many more words. For example, if you learn that *pre-* means "before," then you can begin to figure out hundreds of words that begin with *pre-* (*premarital, premix, preemployment*).

In this chapter you will learn about compound words and about the beginnings, middles, and endings of words called prefixes, roots, and suffixes.

Suppose that you came across the following sentence in a human anatomy textbook:

> Trichromatic plates are used frequently in the text to illustrate the position of body organs.

If you did not know the meaning of *trichromatic*, how could you determine it? There are no clues in the sentence context. One solution is to look up the word in a dictionary. An easier and faster way is to break the word into parts and analyze the meaning of each part. Many words in the English language are made up of word parts called **prefixes**, **roots**, and **suffixes**. These word parts have specific meanings that, when added together, can help you determine the meaning of the word as a whole.

The word *trichromatic* can be divided into three parts: its *prefix*, *root*, and *suffix*.

Prefix	+	Root	+	Suffix	=	**New word**
tri	+	chrom	+	atic	=	**trichromatic**

Meaning ⟶ three + color + characteristic of = having three colors

You can see from this analysis that *trichromatic* means "having three colors."

Here are a few other examples of words that you can figure out by using prefixes, roots, and suffixes:

> The parents thought the child was **unteachable**.
>
> un- = not
>
> teach = help someone learn
>
> -able = able to do something
>
> unteachable = not able to be taught
>
> The student was a **nonconformist**.
>
> non- = not
>
> conform = go along with others
>
> -ist = one who does something
>
> nonconformist = someone who does not go along with others

The first step in using the prefix root suffix method is to become familiar with the most commonly used word parts. The prefixes and roots listed in Tables 5-1 (p. 150) and 5-2 (p. 154) will give you a good start in determining the meanings of thousands of words without looking them up in the dictionary. For instance, more than ten thousand words can begin with the prefix *non-*. Not all these words are listed in a collegiate dictionary, but they would appear in an unabridged dictionary. Another common prefix, *pseudo-*, is used in more than four hundred words. A small amount of time spent learning word parts can yield a large payoff in new words learned.

Before you begin to use word parts to figure out new words, there are a few things you need to know:

1. **In most cases, a word is built upon at least one root.**
2. **Words can have more than one prefix, root, or suffix.**
   a. Words can be made up of two or more roots (geo/logy).
   b. Some words have two prefixes (in/sub/ordination).
   c. Some words have two suffixes (beauti/ful/ly).
3. **Words do not always have a prefix and a suffix.**
   a. Some words have neither a prefix nor a suffix (read).
   b. Others have a suffix but no prefix (read/ing).
   c. Others have a prefix but no suffix (pre/read).
4. **The spelling of roots may change as they are combined with suffixes.**
   Some common variations are included in Table 5-2.
5. **Different prefixes, roots, or suffixes may have the same meaning.**
   For example, the prefixes *bi-*, *di-*, and *duo-* all mean "two."

6. **Sometimes you may identify a group of letters as a prefix or root but find that it does not carry the meaning of that prefix or root.** For example, the letters *mis* in the word *missile* are part of the root and are not the prefix *mis-*, which means "wrong, bad."

Prefixes

Prefixes appear at the beginning of many English words: they alter the meaning of the root to which they are connected. For example, if you add the prefix *re-* to the word *read*, the word *reread* is formed, meaning "to read again." If *pre-* is added to the word *reading*, the word *prereading* is formed, meaning "before reading." If the prefix *post-* is added, the word *postreading* is formed, meaning "after reading." In Table 5-1 (p. 150), more than 40 common prefixes are grouped according to meaning.

EXERCISE 5-1   Using Prefixes

Directions: Using the list of common prefixes in Table 5-1, match each word in Column A with its meaning in Column B. Write the letter of your choice in the space provided.

Column A	Column B
_____ 1. misplaced	a. half of a circle
_____ 2. postgraduate	b. build again
_____ 3. dehumidify	c. tiny duplicate of printed material
_____ 4. semicircle	d. continuing studies past graduation
_____ 5. nonprofit	e. not fully developed
_____ 6. reconstruct	f. put in the wrong position
_____ 7. triathlete	g. build up electrical power again
_____ 8. microcopy	h. not for making money
_____ 9. recharge	i. to remove moisture from
_____ 10. immature	j. one who participates in three-part sporting events

TABLE 5-1   Common Prefixes

Prefix	Meaning	Sample Word
Prefixes referring to amount or number		
mono/uni	one	monocle/unicycle
bi/di/du	two	bimonthly/divorce/duet
tri	three	triangle
quad	four	quadrant
quint/pent	five	quintet/pentagon
deci	ten	decimal
centi	hundred	centigrade
milli	thousand	milligram
micro	small	microscope
multi/poly	many	multipurpose/polygon
semi	half	semicircle
equi	equal	equidistant
Prefixes meaning "not" (negative)		
a	not	asymmetrical
anti	against	antiwar
contra	against, opposite	contradict
dis	apart, away, not	disagree
in/il/ir/im	not	incorrect/illogical/irreversible/impossible
mis	wrongly	misunderstand
non	not	nonfiction
pseudo	false	pseudoscientific
un	not	unpopular
Prefixes giving direction, location, or placement		
ab	away	absent
ad	toward	adhesive
ante/pre	before	antecedent/premarital
circum/peri	around	circumference/perimeter
com/col/con	with, together	compile/collide/convene
de	away, from	depart
dia	through	diameter
ex/extra	from, out of, former	ex-wife/extramarital
hyper	over, excessive	hyperactive
inter	between	interpersonal
intro/intra	within, into, in	introduction/intramural
post	after	posttest
re	back, again	review
retro	backward	retrospect
sub	under, below	submarine
super	above, extra	supercharge
tele	far	telescope
trans	across, over	transcontinental

EXERCISE **5-2**   **Using Prefixes**

Directions: Use the list of common prefixes in Table 5-1 (p. 150) to determine the meaning of each of the following words. Write a brief definition or synonym for each. If you are unfamiliar with the root, you may need to check a dictionary.

1. interoffice: _____

2. supernatural: _____

3. nonsense: _____

4. introspection: _____

5. prearrange: _____

6. reset: _____

7. subtopic: _____

8. transmit: _____

9. multidimensional: _____

10. imperfect: _____

EXERCISE **5-3**   **Using Prefixes to Write Brief Definitions**

Directions: Write a brief definition for each word in boldfaced type.

1. an **atypical** child: _____

2. to **hyperventilate**: _____

3. an **extraordinary** request: _____

4. **semisoft** cheese: _____

5. **antisocial** behavior: _____

6. to **circumnavigate** the globe: _____

7. a **triweekly** publication: _____

8. an **uneventful** weekend: _____

9. a **disfigured** face: _____

10. to **exhale** smoke: _____

EXERCISE **5-4**   **Using Prefixes**

Directions: Read each of the following sentences. Use your knowledge of prefixes to fill in the blank to complete the word.

1. A person who speaks two languages is _____**lingual.**

2. A letter or number written beneath a line of print is called a _____ **script.**

3. The new sweater had a snag, and I returned it to the store because it was _____ **perfect.**

4. The flood damage was permanent and _____ **reversible.**

5. I was not given the correct date and time; I was _____ **informed.**

6. People who speak several different languages are _____ **lingual.**

7. A musical _____ **lude** was played between the events in the ceremony.

8. I decided the magazine was uninteresting, so I _____ **continued** my subscription.

9. Merchandise that does not pass factory inspection is considered _____ **standard** and sold at a discount.

10. The tuition refund policy approved this week will apply to last year's tuition as well; the policy will be _____ **active** to January 1 of last year.

11. The elements were _____ **acting** with each other when they began to bubble and their temperature rose.

12. _____ **ceptives** are widely used to prevent unwanted pregnancies.

13. All of the waitresses were required to wear the restaurant's _____ **form.**

14. The _____ **viewer** asked the presidential candidates unexpected questions about important issues.

15. The draperies were _____ **colored** from long exposure to the sun.

EXERCISE 5-5   **Using Prefixes**

Directions: Use your knowledge of prefixes to supply the missing word in each sentence. Write the word in the space provided.

1. Our house is a duplex. The one next door with three apartments is
   a _____.

2. A preparation applied to the skin to reduce or prevent perspiration is called
   an _____.

3. A person who cannot read or write is _____.

4. I did not use my real name; instead I gave a _____.

5. If someone seems to have greater powers than do normal humans, he or she
   might be called _____.

6. If you plan to continue to take college courses after you graduate, you will be
   taking _____ courses.

7. Substances that fight bacteria are known as _____drugs.

8. The branch of biology that deals with very small living organisms is
   _____.

9. In the metric system a _____ is one one-hundredth of a meter.

10. One one-thousandth of a second is called a _____.

EXERCISE 5-6   **Using Prefixes**

Directions: Working in teams of two, list as many words as you can think of for two of the following prefixes: *multi-, mis-, trans-, com-, inter-*. Then share your lists with the class.

Roots

Roots carry the basic or core meaning of a word. Hundreds of root words are used to build words in the English language. More than 30 of the most common and most useful are listed in Table 5-2. Knowledge of the meanings of these roots will enable you to unlock the meanings of many words. For example, if you know that the root *dic/dict* means "tell or say," then you would

TABLE 5-2   Common Roots

Common Root	Meaning	Sample Word
aster/astro	star	astronaut
aud/audit	hear	audible
bene	good, well	benefit
bio	life	biology
cap	take, seize	captive
chron/chrono	time	chronology
cog	to learn	cognitive
corp	body	corpse
cred	believe	incredible
dict/dic	tell, say	predict
duc/duct	lead	introduce
fact/fac	make, do	factory
geo	earth	geophysics
graph	write	telegraph
log/logo/logy	study, thought	psychology
mit/miss	send	permit/dismiss
mort/mor	die, death	immortal
path	feeling	sympathy
phono	sound, voice	telephone
photo	light	photosensitive
port	carry	transport
scop	seeing	microscope
scrib/script	write	inscription
sen/sent	feel	insensitive
spec/spic/spect	look, see	retrospect
tend/tens/tent	stretch or strain	tension
terr/terre	land, earth	territory
theo	god	theology
ven/vent	come	convention
vert/vers	turn	invert
vis/vid	see	invisible/video
voc	call	vocation

have a clue to the meanings of such words as *dictate* (to speak for someone to write down), *diction* (wording or manner of speaking), or *dictionary* (book of what words "say").

EXERCISE 5-7 **Using Roots**

Directions: Using the list of common roots in Table 5-2 (p. 154), match each word in Column A with its meaning in Column B. Write the letter of your choice in the space provided.

Column A

_____ 1. benediction

_____ 2. audible

_____ 3. missive

_____ 4. telemarketing

_____ 5. mortician

_____ 6. intervene

_____ 7. reverted

_____ 8. aqueduct

_____ 9. photoactive

_____ 10. vocalize

Column B

a. undertaker

b. went back to

c. able to respond to light

d. come between two things

e. channel or pipe that brings water from a distance

f. use the voice

g. blessing

h. letter or message

i. can be heard

j. selling a product by phone

EXERCISE 5-8 **Using Roots**

Directions: Use the list of common roots in Table 5-2 (p. 154) to determine the meanings of the following words. Write a brief definition or synonym for each, checking a dictionary if necessary.

1. dictum: _____

2. biomedicine: _____

3. photocopy: _____

4. porter: _____

5. visibility: _____

6. credentials: _____

7. speculate: _____

8. terrain: _____

9. audition: _____

10. sentiment: _____

11. astrophysics: _____

12. capacity: _____

13. chronicle: _____

14. corporation: _____

15. facile: _____

16. autograph: _____

17. sociology: _____

18. phonometer: _____

19. sensation: _____

20. vocal: _____

EXERCISE **5-9** **Completing Sentences**

Directions: Complete each of the sentences on the next page with one of the words listed below.

apathetic	dictated	graphic	scriptures	tendon
captivated	extensive	phonics	spectators	verdict
deduce	extraterrestrial	prescribed	synchronized	visualize

1. The jury brought in its _____ after one hour of deliberation.

2. Religious or holy writings are called _____.

3. She closed her eyes and tried to _____ the license plate number.

4. The _____ watching the football game were tense.

5. The doctor _____ two types of medication.

6. The list of toys the child wanted for his birthday was _____.

7. The criminal appeared _____ when the judge pronounced the sentence.

8. The runners _____ their watches before beginning the race.

9. The textbook contained numerous _____ aids, including maps, charts, and diagrams.

10. The study of the way different parts of words sound is called _____.

11. The athlete strained a(n) _____ and was unable to continue training.

12. The movie was about a(n) _____ ,a creature not from earth.

13. The district manager _____ a letter to her secretary, who then typed it.

14. Through his attention-grabbing performance, he _____ the audience.

15. By putting together the clues, the detective was finally able to _____ who committed the crime.

EXERCISE 5-10   Using Roots

Directions: List two words for each of the following roots: *dict/dic*, *spec/spic/spect*, *fact/fac*, *phono*, *scrib/script*.

Suffixes

Suffixes are word endings that often change the part of speech of a word. For example, adding the suffix -*y* to the noun *cloud* forms the adjective *cloudy*. Accompanying the change in part of speech is a shift in meaning (*cloudy* means "resembling clouds; overcast with clouds; dimmed or dulled as if by clouds").

Often, several different words can be formed from a single root word by adding different suffixes.

Root	+	Suffix	=	New word
class	+	ify	=	classify
class	+	ification	=	classification
class	+	ic	=	classic
right	+	ly	=	rightly
right	+	ful	=	rightful
right	+	eous	=	righteous

If you know the meaning of the root word and the ways in which different suffixes affect the meaning of the root word, you will be able to figure out a word's meaning when a suffix is added. A list of common suffixes and their meanings appears in Table 5-3 (p. 159).

You can expand your vocabulary by learning the variations in meaning that occur when suffixes are added to words you already know. When you find a word that you do not know, look for the root. Then, using the sentence the word is in (its context; see Chapter 4), figure out what the word means with the suffix added. Occasionally you may find that the spelling of the root word has been changed. For instance, a final *e* may be dropped, a final consonant may be doubled, or a final *y* may be changed to *i*. Consider the possibility of such changes when trying to identify the root word.

The article was a **compilation** of facts.

root + suffix

compil(e) + -ation = something that has been compiled, or put together into an orderly form

We were concerned with the **legality** of our decision to change addresses.

root + suffix

legal + -ity = something pertaining to legal matters

Our college is one of the most **prestigious** in the state.

root + suffix

prestig(e) + -ious = having prestige or distinction

TABLE 5-3   Common Suffixes

Suffix	Sample Word
Suffixes that refer to a state, condition, or quality	
able	touchable
ance	assistance
ation	confrontation
ence	reference
ible	tangible
ion	discussion
ity	superiority
ive	permissive
ment	amazement
ness	kindness
ous	jealous
ty	loyalty
y	creamy
Suffixes that mean "one who"	
an	Italian
ant	participant
ee	referee
eer	engineer
ent	resident
er	teacher
ist	activist
or	advisor
Suffixes that mean "pertaining to or referring to"	
al	autumnal
ship	friendship
hood	brotherhood
ward	homeward
Suffixes that mean "without"	
less	guiltless

EXERCISE **5-11**   **Using Suffixes**

Directions: For each suffix shown in Table 5-3, write another example of a word you know that has that suffix.

EXERCISE **5-12**   **Creating New Words by Adding Suffixes**

Directions: For each of the words listed, add a suffix so that the word will complete the sentence. Write the new word in the space provided. Check a dictionary if you are unsure of the spelling.

1. converse

   Our phone _____ lasted ten minutes.

2. assist

   The medical _____ labeled the patient's blood samples.

3. qualify

   The job applicant outlined his _____ to the interviewer.

4. intern

   The doctor completed her _____ at Memorial Medical Center.

5. eat

   We did not realize that the blossoms of the plant could be _____.

6. audio

   She spoke so softly that her voice was not _____.

7. season

   It is usually very dry in July, but this year it has rained constantly. The weather is not very _____.

8. permit

   The professor granted her _____ to miss class.

9. instruct

   The lecture on Freud was very _____.

10. remember

    The wealthy businessman donated the building in _____ of his deceased father.

11. mortal

The _____ rate in Ethiopia is very high.

12. president

The _____ race held many surprises.

13. feminine

She called herself a _____ ,although she never actively supported the movement for equal rights for women.

14. hazard

The presence of toxic waste in the lake is _____ to health.

15. destine

The young man felt it was his _____ to become a priest.

EXERCISE 5-13 **Adding Suffixes**

Working Together

Directions: Working with a classmate, for each word listed below, write as many new words as you can create by adding suffixes. Share your findings with the class.

1. compare: _____

2. adapt: _____

3. right: _____

4. identify: _____

5. will: _____

6. prefer: _____

7. notice: _____

8. like: _____

9. pay: _____

10. promote: _____

How to Use Word Parts

Think of roots as being at the root or core of a word's meaning. There are many more roots than are listed in Table 5-2. You already know many of these because they are used in everyday speech. Think of prefixes as word parts that are added before the root to qualify or change its meaning. Think of suffixes as add-ons that make the word fit grammatically into the sentence in which it is used.

When you come upon a word you do not know, keep the following pointers in mind:

Using Word Parts

1. **First, look for the root.** Think of this as looking for a word inside a larger word. Often a letter or two will be missing.

un/utter/able	defens/ible
inter/colleg/iate	re/popular/ize
post/operat/ive	non/adapt/able
im/measur/ability	non/commit/tal

2. **If you do not recognize the root, then you will probably not be able to figure out the word.** The next step is to check its meaning in a dictionary.

3. **If you did recognize the root word, look for a prefix.** If there is one, determine how it changes the meaning of the word.

un/utterable	un- = not
post/operative	post- = after

4. **Locate the suffix.** Determine how it further adds to or changes the meaning of the root word.

unutter/able	-able = able to
postoperat/ive	-ive = state or condition

5. **Next, try out the meaning in the sentence in which the word was used.** Substitute your meaning for the word, and see whether the sentence makes sense.

> Some of the victim's thoughts were **unutterable** at the time of the crime.
>
> unutterable = cannot be spoken
>
> My sister was worried about the cost of **postoperative** care.
>
> postoperative = describing state or condition after an operation

EXERCISE **5-14**   **Identifying Roots and Writing Definitions**

Directions: Use the steps listed previously to determine the meaning of each bold-faced word. Underline the root in each word, and then write a brief definition of the word that fits its use in the sentence.

1. The doctor felt the results of the X-rays were **indisputable**

   _____

2. The **dissimilarity** among the three brothers was surprising.

   _____

3. The **extortionist** demanded two payments of $10,000 each, threatening physical harm if he was not paid on time.

   _____

4. It is **permissible** to camp in most state parks.

   _____

5. The student had an unusually **retentive** memory.

   _____

6. The **traumatic** event changed the child's attitude toward animals.

   _____

7. We were surprised by her **insincerity**.

   _____

8. The child's **hypersensitivity** worried his parents.

   _____

9. The English instructor told Peter that he had written a **creditable** paper.

   _____

10. The rock group's agent hoped to **repopularize** their first hit song.

    _____

11. The gambler was filled with **uncertainty** about the horse race.

    _____

12. The **nonenforcement** of the speed limit led to many deaths.

    _____

13. The effects of the disease were **irreversible**.

    _____

14. The mysterious music seemed to **foretell** the murder of the movie's heroine.

    _____

15. The **polyphony** filled the concert hall.

    _____

16. Sailors used to think the North Sea **unnavigable**.

    _____

17. She received a **dishonorable** discharge from the Marines.

    _____

18. The criminal was **unapologetic** to the judge about the crimes he had committed.

    _____

19. A systems analysis revealed that the factory was **underproductive**.

    _____

20. He rotated the dial **counterclockwise**.

    _____

EXERCISE 5-15   **Using Word Parts**

Directions: Read each of the following paragraphs and determine the meaning of each boldfaced word. Write a brief definition for each in the space provided.

A.   The values and norms of most **subcultures** blend in with mainstream society. In some cases, however, some of the group's values and norms place it at odds with the dominant culture. **Sociologists** use the term **counterculture** to refer to such groups. To better see this distinction, consider motorcycle enthusiasts and motorcycle gangs. Motorcycle **enthusiasts**—who emphasize personal freedom and speed and **affirm** cultural values of success through work or education—are members of a subculture. In contrast, the Hell's Angels, Pagans, and Bandidos not only stress freedom and speed but also value dirtiness and contempt toward women, work, and education. This makes them a counterculture. Countercultures do not have to be negative, however. Back in the 1800s, the Mormons were a counterculture that challenged the dominant culture's core value of **monogamy**.

—Henslin, *Sociology*, p. 52

What is the purpose of this photo and caption?

Why is professional dancing a subculture and not a counterculture?

1. subcultures

_____

2. sociologists

_____

3. counterculture

_____

4. enthusiasts

_____

5. affirm

_____

6. monogamy

_____

B.   Our **perception** of the richness or quality of the material in clothing, bedding, or upholstery is linked to its "feel," whether rough or smooth, flexible or **inflexible**. We **equate** a smooth fabric, such as silk, with luxury, whereas we consider denim to be practical and **durable**. Fabrics composed of **scarce** materials or that require a high degree of processing to achieve their smoothness or fineness tend to be more expensive and thus we assume they are of a higher class.

—adapted from Solomon, *Consumer Behavior*, pp. 62–63

7. perception

_____

8. inflexible

_____

9. equate

_____

10. durable

_____

11. scarce

_____

C.   The college years mark a critical **transition** period for young adults as they move away from families and establish themselves as **independent** adults. The transition to independence will be easier for those who have successfully accomplished earlier developmental tasks, such as learning how to solve problems, make and evaluate decisions, define and **adhere** to personal values, and establish both casual and **intimate** relationships. People who have not fulfilled these earlier tasks may find their lives interrupted by **recurrent** "crises" left over from earlier stages. For example, if they did not learn to trust others in childhood, they may have difficulty establishing intimate relationships as adults.

—Donatelle, *Health*, p. 34

12. transition

_____

13. independent

_____

14. adhere

_____

15. intimate

_____

16. recurrent

_____

D. An ecosystem is a group of living organisms and the **abiotic** spheres with which they interact. **Ecology** is the scientific study of ecosystems. Ecologists study **interrelationships** between living organisms and their environments within particular ecosystems, as well as interrelationships among various ecosystems in the **biosphere**.

—Rubenstein, *Contemporary Human Geography*, p. 25

17. abiotic

_____

18. ecology

_____

19. interrelationships

_____

20. biosphere

_____

EXERCISE 5-16 **Using Prefixes to Change Meaning**

Directions: Write a sentence using each of the key words listed below. Exchange your sentences with a partner. Read each sentence and change the meaning of the key word by adding a prefix and/or suffix, and then rewrite the sentence to reflect the change in meaning. Exchange sentences to check each other's work.
Key Words: allow interest regular agree direct

LEARN NEW WORDS

2 LEARNING GOAL
Learn new words

Most people think they have just one category of vocabulary and that this can be characterized as large or small, strong or weak. Actually, everyone has at least four categories of vocabulary, and each varies in strength:

1. Words you use in everyday speech or writing

   Examples: decide, death, daughter, damp, date

2. Words you know but seldom or never use in your own speech or writing

   Examples: demonstrate, diminish, delicacy, distinguish, dependent

3. Words you have heard or seen before but cannot fully define

Examples: denounce, deficit, decadent, deductive, decisive

4. Words you have never heard or seen before

Examples: doggerel, dogma, denigrate, deleterious, diatropism

In the spaces provided, list five words that fall under each of these four categories. It will be easy to think of words for Category 1. Words for Categories 2–4 may be taken from the following list:

contort	garbanzo	voluntary	impertinent
continuous	logic	resistance	delicacy
credible	connive	alien	impartial
activate	congruent	meditate	delve
deletion	demean	fraught	attentive
focus	liberate	gastronome	osmosis
manual	heroic	havoc	

Category 1	Category 2	Category 3	Category 4
_____	_____	_____	_____
_____	_____	_____	_____
_____	_____	_____	_____
_____	_____	_____	_____
_____	_____	_____	_____

To build your vocabulary, try to shift as many words as possible from a less familiar to a more familiar category. Use the following steps:

1. Start by noticing words.
2. Question, check, and remember their meanings.
3. Record new words and their meanings in a log, notebook, or computer file.
4. Use these new words often in your speech and writing.

SELECT AND USE A DICTIONARY AND THESAURUS

3 LEARNING GOAL

Use a dictionary and thesaurus effectively

Every college student needs to use a dictionary, not only to check meanings, but also to check spellings and the appropriate use of words. A student also needs to use a thesaurus, a dictionary of synonyms (words with similar meanings).

Many general dictionaries are available on the Internet and as apps for your tablet or smart phone. Two of the most widely used English print dictionaries, those by Merriam-Webster and American Heritage, have Internet versions. Other dictionary sites, such as Wiktionary.org. and Dictionary.com, do not have a print version.

In addition, many word-processing programs, tablets, and e-book readers have built-in dictionaries. By right-clicking on a word, you can look up its definition.

Online dictionaries have several important advantages over print dictionaries.

- **Audio component.** Many online dictionaries, such as Merriam-Webster and American Heritage, feature an audio component that allows you to hear how the word is pronounced.

- **Multiple dictionary entries.** Some sites, such as Dictionary.com, display entries from several dictionaries at once for a particular word.

- **Tolerance for misspellings.** If you aren't sure of how a word is spelled or you mistype it, several suggested words will be returned.

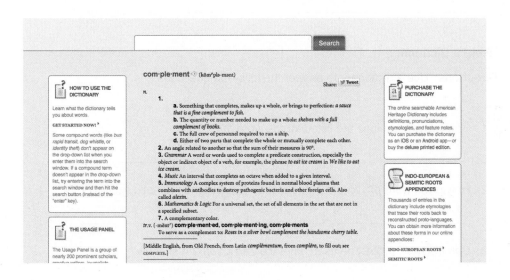

The American Heritage® Dictionary of the English Language, Fifth Edition copyright ©2014 by Houghton Mifflin Harcourt Publishing Company. All rights reserved.

ESL Dictionaries

If you are an ESL student, you may wish to use an ESL dictionary. Numerous ESL dictionaries are available in paperback and online editions, including *The Longman Dictionary of Contemporary English*.

EXERCISE 5-17   Using a Dictionary

Directions: Use the sample dictionary entry on the previous page to complete the following items.

1. Which two parts of speech can the word *complement* be used as?

   _____

2. Find three meanings for *complement* and write a sentence using each.

   _____

3. Based on definition 2, in which college discipline do you think the word *complement* is often used?

   _____

EXERCISE 5-18   Using a Dictionary

Directions: Use a dictionary to answer the following questions:

1. How many meanings are listed for the word *fall*?

   _____

2. How is the word *phylloxera* pronounced? (Record the phonetic spelling.)

   _____

3. Can the word *protest* be used other than as a verb? If so, how?

   _____

4. The word *prime* can mean first or original. List some of its other meanings.

   _____

5. What does the French expression *savoir faire* mean?

   _____

6. List three meanings for the word *fault.*

   _____

7. List several words that are formed using the word *dream.*

   _____

8. What is the plural spelling of *addendum*?

   _____

9. Explain the meaning of the idiom *turn over a new leaf.*

   _____

10. Define the word *reconstituted* and write a sentence using the word.

    _____

    _____

Finding the Right Meaning

Most words have more than one meaning. When you look up the meaning of a new word, you must choose the meaning that fits the way the word is used in the sentence context. The meanings are often grouped by part of speech and are numbered consecutively in each group. Generally, the most common meanings of the word are listed first, with more specialized, less-common meanings appearing toward the end of the entry.

Here are a few suggestions for choosing the correct meaning from among those listed in an entry:

Finding Correct Meanings

1. **If you are familiar with the parts of speech, try to use these to locate the correct meaning.** For instance, if you are looking up the meaning of a word that names a person, place, or thing, you can save time by reading only those entries given after *n* (noun).

2. **For most types of college reading, you can skip definitions that give slang and colloquial (abbreviated *colloq.*) meanings.** Colloquial meanings refer to informal or spoken language.

3. **If you are not sure of the part of speech, read each meaning until you find a definition that seems correct.** Skip over restrictive meanings that are inappropriate.

4. **Test your choice by substituting the meaning in the sentence with which you are working.** Substitute the definition for the word and see whether it makes sense in the context (see Chapter 4).

Suppose you are looking up the word *oblique* to find its meaning in this sentence:

My sister's **oblique** answers to my questions made me suspicious.

Oblique is used in the above sentence as an adjective. Looking at the entries listed after *adj.* (adjective) below, definition 2a (not straightforward, indirect) best fits the way *oblique* is used in the sentence.

oblique   *adjective* \ō-'blēk, ə-, -'blik; *military usually* ī\
1 a : neither perpendicular nor parallel : inclined
b : having the axis not perpendicular to the base <an *oblique* cone>
c : having no right angle <an *oblique* triangle>
2 a : not straightforward : indirect; *also* : obscure
b : devious, underhanded
3 : situated at an angle and having one end not inserted on bone <*oblique* muscles>
4 : taken from an airplane with the camera directed horizontally or diagonally downward <an *oblique* photograph>
— **oblique·ly** *adverb*
— **oblique·ness** *noun*
Origin of OBLIQUE
Middle English *oblike*, from Latin *obliquus*
First Known Use: 15th century
oblique
noun \ō-'blēk, ə-, -'blik; *military usually* ī\
1 : something (as a line) that is oblique
2 : any of several oblique muscles; *especially* : any of the thin flat muscles forming the middle and outer layers of the lateral walls of the abdomen

—By permission. From *Merriam-Webster's Collegiate® Dictionary, 11th Edition* © 2013 by Merriam-Webster, Inc. (www.Merriam-Webster.com).

EXERCISE **5-19** **Finding Multiple Meanings**

Directions: The following words have two or more meanings. Look them up in your dictionary, and write two sentences with different meanings for each word.

1. culture: _____

_____

2. perch: _____

_____

3. surge: _____

_____

4. apron: _____

_____

5. irregular: _____

_____

EXERCISE **5-20** **Finding the Right Meaning**

Directions: Use a dictionary to help you write an appropriate meaning for the bold-faced word in each of the following sentences.

1. The last contestant did not have a **ghost** of a chance. _____

2. The race car driver won the first **heat**. _____

3. The police took all possible **measures** to protect the witness.

_____

4. The orchestra played the first **movement** of the symphony.

_____

5. She tried to **couch** her criticism in polite language.

_____

Subject Area Dictionaries

Many academic disciplines have specialized dictionaries that list important terminology used in that field. They give specialized meanings and suggest how and when to use a word. For the field of music there is the *New Grove Dictionary of Music and Musicians*, which lists and defines the specialized vocabulary of music. Other subject area dictionaries include *Taber's Cyclopedic Medical Dictionary*, *A Dictionary of Anthropology*, and *A Dictionary of Economics*. Many of these dictionaries are available in hardbound copies and electronic versions. Your school's library may own the hardcopy, a subscription to the electronic edition, or both.

Using a Thesaurus

A thesaurus is a dictionary of synonyms. It groups words with similar meanings together. A thesaurus is particularly useful when you want to do the following:

- Locate the precise term to fit a particular situation
- Find an appropriate descriptive word
- Replace an overused or unclear word
- Convey a more specific shade of meaning

Suppose you are looking for a more precise word for the expression *tell us about* in the following sentence:

> In class today, our chemistry instructor will **tell us about** our next assignment.

Among the choices a thesaurus may list are *explain, spell out, comment on, annotate, restate, unravel, transcribe,* and so forth.

Some choices, such as *explain,* fit well. Others such as *unravel* or *transcribe* do not. Be sure to choose a word that fits the context in which you will use it. The most widely used thesaurus is *Roget's Thesaurus*. Inexpensive paperback editions are available in most bookstores; you can also access thesauruses online.

EXERCISE **5-21**　**Using a Thesaurus**

Directions: Using a print or online thesaurus, replace the boldfaced word or phrase in each sentence with a more precise or descriptive word. Write the word in the space provided. Rephrase the sentence, if necessary.

1. Although the movie was **good**, it lasted only an hour.

   _____

2. The judge **looked at** the criminal as she pronounced the sentence.

   _____

3. The accident victim was awarded a **big** cash settlement.

   _____

4. The lottery winner was **happy** to win the $100,000 prize, but he was surprised to learn that a sizable portion had already been deducted for taxes.

   _____

5. On the first day of class, the instructor **talked to** the class about course requirements.

   _____

PRONOUNCE UNFAMILIAR WORDS

Pronounce
unfamiliar words

At one time or another, we come across words that we are unable to pronounce. To pronounce an unfamiliar word, sound it out syllable by syllable. Here are a few simple guidelines for dividing words into syllables:

1. **Divide compound words between the individual words that form the compound word.**

house/broken	house/hold	space/craft
green/house	news/paper	sword/fish

2. **Divide words between prefixes (word beginnings) and roots (base words) and/or between roots and suffixes (word endings).**

Prefix + Root

pre/read	post/pone	anti/war

Root + Suffix

sex/ist	agree/ment	list/ing

3. **Each syllable is a separate, distinct speech sound.** Pronounce the following words and try to hear the number of syllables in each.

expensive	ex/pen/sive = 3 syllables
recognize	rec/og/nize = 3 syllables
punctuate	punc/tu/ate = 3 syllables
complicated	com/pli/cat/ed = 4 syllables

4. **Each syllable has at least one vowel and usually one or more consonants.** (The letters *a, e, i, o, u,* and sometimes *y* are vowels. All other letters are consonants.)

as/sign	re/act	cou/pon	gen/er/al

5. **Divide words before a single consonant, unless the consonant is the letter *r*.**

hu/mid	re/tail	fa/vor	mor/on

6. **Divide words between two consonants appearing together.**

pen/cil	lit/ter	lum/ber	sur/vive

7. **Divide words between two vowel sounds that appear together.**

te/di/ous	ex/tra/ne/ous

These rules will prove helpful but, as you no doubt already know, there will always be exceptions.

EXERCISE **5-22**   **Syllabication**

Directions: Use vertical marks (|) to divide each of the following words into syllables.

1. polka
2. pollute
3. ordinal
4. hallow
5. judicature
6. innovative
7. obtuse
8. germicide
9. futile
10. extol

11. tangelo
12. symmetry
13. telepathy
14. organic
15. hideous
16. tenacity
17. mesmerize
18. intrusive
19. infallible
20. fanaticism

EXERCISE **5-23**   **Pronouncing Words**

Directions: Locate ten words that you find difficult to pronounce. Sources may be a dictionary, a textbook, or one of the reading selections in Parts Five or Six of this text. Write each of the ten words on a separate index card, and then create a list of the words and how they are pronounced. Your instructor will form groups. Pass the cards around the group. Each student should attempt a pronunciation. The student who pronounces the word correctly keeps the card. Make a note of words that you were unable to pronounce; check their pronunciation in your dictionary.

RESOURCES FOR LEARNING NEW WORDS

5 LEARNING GOAL

Develop a system for learning new words

As you read textbook assignments and reference sources and while listening to your instructors' class presentations, you are constantly exposed to new words. Unless you make a deliberate effort to remember and use these words, many of them will probably fade from your memory. Be sure to highlight them in textbooks and record them in your notes.

The Flash Card System

Once you have identified and marked new terminology, both in your lecture notes and in your textbook, the next step is to organize the words for study and review. One of the most efficient and practical ways to accomplish this is the flash card system. You can use flash cards available online or create your own. The system is described on the next page.

1. **Whenever you hear or read a new word that you intend to learn,** jot it down in the margin of your notes or mark it some way in the material you are reading.

2. **Later, write the word on the front of an index card.** Then look up its meaning and write it on the back of the card. Also, record a phonetic key for the word's pronunciation, its part of speech, other forms the word may take, and a sample sentence or example of how the word is used. Your cards should look like the one in Figure 5-1.

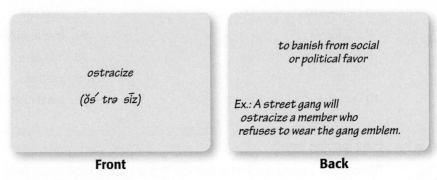

ostracize

(ŏs′ trə sīz)

to banish from social or political favor

Ex.: A street gang will ostracize a member who refuses to wear the gang emblem.

Front   **Back**

Figure 5-1 Sample Flash Card

3. **Once a day, take a few minutes to go through your pack of flash cards.** For each card, look at the word on the front and try to recall its meaning on the back. Then check the back of the card to see whether you were correct. If you were unable to recall the meaning or if you confused the word with another word, retest yourself. Shuffle the cards after each use.

4. **After you have gone through your pack of cards several times, sort the cards into two piles—words you know and words you have not learned.** Then, putting the known words aside, concentrate on the words still to be learned.

5. **Once you have learned the entire pack of words, review them often to refresh your memory.**

This flash card system is effective for several reasons. First, you can review the cards in the spare time that is often wasted waiting for a class to begin, riding a bus, and so on. Second, the system enables you to spend time learning what you do *not* know rather than wasting time studying what you already know. Finally, the system overcomes a major problem that exists in learning information that appears in list form. If the material to be learned is presented in a fixed order, you tend to learn it in that order and may be unable to recall individual items when they appear alone or out of order. By shuffling the cards, you scramble the order of the words and thus avoid this problem.

Many publishers now provide free electronic flash cards with the Web materials that accompany the textbook. Check the book's preface or Web site for a list of the available study materials.

Several commercial web sites also enable you to create your own flash cards electronically. These include Cram.com and Quizlet.

EXERCISE 5-24   ## Using the Flash Card System

Directions: Make a set of at least 20 word cards, choosing words from one of your textbooks or from one of the reading selections in Part Six of this text. Then study the cards using the method described in this chapter.

Vocabulary Enrichment with Electronic Sources

Many electronic textbooks (e-books, e-readers, etc.) allow you to highlight terminology that is important to learn. You can use this feature to test yourself. For a word you have highlighted, try to recall its definition, and then click on the word and compare your definition with the one that pops up.

Various Web sites are useful for vocabulary building. The Merriam-Webster Web site, for example, offers a word of the day. Wordsmith allows you to sign up to receive a word of the day via e-mail. A variety of other Web sites offer assistance with idioms, frequently confused words, and so forth. Do a Google search to locate useful sites.

LEARNING STYLE TIPS

If you tend to be a(n) . . .	Then strengthen your vocabulary by . . .
Social learner	Studying with a group of classmates
Independent learner	Making up review tests, or asking a friend to do so, and practice taking the tests
Creative learner	Experimenting with new words in both speech and writing
Pragmatic learner	Creating lists or computer files of words you need to learn and use

SELF-TEST SUMMARY

1	**What are prefixes, roots, and suffixes and why are they useful?**	Prefixes are beginnings of words, roots are middles of words, and suffixes are endings of words. They unlock the meanings of thousands of English words.
2	**How many categories of vocabulary does a person have?**	Everyone has at least four categories of vocabulary: everyday words, words you know but seldom use, words you have heard before but cannot define, and words you have never heard.
3	**What reference sources are useful in building a strong vocabulary?**	Print and online dictionaries, ESL dictionaries, subject area dictionaries, and the thesaurus are all useful in building a strong vocabulary.
4	**How do you pronounce unfamiliar words?**	To pronounce unfamiliar words, use the pronunciation key in your dictionary and apply the seven rules listed in this chapter (see pages 175–176).
5	**Describe a system for learning new words.**	The flash card system is a method of learning vocabulary. Write a word on the front of the flash card and its meaning on the back. Study the cards by sorting them into two piles—known and unknown words.

GOING ⊙ ONLINE

1. **Pronunciation**

   Many online reference works (encyclopedias, wikis, dictionaries, etc.) offer an audio feature. Look for the audio icon and click on it to hear the word pronounced. Find an online reference work with an audio feature and listen to the pronunciations of these words: *Kyrgyzstan, queue, aporia, munificent, logorrhea.*

2. **Slang**

   Many idiomatic words and phrases fall into the category of *slang*, which is composed of informal words and phrases that are used much more often in speech than in writing. The Web offers many sites that help define slang words. Find a site and list five common (or uncommon) slang words/phrases and their meanings. Share these with a small group or the class. Can any classmates define these idioms?

3. **Word Meanings**

   Quiz yourself on word meanings with the online game called Free Rice (freerice .com). The difficulty of the multiple-choice questions adjusts to your level. For every answer that you get right, the nonprofit site donates ten grains of rice to help end world hunger. Watch bowls fill up with rice as you learn new vocabulary words.

MASTERY TEST 1 Reading Selection

The "McDonaldization" of Society

John J. Macionis

Before Reading

This selection appeared in a sociology textbook, *Society: The Basics*, by John Macionis. Read the selection to find out how the concept behind McDonald's has had an effect on American society.

Previewing the Reading

Using the steps listed on pages 49–50, preview the reading selection. When you have finished, complete the following items.

1. Which fast-food chain inspired the selection? _____

2. In which city is the world's largest McDonald's located? _____

3. List the four basic principles of McDonaldization:

   a. _____
   b. _____
   c. _____
   d. _____

5. Which sociologist expressed serious concerns about the world's "increasing rationalization"? _____

Predicting and Connecting

1. What is your favorite fast-food chain? What similarities do you see between different stores in the same chain? Do you see any differences?

2. Which would be a better way to study this selection: paraphrasing the opening and closing paragraphs, or preparing an outline? Why?

> **Vocabulary Preview**
>
> **rationalization** (par. 13) replacing traditional beliefs and emotions with those that are planned and calculated

1   McDonald's has enjoyed enormous success, now operating more than 33,000 restaurants in the United States and around the world. Japan has more than 3,300 Golden Arches, and the world's largest McDonald's, which seats more than 1,500 customers, is found in London.

2   McDonald's is far more than a restaurant chain; it is a symbol of U.S. culture. Not only do people around the world associate McDonald's with the United States, but also here at home, one poll found that 98 percent of schoolchildren could identify Ronald McDonald, making him as well known as Santa Claus.

3   Even more important, the organizational principles that underlie McDonald's are coming to dominate our entire society. Our culture is becoming "McDonaldized," an awkward way of saying that we model many aspects of life on the approach taken by this restaurant chain: Parents buy toys at worldwide chain stores all carrying identical merchandise; we drop in at a convenient shop for a ten-minute drive-through oil change; face-to-face communication is being replaced more and more with electronic methods such as voice mail, e-mail, and instant messaging; more vacations take the form of resorts and tour packages; television packages the news in the form of ten-second sound bites; college admissions officers size up applicants they have never met by glancing at their GPA and SAT scores.

4   Can you tell what all these developments have in common?

Four Principles

5   According to George Ritzer, who wrote a book about the McDonaldization of society, four basic organizational principles are involved.

6   1. **Efficiency.** Ray Kroc, the marketing genius behind the expansion of McDonald's, set out to serve a hamburger, French fries, and a milkshake to a customer in fifty seconds. Today, one of the company's most popular items is the Egg McMuffin, an entire breakfast packaged into a single sandwich. In the restaurant, customers pick up their meals at a counter, dispose of their own trash, and stack their own trays as they walk out the door or, better still, drive away from the pickup window taking whatever mess they make with them. Such efficiency is now central to our way of life. We tend to think that anything done quickly is, for that reason alone, good.

7   **2. Predictability.** An efficient organization wants to make everything it does as predictable as possible. McDonald's prepares all food using set formulas. Company policies guide the performance of every job.

8   **3. Uniformity.** The first McDonald's operating manual declared the weight of a regular raw hamburger to be 1.6 ounces, its size to be 3.875 inches across, and its fat content to be 19 percent. A slice of cheese weighs exactly half an ounce, and French fries are cut precisely 9/32 inch thick.

9   Think about how many of the objects we see every day around the home, the workplace, and the campus are designed and mass-produced uniformly according to a standard plan. Not just our environment but our everyday life experiences—from traveling the nation's interstates to sitting at home viewing national TV shows—are more standardized than ever before.

10   Almost anywhere in the world, a person can walk into a McDonald's restaurant and buy the same sandwiches, drinks, and desserts prepared in the same way. Uniformity results from a highly rational system that specifies every action and leaves nothing to chance.

11   **4. Control.** The most unreliable element in the McDonald's system is human beings. After all, people have good and bad days, and they sometimes let their minds wander or decide to do something a different way. To minimize the unpredictable human element, McDonald's has automated its equipment to cook food at a fixed temperature for a set length of time. Even the cash registers at McDonald's are keyed to pictures of the menu items so that ringing up a customer's order is as simple as possible.

12   Similarly, automatic teller machines are replacing bank tellers, highly automated bakeries produce bread while people stand back and watch, and chickens and eggs (or is it eggs and chickens?) emerge from automated hatcheries. In supermarkets, laser scanners at self-checkouts are phasing out human checkers. Much of our shopping now occurs in malls, where everything from temperature and humidity to the kinds of stores and products sold are subject to continuous control and supervision.

Can Rationality Be Irrational?

13   There is no doubt about the popularity or efficiency of McDonald's. But there is another side to the story. Max Weber* was alarmed at the increasing rationalization of the world, fearing that formal organizations would cage our imaginations and crush the human spirit. As he saw it, rational systems are efficient but dehumanizing. McDonaldization bears him out. Each of the principles we have just discussed limits human creativity, choice, and freedom. Echoing Weber, Ritzer states that "the ultimate irrationality of McDonaldization is that people could lose control over the system and it would come to control us."

*Max Weber, an influential sociologist, is often considered to be one of the founding fathers of sociology.

Perhaps even McDonald's understands the limits of rationalization—the company has now expanded its offerings of more upscale foods, such as premium roasted coffee and salad selections that are more sophisticated, fresh, and healthful.

—Macionis, *Society*, pp. 121–122

After Reading

Checking Your Comprehension

_____ 1. The main point of the article is that our society
   a. is becoming similar to McDonald's, with everything the same.
   b. has too much fast food in our diet because of McDonald's.
   c. does not allow children to have good role models.
   d. emphasizes commercial success more than any other type of success.

_____ 2. According to this article, people have come to believe that if something is done speedily that it is done
   a. poorly.
   b. incompletely.
   c. cheaply.
   d. well.

_____ 3. When products become standardized it means
   a. employees work less.
   b. there is a loss of efficiency.
   c. items are produced identically.
   d. nothing can be automated.

_____ 4. The most unreliable part of McDonald's system is its
   a. food quality.
   b. employees.
   c. packaging.
   d. profits.

_____ 5. Max Weber believed that systems like McDonald's work well but have the effect of being
   a. expensive.
   b. unproductive.
   c. dehumanizing.
   d. polluting.

Applying Your Skills: Using Word Parts and Learning New Words

_____ 6. The root word of *irrationality* (par. 13) means
   a. attractive.
   b. sudden.
   c. competent.
   d. reasonable.

_____ 7. The root of the word *standardized* (par. 9) means
   a. heatedly discussed.
   b. the same or very similar.
   c. used by different people for different purposes.
   d. easily changed or altered.

_____ 8. The prefix of the word *unpredictable* (par. 11) means
   a. not.
   b. for.
   c. after.
   d. away.

_____ 9. The prefix of the word *automated* (par. 11) means
   a. against.
   b. false.

c. self-acting.

d. out of.

Studying Words

_____10. The word *applicant* (par. 3) means a
a. person who is praying.
b. person seeking admission.
c. relative you don't know.
d. stranger asking for a favor.

_____11. The word *expansion* (par. 6) means
a. study.
b. idea.
c. expense.
d. growth.

_____12. The word *formulas* as used in paragraph 7 means
a. clear methods.
b. infant beverages.

c. mathematical equations.

d. chemical representations.

_____13. The word *manual* as used in paragraph 8 means
a. done by hand.
b. a book or guide.
c. a type of transmission.
d. method for holding a rifle.

_____14. The word *minimize* (par. 11) means to make
a. larger.
b. smaller.
c. different.
d. the same.

For more practice, ask your instructor for an opportunity to work on the mastery tests that appear in the Test Bank.

Thinking Visually

1. What does the photograph contribute to the reading?

2. Does the photograph demonstrate any the four principles of McDonaldization? If so, which ones, and how?

Thinking Critically About the Reading

1. Why does the author mention the statistic about children and Ronald McDonald? How would you describe the author's feelings about this?

2. In paragraph 3, the author discusses examples of McDonaldization in our society. What is the author's attitude about these changes?

Academic Application: Summarizing the Reading

Directions: The night before an exam, you decide to write a summary of the reading to evaluate how well you remember it. Complete the following summary by filling in the blanks. Note that you will have to write complete sentences for the second half of the reading.

McDonald's is a company known across many _____ and is also a symbol of _____. Many parts of _____ follow the approach taken by _____, using its four _____: efficiency, _____, _____, and _____. _____

_____

_____

_____

_____

MASTERY TEST 2 Reading Selection

How Can You Study When You Can't Eat?

The Invisible Problem of Hunger on Campus

Stacia L. Brown

Before Reading

This selection originally appeared on Salon.com, a popular online magazine. The author is a college instructor and blogger.

Previewing the Reading

Using the steps listed on pages 49–50, preview the reading selection. As part of your preview, read the first sentence of each paragraph. When you have finished, complete the following items.

1. The topic of the selection is _____.
2. Indicate whether each statement is true (T) or false (F).
    _____ a. College student hunger and homelessness are on the rise.
    _____ b. The author teaches at a college that recently opened a food bank on campus.

Predicting and Connecting

1. If you did not have enough money to buy food, would you be reluctant to admit it? Why or why not?
2. Do you expect the reading to be fairly easy to understand, of moderate difficulty, or challenging? Why?

Vocabulary and Concept Preview

Bridge Card (par. 1) a Michigan food assistance-program

gauge (par. 1) measure

cynicism (par. 1) skepticism

manifest (par. 4) show

stigma (par. 5) shame

Great Recession (par. 6) major U.S. economic downturn from 2007–2009

SNAP (par. 6) the federal Supplemental Nutrition Assistance Program

---

During Reading

As you read the selection, complete each of the following. When highlighting, use a different color highlighter for each task.

a. Highlight the topic sentence of each paragraph. If the main idea is unstated, write a sentence that states it.

b. Highlight the most important details in each paragraph.

c. Highlight useful transitional words and phrases that help you understand and connect the author's ideas.

d. Read and respond to the questions in the margin

Thousands of students around the country are homeless or hungry, and their classmates and colleges might never know.

1   For three years, I've been showing my English composition classes news clips about college students and food stamps. The first is a segment on alleged Bridge Card abuse in Western Michigan, followed by a campus response clip from students at Michigan State who lost their food assistance after a statewide reform. Then we watch a report on a northern California college so supportive of student food stamp use that it offers applications in one of its administrative offices. Classroom response can be hard to gauge; after discussion, my classes seem to agree that a student in need should not be denied government food assistance—but there's also a bit of cynicism there. College students who look no different than themselves couldn't be that hungry—food-stamp hungry—could they?

> What are food stamps?

> Why does the author begin by summarizing her students' reaction to the problem?

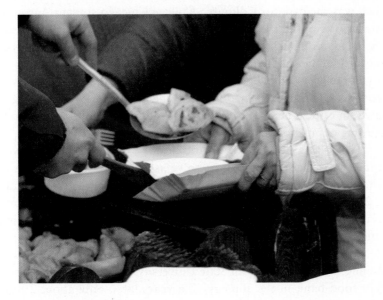

> What feeling does this photograph create?

> Underline the sentence in paragraph 2 that tells you that the author is shifting to a new idea.

2   In fact, college student hunger and homelessness are on the rise. But it's no surprise that some of my students have a hard time believing it. Until very recently, neither situation has been thoroughly investigated. Colleges are not required to track student homelessness; the best—and only—national measure available is via the Free Application for Federal Student Aid. Currently, about 58,000 students have self-identified as homeless on their FAFSA forms. But the number is likely higher, as FAFSA does not always account for non-degree students and not all students without a permanent residence self-identify as homeless.

> What is "higher education"?

3   Food insecurity is even more difficult to gauge. Whereas K–12 school systems evaluate students to determine eligibility for free and reduced-price lunch programs, no comparable assessment exists in higher education. Without reliable, regulated programs in place, it can be difficult to get reluctant students to out themselves as food insecure.

> What is meant by "emaciated stoicism"?

4   Hunger is difficult to spot without their input. It has no universal profile. It doesn't present the same way for every student. This is often what hinders my own classes from accepting the seriousness of the problem during our college-kids-on-food-stamps discussions. They expect hunger to manifest as emaciated stoicism, listlessness, or fidgety desperation, thereby making it easy to detect. But students who don't want their professors or peers to know that meals aren't consistently accessible to them can easily conceal their reality.

> Why is this example included?

5   Placing the onus solely on the homeless or hungry student to self-identify ensures that the needs of both populations will go underaddressed. Some are reluctant to confide in peers for fear of stigma and ostracism. Such was the case for Columbia College Chicago student Aaron James Flowers, who told the institution's student-run newspaper last year that his friends stopped inviting him to events when they discovered his disadvantage and began "treating him like a bum."

6   In the years following the Great Recession—and now in the wake of steep SNAP benefit cuts nationwide—college campuses are finding themselves in critical need of immediate on-site resources to accommodate a growing population that's hesitant to reveal itself.

> How do the examples in this paragraph help the author make her point?

7   This isn't a new problem. Anecdotally, college faculties have long traded stories about students who've asked to share their lunch or for whom they keep a small stash of non-perishables in their office drawers. In 2004, *The Progressive* published a feature on college homelessness and faculty who went as far as clandestinely allowing students to sleep in their offices for months.

8   What's unclear is why provision for these kids has been so slow in coming. In 1993, Michigan State University created the first college student food bank in the country. Ten years later, only about 20 known

higher ed institutions have followed suit, according to MSU's College and University Food Bank Alliance.

9   My own college recently joined the right for food justice on campus, opening a food bank in its student lounge. Its first student-run food drive started last Friday, just in time for the holidays. The presence of a campus food bank invites hungry students to come out of hiding and destigmatizes their needs by publicly acknowledging them. Most important, the frequency of its use provides colleges with a solid gauge of campus-wide hunger. And it helps teach students what hunger looks like: It looks just like them.

> Summarize the benefits of the food bank.

—Brown, *Salon*, Nov. 2013

After Reading

Checking Your Comprehension

_____ 1. The author's students tend to react to stories about students' needs for food assistance with a mixture of _____ and _____.
   a. neutrality, passion.
   b. anger, political activism.
   c. concern, skepticism.
   d. apathy, disbelief.

_____ 2. The author's two key concerns are _____ and _____.
   a. tuition, commuting time.
   b. college administrators, high-school teachers.
   c. faculty, students.
   d. hunger, homelessness.

_____ 3. The first student food bank in the country was established at
   a. Columbia College.
   b. University of California at Berkeley.
   c. University of Michigan.
   d. Kalamazoo College.

_____ 4. The author thinks hungry students are often unwilling to admit their hunger because they
   a. see their hunger as a personal failing.
   b. do not want to apply for government assistance.
   c. are trying to protect their parents from criticism.
   d. feel embarrassed to do so.

_____ 5. The reading cites all of the following examples of how college faculty have helped hungry or homeless students *except*
   a. faculty who have allowed homeless students to sleep in their offices.
   b. faculty who keep non-perishable foods on hand to give to hungry students.
   c. faculty who notify the student's parents regarding the student's difficult situation.
   d. faculty who have had students ask to share the faculty member's lunch.

Applying Your Skills: Using Word Parts and Learning New Words

_____ 6. In the word *homelessness* (par. 2), the _____ "less" means "without."
   a. prefix.
   b. root.
   c. suffix.

_____ 7. In the word *self-identify* (par. 2), "identify" is the _____.
   a. prefix.
   b. root.
   c. suffix.

_____ 8. In the word *insecurity* (par. 3), the prefix "in" means _____.
   a. not.
   b. above.
   c. many.
   d. through.

_____ 9. In the word *disadvantage* (par. 5), "dis" is a _____ meaning _____.
   a. prefix; not.
   b. root; core.
   c. suffix; state of.

_____ 10. In the word *non-perishables* (par. 7), the root is _____, the suffix is _____, and the prefix is _____.
   a. able, non, perish.
   b. non, able, perish.
   c. perish, able, non.
   d. non, perish, able.

Studying Words

Using your understanding of word parts (prefixes, roots, and suffixes), define each of the following words or phrases as it is used in the reading.

11. non-degree students (par. 2) _____

12. listlessness (par. 4) _____

13. accessible (par. 4) _____

14. underaddressed (par. 5) _____

15. destigmatizes (par. 9) _____

Thinking Visually

1. How does the photo illustrate the content of the selection?

2. Describe at least two other photos, graphs, or visual aids that could be used to emphasize the reading's key points.

Thinking Critically About the Reading

1. Identify at least three opinions in the reading.

2. How would you describe the author's attitude toward the subject matter? If you were her student, would you find her to be a sympathetic teacher?

3. What does the author mean when she says in the last sentence of the reading, "It [hunger] looks just like them"?

4. The reading begins with a boldfaced statement, "Thousands of students around the country are homeless or hungry, and their classmates and colleges might never know." How does this statement relate to the reading as a whole?

Academic Application: Writing a Paraphrase

Directions: You receive the following assignment: "Write a paraphrase of paragraph 4, which explains why it can be difficult to identify hungry and homeless students." Complete the following paraphrase by filling in the blanks.

We need _____ to tell us when they are hungry, because _____ shows itself differently for each student. This fact is the cause of my students' _____ regarding the existence of the student-hunger problem. My students think that hungry people should show their hunger by being extremely _____, having no _____, or being jumpy and hopeless, but the reality is much more complicated. And students who want to _____ their hunger find it easy to do so.

CHAPTER

6

Understanding Paragraphs: Topics and Main Ideas

LEARNING GOALS

This chapter will show you how to

1 Understand general and specific ideas

2 Identify topics

3 Identify stated main ideas in paragraphs

4 Recognize topic sentences

5 Understand implied main ideas

Focusing on . . . Topics and Main Ideas

The newspaper headline above announces what the article is about. It suggests the main point the author wants to make about the topic. Paragraphs work the same way. Each is built around a topic—the one thing the paragraph is about—and each paragraph presents a main point—or main idea—about the topic. This chapter will show you how to identify topics and main ideas.

Understanding a paragraph is a step-by-step process. The first thing you need to know is what the paragraph is about. Then you have to understand what each sentence is saying. Next, you have to see how the sentences relate to one another. Finally, to understand the main point of the paragraph, you have to consider what all the sentences, taken together, mean.

The one subject the whole paragraph is about is called the **topic**. The point that the whole paragraph makes about the topic is called the **main idea**. The sentences that explain the main idea are called **details**. To connect their ideas, writers use words and phrases known as **transitions**.

A paragraph, then, is a group of related sentences about a single topic. It has four essential parts: (1) topic, (2) main idea, (3) details, and (4) transitions. To read paragraphs efficiently, you will need to become familiar with each part of a paragraph and be able to identify and use these parts as you read.

This chapter concentrates on understanding main ideas, both stated and implied. The next chapter, Chapter 7, focuses on supporting details and transitions.

GENERAL AND SPECIFIC IDEAS

1 LEARNING GOAL
Understand general and specific ideas

To identify topics and main ideas in paragraphs, it will help you to understand the difference between **general** and **specific**. A general idea is a broad idea that applies to a large number of individual items. The term *clothing* is general because it refers to a large collection of individual items—

pants, suits, blouses, shirts, scarves, and so on. A specific idea or term is more detailed or particular. It refers to an individual item. The word *scarf*, for example, is a specific term. The phrase *red plaid scarf* is even more specific.

General:	pies	**General:**	countries
Specific:	chocolate cream	**Specific:**	England
	apple		Finland
	cherry		Brazil
General:	types of context clues	**General:**	word parts
Specific:	definition	**Specific:**	prefix
	example		root
	contrast		suffix

EXERCISE **6-1**   **Analyzing General and Specific Ideas**

Directions: Read each of the following items and decide what term(s) will complete the group. Write the word(s) in the spaces provided.

1. General: college courses
   Specific: math

   _____

2. General: _____
   Specific: roses
              tulips
              daffodils

3. General: musical groups
   Specific: _____

   _____

4. General: celebrities
   Specific: Angelina Jolie

   _____

   _____

5. General: types of movies
   Specific: comedies

   _____

   _____

EXERCISE **6-2**   **Identifying General Ideas**

Directions: For each set of specifics, select the general idea that best describes it.

_____ 1. Specific ideas: Michelle Obama, Laura Bush, Nancy Reagan
        a. famous twentieth-century women
        b. famous American parents
        c. famous wives
        d. wives of American presidents

_____ 2. Specific ideas: touchdown, home run, 3-pointer, 5 under par
    a. types of errors in sports
    b. types of activities
    c. types of scoring in sports
    d. types of sports

_____ 3. Specific ideas: for companionship, to play with, because you love animals
    a. reasons to visit the zoo
    b. reasons to feed your cat
    c. reasons to get a pet
    d. ways to solve problems

_____ 4. Specific ideas: taking a hot bath, going for a walk, watching a video, listening to music
    a. ways to relax
    b. ways to help others
    c. ways to listen
    d. ways to solve problems

_____ 5. Specific ideas: listen, be helpful, be generous, be forgiving
    a. ways to get a job
    b. ways to keep a friend
    c. ways to learn
    d. ways to appreciate a movie

EXERCISE 6-3   Identifying General Terms

Directions: Underline the most general term in each group of words.

1. pounds, ounces, kilograms, weights

2. soda, coffee, beverages, wine

3. soap operas, news, TV programs, sports specials

4. home furnishings, carpeting, drapes, wall hangings

5. sociology, social sciences, anthropology, psychology

Applying General and Specific to Paragraphs

Now we will apply the idea of general and specific to paragraphs. The main idea is the most general statement the writer makes about the topic. Pick out the most general statement among the following sentences:

1. People differ according to height.
2. Hair color distinguishes some people from others.
3. People differ in a number of ways.
4. Each person has his or her own personality.

Did you choose item 3 as the most general statement? Now we will change this list into a paragraph by rearranging the sentences and adding a few facts.

People differ in a number of ways. They differ according to physical characteristics, such as height, weight, and hair color. They also differ in personality. Some people are friendly and easygoing. Others are more reserved and formal.

In this brief paragraph, the main idea is expressed in the first sentence. This sentence is the most general statement expressed in the paragraph. All the other statements are specific details that explain this main idea.

EXERCISE **6-4**   **Identifying General Statements**

Directions: For each of the following groups of sentences, select the most general statement the writer makes about the topic.

_____ 1. a. Brightly colored annuals, such as pansies and petunias, are often used as seasonal accents in a garden.
     b. Most gardens feature a mix of perennials and annuals.
     c. Some perennials prefer shade, while others thrive in full sun.
     d. Butterfly bushes are a popular perennial.

_____ 2. a. Hiring a housepainter is not as simple as it sounds.
     b. You should try to obtain a cost estimate from at least three painters.
     c. Each painter should be able to provide reliable references from past painting jobs.
     d. The painter must be able to work within the time frame you desire.

_____ 3. a. Flaxseed is an herbal treatment for constipation.
b. Some people use Kava to treat depression.
c. Gingko biloba is a popular remedy for memory loss.
d. A growing number of consumers are turning to herbal remedies to treat certain ailments.

_____ 4. a. Many students choose to live off-campus in apartments or rental houses.
b. Most colleges and universities offer a variety of student housing options.
c. Sororities and fraternities typically allow members to live in their organization's house.
d. On-campus dormitories provide a convenient place for students to live.

_____ 5. a. Try to set exercise goals that are challenging but realistic.
b. Increase the difficulty of your workout gradually.
c. Several techniques contribute to success when beginning an exercise program.
d. Reduce soreness by gently stretching your muscles before you exercise.

IDENTIFY THE TOPIC

2 LEARNING GOAL
Identify topics

The **topic** is the subject of the entire paragraph. Every sentence in a paragraph in some way discusses or explains this topic. If you had to choose a title for a paragraph, the one or two words you would choose are the topic.

To find the topic of a paragraph, ask yourself: What is the one thing the author is discussing throughout the paragraph?

Now read the following paragraph with that question in mind:

What causes asthma?

Asthma is caused by inflammation of the airways in the lungs, leading to wheezing, chest tightness, shortness of breath, and coughing. In most people, asthma is brought on by allergens or irritants in the air; some people also have exercise-induced asthma. People with asthma can generally control their symptoms through the use of inhaled medications, and most asthmatics keep a "rescue" inhaler of medication on hand to use in case of a flare-up.

—adapted from Donatelle, *Health*, p. 424

In this example, the author is discussing one topic—asthma—throughout the paragraph. Notice that the word *asthma* is used several times. Often the repeated use of a word can serve as a clue to the topic.

EXERCISE 6-5   **Identifying the Topic**

Directions: Read each of the following paragraphs and then select the topic of the paragraph from the choices given.

_____   1.   People have been making glass in roughly the same way for at least 2,000 years. The process involves melting certain Earth materials and cooling the liquid quickly before the atoms have time to form an orderly crystalline structure. This is the same way that natural glass, called obsidian, is generated from lava. It is possible to produce glass from a variety of materials, but most commercial glass is produced from quartz sand and lesser amounts of carbonate minerals.

—Lutgens et al., *Essentials of Geology*, p. 62

   a. earth
   b. glass
   c. atoms
   d. lava

_____   2.   The large majority of shoplifting is not done by professional thieves or by people who genuinely need the stolen items. About 2 million Americans are charged with shoplifting each year, but analysts estimate that for every arrest, 18 unreported incidents occur. About three-quarters of those caught are middle- or high-income people who shoplift for the thrill of it or as a substitute for affection. Shoplifting is also common among adolescents. Research evidence indicates that teen shoplifting is influenced by factors such as having friends who also shoplift.

—Solomon, *Consumer Behavior*, p. 35

   a. shoplifting
   b. shopping
   c. professional thieves
   d. adolescents

_____   3.   Kidney transplants are performed when the kidneys fail due to kidney disease. The kidneys are a pair of bean-shaped organs located under the rib cage by the small of the back. Each kidney is a little smaller than a fist and functions as a filter to remove toxins and wastes from the blood. When kidneys fail, waste products build up in the blood, which can be toxic.

—adapted from Belk and Maier, *Biology*, p. 438

a. organ transplants
b. organ disease
c. kidneys
d. toxins

_____ 4.   In order to survive, hunting and gathering societies depend on hunting animals and gathering plants. In some groups, the men do the hunting, and the women the gathering. In others, both men and women (and children) gather plants, the men hunt large animals, and both men and women hunt small animals. Hunting and gathering societies are small, usually consisting of only 25 to 40 people. These groups are nomadic. As their food supply dwindles in one area, they move to another location. They place high value on sharing food, which is essential to their survival.

—adapted from Henslin, *Sociology*, p. 148

a. hunters
b. food supplies
c. survival
d. hunting and gathering societies

_____ 5.   People who call themselves **freegans** are modern-day scavengers who live off discards as a political statement against corporations and consumerism. They forage through supermarket trash and eat the slightly bruised produce or just-expired canned goods that we routinely throw out, and obtain surplus food from sympathetic stores and restaurants. Freegans dress in castoff clothes and furnish their homes with items they find on the street. They get the word on locations where people are throwing out a lot of stuff by checking out postings at freecycle.org and at so-called *freemeets* (flea markets where no one exchanges money).

—adapted from Solomon, *Consumer Behavior*, pp. 392–393

a. scavengers
b. freegans
c. recycling
d. freemeets

Notice that the photograph helps you identify the topic of the paragraph.

EXERCISE 6-6   **Identifying the Topic**

Directions: Read each of the following paragraphs and then write the topic of the paragraph in the space provided.

A.   The word **locavore** has been coined to describe people who eat only food grown or produced locally, usually within close proximity to their homes. Locavores rely on farmers' markets, homegrown foods, or foods grown by independent farmers. Locavores prefer these foods because they are thought to be fresher, more environmentally friendly, and require far fewer resources to get them to market and keep them fresh for longer periods of time. Locavores believe that locally grown organic food is preferable to large corporation- or supermarket-based organic foods, as local foods have a smaller impact on the environment.

—adapted from Donatelle, *Health*, p. 282

Topic: _____

B.   A monopoly exists when an industry or market has only one producer (or else is so dominated by one producer that other firms cannot compete with it). A sole supplier enjoys nearly complete control over the prices of its products. Its only constraint is a decrease in consumer demand due to increased prices or government regulation. In the United States, laws forbid many monopolies and regulate prices charged by natural monopolies—industries in which one company can most efficiently supply all needed goods or services. Many electric companies are natural monopolies because they can supply all the power needed in a local area.

—adapted from Ebert and Griffin, *Business Essentials*, p. 12

Topic: _____

C.   Values represent cultural standards by which we determine what is good, bad, right, or wrong. Sometimes these values are expressed as proverbs or sayings that teach us how to live. Do you recognize the phrase, "Life is like a box of chocolates—you never know what you're going to get"? This modern-day saying is popular among those who embrace life's unpredictability. Cultures are capable of growth and change, so it's possible for a culture's values to change over time.

—Carl, *THINK Sociology*, p. 51

Topic: _____

D.   They go by many different names—capsule hotels, modular hotels, and pod hotels—but they all have one thing in common: very efficient use of space in a small footprint. The concept of modular hotels was pioneered by the Japanese, but the idea is sweeping across the world. Priced well below most competitors, these small, 75- to 100-square-foot rooms don't waste any space. Most modular units include the basics: private bathrooms, beds that are designed for two, flat-screen televisions, and a small work space. Weary travelers looking for nothing more than a place to sleep are finding that modular hotels "fit the bill."

—adapted from Cook et al., *Tourism*, p. 347

Topic: _____

E.   Television commercials provide a rich source of material to analyze. Begin by asking, "What reasons am I being given to lead me to want to buy this product?" Often, commercials do not overtly state the reasons; instead, they use music, staging, gestures, and visual cues to suggest the ideas they want us to have. We probably will not find a commercial that comes right out and says that buying someone a bottle of perfume or piece of jewelry will lead to a fulfilling love life, but several holiday commercials certainly imply as much.

—adapted from Facione, *Think Critically*, p. 90

Topic: _____

FIND THE STATED MAIN IDEA

3 LEARNING GOAL

Identify stated main ideas in paragraphs

The **main idea** of a paragraph is the most important idea; it is the idea that the whole paragraph explains or supports. Usually it is expressed in one sentence called the **topic sentence**. To find the main idea, use the following suggestions.

Locate the Topic

You have learned that the topic is the subject of a paragraph. The main idea is the most important thing the author wants you to know about the topic. To find the main idea, ask yourself, "What is the one most important thing to know about the topic?" Read the following paragraph and then answer this question.

Rather than traveling for rest and relaxation, more and more of the world's population is traveling for sport-related reasons. Sport tourism has exploded in the last ten years and is now seen as a major form of special-interest tourism. Sport tourism is travel away from home to play sport, watch sport, or to visit a sport attraction including both competitive and noncompetitive activities. Think of the vast array of travel that is included in this definition. Sport team members traveling to out-of-town tournaments are included; booster and alumni clubs trekking to "bowl" games are included; golf fans traveling to the British Open are included; a snowboard/ski club traveling to the Rockies for spring break is included!

—Cook et al., *Tourism*, p. 52

In this example, the topic is sport tourism. The most important point the author is making is that sport tourism has become a popular form of travel.

Locate the Most General Sentence

The most general sentence in the paragraph expresses the main idea. This sentence is called the topic sentence. This sentence must be broad enough to include or cover all the other ideas (details) in the paragraph. In the paragraph on the preceding page, the second sentence makes a general statement about sport tourism—that it is becoming more and more popular. The rest of the sentences provide specifics.

Study the Rest of the Paragraph

The main idea must connect, draw together, and make meaningful the rest of the paragraph. You might think of the main idea as the one that all the details, taken together, add up to, explain, or support. In the paragraph on the preceding page, sentence one serves as an introductory sentence. Sentence three offers a definition of sports tourism. Sentences four and five provide examples.

EXERCISE 6-7 **Writing Main Ideas**

Directions: Bring to class a list of bumper sticker or T-shirt messages you have recently seen. Form groups of three or four students. Each group should select three messages. For each, identify the topic and write a sentence that states its main idea. Groups should share their work with the class. The class may choose to select the most fun, innovative, or effective message and corresponding main idea.

IDENTIFY TOPIC SENTENCES

4 LEARNING GOAL
Recognize topic sentences

The topic sentence can be located anywhere in the paragraph. However, there are several positions where it is most likely to be found.

Topic Sentence
Detail
Detail
Detail

Topic Sentence First

Most often the topic sentence is placed first in the paragraph. In this type of paragraph, the author first states his or her main point and then explains it.

> The extended family consists of two or more closely related families who share a household and are economically bound to others in the group. For example, among the Navajo, relationships among sisters and other female kin often take precedence over the husband-wife relationships, not only because these relationships are defined as more satisfying but because women—not husbands and wives—live and work together and own property in common. Extended families take two major forms: *vertical extended families*, which include three or more generations—parents, their married children, grandchildren, and so on—and *joint families*, consisting of siblings and their spouses and their children.
>
> —Thompson and Hickey, *Society in Focus*, p. 360

Here the writer first defines an extended family. The rest of the paragraph offers more details about specific types of extended families.

Topic Sentence Last

The second most likely place for a topic sentence to appear is last in the paragraph. When using this arrangement, a writer leads up to the main point and then directly states it at the end.

Detail
Detail
Detail
Topic Sentence

> Art can inform, embellish, inspire, arouse, awaken, and delight us. Art can challenge us to think and see in new ways, and help each of us to develop a personal sense of beauty and truth. It can also deceive, humiliate, and anger us. A given work of art may serve several functions all at once.
>
> —Frank, *Prebles' Artforms*, p. 5

This paragraph first describes the positive effects that art can have on us, then describes other effects that are more negative. The paragraph ends with a general statement about the many functions of art.

Topic Sentence in the Middle

If it is placed neither first nor last, then the topic sentence appears somewhere in the middle of the paragraph. In this arrangement, the sentences before the topic sentence lead up to or introduce the main idea. Those that follow the main idea explain or describe it.

Detail
Detail
Topic Sentence
Detail
Detail

> If a person won the lottery or invested in the right stocks, his or her social class could change in an upward direction in an instant. Likewise, the mortgage crisis and corporate downsizing have sent many middle-class families plummeting into poverty. <u>Social mobility is a term that describes social class change, either upward or downward.</u> Wherever we are in life, then, there's always the chance that something could happen to us that would change our status. If social class is a ladder, social mobility occurs when we are moved either up or down it.
>
> —adapted from Carl, *THINK Sociology*, p. 128

In this paragraph, the author begins with examples of upward as well as downward mobility. He then states his main point and follows it with a general statement about status.

Topic Sentence First and Last

Occasionally the main idea will appear at the beginning of a paragraph and again at the end. Writers may use this organization to emphasize an important idea or to explain an idea that needs clarification.

Topic Sentence
Detail
Detail
Detail
Topic Sentence

> <u>Modeling, or learning behaviors by watching others perform them, is one of the most effective strategies for changing behavior.</u> For example, suppose that you have trouble talking to people you don't know very well. One of the easiest ways to improve your communication skills is to select friends whose social skills you envy. Observe them. Do they talk more or listen more? How do people respond to them? Why are they such good communicators? <u>If you observe behaviors you admire, you can model the steps of your behavior-change technique on a proven success.</u>
>
> —adapted from Donatelle, *Health*, p. 18

The first and last sentences both state, in slightly different ways, that modeling can be an effective way to change behavior.

EXERCISE **6-8**   **Identifying Topic Sentences**

Directions: Underline the topic sentence(s) in each of the following paragraphs.

A. Sociologists have several different ways of defining poverty. *Transitional poverty* is a temporary state that occurs when someone loses a job for a short time. *Marginal poverty* occurs when a person lacks stable employment (for example, if your job is lifeguarding at a pool during the summer season, you might experience marginal poverty when the season ends). The next, more serious level, *residual poverty*, is chronic and multigenerational. A person who experiences *absolute poverty* is so poor that he or she doesn't have resources to survive. *Relative poverty* is a state that occurs when we compare ourselves with those around us.

—adapted from Carl, *THINK Sociology*, p. 122

B.   A few years ago, the CBS-TV megahit series *NCIS: Naval Criminal Investigative Service* was recognized by the Paley Center for Media in Los Angeles as the most popular scripted TV show in the world. With more than 20 million dedicated viewers in the United States alone, the show has achieved heights that most other shows can't even dream of. Another immensely popular series on the same network, *CSI*, which follows teams of crime-scene investigators, now includes shows featuring New York City and other locales, and it is available to a global audience of nearly 2 billion viewers in 200 countries. The popularity of prime-time television crime shows is not limited to *NCIS* and *CSI*, as other widely followed series demonstrate. Social commentators note that the plethora of crime shows bombarding the airwaves today reveals a penchant among American TV viewers for crime-related entertainment and a fascination with police work and the criminal justice system.

—adapted from Schmalleger, *Criminal Justice*, p. 23

C.   Elections serve a critical function in American society. They make it possible for most political participation to be channeled through the electoral process rather than bubbling up through demonstrations, riots, or revolutions. Elections provide regular access to political power, so that leaders can be replaced without being overthrown. This is possible because elections are almost universally accepted as a fair and free method of selecting political leaders. Furthermore, by choosing who is to lead the country, the people—if they make their choices carefully—can also guide the policy direction of the government.

—adapted from Edwards et al., *Government in America*, p. 306

D.   Whether you realize it or not, you have probably been eating genetically modified foods for your entire life. Some genetic modifications involve moving genes between organisms in labs. Other modifications have occurred over the last several thousand years due to farmers' use of selective breeding techniques—breeding those cattle that produce the most milk or crossing crop plants that are easiest to harvest. While this artificial selection does not involve moving a gene from one organism to another, it does change the overall frequency of certain alleles for a gene in the population. Unless you eat only certified organic foods, you have been eating food that has been modified.

—adapted from Belk and Maier, *Biology*, p. 208

E.   People have not limited themselves to investigating nature. To try to understand life, they have also developed fields of science that focus on the social world. The social sciences examine human relationships. Just as the natural sciences attempt to understand the world of nature, the social sciences attempt to understand the social world. Just as the world of nature contains relationships that are not obvious but must be discovered through controlled observations, so the relationships of the human or social world are not obvious and must be revealed by means of repeated observations.

—adapted from Henslin, *Sociology*, p. 6

F.   Darwin hypothesized sexual selection as an explanation for differences between males and females within a species. For instance, the enormous tail on a male peacock results from female peahens that choose mates with showier tails. Because large tails require so much energy to display and are more conspicuous to their predators, peacocks with the largest tails must be both physically strong and smart to survive. Peahens can use the size of the tail, therefore, as a measure of the "quality" of the male. When a peahen chooses a male with a large tail, she is making sure that her offspring will receive high-quality genes. Sexual selection explains the differences between males and females in many species.

—adapted from Belk and Maier, *Biology*, p. 305

G.   In Japan, it's called *kuroi kiri* (black mist); in Germany, it's *schmiergeld* (grease money), whereas Mexicans refer to *la mordida* (the bite), the French say *pot-de-vin* (jug of wine), and Italians speak of the *bustarella* (little envelope). They're all talking about *baksheesh*, the Middle Eastern term for a "tip" to grease the wheels of a transaction. Giving "gifts" in exchange for getting business is common and acceptable in many countries, even though this may be frowned on elsewhere.

—adapted from Solomon, *Consumer Behavior*, p. 21

H.   When you hear the word *bird*, what mental image comes to mind? Does it resemble an ostrich? Or is your image closer to a robin, sparrow, or blue jay? The likely image that comes to mind at the suggestion to imagine a bird is what psychologists call a prototype. **Prototypes** are mental representations of an average category member. If you took an average of the three most familiar birds, you would get a prototypical bird. Prototypes allow for classification by resemblance. When you encounter a little creature you have never seen before, its basic shape—maybe just its silhouette—can be compared to your prototype of a bird. A match will then be made and you can classify the creature as a bird.

—Krause and Corts, *Psychological Science*, pp. 273–274

What aspect of geology does this photograph illustrate?

I. The standards of our peer groups tend to dominate our lives. If your peers, for example, listen to rap, rock and roll, country, or gospel, it is almost inevitable that you also prefer that kind of music. In high school, if your friends take math courses, you probably do too. It is the same for clothing styles and dating standards. Peer influences also extend to behaviors that violate social norms. If your peers are college-bound and upwardly striving, that is most likely what you will be; but if they use drugs, cheat, and steal, you are likely to do so too.

—adapted from Henslin, *Sociology*, p. 85

J. In the western and southwestern United States, sedimentary rocks often exhibit a brilliant array of colors. In the walls of Arizona's Grand Canyon we can see layers that are red, orange, purple, gray, brown, and buff. Some of the sedimentary rocks in Utah's Bryce Canyon are a delicate pink color. Sedimentary rocks in more humid places are also colorful but they are usually covered by soil and vegetation.

—Lutgens et al., *Essentials of Geology*, p. 144

LEARNING STYLE TIPS

If you tend to be a . . .	Then find topic sentences by . . .
Creative learner	Looking away from the paragraph and stating its main point in your own words. Find a sentence that matches your statement.
Pragmatic learner	Reading through the paragraph, sentence by sentence, evaluating each sentence.

EXERCISE **6-9** **Writing Main Ideas**

Working Together

Directions: Form groups of three students. Each group writes a topic at the top of a sheet of paper. Groups exchange papers and each group then writes a topic sentence based on the topic. Groups continue to exchange papers and write topic sentences until every group has written a topic sentence for each topic, and then papers are returned to the groups that wrote the original topic. Groups then read aloud the topic and suggested topic sentences. The class evaluates the topic sentences and selects the most effective ones for each topic.

IMPLIED MAIN IDEAS

When you **imply** something, you suggest an idea, but you do not state it outright. Study the cartoon below. The point the cartoonist is making is clear—conflicts are difficult to resolve. Notice, however, that this point is not stated directly. To get the cartoonist's point, you had to study the details and read the caption of the cartoon, and then reason out what the cartoonist is trying to say. You need to use the same reasoning process when reading paragraphs that lack a topic sentence. You have to study the details and figure out what all the details mean when considered together. This section will show you how to figure out main ideas that are suggested (implied) but not directly stated in a paragraph.

"Aren't you glad we had this meeting to resolve our conflict?"

What Does *Implied* Mean?

Suppose your favorite shirt is missing from your closet and you know that your roommate often borrows your clothes. You say to your roommate, "If that blue plaid shirt is back in my closet by noon, I'll forget that it was missing." Now, you did not directly accuse your roommate of borrowing your shirt, but your message was clear—return my shirt! Your statement implied, or suggested, that your roommate had borrowed it and should return it. Your roommate, if he understood your message, inferred (reasoned out) that you suspected that he had borrowed your shirt and that you want it back.

Speakers and writers imply ideas. Listeners and readers must make inferences in order to understand them. Here are two important terms you need to know:

> Imply   means   to suggest an idea but not state it directly.
>
> Infer   means   to reason out something based on what has been said.

Here is another statement; what is the writer implying?

> I wouldn't feed that cake to my dog.

No doubt you inferred that the writer dislikes the cake and considers it inedible, but notice that the writer did not say that.

EXERCISE 6-10   Identifying Implications

Directions: For each of the following statements, select the choice that best explains what the writer is implying but has not directly stated.

_____ 1. Jane's hair looks as if she just came out of a wind tunnel.
  a. Jane's hair needs rearranging.
  b. Jane's hair needs coloring.
  c. Jane's hair needs styling.
  d. Jane's hair is messy.

_____ 2. I would not recommend Professor Wright's class to my worst enemy.
  a. The writer likes Professor Wright's class.
  b. The writer dislikes Professor Wright's class.
  c. Professor Wright's class is popular.
  d. Professor Wright's class is unpopular.

_____ 3. The steak was overcooked and tough; the mashed potatoes were cold; the green beans were withered; and the chocolate pie was mushy.
  a. The dinner was tasty.
  b. The dinner was prepared poorly.
  c. The dinner was nutritious.
  d. The dinner was served carelessly.

_____ 4. Professor Rodriguez assigns three 5-page papers, gives weekly quizzes, and requires both a midterm and final exam. In addition to weekly assigned chapters in the text, we must read three or four journal articles each week. It is difficult to keep up.
   a. Professor Rodriguez's course is demanding.
   b. Professor Rodriguez is not a good teacher.
   c. Professor Rodriguez likes to give homework.
   d. Professor Rodriguez's course is unpopular.

_____ 5. It was my favorite time of year. The lilacs were blooming—finally!—and even though we still wore sweaters, the breeze held the promise of warm days to come.
   a. It was autumn.
   b. It was springtime.
   c. It was summertime.
   d. There was a storm coming.

_____ 6. When Alton got the estimate for repairing his car, he knew he had a tough decision to make.
   a. Alton was going to repair his own car.
   b. Alton would have to find another car repair shop.
   c. Alton's car repairs were going to be inexpensive.
   d. Alton would have to decide whether to repair the car or buy a different one.

_____ 7. Charlie limped over to the couch and lay down. He put his foot up on a pillow and carefully placed the ice pack on his ankle.
   a. Charlie is getting ready to take a nap.
   b. Charlie has the flu.
   c. Charlie has an injured ankle.
   d. Charlie has been running.

_____ 8. After the girls' sleepover party last Saturday, it looked like a bomb had gone off in the basement.
   a. The girls made a mess in the basement.
   b. The electricity went out during the sleepover party.
   c. There was an explosion in the basement after the sleepover party.
   d. The sleepover party was too loud.

_____ 9. When it was Kei's turn to give her speech, her stomach did a flip, and her face felt as if it were on fire.
   a. Kei looked forward to giving her speech.
   b. Kei was experienced at giving speeches.
   c. Kei was nervous about giving her speech.
   d. Kei enjoyed giving speeches.

_____ 10. People filed out of the movie theater slowly and quietly; many of them wiped their eyes and noses with tissues as they walked to their cars.
   a. The movie was sad.
   b. The movie was funny.
   c. The theater was cold.
   d. The moviegoers were disappointed.

Figuring Out Implied Main Ideas

Implied main ideas, when they appear in paragraphs, are usually larger, more important ideas than the details. You might think of **implied ideas** as general ideas that are suggested by specifics.

What larger, more important idea do these details point to?

> The wind was blowing at 35 mph.
>
> The windchill was 5 degrees below zero.
>
> Snow was falling at the rate of 3 inches per hour.

Together these three details suggests that a snowstorm or blizzard was occurring. You might visualize this as follows:

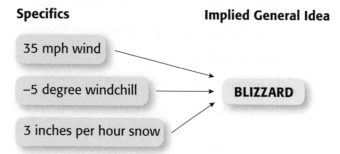

Now what idea does the following set of specifics suggest?

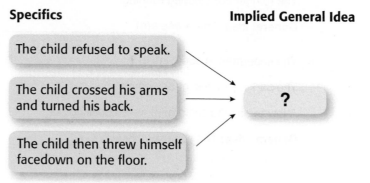

You probably determined that the child was angry or having a temper tantrum.

EXERCISE **6-11**   **Inferring General Ideas**

Directions: Find a word from the list below that describes the larger idea or situation each set of specifics suggests. Each will require you to infer a general idea.

tonsillitis	closed	dying	flu
power outage	accident	burglary	going too fast

1. The child has a headache.

   The child has a queasy stomach.

   The child has a mild fever.

   General idea: The child has the _____.

2. The plant's leaves were withered.

   The blossoms had dropped.

   Its stem was drooping.

   General idea: The plant was _____.

3. The windshield of the car was shattered.

   The door panel was dented.

   The bumper was crumpled.

   General idea: The car had been in a(n) _____.

4. The lights went out.

   The television shut off.

   The refrigerator stopped running.

   General idea: There was a(n) _____.

5. The supermarket door was locked.

   The parking lot was nearly empty.

   A few remaining customers were checking out.

   General idea: The supermarket was _____.

Implied Ideas in Paragraphs

In paragraphs, writers sometimes leave their main idea unstated. The paragraph contains only details. It is up to you, the reader, to infer the writer's main point. You can visualize this type of paragraph as follows:

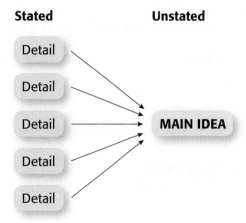

The details, when taken together, all point to a larger, more important idea. Think of the paragraph as a list of facts that you must add up or put together to determine the meaning of the paragraph as a whole. Use the following steps as a guide to find implied main ideas:

1. **Find the topic.** Ask yourself, "What is the one thing the author is discussing throughout the paragraph?"
2. **Decide what the writer wants you to know about that topic.** Look at each detail and decide what larger general idea each explains.
3. **Express this idea in your own words.** Make sure the main idea is a reasonable one. Ask yourself, "Does it apply to all the details in the paragraph?"

Read the following paragraph; then follow the three steps listed above.

Some advertisers rely on star power. Commercials may use celebrities to encourage consumers to purchase a product. Other commercials may use an "everyone's buying it" approach that argues that thousands of consumers could not possibly be wrong in their choice, so the product must be worthwhile. Still other commercials may use visual appeal to catch the consumers' interest and persuade them to make purchases.

The topic of this paragraph is commercials. More specifically it is about devices advertisers use to build commercials. Three details are given: use of star power, an everyone's-buying-it approach, and visual appeal. Each of the three details is a different persuasive device. The main point the writer is trying to make, then, is that commercials use various persuasive devices to appeal to consumers. Notice that no single sentence states this idea clearly.

You can visualize this paragraph as follows:

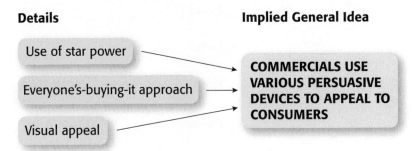

Details

- Use of star power
- Everyone's-buying-it approach
- Visual appeal

Implied General Idea

COMMERCIALS USE VARIOUS PERSUASIVE DEVICES TO APPEAL TO CONSUMERS

Here is another paragraph. Read it and then fill in the diagram that follows:

Yellow is a bright, cheery color; it is often associated with spring and hopefulness. Green, since it is a color that appears frequently in nature (trees, grass, plants), has come to suggest growth and rebirth. Blue, the color of the sky, may suggest eternity or endless beauty. Red, the color of both blood and fire, is often connected with strong feelings such as courage, lust, and rage.

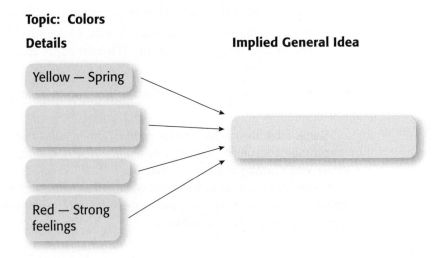

Topic: Colors

Details

- Yellow — Spring
-
-
- Red — Strong feelings

Implied General Idea

How to Know if You Have Made a Reasonable Inference

There is a test you can perform to discover whether you inferred a reasonable main idea. The idea you infer to be the main idea should be broad enough so that every sentence in the paragraph explains the idea you have chosen. Work through the paragraph, sentence by sentence. Check to see that each sentence explains or gives more information about the idea you have chosen. If some sentences do not explain your chosen idea, your main idea probably is not broad enough. Work on expanding your idea and making it more general.

EXERCISE 6-12   **Completing Paragraph Diagrams**

Directions: Read each of the following paragraphs and complete the diagram that follows.

A.   Workers in the **primary sector** of an economy extract resources directly from the earth. Most workers in this sector are usually in agriculture, but the sector also includes fishing, forestry, and mining. Workers in the **secondary sector** transform raw materials produced by the primary sector into manufactured goods. Construction is included in this sector. All other jobs in an economy are within the **tertiary sector**, sometimes called the **service sector**. The tertiary sector includes a great range of occupations, from a store clerk to a surgeon, from a movie ticket seller to a nuclear physicist, from a dancer to a political leader.

—Bergman and Renwick, *Introduction to Geography*, p. 365

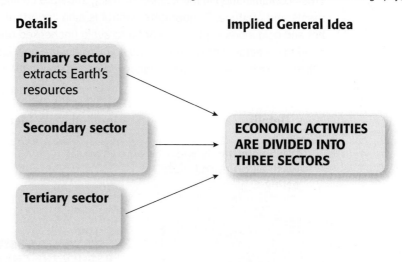

B.   Among many other activities, urban gangs fight among themselves and prey on the weak and vulnerable. They delight in demonstrating ownership and control of their "turf," and they sometimes turn neighborhoods into war zones in defense of it. Once gangs form, their graffiti soon adorn buildings and alleyways, and membership is displayed through hand signs, clothing, and special colors. As a newly formed gang grows in reputation and confidence, it soon finds itself attracting those who would like to be members in order to reap the benefits: safety, or girlfriends, or a reputation for toughness.

—Barlow, *Criminal Justice in America*, p. 271

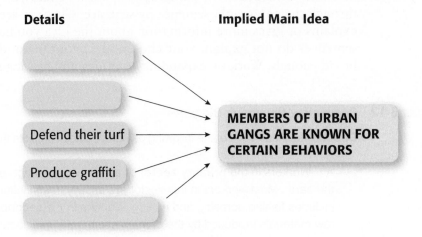

C.   More than 30 percent of all foodborne illnesses result from unsafe handling of food at home. What can you do to prevent such illnesses? Among the most basic of precautions are to wash your hands and to wash all produce before eating it. Avoid cross-contamination in the kitchen by using separate cutting boards and utensils for meats and produce. Temperature control is also important; hot foods must be kept hot and cold foods kept cold in order to avoid unchecked bacterial growth. Leftovers need to be eaten within 3 days, and if you're unsure how long something has been sitting in the fridge, don't take chances. When in doubt, throw it out.

—adapted from Donatelle, *Health*, p. 280

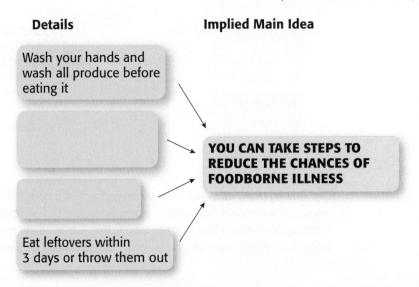

D. How should you present your speech? Let's consider your options. An **impromptu speech** is delivered on the spur of the moment, without preparation. The ability to speak off the cuff is useful in an emergency, but impromptu speeches produce unpredictable outcomes. It's certainly not a good idea to rely on impromptu speaking in place of solid preparation. Another option is a **memorized speech**. Speakers who use memorized presentations are usually most effective when they write their speeches to sound like informal and conversational speech rather than formal, written essays. A **manuscript speech** is written out beforehand and then read from a manuscript or teleprompter. When extremely careful wording is required (for example, when the president addresses Congress), the manuscript speech is appropriate. However, most speeches that you'll deliver will be extemporaneous. An **extemporaneous speech** is one that is prepared in advance and presented from abbreviated notes. Extemporaneous speeches are nearly as polished as memorized ones, but they are more vigorous, flexible, and spontaneous.

—German et al., *Principles of Public Speaking*, pp. 190–191

Details   **Implied Main Idea**

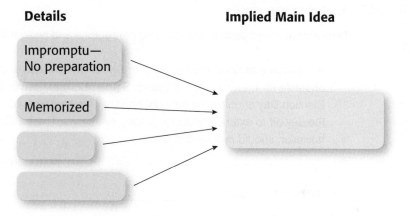

Impromptu—
No preparation

Memorized

E. In order to measure social class standing, sociologists may use the *objective* method, which ranks individuals into classes on the basis of measures such as education, income, and occupational prestige. Sociologists may also use the *reputational* method, which places people into various social classes on the basis of reputation in the community. A third method, *self-identification*, allows people to place themselves in a social class. Although people can readily place themselves in a class, the results are often difficult to interpret. People might be hesitant to call themselves upper-class for fear of appearing snobbish, but at the same time they might be reluctant to call themselves lower-class for fear of being stigmatized. The net result is that the method of self-identification substantially overestimates the middle portion of the class system.

—Curry et al., *Sociology for the 21st Century*, p. 138

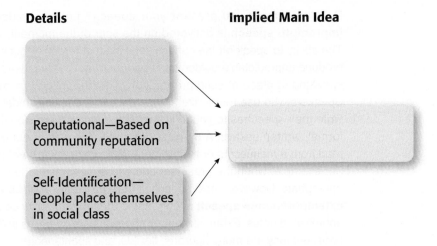

Details   **Implied Main Idea**

Reputational—Based on community reputation

Self-Identification— People place themselves in social class

EXERCISE **6-13**   **Analyzing Paragraphs**

Directions: Read each of the following paragraphs and answer the questions that follow.

A.   Since elections traditionally are held on Tuesdays, the busy workday is an obstacle for many would-be voters. Some reformers have, therefore, proposed that Election Day should be a national holiday. This strategy could backfire if people used the day off to extend vacations or long weekends. The tradition of Tuesday elections, however, should reduce this risk.

—O'Connor et al., *American Government*, p. 383

1. What is the topic? _____

2. What is the implied main idea? _____

   _____

B.   Research suggests that women who are considered attractive are more effective in changing attitudes than are women thought to be less attractive. In addition, more attractive individuals are often considered to be more credible than less attractive people. They are also perceived to be happier, more popular, more sociable, and more successful than are those rated as being less attractive. With respect to shape and body size, people with fat, round silhouettes are consistently rated as older, more old-fashioned, less good-looking, more talkative, and more good-natured. Athletic, muscular people are rated as more mature, better looking, taller, and more adventurous. Tall and thin people are rated as more ambitious, more suspicious of others, more tense and nervous, more pessimistic, and quieter.

—Beebe and Masterson, *Communicating in Small Groups*, p. 150

How do these photographs suggest the implied main idea of paragraph C?

3. What is the topic? _____

4. What is the implied main idea? _____

_____

C.   Any zookeeper will tell you that the primate house is their most popular exhibit. People love apes and monkeys. It is easy to see why—primates are curious, playful, and agile. In short, they are fun to watch. But something else drives our fascination with these wonderful animals: We see ourselves reflected in them. The placement of their eyes and their small noses appear humanlike. They have hands with fingernails instead of paws with claws. Some can stand and walk on two legs for short periods. They can finely manipulate objects with their fingers and opposable thumbs. They show extensive parental care, and even their social relations are similar to ours—they tickle, caress, kiss, and pout.

—adapted from Belk and Maier, *Biology*, p. 236

5. What is the topic? _____

6. What is the implied main idea? _____

_____

D.   The Web has enabled people to work, "talk" to friends across town and across the ocean, and buy goods from online retailers without leaving their houses. It has also made some criminal enterprises and unethical behavior easier to accomplish and harder to trace—for example, people can scam others out of large sums of money, buy college term papers, and learn how to build a bomb.

—adapted from Divine et al., *America Past and Present*, p. 449

7. What is the topic? _____

8. What is the implied main idea? _____

E.   Sleep conserves body energy so that we are rested and ready to perform during high-performance daylight hours. Sleep also restores the neurotransmitters that have been depleted during the waking hours. This process clears the brain of unimportant details as a means of preparing for a new day. Getting enough sleep to feel ready to meet daily challenges is a key factor in maintaining optimal physical and psychological status.

—adapted from Donatelle and Davis, *Access to Health*, p. 42

9. What is the topic? _____

10. What is the implied main idea? _____

_____

EXERCISE **6-14** **Writing Implied Main Ideas**

Directions: None of the following paragraphs has a topic sentence. Read each paragraph and, in the space provided, write a sentence that expresses the main idea.

A. More than 32,000 people in the U.S. take their own lives every year, and for every death there are at least another eight attempted suicides. College students are more likely than the general population to try to take their own lives, and some, unfortunately, succeed. Suicide is the second leading cause of death on college campuses, and more than 6% of students said they had seriously considered attempting suicide in the past year.

—Lynch et al., *Choosing Health*, p. 35

Implied main idea: _____

B. Governments in this country spend billions of dollars on schools, libraries, hospitals, and dozens of other public institutions. Some of these services, like highways and public parks, can be shared by everyone and cannot be denied to anyone. These kinds of services are called public goods. Other services, such as a college education or medical care, can be restricted to individuals who meet certain criteria and may be provided by the private sector as well. Governments typically provide these services to make them accessible to people who may not be able to afford privately available services.

—Edwards et al., *Government in America*, p. 9

Implied main idea: _____

C. Sociologists use the term **norms** to describe the rules of behavior that develop out of a group's values. The term **sanctions** refers to the reactions people receive for following or breaking norms. A positive sanction expresses approval for following a norm, and a negative sanction reflects disapproval for breaking a norm. Positive sanctions can be material, such as a prize, a trophy, or money, but in everyday life they usually consist of hugs, smiles, a pat on the back, or even handshakes and "high fives." Negative sanctions can also be material—being fined in court is one example—but negative sanctions, too, are more likely to be symbolic: harsh words, or gestures such as frowns, stares, clenched jaws, or raised fists.

—adapted from Henslin, *Sociology*, p. 46

Implied main idea: _____

D. The amount of air forced past the vocal cords determines the volume of our speech, while muscles that control the length of the vocal cords help to determine the pitch of our speech. The shape of our mouths, lips, and tongue and the position of our teeth determine the actual sound that is produced. Sustained exposure to tobacco smoke can cause parts of the larynx to become covered with scar tissue, often making long-time smokers sound quite hoarse.

—Belk and Borden Maier, *Biology*, p. 447

Implied main idea: _____

E.   Most sporting goods manufacturers have long sold products for women, but this often meant simply creating an inferior version of the male product and slapping a pink label on it. Then the companies discovered that many women were buying products intended for boys because they wanted better quality, so some of them figured out that they needed to take this market segment seriously. Burton Snowboard Company was one of the early learners. When the company started to offer high-quality clothing and gear made specifically for women, female boarders snapped them up. Burton also changed the way it promotes these products and redesigned its Web site after getting feedback from female riders.

—adapted from Solomon, *Consumer Behavior*, p. 189

Implied main idea: _____

_____

F.   If you've ever noticed that you feel better after a belly laugh or a good cry, you aren't alone. Old adages such as "laughter is the best medicine" and "smile and the world smiles with you" didn't just evolve out of the blue. Scientists have long recognized that smiling, laughing, singing, dancing, and other actions can elevate our moods, help us live longer, and help us improve our relationships. Crying can have similar positive physiological effects. Recent research has shown that laughter and joy can increase endorphin levels, increase oxygen levels in the blood, increase immune system functioning, decrease stress levels, relieve pain, enhance productivity, reduce risks of heart disease, and help fight cancer.

—Donatelle, *Health*, p. 71

Implied main idea: _____

_____

G.   As the effects of caffeine begin to wear off, users may feel let down, mentally or physically depressed, exhausted, and weak. To counteract these effects, people commonly choose to drink another cup of coffee. But before you say yes to another cup of coffee, consider this. Although you would have to drink between 66 and 100 cups of coffee in a day to produce a fatal overdose of caffeine, you may experience sensory disturbances after consuming only 10 cups of coffee within a 24-hour period. These symptoms include tinnitus (ringing in the ears), spots before the eyes, numbness in arms and legs, poor circulation, and visual hallucinations. Because

10 cups of coffee is not an extraordinary amount for many people to drink within a 24-hour period, caffeine use is clearly something to think about.

—Donatelle and Davis, *Access to Health*, pp. 289–290

Implied main idea: _____

H.   In 1946, the Levitt Company was finishing up Levittown. Practically overnight, what was formerly a Long Island potato field 25 miles east of Manhattan became one of America's newest suburbs, changing the way homes were built. The land was bulldozed and the trees removed, and then trucks dropped building materials at precise 60-foot intervals. Construction was divided into 26 distinct steps. At the peak of production, the company constructed 30 new single-family homes each day.

—Bergman and Renwick, *Introduction to Geography*, p. 422

Implied main idea: _____

_____

I.   Children who exercise are more likely to continue exercising in adulthood than children who do not exercise. In a country where most adults do not get the recommended 30 to 60 minutes of exercise most days of the week, it makes sense to encourage everyone to become more athletic. When good exercise habits are carried into adulthood, there is a decreased risk of heart disease, obesity, diabetes, and many cancers. Additional benefits include lowered cholesterol, and studies suggest that exercise may decrease anxiety and depression.

—Belk and Borden Maier, *Biology*, p. 509

Implied main idea: _____

J.   *Turn-requesting cues* tell the speaker that you, as a listener, would like to take a turn as speaker; you might transmit these cues by using some vocalized "er" or "um" that tells the speaker that you would now like to speak, by opening your eyes and mouth as if to say something, by beginning to gesture with a hand, or by leaning forward.

Through *turn-denying cues* you indicate your reluctance to assume the role of speaker by, for example, intoning a slurred "I don't know"; giving the speaker some brief grunt that signals you have nothing to say; avoiding eye contact with the speaker who wishes you now to take on the role of speaker; or engaging in some behavior that is incompatible with speaking—for example, coughing or blowing your nose.

Through *backchanneling cues* you communicate various meanings back to the speaker—but without assuming the role of the speaker. For example, you can indicate your *agreement* or *disagreement* with the speaker through smiles or frowns, nods of approval or disapproval; brief comments such as "right," "exactly," or "never"; or vocalizations such as "uh-huh" or "uh-uh."

—DeVito, *Messages*, pp. 224–225

Implied main idea: _____

_____

EXERCISE **6-15** **Identifying Main Ideas**

Working Together

Directions: Separate into groups. Using a reading selection from Part Six of this text, work with your group to identify and underline the topic sentence of each paragraph. If any of the main ideas are unstated, write a sentence that states the main idea. When all the groups have completed the task, the class should compare the findings of the various groups.

SELF-TEST SUMMARY

1	**What are general and specific ideas?**	A general idea is broad and can apply to many things. A specific idea is detailed and refers to a smaller group or an individual item.
2	**How can you identify the topic of a paragraph?**	Look for the one idea the author is discussing throughout the entire paragraph.
3	**How can you find the stated main idea of a paragraph?**	Find the topic and then locate the one sentence in the paragraph that is the most general. Check to be sure that this one sentence relates to all the details in the paragraph.
4	**What is a topic sentence?**	The topic sentence states the main idea of a paragraph. The topic sentence can be located anywhere in the paragraph. The most common positions are first or last, but the topic sentence can also appear in the middle of the paragraph, or as the first and last sentences of the paragraph.
5	**How can you figure out implied main ideas?**	Implied main ideas are suggested but not directly stated in a paragraph. To find implied main ideas, • find the topic • figure out what general idea the paragraph explains • express the idea in your own words

GOING  ONLINE

1. **Main Ideas in Electronic Communications**

   Imagine the following situation: You need to communicate with a group of friends or classmates about several important matters. For this reason, you need to compose an e-mail rather than send a text message. What can you do to make sure the main ideas or topic sentences of your email "pop off the screen" (i.e., get your readers' attention)?

2. **Implied Ideas and Emoticons**

   You have seen *emoticons*—small symbols like ☺ used in electronic communications. Many people believe emoticons have become popular because they help readers better understand the writer's emotions and intentions. For example, on a text message, a writer may use the ☺ emoticon to suggest "I am kidding." Abbreviations such as LOL ("laughing out loud") are also common. With a group of classmates, brainstorm a list of five common emoticons or abbreviations, and provide a definition of each. Write a sentence that uses each. Does including an emoticon or abbreviation help you better express yourself?

CHAPTER

6

MASTERY TEST 1 Reading Selection

Communicating Through Objects

Joseph A. DeVito

Before Reading

This selection is an excerpt from a communications textbook, *Human Communication: The Basic Course*. It appeared in a chapter titled "Nonverbal Messages."

Previewing the Reading

Using the steps listed on pages 49–50, preview the reading selection. When you have finished, complete the following items.

1. _____ communication is via objects made by human hands.

2. The three types of communication discussed in this article are color communication, _____ , and _____.

Predicting and Connecting

1. How would you describe your "personal style" in terms of your clothing, hairstyle, and so on? Do you tend to favor any particular colors when dressing or decorating?

2. Does the format of this reading lend itself to outlining? Why or why not?

> **Vocabulary Preview**
> **physiologically** (par. 2) bodily, biologically
> **inferences** (par. 4) deductions
> **hierarchy** (par. 4) pecking order, chain of command
> **mahogany** (par. 8) a reddish-brown wood
> **conscientiousness** (par. 10) diligence
> **extroversion** (par. 10) degree to which a person is outgoing

Communicating Through Objects

1   **Artifactual communication** is communication via objects made by human hands. Thus, color, clothing, jewelry, and the decoration of space would be considered artifactual. Let's look at each of these briefly.

Color Communication

2   There is some evidence that colors affect us physiologically. For example, respiratory movements increase with red light and decrease with blue light. Similarly, eye blinks increase in frequency when eyes are exposed to red light and

227

decrease when exposed to blue. These responses seem consistent with our intuitive feelings about blue being more soothing and red more arousing. When a school changed the color of its walls from orange and white to blue, the blood pressure of the students decreased and their academic performance increased (Ketcham, 1958; Malandro, Barker, & Barker, 1989).

3   Color also influences perceptions and behaviors (Kanner, 1989). People's acceptance of a product, for example, is largely determined by its packaging—especially its color. In one study the very same coffee taken from a yellow can was described as weak, from a dark brown can as too strong, from a red can as rich, and from a blue can as mild. Even your acceptance of a person may depend on the colors he or she wears. Consider, for example, the comments of one color expert (Kanner, 1989): "If you have to pick the wardrobe for your defense lawyer heading into court and choose anything but blue, you deserve to lose the case." Black is so powerful it could work against the lawyer with the jury. Brown lacks sufficient authority. Green would probably elicit a negative response.

Clothing and Body Adornment

4   People make inferences about who you are, at least in part, from the way you dress. Your socioeconomic class, your seriousness, your attitudes (e.g., whether you're conservative or liberal), your concern for convention, your sense of style, and perhaps even your creativity will all be judged in part by the way you dress (Burgoon, Guerrero, & Floyd, 2010; Knapp & Hall, 2010; Molloy, 1981). In the business world, your clothing may communicate your position within the hierarchy and your willingness and desire to conform to the norms of the organization.

5   The way you wear your hair says something about your attitudes—from a concern about being up to date, to a desire to shock, to perhaps a lack of interest in appearances. Men with long hair will generally be judged as less conservative than those with shorter hair. Your jewelry also communicates about you. Wedding and engagement rings are obvious examples that communicate specific messages. College rings and political buttons likewise communicate specific messages. If you wear a Rolex watch or large precious stones, others are likely to infer that you're rich.

6   Body piercings are now common, especially among theyoung. Nose, nipple, tongue, and belly button jewelry (among other piercings) send a variety of messages. Although people wearing such jewelry may wish to communicate positive meanings, research indicates that those interpreting these messages seem to infer that the wearer is communicating an unwillingness to conform to social norms and a willingness to take greater risks than people without such piercings (Forbes, 2001). And in health-care situations, tattoos and piercings may communicate such undesirable traits as impulsiveness, unpredictability, and

a tendency toward being reckless or violent (Rapsa & Cusack, 1990; Smith, M. H., 2003). This situation and these impressions may well change as body jewelry becomes more and more common.

7   Tattoos, whether temporary or permanent, likewise communicate a variety of messages—often the name of a loved one or some symbol of allegiance or affiliation. Tattoos also communicate to the wearers themselves. For example, tattooed students see themselves (and perhaps others do as well) as more adventurous, creative, individualistic, and risk-prone than those without tattoos (Drews, Allison, & Probst, 2000). Attitudes toward tattoos are also likely to change as they become more popular with both men and women.

Space Decoration

8   The way you decorate your private spaces also communicates about you. The office with a mahogany desk and bookcases and oriental rugs communicates your importance and status within an organization, just as a metal desk and bare floor indicate a worker much further down in the hierarchy.

9   Similarly, people will make inferences about you based on the way you decorate your home. The expensiveness of the furnishings may communicate your status and wealth; their coordination may convey your sense of style. The magazines may reflect your interests, and the arrangement of chairs around a television set may reveal how important watching television is to you. The contents of bookcases lining the walls reveal the importance of reading in your life. In fact, there's probably little in your home that will not send messages from which others will draw inferences about you. Similarly, the absence of certain items will communicate something about you. Consider what messages you'd get from a home where no television, phone, or books can be seen.

10   People will also make judgments as to your personality on the basis of room decorations. They will evaluate your openness to new experiences (distinctive decorating usually communicates this, as would different types of books and magazines and travel souvenirs) and even about your conscientiousness, emotional stability, degree of extroversion, and agreeableness. Not surprisingly, bedrooms prove more revealing of personality than offices (Gosling, Ko, Mannarelli, & Morris, 2002).

—DeVito, *Human Communication*, pp. 133–134

After Reading

Checking Your Comprehension

_____ 1. Which of the following colors is considered the most soothing and relaxing?
   a. red.
   b. white.
   c. blue.
   d. orange.

_____ 2. According to the reading, which of the following is generally considered a sign of wealth?
   a. large gems or precious stones.
   b. long hair.
   c. a conservative wardrobe.
   d. tattoos.

_____ 3. In general, most people perceive body piercings to be an indicator of
   a. ethnic heritage.
   b. social class.
   c. nonconformity.
   d. an artistic nature.

_____ 4. People with tattoos often see themselves as all of the following _except_
   a. individualistic.
   b. creative.
   c. adventurous.
   d. politically liberal.

_____ 5. Which of the following tends to _least_ reflect a person's individual personality?
   a. his or her bedroom.
   b. choice of body adornment.
   c. his or her office space.
   d. size and type of tattoo.

Applying Your Skills: Topics and Main Ideas

_____ 6. The topic of paragraph 2 is
   a. red and blue.
   b. bodily responses to colors.
   c. school colors.
   d. academic performance.

_____ 7. All of the following words are used in paragraph 3. Three words are specific, and one is general. Which is the general word?
   a. color.
   b. black.
   c. brown.
   d. green.

_____ 8. Which of the following best states the implied main idea of paragraph 5?
   a. Hairstyle is a key indicator of political beliefs.
   b. People choose their hairstyles for a variety of reasons.
   c. Hairstyles and jewelry send specific messages.
   d. To be perceived as rich, wear a Rolex watch.

_____ 9. The topic sentence of paragraph 9 is found in the
   a. first sentence.
   b. third sentence.
   c. fourth sentence.
   d. last sentence.

_____ 10. The topic sentence of paragraph 10 is found in the
   a. first sentence.
   b. second sentence.
   c. third sentence.
   d. first and third sentences.

Studying Words

_____11. The word *respiratory* (par. 2) means
  a. related to sight.
  b. related to sound.
  c. related to breathing.
  d. related to thinking.

_____12. The word *convention* (par. 4) means
  a. social customs.
  b. large gathering of people.
  c. fashion.
  d. political statement.

_____13. The word *trait* (par. 6) means
  a. crime.
  b. characteristic.
  c. habit.
  d. constraint.

_____14. The word *allegiance* (par. 7) means
  a. patriotism.
  b. ownership.
  c. independence.
  d. loyalty.

_____15. The word *distinctive* (par. 10) means
  a. unique.
  b. odd.
  c. inexpensive.
  d. colorful.

For more practice, ask your instructor for an opportunity to work on the mastery tests that appear in the Test Bank.

Thinking Visually

1. What is your reaction to the photo on page 229? What assumptions do you make about the person shown in the photo based on her body adornments? Do your assumptions match those summarized in the reading?

2. Suppose you want to illustrate the section of the reading titled "Space Decoration" with two photos. What types of photos would you use? Describe their contents. Write a caption that ties each photo to the content of the reading.

3. Create a map of the reading, following the directions on page 96.

Thinking Critically About the Reading

1. Examine the decorations in the room you are sitting in right now. What messages do those decorations send?

2. In the reading, you no doubt noticed the names and dates in parentheses. For example, paragraph 10 refers to "Gosling, Ko, Mannarelli, & Morris, 2002." To what do these names and date refer?

3. Reread the last sentences of paragraphs 6 and 7. Why do you think the author included these sentences?

4. Describe the author's approach to his topic. Which word best describes his tone: humorous, scholarly, unconventional, or vague?

Academic Application: Summarizing the Reading

Directions: Imagine your instructor has asked you to write a one-paragraph summary of the section titled "Color Communication." Complete the following summary by filling in the blanks.

Our _____ react to colors. Breathing and eye blinks increase with red light, but decrease with _____ light. These observations are evidence for the idea that blue is a more soothing color, while red is more _____. Color also influences perceptions and _____. The color of a product's _____ usually predicts its acceptance by consumers. The color of a person's _____ may affect the way people respond to him or her. For example, the best color for a defense attorney to wear in a courtroom is _____.

MASTERY TEST 2 Reading Selection

What Is Veiling?

Banu Gökariksel

Before Reading

This selection originally appeared in an introductory geography textbook in a chapter that explores cultures from around the world.

Previewing the Reading

Using the steps listed on pages 49–50, preview the reading selection. When you have finished, complete the following items.

1. Which question will this selection answer? _____

2. Three key topics that will be discussed in the selection are the concept of veiling in Islam, the veil as a _____, and _____
_____.

3. Indicate whether each statement is true (T) or false (F).
   _____ a. Veiling is an application of the Islamic code of hospitality.
   _____ b. The veil has become an object of fashion.
   _____ c. Veiling often creates a private space for women.

Predicting and Connecting

1. How much do you know about Islam? Do you know or understand why Muslim women wear veils in public?

2. Do you expect the reading to be fairly easy to understand, of moderate difficulty, or challenging? Why?

> **Vocabulary and Concept Preview**
> **pious** (par. 1) religious, devout
> **Qur'an** (par. 2) the holy book of Islam; also spelled Koran
> **mandates** (par. 2) requires
> **chic** (par. 4) fashionable
> **fluid** (par. 5) changing

Think As You Read
Read • Respond

During Reading

As you read the selection, complete each of the following. When highlighting, use a different color highlighter for each task.

a. Highlight the topic sentence of each paragraph. If the main idea is unstated, write a sentence that states it.

b. Highlight the most important details in each paragraph.

c. Highlight useful transitional words and phrases that help you understand and connect the author's ideas.

d. Read and respond to the questions in the margin

Circle the two key issues in paragraph 1 that the author will discuss in this reading.

1   In recent years, there has been an emphasis on veiling as an Islamic requirement for pious Muslims. The emergence of veiling as a religious, political, and cultural issue is linked to two related issues in the Muslim world. The first is the rise of broad Islamic-oriented social and political movements across most Muslim countries. These movements share an emphasis on living according to the tenets of Islam, but vary in terms of specific political goals and strategies. The second issue is the growth of an "Islamic" consumer market that includes a fashion industry.

2   **THE CONCEPT OF VEILING IN ISLAM** Veiling is an application of the Islamic code of modesty. The Qur'an specifies modesty for both men and women, including virtues such as humility, moderation, and not drawing attention to oneself in public. The same code mandates women's covering their "ornaments" or "jewels" in public spaces or in the presence of unrelated men. Debates continue about the interpretation of Qur'anic injunctions about veiling, which has led to different practices in different places.

3   Interpretations of modest dress differ across Muslim communities. These are often linked to cultural concepts such as honor, respectability, femininity, and social class. Historically in Egypt, upper-class urban women were fully covered. For many centuries in Indonesia, Muslim women did not cover their hair and shoulders in their daily practice. Only recently have young Indonesian women accepted veiling as an important religious requirement.

Why does the author include these examples?

4   **THE VEIL AS A FASHION OBJECT** Muslim women's veiling practices are increasingly varied as a result of the rise of a growing fashion industry that targets devout Muslim women and offers designs for chic headscarves and modest clothing. The veil as fashion object has not gone without criticism. Veiled women in Turkey, for example, question whether

Figure 1 Muslim women, both veiled and unveiled, on a city street in Italy.

What feeling does this photograph create?

Figure 2 A Muslim couple in Morocco. The Qur'an calls for modesty for both men and women, including virtues such as humility, moderation, and not drawing attention to oneself in public.

the products of veiling-fashion are actually modest. They remain skeptical of growing consumerism, showiness, and materialism—even as some follow modern fashion trends in veiling. These criticisms have broad relevance concerning religious commodities and today's worldwide markets.

What is the author suggesting?

5   **VEILING AS A SPATIAL PRACTICE** Veiling is inherently a spatial practice that creates a boundary between inner/outer and private/public spaces, and serves as a means to navigate those spaces. Veiling the body defines it as a site of piety, and indicates how a veiled woman sees herself and her role, how she relates to her body, and how others see and interact with her. Like any other spatial boundary, the boundaries created by

Summarize this paragraph in your own words.

Figure 3 A variety of colorful headscarves on display at a clothing store. A growing fashion market targeted at devout Muslim women offers designs for chic headscarves and modest clothing.

veiling are not fixed but fluid and incomplete. In fact, the management of this boundary becomes very important for women's practice of piety as they try to harmonize inner piety and outer appearance.

6   The many meanings and experiences of veiling depend on different cultural and national contexts and expectations. Where women's presence in public spaces is limited, veiling creates a private space for women and enables them to travel with ease. In Turkey, as well as in France where headscarves are banned from schools, a young woman wearing a headscarf may have a very different understanding and experience concerning this practice than women in Iran and Saudi Arabia where women are required to veil. It is important to develop a cultural geographic understanding of the complexities of veiling concerning its role in producing spaces and identities as well as its varied role in religion, the fashion industry, and politics.

—Dahlman and Renwick, *Introduction to Geography*, pp. 274–275

> Why is the last sentence an effective way to end the selection?

After Reading

Checking Your Comprehension

_____ 1. Veiling is an application of the Islamic principle of
a. charity.
b. modesty.
c. faith.
d. pilgrimage.

_____ 2. In which country did Muslim women not cover their hair and shoulders in daily life, a practice that has changed recently?
a. Indonesia
b. Saudi Arabia
c. Egypt
d. Yemen

_____ 3. Critics of fashionable headscarves believe that such scarves are all of the following _except_
a. consumerist.
b. showy.
c. traditional.
d. materialistic.

_____ 4. In which country are headscarves banned from schools?
a. the United States
b. France
c. Indonesia
d. the United Kingdom

_____ 5. According to the author, the veil is
a. a source of frustration for the Muslim women who must wear it against their will at home and in public.

b. a means of allowing Muslim men to discriminate against women with regard to job and schooling opportunities.
c. a spatial boundary that allows Muslim women to harmonize inner piety with outer appearance.
d. a modern practice that has only recently gained popularity as Muslim women rediscover their religious values.

Applying Your Skills: Topics and Main Ideas

_____ 6. Which of the following words from paragraph 2 is the most general? (Hint: One word is general, while the other three are specific.)
a. modesty.
b. virtue.
c. humility.
d. moderation.

_____ 7. In paragraph 2, the main idea is found in the
a. first sentence.
b. second sentence.
c. third sentence.
d. last sentence.

_____ 8. In paragraph 3, the most general statement is found in the
a. first sentence.
b. third sentence.
c. fourth sentence.
d. last sentence.

_____ 9. The heading before paragraph 4, "The Veil as a Fashion Object" is also
   a. a paraphrase of paragraph 4.
   b. the implied main idea of paragraph 4.
   c. the topic of paragraph 4.
   d. a summary of paragraph 4.

_____ 10. In which paragraph is the main idea found in both the first and last sentence?
   a. paragraph 1.
   b. paragraph 2.
   c. paragraph 3.
   d. paragraph 6.

Studying Words

Using context or a dictionary, define each of the following words as it is used in the reading.

11. tenet (par. 1) _____

12. injunction (par. 2) _____

13. commodities (par. 4) _____

14. harmonize (par. 5) _____

15. piety (par. 5) _____

Thinking Visually

1. How do the photos on pages 235–236 illustrate the content of the selection? How does the content tie to the text?

2. What other types of photos or visual aids might the author have used to illustrate the selection?

3. Draw a map of the reading, following the instructions on page 96.

Thinking Critically About the Reading

1. Would you describe this selection as primarily fact based or primarily opinion based? Explain.

2. How would you describe the author's approach to veiling?

3. What was the author's purpose for writing this selection?

4. Does the selection strike you as fair and unbiased? Or does the author have a hidden agenda?

Academic Application: Writing an Outline

Directions: You are conducting research for a paper on veiling. To help you remember the contents of this selection, you decide to outline it. The first part of the outline has been created for you. Complete the rest of the outline.

What Is Veiling?

Introduction: Veiling as religious requirement
- Two key issues
    Rise of Islamic social and political movements
    Growth of Islamic consumer market and fashion industry

The Concept of Veiling in Islam
- Veiling as application of modesty
-
-

Understanding Paragraphs: Supporting Details and Transitions

Focusing on . . . Supporting Details and Transitions

Pasta with Broccoli

In a large pan, heat the olive oil over medium heat and add the garlic and red pepper flakes. Cook for two minutes. Add broccoli to the pan and cook until it is al dente, stirring. Add the red bell pepper and salt and pepper. Add the vinegar and pasta water and turn the heat up, tossing the vegetables until coated and shiny, about one minute. Stir in the pasta and stir until all the ingredients are combined. Add cheese for topping.

To produce the pasta dish shown in the photo, the cook had to follow the recipe closely, paying attention to each

1/3 cup olive oil
2 cloves of garlic, minced
1/4 teaspoon red pepper flakes
1/4 teaspoon Italian herb mix
1/4 head of broccoli, stems removed, cut into florets
1/4 red bell pepper diced
Salt and pepper to taste
2 teaspoons red wine vinegar
2 cups penne pasta, cooked, with 2 tablespoons of pasta cooking water reserved
Parmesan cheese for topping

detailed step. The cook also had to complete each step in the order presented. Reading a paragraph involves a similar process. The reader must pay attention to all the details that support the main idea. Also, the reader must pay attention to the order of details and their relationship to one another, often signaled by the use of connecting words called *transitions*.

Suppose you read the following sentence in a business communication textbook. It appears as the opening sentence of a paragraph.

> Distractions are a major problem in business communication, but everyone in an organization can help minimize them.

After reading this sentence you are probably wondering how distractions can be minimized. Only poor writers make statements without supporting them. So you expect, then, that in the remainder of the paragraph the author will support the statement about eliminating distractions. Here is the full paragraph.

> Distractions are a major problem in business communication, but everyone in an organization can help minimize them. A small dose of common sense and courtesy goes a long way. Turn off that mobile phone before you step into a meeting. Don't talk across the tops of other people's cubicles. Be sensitive to personal differences, too; for instance, some people enjoy working with music on, but music is an enormous distraction for others.
>
> —Thill and Bovée, *Excellence in Business Communication*, p. 14

In this paragraph, the authors explained their statement by giving examples of how distractions can be minimized. The first sentence expresses the main idea; the remaining sentences are supporting details. You will recall from Chapter 6 that a paragraph has four essential elements:

- **topic**—the one thing the whole paragraph is about
- **main idea**—the broad, general idea the whole paragraph is concerned with
- **supporting details**—the ideas that explain or support the main idea
- **transitions**—the words or phrases that link ideas together

This chapter will focus on how to recognize supporting details and how to use transitions to guide your reading.

RECOGNIZE SUPPORTING DETAILS

1 LEARNING GOAL
Recognize supporting details

Supporting details are those facts and ideas that prove or explain the main idea of a paragraph. While all the details in a paragraph support the main idea, not all details are equally important. As you read, try to identify and pay attention to the most important details. Pay less attention to details of lesser importance.

The key details directly explain the main idea. Other minor details may provide additional information, offer an example, or further explain one of the key details.

The diagram in Figure 7-1 shows how details relate to the main idea and how details range in degree of importance. In the diagram, less important details appear below the important details they explain.

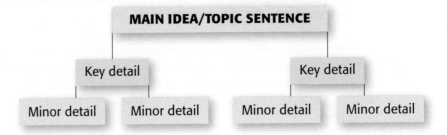

Figure 7-1

Read the following paragraph and study the diagram that follows.

The skin of the human body has several functions. First, it serves as a protective covering. In doing so, it accounts for 17 percent of body weight. Skin also protects the organs within the body from damage or harm. The skin serves as a regulator of body functions. It controls body temperature and water loss. Finally, the skin serves as a receiver. It is sensitive to touch and temperature.

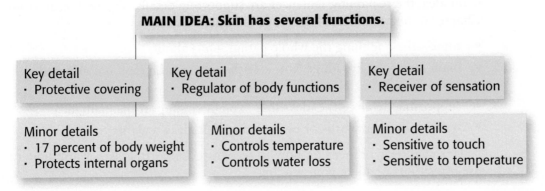

Figure 7-2

From the diagram in Figure 7-2 on the previous page you can see that the details that state the three functions of skin are the key details. Other details, such as "protects internal organs," provide further information and are at a lower level of importance.

Read the following paragraph and try to pick out the more important details.

> The history of the feminist movement goes back to the eighteenth century. Mary Wollstonecraft's famous essay "A Vindication of the Rights of Woman" is one of the earliest examples of western feminist thought. It predates modern feminism, which can be divided into three "waves." What is considered the first wave began in the late 19th and early 20th centuries and revolved around the women's suffrage movement. The fight for women's right to vote began in 1848 with activists such as Susan B. Anthony and Elizabeth Cady Stanton. The second wave of feminism occurred during the women's liberation movement that began in the 1960s. Second-wave feminism also included equality in the workplace, equality in education and social independence from men. Beginning in the 1990s, the third wave of feminism branched out to include multiple racial and socioeconomic groups and connected topics like race, capitalism and gender.
>
> —adapted from Carl, *THINK Sociology*, p. 200

This paragraph could be diagrammed as shown in Figure 7-3 below:

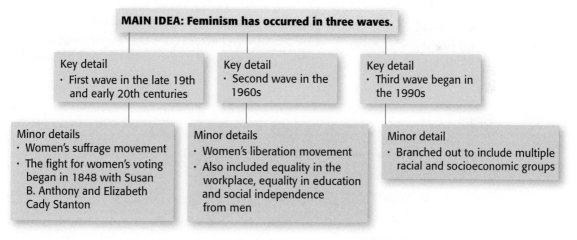

Figure 7-3

EXERCISE **7-1**   **Identifying Key and Minor Details**

Directions: Read each of the following paragraphs, and then answer the multiple-choice questions about the diagram that follows.

Paragraph 1

What does it mean to be a vegetarian? For some, it's an eating style, for others a lifestyle. In its broadest description, vegetarian means avoiding foods from animal sources: red meat, poultry, seafood, eggs, and dairy products. But the term has many subcategories:

- The strictest vegetarians are *vegans*. They consume no animal products—no red meat, poultry, seafood, eggs, milk, cheese, or other dairy products.
- More moderate vegetarians are *lacto-ovo-vegetarians*. They avoid red meat, poultry, and seafood but will consume dairy products and eggs.
- *Pesco-vegetarians* avoid red meat and chickens but will eat seafood (*pesce* means fish), dairy products, and eggs.
- *Semivegetarians* (also called *flexitarians*) may avoid only red meat, or may eat animal-based foods only once or twice a week.

—Lynch et al., *Choosing Health*, p. 83

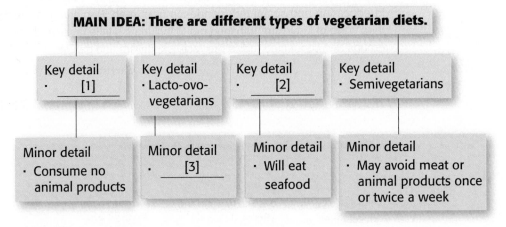

MAIN IDEA: There are different types of vegetarian diets.

| Key detail · ___[1]___ | Key detail · Lacto-ovo-vegetarians | Key detail · ___[2]___ | Key detail · Semivegetarians |

| Minor detail · Consume no animal products | Minor detail · ___[3]___ | Minor detail · Will eat seafood | Minor detail · May avoid meat or animal products once or twice a week |

Figure 7-4

_____ 1. The correct word to fill in the blank labeled [1] is

    a. Flexitarians.

    b. Vegans.

    c. Eggs.

    d. Moderate.

_____ 2. The correct word or phrase to fill in the blank labeled [2] is

    a. Vegans.

    b. Dairy products.

    c. Pesco-vegetarians.

    d. Poultry.

_____ 3. The correct phrase to fill in the blank labeled [3] is

     a. Will eat seafood.

     b. Will not eat eggs.

     c. Consume red meat.

     d. Consume dairy products and eggs.

Paragraph 2

     Advertising is not a one-size-fits-all proposition; rather, it comes in so many forms and options that the types of advertising seem to be limitless. However, there continue to be two primary kinds: institutional advertising and product advertising. **Institutional advertising** provides information about an organization rather than a specific product, and is intended to create awareness about the firm and enhance its image. This advertising is exemplified by the Bank of America ads that focus on the company as the "bank of opportunity" rather than promoting particular financial products. Such advertising is designed to build general credibility and recognition for specific products or services. **Product advertising** is designed to create awareness, interest, purchasing behavior, and post-purchase satisfaction for specific products and services. Typically, small, entrepreneurial companies expend their advertising resources on product advertising. For example, they may want to promote the sale of a particular item, or a store-wide sale.

—Mariotti and Glackin, *Entrepreneurship & Small Business Management*, p. 216

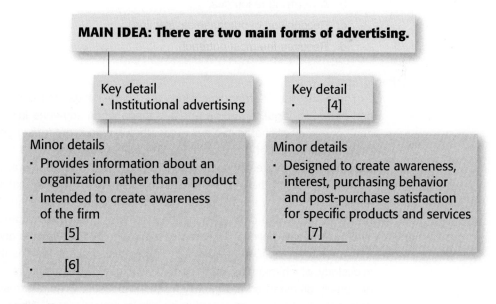

MAIN IDEA: There are two main forms of advertising.

Key detail
- Institutional advertising

Key detail
-    [4]

Minor details
- Provides information about an organization rather than a product
- Intended to create awareness of the firm
-    [5]

-    [6]

Minor details
- Designed to create awareness, interest, purchasing behavior and post-purchase satisfaction for specific products and services
-    [7]

Figure 7-5

_____ 4. The correct phrase to fill in the blank labeled [4] is

    a. Satisfaction.

    b. Purchasing behavior.

    c. Product advertising.

    d. Financial products.

_____ 5. The correct phrase to fill in the blank labeled [5] is

    a. Bank of opportunity.

    b. Financial products.

    c. The most popular form of advertising.

    d. Bank of America is an example.

_____ 6. The correct phrase to fill in the blank labeled [6] is

    a. Image enhancement.

    b. Designed to build general credibility and recognition.

    c. Cost-prohibitive.

    d. Works best with social media.

_____ 7. The correct phrase to fill in the blank labeled [7] is

    a. Used most by small entrepreneurial companies.

    b. Advertising resources.

    c. Recognition of purchase satisfaction.

    d. Requires the most outreach.

Paragraph 3

There are four different dimensions of an arrest: legal, behavioral, subjective, and official. In **legal** terms, an arrest is made when someone lawfully deprives another person of liberty; in other words, that person is not free to go. The actual word *arrest* need not be uttered, but the other person must be brought under the control of the arresting individual. The **behavioral** element in arrests is often nothing more than the phrase "You're under arrest." However, that statement is usually backed up by a tight grip on the arm or collar, or the drawing of an officer's handgun, or the use of handcuffs. The **subjective** dimension of arrest refers to whenever people believe they are not free to leave; to all intents and purposes, they are under arrest. In any case, the arrest lasts only as long as the person is in custody, which might be a matter of a few minutes or many hours. Many people are briefly detained on the street and then released. **Official** arrests are those detentions that the police record in an administrative record. When a suspect is "booked" at the police station, a record is made of the arrest.

—adapted from Barlow, *Criminal Justice in America*, p. 238

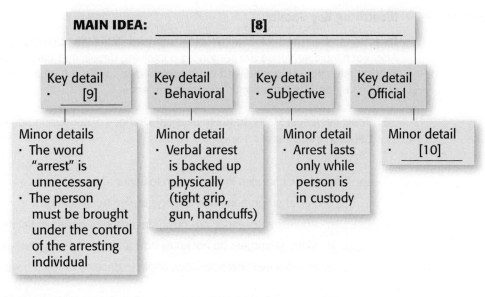

MAIN IDEA: _____ [8] _____

Key detail
· [9]

Key detail
· Behavioral

Key detail
· Subjective

Key detail
· Official

Minor details
· The word "arrest" is unnecessary
· The person must be brought under the control of the arresting individual

Minor detail
· Verbal arrest is backed up physically (tight grip, gun, handcuffs)

Minor detail
· Arrest lasts only while person is in custody

Minor detail
· [10]

Figure 7-6

_____ 8. The correct sentence to fill in the blank labeled [8] is

    a. When a person is lawfully deprived of freedom, it is not necessary to use the word *arrest*.

    b. The four different dimensions of an arrest are legal, behavioral, subjective, and official.

    c. People can be subjectively under arrest even when they are not officially under arrest.

    d. The only official arrests are those that are recorded at the police station.

_____ 9. The correct word or phrase to fill in the blank labeled [9] is

    a. Dimensions.

    b. Liberty.

    c. Not free to go.

    d. Legal.

_____ 10. The correct word or phrase to fill in the blank labeled [10] is

    a. Arrest is recorded at police station.

    b. Detentions.

    c. Briefly detained.

    d. Booked.

EXERCISE 7-2   **Identifying Key Details**

Directions: Each of the following topic sentences states the main idea of a paragraph. After each topic sentence are sentences containing details that may or may not support the topic sentence. Read each sentence and write a *K* beside those that contain **key details** that support the topic sentence.

1. *Topic sentence:* Many dramatic physical changes occur during adolescence between the ages of 13 and 15.

   Details:

   _____ a. Voice changes in boys begin to occur at age 13 or 14.

   _____ b. Facial proportions may change during adolescence.

   _____ c. Adolescents, especially boys, gain several inches in height.

   _____ d. Many teenagers do not know how to react to these changes.

   _____ e. Primary sex characteristics begin to develop for both boys and girls.

2. *Topic sentence:* The development of speech in infants follows a definite sequence or pattern of development.

   Details:

   _____ a. By the time an infant is six months old, he or she can make 12 different speech sounds.

   _____ b. Mindy, who is only three months old, is unable to produce any recognizable syllables.

   _____ c. During the first year, the number of vowel sounds a child can produce is greater than the number of consonant sounds he or she can make.

   _____ d. Between 6 and 12 months, the number of consonant sounds a child can produce continues to increase.

   _____ e. Parents often reward the first recognizable word a child produces by smiling or speaking to the child.

3. *Topic sentence:* The main motives for attending a play are the desire for recreation, the need for relaxation, and the desire for intellectual stimulation.

   Details:

   _____ a. By becoming involved with the actors and their problems, members of the audience temporarily forget about their personal cares and concerns and are able to relax.

   _____ b. In America today, the success of a play is judged by its ability to attract a large audience.

   _____ c. Almost everyone who attends a play expects to be entertained.

   _____ d. Even theater critics are often able to relax and enjoy a good play.

   _____ e. There is a smaller audience that looks to theater for intellectual stimulation.

4. *Topic sentence:* Licorice is used in tobacco products because it has specific characteristics that cannot be found in any other single ingredient.

   Details:

   _____ a. McAdams & Co. is the largest importer and processor of licorice root.

   _____ b. Licorice blends with tobacco and provides added mildness.

   _____ c. Licorice provides a unique flavor and sweetens many types of tobacco.

   _____ d. The extract of licorice is present in relatively small amounts in most types of pipe tobacco.

   _____ e. Licorice helps tobacco retain the correct amount of moisture during storage.

5. *Topic sentence:* An oligopoly is a market structure in which only a few companies sell a certain product.

   Details:

   _____ a. The automobile industry is a good example of an oligopoly, even though it gives the appearance of being highly competitive.

   _____ b. The breakfast cereal, soap, and cigarette industries, although basic to our economy, operate as oligopolies.

   _____ c. Monopolies refer to market structures in which only one industry produces a particular product.

   _____ d. Monopolies are able to exert more control and price fixing than oligopolies.

   _____ e. In the oil industry there are only a few producers, so each producer has a fairly large share of the sales.

> Which characteristics of tourism does each photograph illustrate?

EXERCISE **7-3**   **Identifying Key Details**

Directions: Read each of the following paragraphs and write the numbers of the sentences that contain only the most important key details.

Paragraph 1

[1]There are four main characteristics of a tourism product. [2]The first is service, which is intangible because it cannot be inspected physically. [3]For example, a tourist cannot sample a Caribbean cruise or a European tour before purchasing one. [4]The second characteristic is that the tourism product is largely psychological in its attraction. [5]It is more than airline seats or car rentals; it is the temporary use of a different environment, its culture, heritage, and experiences. [6]A third characteristic is that the product frequently varies in quality and standards. [7]A tourist's hotel experience may be excellent one time and not so good at the next visit. [8]A fourth characteristic of the tourism

product is that the supply of the product is fixed. [9]For example, more hotel rooms cannot be instantly created to meet increased demand.

—adapted from Walker and Walker, *Tourism*, p. 11

Key details: _____

Paragraph 2

[1]Political activists depend heavily on the media to get their ideas placed high on the governmental agenda. [2]Their arsenal of weapons includes press releases, press conferences, and letter writing; convincing reporters and columnists to tell their side; trading on personal contacts; and, in cases of desperation, resorting to staging dramatic events. [3]The media are not always monopolized by political elites; the poor and downtrodden have access to them too. [4]Civil rights groups in the 1960s relied heavily on the media to tell their stories of unjust treatment. [5]Many believe that the introduction of television helped to accelerate the movement by showing Americans just what the situation was. [6]Protest groups have learned that if they can stage an interesting event that attracts the media's attention, at least their point of view will be heard. [7]Radical activist Saul Alinsky once dramatized the plight of one neighborhood by having its residents collect rats and dump them on the mayor's front lawn. [8]The story was one that local reporters could hardly resist.

—adapted from Edwards et al., *Government in America*, p. 239

Key details: _____

Paragraph 3

[1]To be patented, an invention must be novel, useful, and nonobvious. [2]An invention is *novel* if it is new and has not been invented and used in the past. [3]If the invention has been used before, it is not novel and cannot be patented. [4]An invention is *useful* if it has some practical purpose. [5]For example, an inventor received a patent for "forkchops," which are a set of chopsticks with a spoon at one handle-end and a fork on the other handle-end. [6]This invention is useful. [7]If the invention is *nonobvious*, it qualifies for a patent; if the invention is obvious, then it does not qualify for a patent. [8]For example, inventors received a patent for a cardboard sleeve that can be placed over a paper coffee cup so that the cup will not be as hot as if there were no sleeve. [9]This invention is novel, useful, and nonobvious.

—adapted from Goldman and Cheeseman, *The Paralegal Professional*, pp. 736–737

Key details: _____

Paragraph 4

[1]People who exercise their mental abilities have been found to be far less likely to develop memory problems and even senile dementias such as Alzheimer's in old age. [2]"Use it or lose it" is the phrase to remember. [3]Working challenging crossword puzzles, for example, can be a major factor in maintaining a healthy level of cognitive function-

ing. [4]Reading, having an active social life, going to plays, taking classes, and staying physically active can all have a positive impact on the continued well-being of the brain.

—adapted from Ciccarelli and White, *Psychology*, p. 249

Key details: _____

Paragraph 5

[1]A general law practice is one that handles all types of cases. [2]This is what people usually think of as the small-town lawyer, the generalist to whom everyone in town comes for advice. [3]The reality is that the same generalists practice in cities as well as small towns throughout the country. [4]Their practices are as diverse as the law itself, handling everything from adoptions to zoning appeals. [5]As general practitioners, they serve the same function in the law as the general family practice doctor does in medicine. [6]Lawyers in this type of practice often work in several areas of law within the same day. [7]Their day may include attending a hearing in small-claims court in the morning, preparing a will before lunch, meeting with an opposing attorney to discuss settlement of an accident case, then helping someone who is forming a corporation, and finally appearing at a municipal government meeting in the evening to seek a zoning approval.

—adapted from Goldman and Cheeseman, *The Paralegal Professional*, p. 81

Key details: _____

TYPES OF SUPPORTING DETAILS

2 LEARNING GOAL

Identify types of supporting details

There are many types of details that a writer can use to explain or support a main idea. As you read, be sure you know *how* a writer supports his or her main idea—or what types of detail he or she uses. As you will see in later chapters, the way a writer explains and supports an idea may influence how readily you accept or agree with it. The most common types of supporting details are (1) examples, (2) facts or statistics, (3) reasons, (4) descriptions, and (5) steps or procedures. Each will be briefly discussed here.

Examples

One way a writer may support an idea is by using examples. **Examples** make ideas and concepts real and understandable. In the following paragraph, an example is used to explain heat and temperature.

> Heat and temperature are measures of energy. **Heat** is the total amount of energy associated with the movements of atoms and molecules in a substance. **Temperature** is a measure of the intensity of heat—for example, how fast the molecules in the substance are moving. When you are swimming in a cool lake, your body has a higher temperature than the water; however, the lake contains

(*Continued*)

> more heat than your body because even though its molecules are moving more slowly, the sum total of molecular movement in its large volume is much greater than the sum total of molecular movements in your much smaller body.
>
> —Belk and Borden Maier, *Biology*, pp. 95–96

In this paragraph the author uses a person swimming in a lake to explain heat and temperature. As you read illustrations and examples, try to see the relationship between the examples and the concepts or ideas they illustrate.

Facts or Statistics

Another way a writer supports an idea is by including **facts** and/or **statistics**. The facts and statistics may provide evidence that the main idea is correct. Or the facts may further explain the main idea. For example, to prove that the divorce rate is high, the author may give statistics about the divorce rate and percentage of the population that is divorced. Notice how, in the following paragraph, the main idea stated in the first sentence is explained using statistics.

> The term **graying of America** refers to the increasing percentage of older people in the U.S. population. In 1900 only 4 percent of Americans were age 65 and older. Today almost 13 percent are. The average 65-year-old can expect to live another eighteen years. U.S. society has become so "gray" that the median age has doubled since 1850, and today there are seven million *more* elderly Americans than teenagers. Despite this change, on a global scale Americans rank fifteenth in life expectancy.
>
> —Henslin, *Sociology*, p. 383

In this paragraph, the main idea that the number of older Americans is increasing is supported using statistics.

Reasons

A writer may support an idea by giving **reasons** *why* a main idea is correct. A writer might explain *why* nuclear power is dangerous or give reasons *why* a new speed limit law should be passed by Congress. In the following paragraph, the author explains why American colonists imported more and more goods from England.

> Eighteenth-century Americans imported more manufactured products from England with every passing year. This practice did not simply reflect the growth of the colonial population, for the rate at which Americans bought British goods exceeded the rate of population increase. Colonists owned more goods, often of

(Continued)

better quality, than their parents and grandparents had possessed. In the less secure economic climate of the seventeenth century, colonists had limited their purchases of goods, investing instead in land to pass on to their children. But by the eighteenth century, prosperous colonists felt secure enough to buy goods to make their lives more comfortable. Tea drinking became more common, and colonial women in particular might host tea parties as a sign of their status and genteel manners. Colonists acquired goods to advertise their more refined style of life.

—Goldfield et al., *The American Journey*, p. 94

Descriptions

When the topic of a paragraph is a person, object, place, or process, the writer may develop the paragraph by describing the object. **Descriptions** are details that help you create a mental picture of the object. In the following paragraph, the author describes a sacred book of the Islamic religion by telling what it contains.

The Koran is the sacred book of the Islamic religion. It was written during the lifetime of Mohammed (570–632) during the years in which he recorded divine revelations. The Koran includes rules for family relationships, including marriage and divorce. Rules for inheritance of wealth and property are specified. The status of women as subordinate to men is well defined.

Steps or Procedures

When a paragraph explains how to do something, the paragraph details are often lists of **steps** or **procedures** to be followed. For example, if the main idea of a paragraph is how to prepare an outline for a speech, then the details would list or explain the steps in preparing an outline. In the following paragraph the author explains how to do an examination of a patient's abdomen.

To palpate the abdomen, use the fingertips of several fingers and gently press into the abdomen in each quadrant. While palpating, feel for rigidity or hardening and ask or observe whether this causes pain for the patient. If the initial gentle palpation does not cause pain or discomfort, you may palpate a bit deeper. Once you have found pain, discomfort, or abnormality, there is no need to palpate further in that area.

—Limmer and O'Keefe, *Emergency Care*, p. 581

EXERCISE **7-4**   **Identifying Types of Details**

Directions: Each topic sentence is followed by a list of details that could be used to support it. Label each detail as example, fact or statistic, reason, description, or step or procedure.

1. *Topic sentence:* People make inferences about you by the way you dress.

   _____ First, they size you up from head to toe.

   _____ College students assume casually dressed instructors are friendly and flexible.

   _____ Robert Molloy wrote a book called *Dress for Success* in which he discusses appropriate business attire.

2. *Topic sentence:* Probably the most spectacular and best known of all optical phenomena in our atmosphere is the rainbow.

   _____ Rainbows are generated because water droplets act like prisms, dispersing sunlight into the spectrum of colors.

   _____ Although the clarity of the colors varies with each rainbow, the observer can usually discern six rather distinct bands of color.

   _____ The angle between the incoming (incident) rays and the dispersed colors that constitute the rainbow is 42° for red light and 40° for violet.

   — Lutgens et al., *The Atmosphere*, pp. 455–456

3. *Topic sentence:* Every April 15th, millions of Americans make their way to the post office to mail their income tax forms.

   _____ Corporate taxes account for about 10 cents of every federal revenue dollar, compared with 47 cents from individual income taxes.

   _____ This year, the Burnette family filed a return that entitles them to a substantial refund on their state income taxes.

   _____ In order to submit an income tax return, you must first obtain the proper forms.

   —Edwards et al., *Government in America*, pp. 458–459

4. *Topic sentence:* Schizophrenia is one of the most difficult psychological disorders to understand.

_____ Diagnosis is difficult due to the lack of physical tests for schizophrenia; researchers do not know if schizophrenia results from a single process or several processes.

_____ Although the rate of schizophrenia is approximately equal in men and women, it strikes men earlier and with greater severity.

_____ After spending time in mental hospitals and homeless shelters, Greg was finally diagnosed with schizophrenia; he has responded well to medication and now lives in a group home.

_____ Schizophrenia involves a range of symptoms, including disturbances in perception, language, thinking, and emotional expression.

—Davis and Palladino, *Psychology*, pp. 563, 564, 566

5. *Topic sentence:* Many Americans are obsessed with losing weight.

_____ Weight loss obsession is often triggered by major events looming in the near future, such as a high school reunion or a "milestone" birthday.

_____ The two ways to lose weight are to lower caloric intake (through improved eating habits) and to increase exercise (expending more calories).

_____ Studies show that on any given day in America, nearly 40 percent of women and 24 percent of men over the age of 20 are trying to lose weight.

_____ Orlando, a college freshman from Raleigh, admits that he has been struggling with a weight problem since he reached puberty.

—Donatelle and Davis, *Access to Health*, pp. 358, 371

6. *Topic sentence:* In the 1920s, many young American writers and artists left their country behind and became expatriates.

_____ One of the most talented of the expatriates was Ernest Hemingway.

_____ The expatriates flocked to Rome, Berlin, and Paris, in order to live cheaply and escape what seemed to them the "conspiracy against the individual" in America.

_____ Some earned a living as journalists, translators, and editors, or made a few dollars by selling a poem to an American magazine or a painting to a tourist.

—Garraty and Carnes, *The American Nation*, p. 706

7. *Topic sentence:* Historical and cultural attractions can be found in a variety of shapes, sizes, and locations throughout the world.

_____ In Europe, for every museum that existed in 1950, there are now more than four.

_____ Living History Farms, located near Des Moines, Iowa, is an attraction that offers a "hands-on" experience for visitors.

_____ More and more communities and countries are taking action to preserve historical sites because they attract visitors and generate income for local residents.

—Cook et al., *Tourism*, p. 209

8. *Topic sentence:* Knitting has become a popular hobby for many young career women.

_____ Typically, aspiring knitters begin by visiting a yarn shop and then enrolling in a knitting class.

_____ Knitting is popular because it provides a relaxing outlet and an opportunity to create something beautiful as well as useful.

_____ Far from the image of the grandmotherly knitter, today's devoted knitters include a wide range of women, from Wall Street stockbrokers to movie stars like Julia Roberts.

9. *Topic sentence:* Search engines have become one of the most popular ways for people to access information.

_____ The first few results from an Internet search may provide basic information. Continue reading through several pages of results to get in-depth information.

_____ In 2012, Google performed 70 percent of all Internet searches.

_____ Search engines are primarily used for research, shopping, and entertainment.

10. *Topic sentence:* The Anasazi Indians are best known for their artistic, architectural, and technological achievements.

_____ The Anasazi used all of the available materials to build their settlements; with wood, mud, and stone, they erected cliff dwellings and the equivalent of terraced apartment houses.

_____ The Anasazi built one structure with 500 living units; it was the largest residential building in North America until the completion of an apartment house in New York in 1772.

_____ One example of their technological genius was their use of irrigation: they constructed sand dunes at the base of hills to hold the runoff from the sometimes torrential rains.

_____ The Anasazi produced pottery that could rank in beauty with any in the world.

—Brummet et al., *Civilization*, p. 348

EXERCISE 7-5   Identifying Types of Details

Directions: For each paragraph in Exercise 7-3 on pages 249–251, identify the type or types of details used to support the main idea. Write your answers below.

1. Type(s) of details: _____

2. Type(s) of details: _____

3. Type(s) of details: _____

4. Type(s) of details: _____

5. Type(s) of details: _____

EXERCISE 7-6   Writing Supporting Details

Working Together

Directions: Write a topic sentence on one of following topics:

1. one value or danger of social networking
2. driving and the use of cell phones or texting
3. a currently popular movie

Working in groups of three, choose one topic sentence for each topic and generate a list of details that support the chosen topic sentence. Share results with the class. As a class, identify the types of supporting details used.

EXERCISE 7-7   **Identifying Topic Sentences and Supporting Details**

Directions: Form small groups. Using a reading selection from Part Six of this text, work with your group to identify and underline the topic sentence of each paragraph. Try to identify key supporting details and/or the type of supporting details. When all the groups have completed the task, the class should compare the findings of the various groups.

LEARNING STYLE TIPS

If you tend to be a . . .	Then understand supporting details by . . .
Spatial learner	Drawing diagrams that show the relationships among details
Creative learner	Making notes
	Evaluating the appropriateness, accuracy, and sufficiency of details provided

---

TRANSITIONS

3 LEARNING GOAL
Use transitions to guide your reading

Transitions are linking words or phrases used to lead the reader from one idea to another. If you get in the habit of recognizing transitions, you will see that they often guide you through a paragraph, helping you to read it more easily.

In the following paragraph, notice how the circled transitions lead you from one important detail to the next.

> The principle of rhythm and line also contributes to the overall unity of the landscape design. This principle is responsible for the sense of continuity between different areas of the landscape. One way in which this continuity can be developed is by extending planting beds from one area to another. For example, shrub beds developed around the entrance to the house can be continued around the sides and into the backyard. Such an arrangement helps to tie the front and rear areas of the property together. Another means by which rhythm is given to a design is to repeat shapes, angles, or lines between various areas and elements of the design.
>
> —Reiley and Shry, *Introductory Horticulture*, p. 114

Not all paragraphs contain such obvious transitions, and not all transitions serve as such clear markers of major details. Transitions may be used to alert you to what will come next in the paragraph. If you see the phrase *for instance* at the beginning of a sentence, then you know that an example will follow. When you see the phrase *on the other hand*, you can predict that a different, opposing idea will follow. Table 7-1 lists some of the most common transitions used within a paragraph and indicates what they tell you.

TABLE 7-1 Common Transitions

Type of Transition	Examples	What They Tell the Reader
Time/Sequence	first, later, next, finally	The author is arranging ideas in the order in which they happened.
Example	for example, for instance, to illustrate, such as	An example will follow.
Enumeration	first, second, third, last, one, another, next	The author is marking or identifying each major point (sometimes these may be used to suggest order of importance).
Continuation	also, in addition, and, further, another	The author is continuing with the same idea and is going to provide additional information.
Contrast	on the other hand, in contrast, however	The author is switching to a different, opposite, or contrasting idea from that previously discussed.
Comparison	like, likewise, similarly	The writer will show how the previous idea is similar to what follows.
Cause/Effect	because, thus, therefore, since, consequently	The writer will show a connection between two or more things, how one thing caused another, or how something happened as a result of something else.
Summation	to sum up, in conclusion	The writer will draw his or her ideas together.

EXERCISE 7-8 Understanding Transitions

Directions: Match each transition in Column A with a transition of similar meaning in Column B. Write the letter of your choice in the space provided.

Column A	Column B
_____ 1. because	a. therefore
_____ 2. in contrast	b. also
_____ 3. for instance	c. likewise
_____ 4. thus	d. after that
_____ 5. first	e. since
_____ 6. one way	f. in conclusion
_____ 7. similarly	g. on the other hand
_____ 8. next	h. one approach
_____ 9. in addition	i. in the beginning
_____ 10. to sum up	j. for example

EXERCISE **7-9**   **Identifying Types of Transitions**

Directions: Use the list below to identify the type of transition that appears in each of the following sentences. Note that b (Example) and e (Contrast) are each used twice.

a. Time/sequence   b. Example (2)   c. Enumeration   d. Continuation

e. Contrast (2)   f. Comparison   g. Cause/effect   h. Summation

_____   1. The first step in the listening process involves receiving, or hearing, the message.

_____   2. Some people consider computer games a purely passive activity. However, many games actually involve strategy, mathematical skills, and memorization.

_____   3. On election day, several television stations reported a clear winner in the presidential race. Later, those stations were forced to retract their statements and wait—along with the rest of the nation—for a final tally.

_____   4. In conclusion, proper soil preparation is essential to a successful garden.

_____   5. There are many kinds of service dogs. For instance, there are dogs that are trained specifically to assist blind or deaf people as well as therapy dogs that are part of physical rehabilitation programs.

_____   6. Always apply sunscreen before going out in the sun. In addition, a hat and protective clothing are recommended at high altitudes and near water.

_____   7. In contrast to carnivores, *herbivores* eat only plants.

_____   8. Vegetarians typically do not have to worry about elevated cholesterol because cholesterol is found only in animal products.

_____   9. Like Samuel Clemens, who became famous writing under the pen name Mark Twain, Mary Ann Evans found fame as the writer George Eliot.

_____   10. In some communities, judges sentence offenders to community service programs instead of jail time. For example, in one Chicago program, offenders trade a "day for a day"—every day they would have spent in jail equals a day spent doing community service work.

EXERCISE **7-10**   **Choosing Transitional Words**

Directions: Read each of the sentences on the next page. In each blank, write a transitional word or phrase from the list below that makes sense in the sentence.

next	however	for example	another	consequently
because	similarly	such as	to sum up	in addition

1. After a heart attack, the heart muscle is permanently weakened; _____, its ability to pump blood throughout the body may be reduced.

2. Some metals, _____ gold and silver, are represented by symbols derived from their Latin names.

3. In order to sight-read music, you should begin by scanning it. _____, you should identify the key and tempo.

4. The *Oxford English Dictionary*, by giving all present and past definitions of words, shows how word definitions have changed with time. _____, it gives the date and written source where each word appears to have first been used.

5. Some scientists believe intelligence to be determined equally by heredity and environment. _____, other scientists believe heredity to account for about 60 percent of intelligence and environment for the other 40 percent.

6. Tigers tend to grow listless and unhappy in captivity. _____, pandas grow listless and have a difficult time reproducing in captivity.

7. _____, the most important ways to prevent heat stress are to (1) allow yourself time to get used to the heat, (2) wear the proper clothing, and (3) drink plenty of water.

8. Many people who are dissatisfied with the public school system send their children to private schools. _____ option that is gaining in popularity is homeschooling.

9. Studies have shown that it is important to "exercise" our brains as we age. _____, crossword puzzles are a good way to keep mentally fit.

10. Buying smaller-sized clothing generally will not give an overweight person the incentive to lose weight. People with weight problems tend to eat when they are upset or disturbed, and _____ wearing smaller clothing is frustrating and upsetting, overweight people will generally gain weight by doing so.

EXERCISE **7-11**   **Making Predictions**

Directions: Each of the beginnings of paragraphs on the next page uses a transitional word or phrase to tell the reader what will follow in the paragraph. Working in pairs, read each, paying particular attention to the underlined word or phrase. Then discuss what you would expect to find next in the paragraph. Summarize your findings in the space provided.

1. Price is not the only factor to consider in choosing a pharmacy. Many provide valuable services that should be considered. <u>For instance,</u> . . .

_____

2. There are a number of things you can do to prevent a home burglary. <u>First,</u> . . .

_____

3. Most mail order businesses are reliable and honest. <u>However,</u> . . .

_____

4. One advantage of a compact stereo system is that all the components are built into the unit. <u>Another</u> . . .

_____

5. Taking medication can have an effect on your hormonal balance. <u>Therefore,</u> . . .

_____

6. To select the presidential candidate you will vote for, you should examine his or her philosophy of government. <u>Next</u> . . .

_____

7. Eating solely vegetables drastically reduces caloric and fat intake, two things on which most people overindulge. <u>On the other hand,</u> . . .

_____

8. Asbestos, a common material found in many older buildings in which people have worked for decades, has been shown to cause cancer. <u>Consequently,</u> . . .

_____

9. Cars and trucks are not designed randomly. They are designed individually for specific purposes. <u>For instance,</u> . . .

_____

10. Jupiter is a planet surrounded by several moons. <u>Likewise,</u> . . .

_____

EXERCISE **7-12**   **Identifying Transitions**

Directions: Reread each paragraph in Exercise 7-3 on pages 249–251. Underline any transitions that you find.

SELF-TEST SUMMARY

1 **What are supporting details?**	Supporting details explain or add support to a paragraph's main idea.
2 **What are the five types of details used to support the main idea?**	The five types of supporting details are examples, facts or statistics, reasons, descriptions, and steps or procedures.
3 **What are transitions, and what information do they give the reader?**	Transitions are linking words and phrases that lead the reader from one idea to another. They suggest time/sequence, example, enumeration, continuation, contrast, comparison, cause/effect, and summation.

GOING ⊙ ONLINE

1. **Finding Reliable Online Sources of Statistics**

    Facts and statistics are important types of supporting details. In your college courses, you will often need to use statistics in your writing assignments. Conduct a Web search for U.S. government–sponsored sources of facts and statistics. (*Hint:* These Web sites will usually end with .gov.) List at least five reliable online data sources, and work with a group of classmates to present a table summarizing the types of data provided by each source and the types of college courses in which this information might be useful.

MASTERY TEST 1 Reading Selection

Let There Be Dark

Paul Bogard

Before Reading

This selection appeared in *The Los Angeles Times* opinion section in late fall.

Previewing the Reading

Using the steps listed on page 49, preview the reading selection. As part of your pre-view, read the first sentence of each paragraph. When you have finished, complete the following items.

1. What is the topic of the selection? _____

2. What is the winter solstice? _____

3. Indicate whether each statement is true (T) or false (F).

    _____ a. The author believes the darkness can provide the quiet and solitude that human beings need.

    _____ b. The author believes that the night is becoming less dark all over the world.

Predicting and Connecting

1. How do you feel about darkness? Do you find it comforting, or does it make you uneasy? Why?

2. Do you expect the reading to be fairly easy to understand, of moderate difficulty, or challenging? Why?

> **Vocabulary Preview**
>
> **solstice** (par. 2) two times in a year when the sun is farthest from the equator
>
> **carcinogen** (par. 4) something that causes cancer
>
> **crepuscular** (par. 5) active at twilight

1   When I was a child, I knew real darkness.

2   At my family's cabin on a Minnesota lake, I knew woods so dark that my hands disappeared before my eyes. I knew night skies in which meteors left smoky trails across sugary spreads of stars. But now, when 8 of 10 children born in the United States will never know a sky dark enough for the Milky Way, I worry we are rapidly losing night's natural darkness before realizing its worth.

This winter solstice, as we cheer the days' gradual movement back toward light, let us also remember the irreplaceable value of darkness.

3   All life evolved to the steady rhythm of bright days and dark nights. Today, though, when we feel the closeness of nightfall, we reach quickly for a light switch. And too little darkness, meaning too much artificial light at night, spells trouble for all.

4   Already the World Health Organization classifies working the night shift as a probable human carcinogen, and the American Medical Assn. has voiced its unanimous support for "light pollution reduction efforts and glare reduction efforts at both the national and state levels." Our bodies need darkness to produce the hormone melatonin, which keeps certain cancers from developing, and our bodies need darkness for sleep. Sleep disorders have been linked to diabetes, obesity, cardiovascular disease and depression, and recent research suggests one main cause of "short sleep" is "long light." Whether we work at night or simply take our tablets, notebooks and smartphones to bed, there isn't a place for this much artificial light in our lives.

5   The rest of the world depends on darkness as well, including nocturnal and crepuscular species of birds, insects, mammals, fish and reptiles. Some examples are well known—the 400 species of birds that migrate at night in North America, the sea turtles that come ashore to lay their eggs—and some are not, such as the bats that save American farmers billions in pest control and the moths that pollinate 80% of the world's flora. Ecological light pollution is like the bulldozer of the night, wrecking habitat and disrupting ecosystems several billion years in the making. Simply put, without darkness, Earth's ecology would collapse.

6   Darkness shapes our lives in less dramatic ways as well. Consider how it brings us together with those we love, how we illuminate our most intimate experiences with flame or moonlight, with subtlety. What would a winter evening's stroll through the park be without it? Or a candlelight dinner? Or a New Year's bonfire with friends? It's only with night's natural darkness that we appreciate the lights of the city, and of the season. No one thinks much of these lights at noon.

7   In today's crowded, louder, more fast-paced world, night's darkness can provide solitude, quiet and stillness, qualities increasingly in short supply. Every religious tradition has considered darkness invaluable for a soulful life, and the chance to witness the universe has inspired artists, philosophers and everyday stargazers since time began. In a world awash with electric light, St. John of the

Cross could not have offered us the wisdom from his "dark night of the soul." And how would Van Gogh have given the world his "Starry Night"? Who knows what this vision of the night sky might inspire in each of us, in our children or grandchildren?

8   Yet all over the world, our nights are growing brighter. In the United States and Western Europe, the amount of light in the sky increases an average of about 6% every year. Computer images of the United States at night, based on NASA photographs, show that what was a very dark country as recently as the 1950s is now nearly covered with a blanket of light. Much of this light is wasted energy, which means wasted dollars. Those of us over 35 are perhaps among the last generation to have known truly dark nights. Even the northern lake where I was lucky to spend my summers has seen its darkness diminish.

9   It doesn't have to be this way. Light pollution is readily within our ability to solve, using new lighting technologies and shielding existing lights. Already, many cities and towns across North America and Europe are changing to LED streetlights, which offer dramatic possibilities for controlling wasted light. Other communities are finding success with simply turning off portions of their public lighting after midnight. Even Paris, the famed "city of light," which already turns off its monument lighting after 1 A.M., will this summer start to require its shops, offices and public buildings to turn off lights after 2 A.M. Though primarily designed to save energy, such reductions in light will also go far in addressing light pollution. But we will never truly address the problem of light pollution until we become aware of the irreplaceable value and beauty of the darkness we are losing.

10   This winter solstice, this longest night of the year, let us begin.

After Reading

Checking Your Comprehension

_____ 1. The purpose of this selection is to
a. offer suggestions for reducing light pollution at home.
b. explain how darkness can be dangerous.
c. explain the importance of restoring darker nights to our world.
d. discuss how expensive light pollution is.

_____ 2. The main idea of paragraph 4 is that
a. working the night shift may cause cancer.
b. both national and local governments should reduce light pollution.
c. sleep disorders have been linked to serious health problems.
d. too much artificial light is unhealthy for us.

_____ 3. According to the author, solutions to light pollution include
   a. changing to LED streetlights.
   b. shielding existing lights.
   c. turning off public lighting after midnight.
   d. all of the above.

_____ 4. The amount of light in the sky in the United States and Western Europe is
   a. impossible to measure.
   b. increasing every year.
   c. caused entirely by technology.
   d. less than it was in the 1950s.

_____ 5. The main point of paragraph 6 is that
   a. we use light to celebrate holidays.
   b. candlelight is not light pollution.
   c. darkness allows us to appreciate special kinds of light.
   d. it is easier to share things in the dark.

Applying Your Skills: Understanding Paragraphs: Supporting Details and Transitions

_____ 6. The supporting details that the author uses in this selection include
   a. statistics.
   b. examples.
   c. facts.
   d. all of the above.

_____ 7. The second sentence in paragraph 5 is an example of a
   a. main idea.
   b. key detail.
   c. minor detail.
   d. topic sentence.

_____ 8. The author indicates a transition in paragraph 8 with the word
   a. recently.
   b. perhaps.
   c. based.
   d. yet.

_____ 9. In paragraph 3, the transition _though_ indicates that the author is
   a. arranging ideas in order of importance.
   b. continuing with the same idea.
   c. switching to a contrasting idea.
   d. showing how one thing caused another.

_____10. The topic of paragraph 7 is the
   a. decreasing darkness.
   b. benefits of darkness.
   c. ecological effects of darkness.
   d. health benefits of darkness.

Studying Words

_____11. The word _irreplaceable_ (par. 2) means
   a. related to weather.
   b. gradual.
   c. having no substitute.
   d. overrated.

_____12. From context, you can tell that the word _melatonin_ (par. 4) refers to
   a. a hormone.
   b. a disease.
   c. short sleep.
   d. a type of technology.

_____13. The word _disrupting_ (par. 5) means
   a. removing.
   b. calming.
   c. interrupting.
   d. lifting.

_____ 14. The word *illuminate* (par. 6) means
   a. brighten.
   b. discourage.
   c. contact.
   d. allow.

_____ 15. The word *diminish* (par. 8) means
   a. expand.
   b. digitize.
   c. frustrate.
   d. decrease.

For more practice, ask your instructor for an opportunity to work on the mastery tests that appear in the Test Bank.

Thinking Visually

1. What is the purpose of the photo included with this article? How does it illustrate the main point of the article?

2. What other types of photos might help emphasize the author's point?

3. Explain how the title of this article relates to the subject. Can you think of another title that would also work for this selection?

Thinking Critically About the Reading

1. How important is darkness in your life? What does it allow you to do? Describe some activities that would not be the same without darkness.

2. What do you think is beautiful about darkness? How did this article help you appreciate that? Why do you think humans work so hard to eliminate darkness?

3. What could you do in your own life to decrease light pollution? What changes could happen in your own town or city that would reduce light pollution?

Academic Application: Summarizing the Reading

Directions: You are studying with a friend by comparing summaries of the same reading. Your goal is to make sure you picked up on all the important points. Complete the following summary of "Let There Be Dark." Compare it with the summary written by a classmate.

The author has important memories of darkness from his childhood. Today there is less darkness due to artificial light, which negatively affects our health. The lack of darkness also impacts other living creatures, negatively affecting Earth's ecology. Darkness is a valuable part of our lives, allowing us to _____

_____

_____

_____

MASTERY TEST 2 Reading Selection

The Big Win: Life After the Lottery

James M. Henslin

Before Reading

This selection appeared in an introductory sociology textbook in a chapter titled "Social Stratification." In this context, the phrase *social stratification* means social class.

Previewing the Reading

Using the steps listed on page 49, preview the reading selection. Read the first sentence of each paragraph as you preview. When you have finished, complete the following items.

1. What is the topic of the selection? _____

2. Indicate whether each statement is true (T) or false (F).

    _____ a. Many systematic research studies have followed the lives of lottery winners.

    _____ b. The selection will introduce and define the term *anomie*.

    _____ c. Lottery winners' initial reaction is usually shock.

Predicting and Connecting

1. Do you buy lottery tickets? What would you do with your winnings if you won a substantial amount of money?

2. How interesting do you find the topic of this reading selection? How will your answer affect the way you read?

> **Vocabulary Preview**
> **moorings** (par. 6) foundations
> **stingy** (par. 12) cheap; ungenerous
> **replica** (par. 15) reproduction

During Reading

Think As You Read
Read • Respond

As you read the selection, complete each of the following. When highlighting, use a different color highlighter for each task.

a. Highlight the topic sentence of each paragraph. If the main idea is unstated, write a sentence that states it.

b. Highlight the most important details in each paragraph.

c. Highlight useful transitional words and phrases that help you understand and connect the author's ideas.

d. Read and respond to the questions in the margin.

1   "If I just win the lottery, life will be good. These problems I've got, they'll be gone. I can just see myself now."

2   So goes the dream. And many Americans shell out megabucks every week, with the glimmering hope that "Maybe this week, I'll hit it big."

3   Most are lucky to get $20, or maybe just another scratch-off ticket.

What does the phrase "wine, roses, and chocolate" mean? Underline the question that this reading will answer.

4   But some do hit it big p. 305. What happens to these winners? Are their lives all wine, roses, and chocolate afterward?

5   We don't have any systematic studies of the big winners, so I can't tell you what life is like for the average winner. But several themes are apparent from reporters' interviews.

Define *status inconsistency*.

6   The most common consequence of hitting it big is that life becomes topsy-turvy (Bernstein, 2007; Susman, 2012). All of us are rooted somewhere. We have connections with others that provide the basis for our orientations to life and how we feel about the world. Sudden wealth can rip these moorings apart, and the resulting status inconsistency can lead to a condition sociologists call **anomie** (an-uh-mé).

7   First comes the shock. As Mary Sanderson, a telephone operator in Dover, New Hampshire, who won $66 million, said, "I was afraid to believe it was real, and afraid to believe it wasn't." Mary says that she never slept worse than her first night as a multimillionaire. "I spent the whole time crying—and throwing up" (Tresniowski, 1999).

8   Reporters and TV crews appear on your doorstep. "What are you going to do with all that money?" they demand. You haven't the slightest idea, but in a daze you mumble something.

9   Then come the calls. Some are welcome. Your Mom and Dad call to congratulate you. But long-forgotten friends and distant relatives suddenly remember how close they really are to you—and strangely enough, they all have emergencies that your money can solve. You even get calls from strangers who have ailing mothers, terminally ill kids, sick dogs . . .

10   You might be flooded with marriage proposals. You certainly didn't become more attractive or sexy overnight—or did you? Maybe money makes people sexy.

11   You can no longer trust people. You don't know what their real motives are. Before, no one could be after your money because you didn't have any. You may even fear kidnappers. Before, this wasn't a problem—unless some kidnapper wanted the ransom of a 7-year-old car.

12   The normal becomes abnormal. Even picking out a wedding gift becomes a problem. If you give the usual juicer, everyone will think you're stingy. But should you write a check for $25,000? If you do, you'll be invited to every wedding in town—and everyone will expect the same.

13   Here is what happened to some lottery winners:

14   *When Michael Klinebiel of Rahway, New Jersey, won $2 million, his mother, Phyllis, said that half of it was hers, that she and her son had*

pooled $20 a month for years to play the lottery. He said they had done this—but he had bought the winning ticket on his own. Phyllis sued her son ("Sticky Ticket," 1998).

15   *Mack Metcalf, a forklift operator in Corbin, Kentucky, hit the jackpot for $34 million. To fulfill a dream, he built and moved into a replica of George Washington's Mount Vernon home. Then his life fell apart—his former wife sued him, his current wife divorced him, and his new girlfriend got $500,000 while he was drunk. Within three years of his "good" fortune, Metcalf had drunk himself to death (Dao, 2005).*

What feeling does this photograph illustrate?

16   *When Abraham Shakespeare, a dead-broke truck driver's assistant, won $31 million in the Florida lottery, he bought a million dollar home in a gated community. He lent money to friends to start businesses, even paid for funerals (McShane, 2010). This evidently wasn't enough. His body was found buried in the yard of a "friend," who was convicted of his murder (Allen, 2012).*

Why does the author include these mini-case studies?

17   Winners who avoid anomie seem to be people who don't make sudden changes in their lifestyle or their behavior. They hold onto their old friends and routines—the anchors in life that give them identity and a sense of belonging. Some even keep their old jobs—not for the money, of course, but because the job anchors them to an identity with which they are familiar and comfortable.

Summarize the ways that lottery winners can avoid *anomie*.

18   Sudden wealth, in other words, poses a threat that has to be guarded against.

19   And I can just hear you say, "I'll take the risk!"

Why does the author close with this sentence?

After Reading

Checking Your Comprehension

_____ 1. Which of the following does *not* commonly happen to lottery winners?

   a. They are flooded with marriage proposals.

   b. They get phone calls from people who are looking for money.

   c. Their lives continue unchanged for the most part.

   d. Reporters and TV crews appear on their doorsteps.

_____ 2. As used in the reading, the term *anomie* means

   a. a feeling that everything is topsy-turvy.

   b. an understanding of people's greed.

   c. a sense of moral superiority.

   d. an indication that you have made the right decision.

_____ 3. What do the case studies in paragraphs 14–16 all have in common?
   a. They are all examples of female lottery winners.
   b. They are all examples of people who avoided anomie.
   c. They are all examples of people who used lottery winnings to do good for society.
   d. They are all examples of lottery winners who experienced great unhappiness.

_____ 4. People who keep their jobs after winning the lottery often do so because
   a. they enjoy working and are committed to their jobs.
   b. they want time away from their friends and family.
   c. their jobs anchor them to a familiar and comfortable identity.
   d. their supervisors refuse to accept their resignations.

_____ 5. Which lottery winner celebrated the big win by vomiting?
   a. Mary Sanderson
   b. Michael Klinebiel
   c. Mack Metcalf
   d. Abraham Shakespeare

Applying Your Skills: Supporting Details and Transitions

_____ 6. In paragraphs 1–6, which paragraph serves as a transition from the article's introduction into its main content?
   a. paragraph 1
   b. paragraph 2
   c. paragraph 4
   d. paragraph 6

_____ 7. Which type of detail does the author use most frequently in this reading?
   a. steps
   b. procedures
   c. examples
   d. his own personal experience

_____ 8. Paragraph 12 states, "If you give the usual juicer, everyone will think you're stingy." What type of detail is this sentence? (Hint: Think about which statement this sentence supports.)
   a. fact
   b. reason
   c. description
   d. procedure

_____ 9. Which transitional word or phrase in paragraph 17 indicates that the author is showing a cause and an effect? (Hint: See Table 7-1 on p. 259.)
   a. avoid
   b. hold onto
   c. even keep
   d. because

_____ 10. How do the specific numbers for lottery winnings, quoted in paragraphs 14–16, help the author support his thesis?
   a. All of the reported lottery winnings are large amounts, and the author is examining what happens to people who win big.
   b. All of these numbers support the author's thesis that large amounts of money are more easily wasted than small amounts.
   c. These specific numbers support the author's thesis that men are more likely to waste their lottery winnings than women are.
   d. The large lottery winnings are the only three examples of research into winners' lives, justifying the author's thesis that there are few systematic studies of winners.

Studying Words

Using context or a dictionary, define each of the following words as it is used in the reading.

11. megabucks (par. 2) _____

12. terminally ill (par. 9) _____

13. pooled (par. 14) _____

14. evidently (par. 16) _____

15. anchors (par. 17) _____

Thinking Visually

1. How does the photo illustrate the content of the selection?

2. What other types of photos, charts, or visual aids might be useful with this selection?

Thinking Critically About the Reading

1. How would you describe the author's attitude toward the people who are profiled in this reading selection?

2. Paragraph 10 states, "Maybe money makes people sexy." Do you think the author agrees with this statement? Why or why not? What point is the author trying to make?

3. What other types of information would be useful to support the idea that winning the lottery changes one's life?

4. Would you describe this reading as balanced or as biased? That is, does the author present only one side of the story, or does he provide multiple perspectives? (Hint: Think about the people whose stories are told.)

Academic Application: Writing a Paraphrase

Directions: You are preparing an oral presentation in which you discuss the experiences of lottery winners. You want to share the author's overall attitude toward winning the lottery. Paraphrase the last two sentences of the reading.

_____

_____

_____

Following the Author's Thought Patterns

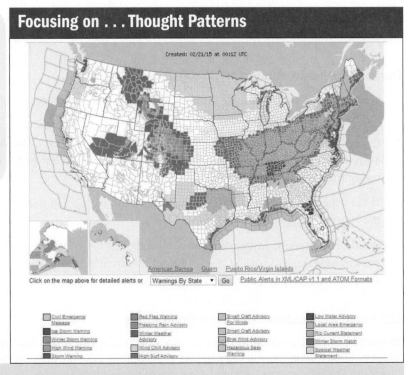

Focusing on . . . Thought Patterns

This map shows a pattern of weather. You can see that a large swath of the country has received a warning or advisory about winter storms. Central Tennessee is anticipating an ice storm, while in Minnesota, wind chill is a greater concern. Just as weather map patterns are useful in helping you understand the weather that is coming your way, patterns in paragraphs are useful in helping you work your way through paragraphs. In this chapter you will see how writers organize their ideas using patterns.

As a way to begin thinking about authors' thought patterns, complete each of the following steps:

1. Study each of the drawings below for a few seconds (count to ten as you look at each one).
2. Cover up the drawings and try to draw each from memory.
3. Check to see how many you had exactly correct.

Most likely you drew all but the fourth correctly. Why did you get that one wrong? How does it differ from the others?

Drawings 1, 2, 3, and 5 have patterns. Drawing 4, however, has no pattern; it is just a randomly jagged line.

From this experiment you can see that it is easier to remember drawings that have a pattern, some understandable form of organization. The same is true of written material. If you can see how a paragraph is organized, it will be easier to understand and remember. Writers often present their ideas in a recognizable order. Once you can recognize the organizational pattern, you will remember more of what you read.

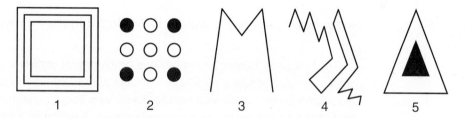

SIX COMMON THOUGHT PATTERNS

1 LEARNING GOAL

Recognize six commonly used thought patterns

This chapter discusses six of the most common thought patterns that writers use and shows how to recognize them: (1) illustration/example, (2) definition, (3) comparison/contrast, (4) cause/effect, (5) classification, and (6) chronological order/process. A brief overview of other useful patterns is provided in the section that follows.

Illustration/Example

One of the clearest, most practical, and most obvious ways to explain something is to give an **example** to illustrate what you are saying. Suppose you had to explain what anthropology is. You might give examples of the topics you study. By using examples, such as the study of apes and early humans, and the development of modern humans, you would give a fairly good idea of what anthropology is all about. When a subject is unfamiliar, an example often makes it easier to understand.

Usually a writer will state an idea first and then follow with examples. Several examples may be given in one paragraph, or a separate paragraph may be used for each example. It may help to visualize the illustration/example pattern this way:

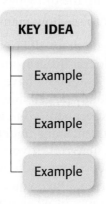

Notice how this thought pattern is developed in the following passage.

> The language barrier is one obvious problem that confronts marketers who wish to break into foreign markets. Travelers abroad commonly encounter signs in tortured English such as a note to guests at a Tokyo hotel that said, "You are invited to take advantage of the chambermaid," a notice at a hotel in Acapulco that proclaimed "The manager has personally passed all the water served here," or a dry cleaner in Majorca that urged passing customers to "drop your pants here for best results."
>
> —Solomon et al., *Marketing*, p. 85

In the preceding passage, the concept of miscommunication due to language barriers is explained through examples. You could visualize the selection as follows:

Here is another passage in which the main idea is explained through example:

> Many companies today are localizing their products, advertising, promotion, and sales efforts to fit the needs of individual regions, cities, and neighborhoods. For example, Walmart operates virtually everywhere but has developed special formats tailored to specific types of geographic locations. In strongly Hispanic neighborhoods, Walmart operates Supermercado de Walmart stores, which feature signage, product assortments, and bilingual staff that are more relevant to local Hispanic customers. In markets where full-size superstores are impractical, Walmart has opened smaller Walmart Market supermarkets and even smaller Walmart Express and Walmart on Campus stores. Similarly, Macy's, the nation's second-largest department store chain, lets its 1,600 district managers around the country customize merchandise in their local stores.
>
> —Armstrong and Kotler, *Marketing*, pp. 165–166

The author explains the way companies localize by offering examples from Walmart and Macy's.

Paragraphs and passages organized using illustration/example often use transitional words and phrases to connect ideas. Examples of such words and phrases include:

for example	for instance	to illustrate

EXERCISE 8-1 **Analyzing Illustration/Example Paragraphs**

Directions: For each of the following paragraphs, underline the topic sentence and list the examples used to explain it.

1. Networking is the process of making informal connections with mutually beneficial business contacts. Networking takes place wherever and whenever people talk: at industry functions, at social gatherings, at sports events and recreational activities, at alumni reunions and so on. Social networks, including Facebook, and business-oriented websites such as LinkedIn, Ryze, and Spoke have become powerful networking resources.

    —adapted from Thill and Bovée, *Excellence in Business Communication*, p. 473

    Examples: _____

2. As part of your day-to-day body functioning, a variety of chemical reactions called *oxidation reactions* continually occur. Although normal, oxidation reactions sometimes produce harmful chemicals called *free radicals*, which can start chain

reactions that can damage cells. It is impossible for you to avoid damage by free radicals; however, certain components of foods can help neutralize them. These substances are generally referred to as *antioxidants* because they work against oxidation. Some antioxidants are nutrients. These include vitamins C and E, beta-carotene (a form of vitamin A), and the mineral selenium. Many other antioxidants are non-nutrients; these include phytochemicals and certain other substances in food.

—adapted from Lynch et al., *Choosing Health*, pp. 75–76

Examples: _____

_____

3.   Problems arise when the marketing of adult products spills over into the children's segment—intentionally or unintentionally. For example, Victoria's Secret targets its highly successful Pink line of young, hip, and sexy clothing to young women from 18 to 30 years old. However, critics charge that Pink is now all the rage among girls as young as 11 years old. Responding to Victoria's Secret's designs and marketing messages, tweens are flocking into stores and buying Pink, with or without their mothers. Critics worry that marketers of everything from lingerie and cosmetics to Barbie dolls are directly or indirectly targeting young girls with provocative products, promoting a premature focus on sex and appearance.

—adapted from Armstrong and Kotler, *Marketing*, p. 181

Examples: _____

EXERCISE 8-2   **Writing an Illustration/Example Paragraph**

Directions: Choose one of the following topics. On a separate sheet of paper, write a paragraph in which you use illustration/example to organize and express your ideas on the topic. Then draw a diagram showing the organization of your paragraph.

1. Parents or friends are helpful (or not helpful) in making decisions.

2. Attending college has (has not) made a major change in my life.

Definition

Another way to provide an explanation is to offer a definition. A **definition** should have two parts: (1) what general group or class an item belongs to and (2) how that item is different or distinguishable from other items in the group.

Let us say that you see an opossum while driving in the country. You mention this to a friend. Since your friend does not know what an opossum is, you have to give a definition. Your definition should include the fact that an opossum is an animal (the general group it belongs to) and a description of the features of an opossum that would help someone tell the difference between it and other animals, such as dogs, raccoons, and squirrels. Thus, you could define an opossum as follows:

> An opossum is an animal with a ratlike tail that lives in trees. It carries its young in a pouch. It is active at night and pretends to be dead when trapped.

This definition can be diagrammed as follows:

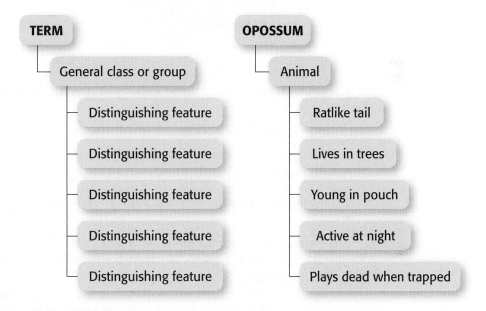

The following passage was written to define the term *ragtime music*.

> Ragtime music is a piano style that developed at the turn of the twentieth century. Ragtime music usually has four themes. The themes are divided into four musical sections of equal length. In playing ragtime music, the left hand plays chords and the right hand plays the melody. There is an uneven accenting between the two hands.

The thought pattern of this passage might be diagrammed as follows:

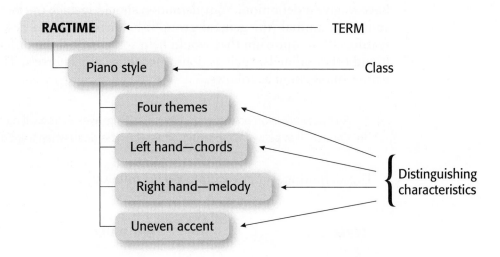

As you read passages that use the definition pattern, keep these questions in mind:

1. What is being defined?
2. What general group or class does it belong to?
3. What makes it different from others in the group?

Read the following passage and apply the above questions.

Nez Perce Indians are a tribe that lives in north-central Idaho. The rich farmlands and forests in the area form the basis for the tribe's chief industries—agriculture and lumber.

The name *Nez Perce* means *pierced nose*, but few of the Indians ever pierced their noses. In 1805, a French interpreter gave the name to the tribe after seeing some members wearing shells in their noses as decorations.

The Nez Perce originally lived in the region where the borders of Idaho, Oregon, and Washington meet. Prospectors overran the Nez Perce reservation after discovering gold there in the 1860s.

Part of the tribe resisted the efforts of the government to move them to a smaller reservation. In 1877, fighting broke out between the Nez Perce and U.S. troops. Joseph, a Nez Perce chief, tried to lead a band of the Indians into Canada. But he surrendered near the United States–Canadian border.

—World Book Online Reference Center

This passage was written to define the Nez Perce. The general group or category is "Indian tribe." The distinguishing characteristics include the source of their name, their original location, and their fight against relocation.

Analyzing Definition Paragraphs

Directions: Read each of the following paragraphs. Then identify the term being defined, its general class, and its distinguishing features.

1.   The Sun's most conspicuous features are large sunspots, caused by magnetic storms on the Sun. Individual sunspots may range in diameter from 10,000 to 50,000 km (6,200 to 31,000 mi), with some growing as large as 160,000 km (100,000 mi), more than 12 times the Earth's diameter. These surface disturbances produce flares and prominences.

—Christopherson, *Elemental Geosystems*, p. 40

Term: _____

General class: _____

Distinguishing features: _____

_____

2.   You may have wondered what it means if someone is "color-blind." Does that person see the world in black and white? No—the term color blindness refers to a vision abnormality that results in an inability to distinguish certain colors from one another. About 8% of males experience some kind of difficulty in distinguishing colors, most commonly red from green. By contrast, fewer than 1% of females suffer from color blindness.

—adapted from Wood, Wood, and Boyd, *Mastering the World of Psychology*, p. 84

Term: _____

General class: _____

Distinguishing features: _____

_____

_____

3.   The Baby Boomer age cohort consists of people whose parents established families following the end of World War II and during the 1950s when the peacetime economy was strong and stable. As teenagers in the 1960s and 1970s, the "Woodstock generation" created a revolution in style, politics, and consumer

attitudes. As they aged, they fueled cultural events as diverse as the Free Speech movement and hippies in the 1960s to Reaganomics and yuppies in the 1980s. Now that they are older, they continue to influence popular culture.

—Solomon, *Consumer Behavior*, p. 508

Term: _____

General class: _____

Distinguishing features: _____

_____

_____

Paragraphs and passages that are organized using definition often use transitional words and phrases to connect ideas. Examples of these transitional words and phrases include:

can be defined as	consists of	involves
is	is called	is characterized by
means	refers to	

EXERCISE **8-4**   **Writing a Definition Paragraph**

Directions: Choose one of the topics listed below. On a separate sheet of paper, write a paragraph in which you define the topic. Be sure to include both the general group and what makes the item different from other items in the same group. Then draw a diagram showing the organization of your paragraph.

1. A type of music

2. Social networks

3. Junk food

Comparison/Contrast

Often a writer will explain something by using **comparison** or **contrast**—that is, by showing how it is similar to or different from a familiar object or idea. Comparison treats similarities, while contrast emphasizes differences. For example, an article comparing two car models might mention these common, overlapping features: radial tires, clock, radio, power steering, and power brakes. The cars may differ in gas mileage, body shape, engine power, braking distance, and so forth. When comparing the two models, the writer would focus on shared features. When contrasting the two cars, the writer would focus on individual differences. Such an article might be diagrammed as follows:

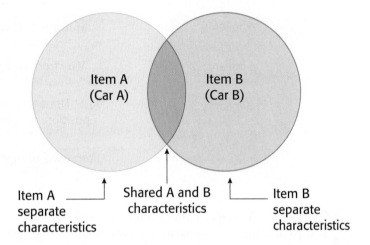

In this diagram, Items A and B are different except where they overlap and share the same characteristics.

In most articles that use the comparison/contrast method, you will find some passages that only compare, some that only contrast, and others that both compare and contrast. To read each type of passage effectively, you must follow the pattern of ideas. Passages that show comparison and/or contrast can be organized in a number of different ways. The organization depends on the author's purpose.

Comparison   If a writer is concerned only with similarities, he or she may identify the items to be compared and then list the ways in which they are alike. The following paragraph shows how permanent and temporary body adornment are similar.

> Every culture has some kind of body adornment. Some are permanent, includ-ing tattoos and piercings. Others are temporary, and include clothing, paint or makeup, and jewelry. Both types of adornment are motivated by specific cultural beliefs and vary from culture to culture. The adornment is often used to indicate social position, rank, religion, or ethnic identity. Adornment of both types is also often used to highlight certain areas of the body that are culturally significant.

Such a pattern can be diagrammed as follows:

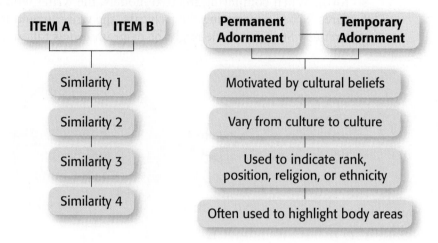

Contrast   A writer concerned only with the differences between sociology and psychology might write the following paragraph:

Sociology and psychology, although both social sciences, are very different fields of study. Sociology is concerned with the structure, organization, and behavior of groups. Psychology, on the other hand, focuses on individual behavior. While a sociologist would study characteristics of groups of people, a psychologist would study the individual motivation and behavior of each group member. Psychology and sociology also differ in the manner in which research is conducted. Sociologists obtain data and information through observation and survey. Psychologists obtain data through carefully designed experimentation.

Such a pattern can be diagrammed as follows:

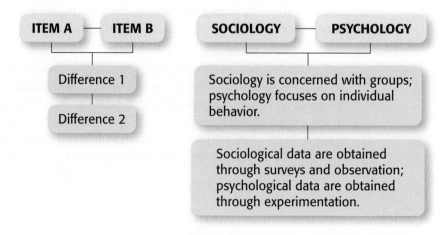

Comparison and Contrast   In many passages, writers discuss both similarities and differences. Suppose you wanted to write a paragraph discussing the similarities and differences between sociology and psychology. You could organize the paragraph in different ways.

1. You could list all the similarities and then all the differences, as shown in this diagram:

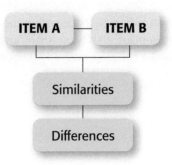

2. You could discuss Item A first, presenting both similarities and differences, and then do the same for Item B. Such a pattern would look like this:

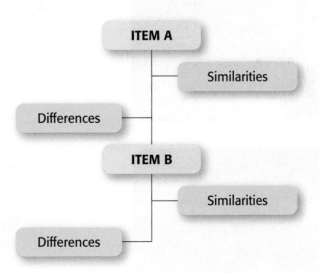

The paragraph on the next page discusses amphibians and reptiles. As you read it, try to visualize its pattern.

Although reptiles evolved from amphibians, several things distinguish the two kinds of animals. Amphibians (such as frogs, salamanders, and newts) must live where it is moist. In contrast, reptiles (which include turtles, lizards and snakes, and crocodiles and alligators) can live away from the water. Amphibians employ external fertilization, as when the female frog lays her eggs on the water and the male spreads his sperm on top of them. By contrast, all reptiles employ internal fertilization—eggs are fertilized inside the female's body. Another difference between amphibians and reptiles is that reptiles have a tough, scaly skin that conserves water, as opposed to the thin amphibian skin that allows water to escape. Reptiles also have a stronger skeleton than amphibians, more efficient lungs, and a better-developed nervous system.

—adapted from Krogh, *Biology*, pp. 466–467, 474

Which contrast between reptiles and amphibians is illustrated by these photos?

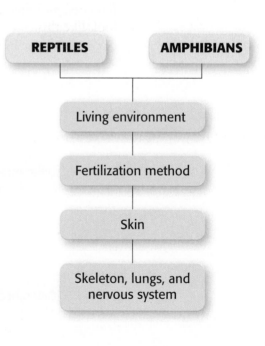

Now read the following passage and decide whether it discusses similarities, differences, or both.

> Groups have two types of leaders. The first is easy to recognize. This person, called an **instrumental leader**, tries to keep the group moving toward its goals. These leaders try to keep group members from getting sidetracked, reminding them of what they are trying to accomplish. The **expressive leader**, in contrast, usually is not recognized as a leader, but he or she certainly is one. This person is likely to crack jokes, to offer sympathy or to do other things that help to lift the group's morale. Both types of leadership are essential: the one to keep the group on track, the other to increase harmony and minimize conflicts.
>
> It is difficult for the same person to be both an instrumental and an expressive leader, for these roles tend to contradict one another. Because instrumental leaders are task oriented, they sometimes create friction as they prod the group to get on with the job. Their actions often cost them popularity. Expressive leaders, in contrast, who stimulate personal bonds and reduce friction, are usually more popular.
>
> —adapted from Henslin, *Sociology*, p. 164

This passage *contrasts* two types of group leaders, focusing on differences between the two types.

Paragraphs and passages that use comparison/contrast often contain transitional words and phrases that guide readers through the material. These include:

Comparison	Contrast
both, in comparison, in the same way, likewise, similarly, to compare	as opposed to, differs from, however, in contrast, instead, on the other hand, unlike

EXERCISE 8-5   Analyzing Comparison/Contrast Paragraphs

Directions: Read each of the following passages and identify the items being compared or contrasted. Then describe the author's approach to the items. Does the author compare, contrast, or both compare and contrast?

1. Congress is bicameral, meaning that it is made up of two houses, the Senate and the House of Representatives. According to the Constitution, all members of Congress must be residents of the states that they have been elected to represent. The Constitution also specifies that representatives must be at least 25 years old and American citizens for 7 years, whereas senators must be at least 30 and American citizens for 9 years. The roles of majority and minority leaders are similar

in both houses, and both use committees to review bills and to set their legislative agenda. Despite these similarities, there are many important differences between the two houses. First, the term of office is two years for representatives but six years for senators. Further, each state is guaranteed two senators but its number of representatives is determined by the state's population; thus, the House of Representatives has 435 members and the Senate has 100. Another difference involves procedure: the House places limits on debate, whereas the Senate allows unlimited debate, which sometimes leads to a filibuster.

Items compared or contrasted: _____

Approach: _____

2.   Whenever direct comparisons are made, the Neanderthals do indeed look primitive in comparison with ancient *Homo sapiens*. Neanderthals thrust spears at prey, but humans developed the valuable technique of *throwing* spears from a distance. The Neanderthals used nothing but stone for their relatively primitive tools, while *H. sapiens* used bone and antler as well as stone in constructing their much finer implements. And the Neanderthals were "foragers," while ancient humans were "collectors." What's the difference? Humans monitored their environments and used "forward planning" by, for example, placing their campsites near animal migration paths. By contrast, Neanderthals do not appear to have timed their migrations in this way. Such differences may have been important to the fate of the Neanderthals, as you'll see.

—Krogh, *Biology*, p. 370

Items compared or contrasted: _____

Approach: _____

3.   The naturalist John Muir, who was strongly influenced by transcendentalist writings and his own experiences in the Sierra Nevada wilderness, advocated the preservationist view that parks and public lands should preserve wild nature in its pristine state. Preservationists believed that humans should have access to wilderness parks for their inspiration and beauty, but that parks should be protected from consumptive uses such as logging or water diversion. To further these goals, Muir and other preservationists founded one of the earliest nongovernmental environmental advocacy organizations, The Sierra Club. The leading spokesman for the opposing view was Gifford Pinchot. Pinchot had studied forestry in Europe and was an ardent critic of the destructive forestry practices widely used at the time. Pinchot articulated the conservationist view that public resources should be used and managed in a sustainable fashion to provide the greatest benefit to the greatest number of people. Conservationists valued nature for the goods and

services it provided to human beings. Preservationists, in contrast, argued that nature had value in its own right and therefore deserved protection.

—Christensen, *The Environment and You,* p. 37

Items compared or contrasted: _____

Approach: _____

EXERCISE 8-6   Writing a Comparison/Contrast Paragraph

Directions: Choose one of the topics listed below. On a separate sheet of paper, write a paragraph in which you compare and/or contrast the two items. Then draw a diagram showing the organization of your paragraph.

1. Two restaurants

2. Two friends

3. Two musical groups

Cause/Effect

The **cause/effect** pattern is used to describe an event or action that is caused by another event or action. A cause/effect passage explains why or how something happened. For example, a description of an automobile accident would probably follow a cause/effect pattern. You would tell what caused the accident and what happened as a result. Basically, this pattern describes four types of relationships:

1. Single cause/single effect

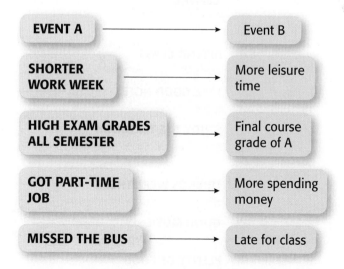

2. Single cause/multiple effects

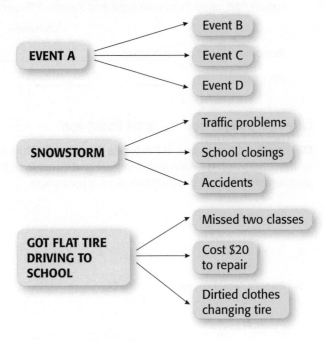

3. Multiple cause/single effect

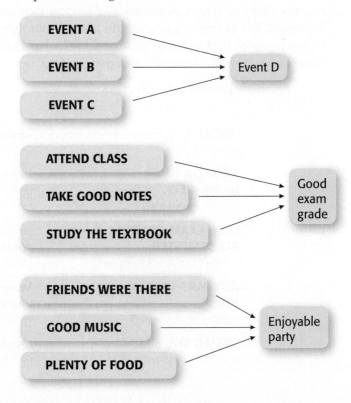

4. Multiple causes/multiple effects

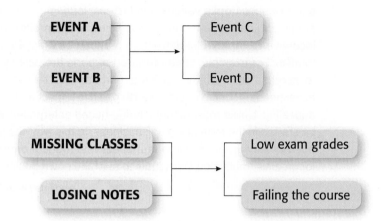

Read the following paragraph and determine which of the four relationships it describes.

> Research has shown that mental illnesses have various causes, but the causes are not fully understood. Some mental disorders are due to physical changes in the brain resulting from illness or injury. Chemical imbalances in the brain may cause other mental illnesses. Still other disorders are mainly due to conditions in the environment that affect a person's mental state. These conditions include unpleasant childhood experiences and severe emotional stress. In addition, many cases of mental illness probably result from a combination of two or more of these causes.

In this paragraph a single effect (mental illness) is stated as having multiple causes (physical and chemical changes, psychological problems).

To read paragraphs that explain cause/effect relationships, pay close attention to the topic sentence. It usually states the cause/effect relationship that is detailed in the remainder of the paragraph. Then look for connections between causes and effects. What event happened as the result of a previous action? How did one event cause the other to happen?

Look for the development of the cause/effect relationship in the following paragraph about tourism.

> Tourism offers several positive economic benefits. First, tourism can provide stability in an economy. Business travel remains relatively constant during changes in economic cycles; and even though people may cut back on the amount they spend on travel during harder economic times, citizens of most industrial nations have come to view vacationing as a necessity of life. Second,

(Continued)

tourism provides economic diversity. A stable economy is one that provides jobs and revenues from a variety of industries; tourism can be added as another economic engine to the industry mix. Third, tourism often provides the economic incentive to improve infrastructure that can be enjoyed by residents as well as tourists. For example, state-of-the-art airports are built by communities primarily to increase accessibility, but the airport can also be used by locals to meet their travel needs. Tourism offers a fourth positive impact that you may find particularly appealing. Unlike most manufacturing-based enterprises, a tourism business can be started in the form of a small business. In this way, the tourism industry can be used to encourage entrepreneurial activity. Tourism provides plenty of chances for creative, motivated individuals to start their own businesses.

—adapted from Cook et al., *Tourism*, p. 282

This paragraph describes the positive effects of tourism. It can be diagrammed as follows:

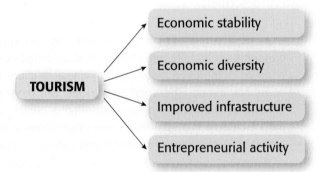

Paragraphs and passages that are organized using cause/effect often use transitional words and phrases to guide the reader. These include:

Cause	Effect
because, because of, for, since, stems from, one cause is, one reason is, for this reason, due to	consequently, one result is, as a result, therefore, thus, hence, results in

EXERCISE **8-7**   **Analyzing Cause/Effect Paragraphs**

Directions: Read each of the following paragraphs and describe the cause/effect relationship in each.

1. The effects of marijuana are relatively mild compared to the other hallucinogens. Most people do report a feeling of mild euphoria and relaxation, along with an altered time sense and mild visual distortions. Higher doses can lead to

hallucinations, delusions, and the all-too-common paranoia. Most studies of marijuana's effects have concluded that while marijuana can create a powerful psychological dependency, it does not produce physical dependency or physical withdrawal symptoms. Newer studies, however, suggest that long-term marijuana use can produce signs of withdrawal such as irritability, memory difficulties, sleep difficulties, and increased aggression. A recent study of the long-term effects of marijuana use has also correlated smoking marijuana with an increased risk of psychotic behavior, with a greater risk for heavier users.

—adapted from Ciccarelli and White, *Psychology*, p. 280

Cause(s): _____

Effect(s): _____

_____

_____

How does this photograph show the cause/effect relationship described in the paragraph?

2. Intermittent fountains in which columns of hot water and steam are ejected with great force, often rising 30 to 60 meters (100 to 200 feet) into the air, are called geysers. After the jet of water ceases, a column of steam rushes out, often with a thunderous roar. Perhaps the most famous geyser in the world is Old Faithful in Yellowstone National Park, which erupts about once each hour. Geysers occur where extensive underground chambers exist within hot igneous rocks. As relatively cool groundwater enters the chambers, it is heated by the surrounding rock. The heating causes the water to expand, and as a result, some of the water is forced out at the surface.

—Lutgens and Tarbuck, *Foundations of Earth Science*, p. 105

Cause(s): _____

Effect(s): _____

3. An important consequence of culture within us is ethnocentrism, a tendency to use our own group's ways of doing things as a yardstick for judging others. All of us learn that the ways of our own group are good, right, and even superior to other ways of life. Ethnocentrism has both positive and negative consequences. On the positive side, it creates in-group loyalties. On the negative side, ethnocentrism can lead to discrimination against people whose ways differ from ours.

—adapted from Henslin, *Sociology*, p. 37

Cause(s): _____

Effect(s): _____

EXERCISE 8-8   **Writing a Cause/Effect Paragraph**

Directions: Choose one of the topics listed below. On a separate sheet of paper, write a paragraph using one of the four cause/effect patterns described on pages 289–292 to explain the topic. Then draw a diagram showing the organization of your paragraph.

1. Why you are attending college

2. Why you chose the college you are attending

3. How a particularly frightening or tragic event happened

Classification

A common way to explain something is **classification**, dividing a topic into parts and explaining each part. For example, you might explain how a home computer works by describing what each major component does. You would explain the functions of the monitor (screen), the disc drive, and the central processing unit. Or you might explain the kinds of courses taken in college by dividing the courses into such categories as electives, required basic courses, courses required for a specific major, and so on, and then describing each category.

Textbook writers use the classification pattern to explain a topic that can easily be divided into parts. These parts are selected on the basis of common characteristics. For example, a psychology textbook writer might explain human needs by classifying them into two categories, primary and secondary. Or in a chemistry textbook, various compounds may be grouped or classified according to common characteristics, such as the presence of hydrogen or oxygen.

The following paragraph explains horticulture. As you read, try to identify the categories into which the topic of horticulture is divided.

> Horticulture, the study and cultivation of garden plants, is a large industry. Recently it has become a popular area of study. The horticulture field consists of four major divisions. First, there is pomology, the science and practice of growing and handling fruit trees. Then there is olericulture, which is concerned with growing and storing vegetables. A third field, floriculture, is the science of growing, storing, and designing flowering plants. The last category, ornamental and landscape horticulture, is concerned with using grasses, plants, and shrubs in landscaping.

This paragraph approaches the topic of horticulture by describing its four areas or fields of study. You could diagram the paragraph as follows:

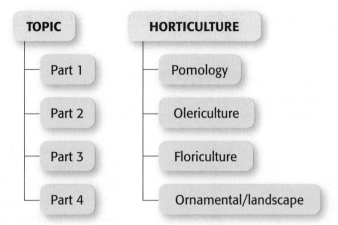

When reading textbook material that uses the classification pattern, be sure you understand *how* and *why* the topic was divided as it was. This technique will help you remember the most important parts of the topic.

Here is another example of the classification pattern:

A newspaper is published primarily to present current news and information. For large city newspapers, more than 2,000 people may be involved in the distribution of this information. The staff of large city papers, headed by a publisher, is organized into departments: editorial, business, and mechanical. The editorial department, headed by an editor-in-chief, is responsible for the collection of news and preparation of written copy. The business department, headed by a business manager, handles circulation, sales, and advertising. The mechanical department is run by a production manager. This department deals with the actual publication of the paper, either print or online.

You could diagram this paragraph as follows:

Paragraphs and passages that are organized using classification frequently use transitional words and phrases to guide the reader. These include:

> another   another kind   classified as   include   is composed of   one types of

---

EXERCISE 8-9   **Analyzing Classification Paragraphs**

Directions: Read each of the following passages. Then identify the topic and the parts into which each passage is divided.

mosses   ferns   conifers   flowering plants
— flowers
— seeds
vascular tissue
— multicellularity
green algae (ancestors)

> Why is this diagram included with the passage?

1.   We can separate the members of the plant kingdom into a mere four types. These are the *bryophytes*, which include mosses; the *seedless vascular plants*, which include ferns; the *gymnosperms*, which include coniferous ("cone-bearing") trees; and the *angiosperms*, a vast division of flowering plants—by far the most dominant on Earth today—that includes not only flowers such as orchids, but also oak trees, rice, and cactus.

—adapted from Krogh, *Biology*, p. 429

Topic: _____

Parts: _____

_____

2.   The amount of space that people prefer varies from one culture to another. North Americans use four different "distance zones." *Intimate distance* extends to about 18 inches from our bodies. We reserve this space for comforting, protecting, hugging, intimate touching, and lovemaking. *Personal distance* extends from 18 inches to 4 feet. We reserve it for friends and acquaintances and ordinary conversations. *Social distance*, extending out from us about 4 to 12 feet, marks impersonal or formal relationships. We use this zone for such things as job interviews. *Public distance*, extending beyond 12 feet, marks even more formal relationships. It is used to separate dignitaries and public speakers from the general public.

—adapted from Henslin, *Sociology*, pp. 109–111

Topic: _____

Parts: _____

What needs does this photograph illustrate?

3. People are born with a need for certain elements necessary to maintain life, such as food, water, air, and shelter. We also can be motivated to satisfy either utilitarian or hedonic needs. When we focus on a *utilitarian need* we emphasize the objective, tangible attributes of products, such as miles per gallon in a car; the amount of fat, calories, and protein in a cheeseburger; or the durability of a pair of blue jeans. *Hedonic needs* are subjective and experiential; here we might look to a product to meet our needs for excitement, self-confidence, or fantasy—perhaps to escape the mundane or routine aspects of life. Of course, we can also be motivated to purchase a product because it provides *both* types of benefits. For example, a woman (perhaps a politically incorrect one) might buy a mink coat because of the luxurious image it portrays and because it also happens to keep her warm through the long, cold winter.

—adapted from Solomon, *Consumer Behavior*, pp. 132, 133

Topic: _____

Parts: _____

EXERCISE 8-10   Writing a Classification Paragraph

Directions: Choose one of the topics listed below. On a separate sheet of paper, write a paragraph explaining the topic, using the classification pattern. Then draw a diagram showing the organization of your paragraph.

1. Advertising

2. Colleges

3. Entertainment

Chronological Order/Process

The terms **chronological order** and **process** both refer to the order in which something is done. Chronological order, also called sequence of events, is one of the most obvious patterns. In a paragraph organized by chronology, the details are presented in the order in which they occur. That is, the event that happened first, or earliest in time, appears first in the paragraph, and so on. Process refers to the steps or stages in which something is done. You might expect to read a description of the events in a World War II battle presented in the order in which they happened—in chronological order. Similarly, in a computer programming manual, the steps to follow to locate an error in a computer program would be described in the order in which you should do them.

Both chronological order and process patterns can be diagrammed as follows:

EVENT OR PROCESS

1. Action or step

2. Action or step

3. Action or step

Read the following paragraph, paying particular attention to the order of the actions or steps.

> In the early 1830s, the newly established Federal Bureau of Narcotics took on a crucial role in the fight against marijuana. Under the directorship of Harry J. Anslinger, a rigorous campaign was waged against the drug and those using it. By 1837, many states had adopted a standard bill making marijuana illegal. In that same year, the federal government stepped in with the Marijuana Tax Act, a bill modeled after the Harrison "Narcotics" Act. Repressive legislation continued, and by the 1850s severe penalties were imposed on those convicted of possessing, buying, selling, or cultivating the drug.
>
> —Barlow, *Criminal Justice in America*, p. 332

This paragraph traces the history of actions taken to limit the use of marijuana. These actions are described in chronological order, beginning with the earliest event and concluding with the most recent.

When reading text material that uses the chronological order/process pattern, pay particular attention to the order of the information presented. Both chronological order and process are concerned with the sequence of events in time.

Paragraphs and passages that use chronological order/process to organize ideas often contain transitional words and phrases to guide the reader. They include:

after	before	by the time	during	finally	first	later
meanwhile	on	second	then	until	when	while

EXERCISE 8-11   **Analyzing Chronological Order/Process Paragraphs**

Directions: Read each of the following paragraphs. Identify the topic and write a list of the actions, steps, or events described in each paragraph.

1.   Two important traditions are typically performed when new lodging properties are constructed. First, when the final floor is completed, an evergreen tree is placed on the top of the building. This act signifies that the building will rise no higher. It also symbolically ties the building safely to the ground through the "roots of the tree." The second important tradition is performed when the ceremonial ribbon is cut on opening day. At that time, the key to the front door is symbolically thrown onto the roof because it will never be used again. This is a symbol signifying that the building is more than just a building. It has become a place that will always be open to those who are seeking a home for the night or more appropriately a "home away from home."

—adapted from Cook et al., *Tourism*, p. 170

Topic: _____

Steps: _____

2.   In jury selection, the pool of potential jurors usually is selected from voter or automobile registration lists. Potential jurors are asked to fill out a questionnaire. Lawyers for each party and the judge can ask questions of prospective jurors to determine if they would be biased in their decision. Jurors can be "stricken for cause" if the court believes that the potential juror is too biased to render a fair verdict. Lawyers may also exclude a juror from sitting on a particular case without giving any reason for the dismissal. Once the appropriate number of jurors is selected (usually six to twelve jurors), they are impaneled to hear the case and are sworn in. The trial is ready to begin.

—adapted from Goldman and Cheeseman, *The Paralegal Professional*, p. 266

Topic: _____

Steps: _____

_____

3.   At 12:30 on the afternoon of May 1, 1915, the British steamship *Lusitania* set sail from New York to Liverpool. The passenger list of 1,257 was the largest since the outbreak of war in Europe in 1914. Six days later, the *Lusitania* reached the coast of Ireland. The passengers lounged on the deck. As if it were peacetime, the ship sailed straight ahead, with no zigzag maneuvers to throw off pursuit. But the submarine U-20 was there, and its commander, seeing a large ship, fired a single torpedo. Seconds after it hit, a boiler exploded and blew a hole in the

Lusitania's side. The ship listed immediately, hindering the launching of lifeboats, and in eighteen minutes it sank. Nearly 1,200 people died, including 128 Americans. As the ship's bow lifted and went under, the U-20 commander for the first time read the name: *Lusitania*.

—adapted from Divine et al., *America Past and Present*, p. 596

Topic: _____

Steps: _____

_____

EXERCISE **8-12** **Writing a Process Paragraph**

Directions: On a separate sheet of paper, write a paragraph explaining how to do something that you do well or often, such as cross-country ski or change a tire, for example. Use the chronological order/process pattern. Then draw a diagram showing the organization of your paragraph.

EXERCISE **8-13** **Identifying Thought Patterns**

Working Together

Directions: Working in pairs or groups of three, read each of the following passages and identify the thought pattern used. Write the name of the pattern in the space provided. Choose from among these patterns: *illustration/example, definition, comparison/contrast, cause/effect, classification,* and *chronological order/process.* Next, write a sentence explaining your choice. Identify any transitions. Then, on a separate sheet of paper, draw a diagram that shows the organization of each selection.

1. **Optimists** are people who always tend to look for positive outcomes. For an optimist, a glass is half full, whereas for a pessimist, the glass is half empty. **Pessimists** seem to expect the worst to happen. Researchers have found that optimism is associated with longer life and increased immune system functioning. Mayo Clinic researchers conducted a study of optimists and pessimists over a period of 30 years. The results for pessimists were not good: They had a much higher death rate than did the optimists, and those that were still living in 1994 had more problems with physical and emotional health, more pain, less ability to take part in social activities, and less energy than optimists. The optimists had a 50 percent lower risk of premature death and were more calm, peaceful, and happy than the pessimists.

—adapted from Ciccarelli and White, *Psychology*, p. 321

Pattern: _____

Reason: _____

A tundra occupies about a fourth of Earth's land surface. What do you think makes up the rest of Earth's land surface?

2.   Along with polar ice, **tundra** is the biome of the far north, stretching in a vast, mostly frozen, ring around the northern rim of the world. So inaccessible is tundra that the average person may never have heard of it, yet it occupies about a fourth of Earth's land surface. The word *tundra* comes from a Finnish word that means "treeless plain," and the description is apt. Its flat terrain stretches out for mile after mile with little change in the vegetational pattern of low shrubs, mosses, lichens, grasses, and the grass-like sedge.

—adapted from Krogh, *Biology*, p. 750

Pattern: _____

Reason: _____

3.   In 1000 B.C., the Cherokee Indians took up residence in the Smoky Mountains. They were virtually isolated until the Spanish conquistadors arrived in 1540, and, more than two hundred years later, other immigrants from the Old World began to settle, first in small groups, and then increasingly in overwhelming numbers. The two groups of people, indigenous and immigrants, lived side by side with only occasional quarreling. In 1838, however, more than 13,000 Cherokee were forced to leave their native lands. Only a few rebellious natives remained along with their Caucasian counterparts.

—adapted from Walker and Walker, *Tourism*, pp. 53–54

Pattern: _____

Reason: _____

4.   Several types of strikes have been held to be illegal and are not protected by federal labor laws. Illegal strikes take the form of violent strikes, sit-down strikes, and partial or intermittent strikes. In **violent strikes**, striking employees cause substantial damage to property of the employer or a third party. Courts usually tolerate a certain amount of isolated violence before finding that the entire strike is illegal. In **sit-down** strikes, striking employees continue to occupy the employer's premises. Such strikes are illegal because they deny the employer's statutory right to continue its operations during the strike. In **partial** or **intermittent strikes**, employees strike part of the day or workweek and work the other part. This type of strike is illegal because it interferes with the employer's right to operate its facilities at full operation.

—adapted from Goldman and Cheeseman, *The Paralegal Professional*, p. 641

Pattern: _____

Reason: _____

5.   Because many natural poisons are alkaloids that occur in plants, it is not surprising that poisons are found in gardens and on farms or ranches. In addition to the toxic pesticides that might be found on a shelf, some of the plants themselves are toxic. For example, oleander (*Nerium oleander*), a beautiful shrub, contains several types of poison, including the potent cardiac glycosides *oleandrin* and *neriine*. (Cardiac glycosides are compounds that have a steroid part and a sugar part and that increase the heart's force of contraction.) Oleander's poisons are so strong that one can be poisoned by eating the honey made by bees that have fed on oleander nectar. Iris, azaleas, and hydrangeas all are poisonous. So are holly berries, wisteria seeds, and the leaves and berries of privet hedges.

—Hill et al., *Chemistry for Changing Times*, p. 682

Pattern: _____

Reason: _____

6.   Behaviors, thoughts, and feelings always occur in a context, that is, in a situation. Situations can be divided into two components: the events that come before and those that come after. *Antecedents* are the setting events for a behavior; they stimulate a person to act in certain ways. Antecedents can be physical events, thoughts, emotions, or the actions of other people. *Consequences*—the results of behavior—affect whether a person will repeat that action. Consequences also can consist of physical events, thoughts, emotions, or the actions of other people.

—Donatelle, *Health*, p. 20

Pattern: _____

Reason: _____

7.   Xylem is the plant tissue through which water moves *up*, from roots through leaves. The flowers we put in vases in our homes have lost their roots, of course, but they haven't lost their xylem, which continues to function long after the flower has been picked. Given this, many flowers can last a long time indoors if we follow a few simple rules. First, realize that the liquid in the xylem is under negative pressure—its natural tendency is to move up *into* the stem, not to flow out of it. As such, if the stems are cut when they are out of water, *air* gets sucked up into the cut ends, creating air bubbles that can then get trapped in the xylem and keep water from rising up through it. When this happens, flowers can wilt, even when their stems are submerged in clean water. Recutting the stem under water can remove this blockage.

—adapted from Krogh, *Biology*, p. 488

Preserving beauty: Following a few simple rules can prolong the life of cut flowers.

Pattern: _____

Reason: _____

8.   The risks of active smoking, in addition to lung and airway damage, include increased rates of throat, bladder, and pancreatic cancer; higher rates of heart attack, stroke, and high blood pressure; and premature aging of the skin. All of these effects occur because many of the components of tobacco smoke can cross into the bloodstream and move throughout the body.

—adapted from Belk and Borden Maier, *Biology*, p. 451

Pattern: _____

Reason: _____

9.   Surveys or questionnaires can be broken down into several types. They may be based on opinion; interpretative; or based on facts. **Opinion surveys** ask respondents questions regarding what they think about particular topics. Answers are based on personal opinion. Therefore, the answers are not necessarily right or wrong. An opinion survey may ask respondents to evaluate a certain topic or express their attitudes and beliefs. **Interpretative surveys** ask respondents to answer why they chose a particular course. For example, a hotel may ask its guests why they chose to stay at the hotel; an airline may ask why passengers chose to fly with them. **Factual surveys** can be thought of as being more concrete in the questions they ask. For example, they may ask travelers what recreational activities they participated in while they were traveling. The answers are based on fact alone, no interpretation or opinion is expressed.

—adapted from Walker and Walker, *Tourism*, p. 241

Pattern: _____

Reason: _____

10.   An organization exists to accomplish something, and this purpose should be clearly stated. Some companies define their missions myopically in product or technology terms ("We are a chemical-processing firm"). But mission statements should be market oriented and defined in terms of satisfying basic customer needs. Facebook doesn't define itself as just an online social network. Its mission is to connect people around the world and help them share important moments in their lives. Likewise, Chipotle's mission isn't to sell burritos. Instead, the restaurant promises "Food with integrity," highlighting its commitment to the immediate and long-term welfare of customers and the environment.

—Kotler and Armstrong, *Principles of Marketing*, pp. 41–42

Pattern: _____

Reason: _____

OTHER USEFUL PATTERNS OF ORGANIZATION

2 LEARNING GOAL

Recognize other useful thought patterns

The patterns presented in the preceding section are the most common. Table 8-1 presents a brief review of those patterns and their corresponding transitional words. However, writers do not limit themselves to these six patterns. Especially in academic writing, you may find one or more of the patterns listed in Table 8-2 (p. 305), as well.

Statement and Clarification

Many writers make a statement of fact and then proceed to clarify or explain that statement. For instance, a writer may open a paragraph by stating that "The best education for you may not be the best education for someone else." The remainder of the paragraph would then discuss that statement and make

TABLE 8-1   A Review of Patterns and Transitional Words

Pattern	Characteristics	Transitional Words
Illustration/ Example	Organizes examples that illustrate an idea or concept	*for example, for instance, such as, to illustrate*
Definition	Explains the meaning of a word or phrase	*are those that, can be defined as, consists of, corresponds to, entails, involves, is, is a term that, is called, is characterized by, is literally, means, occurs when, refers to*
Comparison/ Contrast	Discusses similarities and/or differences among ideas, theories, concepts, objects, or persons	Similarities: *also, as well as, both, correspondingly, in comparison, in the same way, like, likewise, resembles, share, similarly, to compare, too*
		Differences: *as opposed to, despite, differs from, however, in contrast, in spite of, instead, nevertheless, on the other hand, unlike, whereas*
Cause/Effect	Describes how one or more things cause or are related to another	Causes: *because, because of, cause is, due to, for, for this reason, one cause is, one reason is, since, stems from*
		Effects: *as a result, consequently, hence, one result is, results in, therefore, thus*
Classification	Divides a topic into parts based on shared characteristics	*another, another kind, classified as, comprises, different groups that, different stages of, finally, first, include, is composed of, last, one, second, types of, varieties of*
Chronological Order/Process	Describes events, processes, procedures	*after, as soon as, by the time, during, finally, first, following, in, last, later, meanwhile, next, on, second, then, until, when, while*

its meaning clear by explaining how educational needs are individual and based on one's talents, skills, and goals. Here is another example:

> The Constitution of the United States of America is the supreme law of the land. This means that any law—federal, state, or local—that conflicts with the U.S. Constitution is unconstitutional and, therefore, unenforceable. The principles enumerated in the Constitution are extremely broad, because the founding fathers intended them to be applied to evolving social, technological, and economic conditions. The U.S. Constitution often is referred to as a "living document" because it is so adaptable. States also have their own constitutions, often patterned after the U.S. Constitution. Provisions of state constitutions are valid unless they conflict with the U.S. Constitution or any valid federal law.
>
> —adapted from Goldman and Cheeseman, *The Paralegal Professional*, p. 183

Transitional words associated with the statement and clarification pattern are listed in Table 8-2.

TABLE 8-2   A Review of Additional Patterns and Transitional Words

Pattern	Characteristics	Transitional Words
Statement and Clarification	Gives information explaining an idea or concept	*clearly, evidently, in fact, in other words, obviously*
Summary	Provides a condensed review of an idea or piece of writing	*in brief, in conclusion, in short, in summary, on the whole, to sum up, to summarize*
Addition	Provides additional information	*additionally, again, also, besides, further, furthermore, in addition, moreover*
Spatial Order	Describes physical location or position in space	*above, behind, below, beside, in front of, inside, nearby, next to, opposite, outside, within*

Summary

A **summary** is a condensed statement that recaps the key points of a larger idea or piece of writing. The summaries at the end of each chapter of this text provide a quick review of the chapter's contents. Often writers summarize what they have already said or what someone else has said. For example, in a psychology textbook you will find many summaries of research. Instead of asking you to read an entire research study, the textbook author will summarize the study's findings. Other times a writer may repeat in condensed form what he or she has already said as a means of emphasis or clarification. Here is a sample paragraph:

> To sum up, the minimax strategy is a general principle of human behavior that suggests that humans try to minimize costs and maximize rewards. The fewer costs and the more rewards we anticipate from something, the more likely we are to do it. If we believe that others will approve an act, the likelihood increases that we will do it. In short, whether people are playing cards with a few friends or are part of a mob, the principles of human behavior remain the same.
>
> —adapted from Henslin, *Sociology*, p. 637

Transitional words associated with this pattern are listed in Table 8-2 (p. 305).

Addition

Writers often introduce an idea or make a statement and then supply additional information about that idea or statement. For instance, an education textbook may introduce the concept of homeschooling and then provide in-depth information about its benefits. This pattern is often used to expand, elaborate, or discuss an idea in greater detail. Here is an example:

> Mixing alcohol with caffeine does not enable a person to party for a longer period of time than she would without the caffeine. In fact, combining alcohol and caffeine can lead to severe dehydration which, it so happens, is the underlying cause of the constellation of symptoms popularly known as a "hangover." Thus, anyone who wants to avoid a hangover should also avoid mixing caffeine with alcohol. Moreover, caffeine appears to impair drinkers' ability to assess the degree to which they are intoxicated, an effect that leads to poor decision making about driving under the influence of alcohol and other risky behaviors.
>
> —Wood, Wood, and Boyd, *Mastering the World of Psychology*, p. 133

Transitional words associated with this pattern are listed in Table 8-2 (p. 305).

Spatial Order

Spatial order is concerned with the physical location or position in space. Spatial order is used in disciplines in which physical descriptions are important. A photography textbook may use spatial order to describe the parts of a camera.

An automotive technology textbook may use spatial order to describe disk brake operation. Here is a sample paragraph:

> We can taste food because chemoreceptors in the mouth respond to certain chemicals in food. The chemoreceptors for taste are located in structures called **taste buds**, each of which contains 50–150 receptor cells and numerous support cells. At the top of each bud is a pore that allows receptor cells to be exposed to saliva and dissolved food molecules. Each person has over 10,000 taste buds, located primarily on the tongue and the roof of the mouth, but also located in the pharynx.
>
> —Germann and Stanfield, *Principles of Human Physiology*, pp. 303–304

Transitional words associated with this pattern are listed in Table 8-2 (p. 305).

EXERCISE 8-14 **Identifying Thought Patterns**

Directions: For each of the following statements, identify the pattern that is evident and indicate it in the space provided. Choose from among the following patterns:

- a. statement and clarification
- b. summary
- c. addition
- d. spatial order

_____ 1. Short fibers, dendrites, branch out around the cell body and a single long fiber, the axon, extends from the cell body.

_____ 2. Aspirin is not as harmless as people think. It may cause allergic reactions and stomach irritation. In addition, aspirin has been linked to an often fatal condition known as Reye's syndrome.

_____ 3. If our criminal justice system works, the recidivism rate—the percentage of people released from prison who return—should decrease. In other words, in a successful system, there should be a decrease in the number of criminals who are released from prison and then become repeat offenders.

_____ 4. Students who are informed about drugs tend to use them in greater moderation. Furthermore, they tend to help educate others.

_____ 5. To sum up, a successful drug addiction treatment program would offer free or very cheap drugs to addicts.

_____ 6. In conclusion, it is safe to say that crime by women is likely to increase as greater numbers of women assume roles traditionally held by men.

_____ 7. The pollutants we have just discussed all involve chemicals; we can conclude that they threaten our environment and our well-being.

_____ 8. A residual check valve that maintains slight pressure on the hydraulic system is located in the master cylinder at the outlet for the drum brakes.

_____ 9. Sociologists study how we are socialized into sex roles—the attitudes expected of males and females. Sex roles, in fact, identify some activities and behaviors as clearly male and others as clearly female.

_____ 10. The meninges are three membranes that lie just outside the organs of the central nervous system.

EXERCISE 8-15   **Predicting**

Working Together

Directions: Locate and mark five paragraphs in one of your textbooks or in Part Six of this text that are clear examples of the thought patterns discussed in this chapter. Write the topic sentence of each paragraph on a separate index card. Once your instructor has formed small groups, choose a group "reader" who will collect all the cards and read each sentence aloud. Groups should discuss each and predict the pattern of the paragraph from which the sentence was taken. The "finder" of the topic sentence then confirms or rejects the choice, quoting sections of the paragraph if necessary.

Using Transitional Words

As you learned earlier in the chapter, transitional words can help you identify organizational patterns. These words are called **transitional words** because they help you make the transition or connection between ideas. They may also be called *clue words* or *directional words* because they provide readers with clues about what is to follow.

Transitional words are also helpful in discovering or clarifying relationships between and among ideas in any piece of writing. Specifically, transitional words help you grasp connections between and within sentences. Transitional words can help you predict what is to come next within a paragraph. For instance, if you are reading along and come upon the phrase *in conclusion*, you know that the writer will soon present a summary. If you encounter the word *furthermore*, you know that the writer is about to present additional information about the subject at hand. If you encounter the word *consequently* in the middle of a sentence (The law was repealed; consequently, . . .), you know that the writer is about to explain what happened as a result of the repeal. Tables 8-1 and 8-2 on pages 304 and 305 list the transitional words that correspond to the patterns discussed in this chapter.

EXERCISE **8-16**   **Predicting**

Working Together

Directions: Each of the following beginnings of paragraphs uses a transitional word or phrase to tell the reader what will follow in the paragraph. Read each, paying particular attention to the underlined transitional word or phrase. Working with a partner, discuss what you expect to follow. Then, in the space provided, summarize your findings.

1. Many Web sites on the Internet are reliable and trustworthy. <u>However,</u> . . .

   _____

2. One advantage of using a computer to take notes is that you can rearrange information easily. <u>Another</u> . . .

   _____

3. There are a number of ways to avoid catching the cold virus. <u>First of all,</u> . . .

   _____

4. Some pet owners care for their animals responsibly. <u>However,</u> others . . .

   _____

5. When planning a speech, you should choose a topic that is familiar or that you are knowledgeable about. <u>Next,</u> . . .

   _____

6. Following a high-protein diet may be rewarding because it often produces quick weight loss. <u>On the other hand,</u> . . .

   _____

7. The iris is a doughnut-shaped portion of the eyeball. <u>In the center</u> . . .

   _____

8. Price is not the only factor consumers consider when making a major purchase. They <u>also</u> . . .

   _____

9. Cholesterol, commonly found in many fast foods, is associated with heart disease. <u>Consequently,</u> . . .

   _____

10. Many Web sites provide valuable links to related sites. <u>To illustrate,</u> visit . . .

   _____

LEARNING STYLE TIPS

If you tend to be a . . .	Then identify thought patterns by . . .
Spatial learner	Drawing a diagram of the ideas in the passage
Verbal learner	Outlining the passage

SELF-TEST SUMMARY

1 What are the six common thought patterns?

A thought pattern is the way in which an author organizes ideas. The six common thought patterns are

1. **Illustration/example**—The author explains an idea by providing specific instances or experiences that illustrate it.

2. **Definition**—The author explains an object or idea by describing the general class or group to which it belongs and how the item differs from others in the same group (distinguishing features).

3. **Comparison/contrast**—The author explains a new or unfamiliar idea by showing how it is similar to or different from a more familiar idea.

4. **Cause/effect**—The author explains connections between events by showing what caused an event or what happened as a result of a particular event.

5. **Classification**—The author explains an object or idea by dividing it into parts and describing or explaining each.

6. **Chronological order/process**—The author describes events or procedures in the order in which they occur in time.

2 What other thought patterns are used in academic writing?

1. **Statement and clarification**—An explanation will follow a general statement.

2. **Summary**—A condensed view of the subject will be presented.

3. **Addition**—Additional information will follow.

4. **Spatial order**—Physical location or position will be described.

GOING ⊙ ONLINE

1. **Patterns of Organization and Online Images**

   Many photos suggest a pattern of organization. Do a Google Image search for a topic of interest to you, and print out three photos that you find interesting. Then write a sentence (caption) to accompany each photo. Each sentence should use one of the following patterns of organization: illustration/example, definition, comparison/contrast, cause/effect, classification, or chronological order/process. For example, you might use a photo of a maple tree to write a definition or example sentence, such as "The maple is one example of a deciduous tree, which is a type of tree that loses its leaves in the fall."

2. **Comparing and Contrasting Books**

   Go to an online book review Web site and look up reviews of the following two books: *One for the Money* by Janet Evanovich and *An Unsuitable Job for a Woman* by P.D. James. Browse the reviews and, if possible, any sample chapters that may be available for the books. Then, working with a group of classmates, prepare a comparison/contrast of these two books. How are the two books similar? How are they different?

MASTERY TEST 1 Reading Selection

Right Place, Wrong Face

Alton Fitzgerald White

Before Reading

In this selection, the author describes what it was like to be treated as a criminal on the basis of nothing more than having the "wrong face."

Previewing the Reading

Using the steps listed on page 49, preview the reading selection. When you have finished, indicate whether each statement is true (T) or false (F).

_____ a. The author is the youngest of seven children.

_____ b. The reading selection will explain an event that changed the author's life dramatically.

Predicting and Connecting

1. Have you (or someone you know) ever been falsely accused of a crime? What happened, and how did the experience make you feel?

2. What do you know about racial profiling?

> **Vocabulary Preview**
>
> **ovation** (par. 3) enthusiastic, prolonged applause
>
> **overt** (par. 4) not secret, obvious
>
> **splurged** (par. 5) indulged in a luxury
>
> **vestibule** (par. 5) a small entrance hall or passage into the interior of a building
>
> **residue** (par. 9) something that remains after a substance is taken away
>
> **violation** (par. 14) the condition of being treated unfairly or disrespectfully

1   As the youngest of five girls and two boys growing up in Cincinnati, I was raised to believe that if I worked hard, was a good person, and always told the truth, the world would be my oyster. I was raised to be a gentleman and learned that these qualities would bring me respect.

2   While one has to earn respect, consideration is something owed to every human being. On Friday, June 16, 1999, when I was wrongfully arrested at my Harlem apartment building, my perception of everything I had learned as a

Alton Fitzgerald White

young man was forever changed—not only because I wasn't given even a second to use the manners my parents taught me, but mostly because the police, whom I'd always naively thought were supposed to serve and protect me, were actually hunting me.

3   I had planned a pleasant day. The night before was payday, plus I had received a standing ovation after portraying the starring role of Coalhouse Walker Jr. in the Broadway musical *Ragtime*. It is a role that requires not only talent but also an honest emotional investment of the morals and lessons I learned as a child.

4   Coalhouse Walker Jr. is a victim (an often misused word, but in this case true) of overt racism. His story is every black man's nightmare. He is hardworking, successful, talented, charismatic, friendly, and polite. Perfect prey for someone with authority and not even a fraction of those qualities. On that Friday afternoon, I became a real-life Coalhouse Walker. Nothing could have prepared me for it. Not even stories told to me by other black men who had suffered similar injustices.

5   Friday for me usually means a trip to the bank, errands, the gym, dinner, and then off to the theater. On this particular day, I decided to break my pattern of getting up and running right out of the house. Instead, I took my time, slowed my pace, and splurged by making strawberry pancakes. Before I knew it, it was 2:45; my bank closes at 3:30, leaving me less than 45 minutes to get to midtown Manhattan on the train. I was pressed for time but in a relaxed, blessed state of mind. When I walked through the lobby of my building, I noticed two light-skinned Hispanic men I'd never seen before. Not thinking much of it, I continued on to the vestibule, which is separated from the lobby by a locked door.

6   As I approached the exit, I saw people in uniforms rushing toward the door. I sped up to open it for them. I thought they might be paramedics, since many of the building's occupants are elderly. It wasn't until I had opened the door and greeted them that I recognized that they were police officers. Within seconds, I was told to "hold it"; they had received a call about young Hispanics with guns. I was told to get against the wall. I was searched, stripped of my backpack, put on my knees, handcuffed, and told to be quiet when I tried to ask questions.

7   With me were three other innocent black men who had been on their way to their U-Haul. They were moving into the apartment beneath mine, and I had just bragged to them about how safe the building was. One of these gentlemen got off his knees, still handcuffed, and unlocked the door for the officers to get into the lobby where the two strangers were standing. Instead of thanking or even acknowledging us, they led us out the door past our neighbors, who were all but begging the police in our defense.

8   The four of us were put into cars with the two strangers and taken to the precinct station at 165th and Amsterdam. The police automatically linked us,

with no questions and no regard for our character or our lives. No consideration was given to where we were going or why. Suppose an ailing relative was waiting upstairs, while I ran out for her medication? Or young children, who'd been told that Daddy was running to the corner store for milk and would be right back? My new neighbors weren't even allowed to lock their apartment or check on the U-Haul.

9   After we were lined up in the station, the younger of the two Hispanic men was identified as an experienced criminal, and drug residue was found in a pocket of the other. I now realize how naive I was to think that the police would then uncuff me, apologize for their mistake, and let me go. Instead, they continued to search my backpack, questioned me, and put me in jail with the criminals.

10   The rest of the nearly five-hour ordeal was like a horrible dream. I was handcuffed, strip-searched, taken in and out for questioning. The officers told me that they knew exactly who I was, knew I was in *Ragtime*, and that in fact they already had the men they wanted.

11   How then could they keep me there, or have brought me there in the first place? I was told it was standard procedure. As if the average law-abiding citizen knows what that is and can dispute it. From what I now know, "standard procedure" is something that every citizen, black and white, needs to learn, and fast.

12   I felt completely powerless. Why, do you think? Here I was, young, pleasant, and successful, in good physical shape, dressed in clean athletic attire. I was carrying a backpack containing a substantial paycheck and a deposit slip, on my way to the bank. Yet after hours and hours I was sitting at a desk with two officers who not only couldn't tell me why I was there but seemed determined to find something on me, to the point of making me miss my performance.

13   It was because I am a black man!

14   I sat in that cell crying silent tears of disappointment and injustice with the realization of how many innocent black men are convicted for no reason. When I was handcuffed, my first instinct had been to pull away out of pure insult and violation as a human being. Thank God I was calm enough to do what they said. When I was thrown in jail with the criminals and strip-searched, I somehow knew to put my pride aside, be quiet, and do exactly what I was told, hating it but coming to terms with the fact that in this situation I was a victim. They had guns!

15   Before I was finally let go, exhausted, humiliated, embarrassed, and still in shock, I was led to a room and given a pseudo-apology. I was told that I was at the wrong place at the wrong time. My reply? "I was where I live."

16   Everything I learned growing up in Cincinnati has been shattered. Life will never be the same.

—White, *The Nation*

After Reading

Checking Your Comprehension

_____ 1. The author's main purpose in this selection is to
   a. describe his recent experience with racism.
   b. discuss the effects of racism on young people.
   c. criticize the New York police department.
   d. contrast Cincinnati with New York.

_____ 2. Coalhouse Walker Jr. is the name of
   a. the author of the article.
   b. a black actor in New York.
   c. the main character in a Broadway play.
   d. a racist police officer.

_____ 3. The main idea of paragraph 5 is that the author
   a. had errands to take care of.
   b. was making strawberry pancakes.
   c. lives 45 minutes from midtown Manhattan.
   d. changed his routine and was enjoying a leisurely day.

_____ 4. The two strangers in the lobby of the building were
   a. friends of the author.
   b. new residents of the building.
   c. undercover police officers.
   d. suspected criminals.

_____ 5. After opening the door for the police, the author was
   a. thanked by the police and released to go.
   b. assaulted by criminals.
   c. handcuffed and taken away by the police.
   d. harassed by his neighbors.

_____ 6. "Life will never be the same" for the author because he
   a. can no longer trust in what he was raised to believe about manners and respect.
   b. was injured by the police.
   c. does not understand the criminal justice system.
   d. cannot face his neighbors.

Applying Your Skills: Following the Author's Thought Patterns

_____ 7. The main thought pattern used in this selection is
   a. definition.
   b. chronological order.
   c. enumeration.
   d. classification.

_____ 8. In paragraph 2, the transitional word or phrase that indicates the chronological order thought pattern is
   a. while.
   b. on Friday.
   c. because.
   d. but.

_____ 9. In paragraph 9, all of the following transitional words indicate the chronological order thought pattern _except_
   a. after.
   b. now.
   c. then.
   d. instead.

_____10. The main thought pattern used in paragraphs 12 and 13 is
   a. cause/effect.
   b. summary.
   c. enumeration.
   d. definition.

Studying Words

_____11. In paragraph 2, the word *naively* means
a. innocently.
b. negatively.
c. purposely.
d. unfortunately.

_____12. What is the correct pronunciation of the word *charismatic* (par. 4)?
a. KARE iz mat ik
b. kar IZ ma tick
c. kar iz MAT ik
d. kare IZ ma tick

_____13. The word *vestibule* (par. 5) originated from which of the following languages?
a. Latin
b. French
c. German
d. Greek

_____14. What is the best definition of the word *dispute* as it is used in paragraph 11?
a. strive to win
b. question the truth of
c. quarrel angrily
d. engage in discussion

_____15. The prefix of the word *pseudo-apology* (par. 15) indicates that the apology was
a. excessive.
b. false.
c. written.
d. small.

For more practice, ask your instructor for an opportunity to work on the mastery tests that appear in the Test Bank.

Thinking Visually

1. What does the photograph on page 313 contribute to this reading? What details do you notice about it that help you understand the author's story?

2. What does the title of this selection mean? What made the author's face "wrong"?

3. How is White's profession as an actor important to his story? (See p. 313.) Did being a well-known actor seem to help his situation with the police?

Thinking Critically About the Reading

1. Why was it significant that the strangers in the lobby were Hispanic?

2. How do you think you would react in a similar situation?

3. Have you ever been misjudged based on your outward appearance? What was your response? How was it similar to or different from the author's?

Academic Application: Summarizing the Reading

Directions: Academic articles, which often detail the results of original research, often contain an abstract that provides a brief summary of the complete article. Pretend you are writing an abstract of "Right Place, Wrong Face" and complete the following summary of the reading by filling in the blanks. The first three sentences are provided for you; write the remainder of the summary.

On June 16, 1999, Alton Fitzgerald White was starring in the Broadway musical *Ragtime*. On his way out that day, White saw Hispanic strangers in the lobby of his apartment building. Soon after, police officers arrived, responding to a call about Hispanic men with guns. _____

_____

_____

_____

_____

_____

_____

MASTERY TEST 2 Reading Selection

Why More People Are Single

Nijole V. Benokraitis

Before Reading

This selection appeared in a textbook for an introductory sociology course about marriages and families. The book's title is *Marriages and Families: Changes, Choices, and Constraints*. This excerpt comes from the chapter titled "Singlehood, Cohabitation, Civil Unions, and Other Options."

Previewing the Reading

Using the steps listed on page 49, preview the reading selection. When you have finished, complete the following items.

1. What is the topic of the selection? _____

2. Indicate whether each statement is true (T) or false (F).
    _____ a. The selection will discuss the many drawbacks to being single.
    _____ b. Single people tend to be dependent on others.
    _____ c. People with physical or mental handicaps are more likely to get married.

Predicting and Connecting

1. Are you currently single, dating, partnered, or married? In general, how do you personally feel about being single? Are you or would you be comfortable with it?

2. Based on your preview, do you expect the reading to be fairly easy to understand, of moderate difficulty, or challenging? Why?

> **Vocabulary Preview**
>
> **majority** (par. 1) more than half
> **starry-eyed** (par. 4) foolishly optimistic
> **peer** (par. 7) a person of the same age group or social status
> **incentive** (par. 10) motivation
> **domestic** (par. 12) household
> **covet** (par.15) want

During Reading

As you read the selection, complete each of the following. When highlighting, use a different color highlighter for each task.

a.   Highlight the topic sentence of each paragraph. If the main idea is unstated, write a sentence that states it.

b.   Highlight the most important details in each paragraph.

c.   Highlight useful transitional words and phrases that help you understand and connect the author's ideas.

d.   Read and respond to the questions in the margin

---

1   Marriage offers many benefits, but there are also incentives for being single. A majority of adults now believe that being married or being single makes little difference in social status (64 percent), finding happiness (62 percent), or getting ahead in a career (57 percent) (Pew Research Center, 2010). Let's begin with waiting to find an ideal partner, a soul mate, that one true love.

> Underline the two synonyms for "ideal partner."

2   **WAITING FOR A SOUL MATE** Singles sometimes delay marriage because they're waiting to meet their "ideal mate" or "one true love." A national survey found that 31 percent of men and 26 percent of women believed that there was only one true love (Cohn, 2013).

3   Some people believe that waiting for an ideal mate is unrealistic because a marriage involves more than emotional intimacy. If a person decides that a partner is no longer a soul mate, for example, she or he will become disillusioned and bail out. Some self-help authors advise women, especially, to settle for Mr. Not-Quite-Right instead of ending up alone (see Lipka, 2008). Also, the longer one waits to marry, the smaller the pool of eligible partners, especially among the never married.

> What is a "self-help author"?

4   Others contend that waiting for a soul mate isn't necessarily starry-eyed: "Perhaps more than ever before, young people have an opportunity to choose a partner on the basis of personal qualities and shared dreams, not economics or 'gender straitjackets'" (Rivers, 2001).

5   **BEING INDEPENDENT** One of the biggest benefits of singlehood is independence and autonomy because single people can do pretty much what they please. According to a 39-year-old female magazine employee, "Work is very social and I like the peace of coming home and not having to interact with anyone" (Klinenberg, 2012: 113). And as one of my 29-year-old female students once said, "I don't plan to marry until my feet have touched six of the seven continents."

> Is the author unethical or biased in the way she quotes one of her students? Why or why not?

Single professionals often work long hours at their jobs; sometimes this is because they want to advance their careers. Often, however, they are perceived as being less burdened with home and family responsibilities and have nothing better to do.

6   Singles with resources, such as high education levels and high-income jobs, are especially likely to be choosy about marriage partners. If they don't find someone with the traits they seek, both sexes are saying "no thanks" to marriage rather than giving up their freedom.

7   **ENJOYING CLOSE RELATIONSHIPS AND ACTIVITIES** A common reason for getting married is companionship. Singles who are delaying marriage rely on peers rather than a spouse for support and companionship. Especially in large cities, singles have close friends (sometimes called "urban tribes") with whom they socialize. They may meet weekly for dinner at a neighborhood restaurant, sometimes travel together, help move one another's furniture, or join athletic leagues (Watters, 2003). Singles are also involved in many community activities. For example, a friend's single, 50-something nephew coaches Little League and volunteers at a local dog shelter in Brooklyn.

Why is this cartoon amusing?

"We still have a few minor issues to work out: I want a huge wedding and he wants to be single."

8   Being unmarried isn't synonymous with isolation. Many singles are involved in family life, some live with their parents or close friends, and others spend much time with nieces, nephews, and grandchildren. Women, especially, devote much of their time and resources to supporting and caring for other family members.

9   **MAKING A COMMITMENT** There are more never-married men than women in almost all age groups. Why, then, do so many women complain that "there's nothing out there"? One reason is that many men simply don't want to get married.

Does the author's use of humor help you stay interested in the reading?

10   There's an old joke about single guys: "My girlfriend told me I should be more affectionate. So I got two girlfriends!" Some family practitioners believe that men are the foot draggers—especially when there's an abundance of potential girlfriends—because there's little incentive for them to marry. Many men put off marriage because of stagnant wages

and job losses, and they see marriage as a major economic responsibility that they don't want to undertake (Kreider, 2010; Mather and Lavery, 2010). Because of the greater acceptance of premarital sex, most men can have sex and intimate relationships without getting married.

> What is the author implying in the last sentence of this paragraph?

11   **HAVING CHILDREN** Only 44 percent of unmarried Americans believe that having children is a very important reason to marry (Pew Research Center, 2012). Because cohabitation and parenting outside marriage are widely accepted, singles of all ages feel less pressure to get married. The percentage of births to unmarried women rose from 18 percent in 1980 to 41 percent in 2011 (Federal Interagency Forum on Child and Family Statistics, 2013).

12   Some researchers call middle-class, professional, unmarried women who intentionally bear children "single mothers of choice" (Mattes, 1994; Hertz, 2006). Most of these women's first choice is to marry and then have children. However, as one 35-year-old mother said, "You can wait to have a partner and hope you can still have a baby. Or you can choose to let that go and have a baby on your own" (Orenstein, 2000: 149). Even if a woman finds a soul mate, he may not want to participate in child care and other domestic activities that many women now expect men to share.

13   **FEARING DIVORCE** Divorce or prolonged years of conflict between parents can have a negative effect on young adults' perceptions of marriage. Many stay single as long as possible because they worry about divorce. If children have grown up in homes where parents divorced one or more times, they're wary of repeating the same mistake. As one 21-year-old woman said, "My father left my mother when I was 6. I don't believe in divorce" (Herrmann, 2003).

> Write a brief marginal note that summarizes the section titled "Fearing Divorce."

14   Many singles are postponing marriage because they see it as a lifelong commitment that they might not be able to honor. According to a 24-year-old short-order cook who lives with his girlfriend, for instance, "Marriage is a big step. . . . I don't want to be one of those couples that gets married and three years later gets a divorce" (Gibson-Davis et al., 2005: 1309). Thus, many singles are hesitant to marry not because they don't believe in marriage but because they fear divorce.

15   **BEING HEALTHY AND PHYSICALLY ATTRACTIVE** Emotional and physical health and physical appeal also affect singlehood. In the marriage market, most men

Singles in large cities often go to nightclubs to meet people. Despite the racial and ethnic diversity and the large pool of eligible partners, many still can't find a mate. Why not?

are initially drawn only to good-looking women. On a scale of 1 to 10, men who are a 2 or a 3 often go after attractive women who have many options among handsome suitors. In mismatches, "men pursue prizes beyond their grasp, when they could be perfectly content with someone who isn't viewed as a great catch. So these men lose, not only by failing to get what they covet but also in a chance for a happy ending" (Hacker, 2003: 191). People with severe physical or emotional problems are also more likely to remain single longer or not marry at all (Wilson, 2002).

> Why do you think people with physical or emotional problems remain single longer?

—Benokraitis, *Marriages and Families: Changes, Choices, and Constraints*, pp. 250–253

After Reading

Checking Your Comprehension

_____ 1. Which of the following is *not* a reason why people choose to remain single?
   a. They believe that children are better off with only one parent.
   b. They are waiting for their soul mate.
   c. They like being independent.
   d. They fear divorce.

_____ 2. Men put off marriage for all of the following reasons *except*
   a. the relative scarcity of eligible, single women.
   b. they can have intimate relationships and sex without getting married.
   c. they see marriage as a major financial responsibility.
   d. there is little incentive for them to marry.

_____ 3. Which of the following statements is *false*?
   a. Unattractive single men often pursue very attractive women.
   b. Many singles are hesitant to marry not because they don't believe in marriage but because they fear divorce.
   c. Single women often devote much of their time to caring for family members.
   d. The longer one waits to marry, the larger the pool of never-married eligible partners.

_____ 4. The term used in the reading to refer to a group of close friends who live and socialize in a city is
   a. swees (SWIs, or singles with income).
   b. urban tribe.
   c. metropolitan league.
   d. DINKs (dual income, no kids).

_____ 5. Which of the following is true of single people with high levels of resources, such as education and income?
   a. They tend to marry early in life.
   b. They tend to be picky about marriage partners.
   c. They tend to marry a mate who has been chosen by their parents.
   d. They usually prefer to remain childless.

Applying Your Skills: Following the Author's Thought Patterns

_____ 6 The overall thought pattern used in this reading is _____, as signaled by the word "why" in the title.
a. chronological order
b. classification
c. cause/effect
d. definition

_____ 7. The primary thought pattern used in paragraph 12 is
a. definition.
b. spatial order.
c. classification.
d. comparison/contrast.

_____ 8. Paragraph 13 uses all of the following thought patterns _except_
a. cause/effect.
b. illustration/example.
c. definition.
d. statement and clarification.

_____ 9. Which paragraph provides a "reverse definition," defining a term by what it does _not_ mean?
a. paragraph 2
b. paragraph 5
c. paragraph 8
d. paragraph 15

_____ 10. Which of the following transitional words or phrases signals the illustration pattern in paragraph 3?
a. some people
b. because
c. for example
d. also

Studying Words

Using context or a dictionary, define each of the following words as it is used in the reading.

1. disillusioned (par. 3) _____

2. autonomy (par. 5) _____

3. urban (par. 7) _____

4. stagnant (par. 10) _____

5. cohabitation (par. 11) _____

Thinking Visually

1. What point is the cartoonist trying to make in the cartoon on page 320?

2. What other types of photos, charts, or visual aids might be useful with this selection?

3. Write an alternative caption for the photo on page 321. The caption should tie the photo to a key point in the reading.

4. Create a map of the reading, following the directions on page 96.

Thinking Critically About the Reading

1. How would you describe the author's attitude toward singlehood? In general, would you describe her tone as judgmental or nonjudgmental? Why?

2. The reading lists reasons why people choose to remain single. Provide at least five reasons that people choose to marry.

3. The reading identifies two behaviors that may lead to unhappiness, one in paragraph 3 and one in paragraph 15. What are these behaviors?

4. Evaluate the author's use of examples in paragraphs 5 and 13. Do these examples provide enough support for the topic sentence of each paragraph? Why or why not?

Academic Application: Writing an Outline

Directions: You are preparing for an essay exam. You predict the following question will be on the exam: "List and discuss at least five reasons that people may choose to remain single." To study for the exam, you decide to outline the reading selection. Complete the outline that begins below.

Reasons for Remaining Single

1. Waiting for a soul mate
   - looking for one true love
   - some say an ideal mate is unrealistic; others believe you shouldn't settle

2. Being independent
   - _____

3. _____
   - _____

4. _____
   - _____

5. _____
   - _____

CHAPTER

9

Interpreting the Writer's Message and Purpose

Focusing on . . . Interpreting What You Read

"The internet brings everyone closer."

LEARNING GOALS

This chapter will show you how to

1 Understand connotative meanings

2 Make inferences about what you read

3 Understand figurative language

4 Discover the author's purpose

5 Recognize tone

6 Examine language

What point or message does this cartoon convey? While the point is clear, it is not directly stated. You had to use the information in the cartoon to reason out its point. This chapter concentrates on the reasoning processes readers must use to figure out ideas that are not directly stated.

Up to this point, we have been primarily concerned with organizing information for learning and recall, building vocabulary, and understanding a writer's main ideas, details, organizational patterns, and transitions. So far, each chapter has been concerned with understanding what the author says, with factual content. Now our focus must change. To read well, you must go beyond what the author says and also consider what he or she means.

Many writers directly state some ideas but only hint at others. It is left to the reader to pick up the clues or suggestions and use logic and reasoning skills to figure out the writer's unstated message as you did with the cartoon on the first page of this chapter. This chapter will explain several features of writing that suggest meaning. Once you are familiar with these, you will better understand the writer's unstated message. This chapter will also discuss how to discover the author's purpose, recognize the author's tone, and examine the author's language.

CONNOTATIVE MEANINGS

1 LEARNING GOAL

Understand connotative meanings

Which of the following would you like to be a part of: a *crowd*, *mob*, *gang*, *audience*, *congregation*, or *class*? Each of these words has the same basic meaning: "an assembled group of people." But each has a different *shade* of meaning. *Crowd* suggests a large, disorganized group. *Audience*, on the other hand, suggests a quiet, controlled group. Try to decide what meaning each of the other words in the list suggests.

This example shows that words have two levels of meaning—a literal meaning and an additional shade of meaning. These two levels of meaning are called denotative and connotative. A word's **denotative meaning** is the meaning stated in the dictionary—its literal meaning. A word's **connotative meaning** is the additional implied meanings, or nuances, that a word may take on. Often the connotative meaning carries either a positive or negative, favorable or unfavorable impression. The words *mob* and *gang* have a negative connotation because they imply a disorderly, disorganized group. *Congregation*, *audience*, and *class* have a positive connotation because they suggest an orderly, organized group.

Here are a few more examples. Would you prefer to be described as "slim" or "skinny"? As "intelligent" or "brainy"? As "heavy" or "fat"? As "particular" or "picky"? Notice that each pair of words has a similar literal meaning, but that each word within the pair has a different connotation.

Depending on the words they choose, writers can suggest favorable or unfavorable impressions of the person, object, or event they are describing. For example, through the writer's choice of words, the two sentences on the next page create two entirely different impressions. As you read them, underline words that have a positive or negative connotation.

> The unruly crowd forced its way through the restraint barriers and ruthlessly attacked the rock star.
>
> The enthusiastic group of fans burst through the fence and rushed toward the rock star.

When reading any type of informative or persuasive material, pay attention to the writer's choice of words. Often a writer may communicate subtle or hidden messages, or he or she may encourage the reader to feel positive or negative about the subject.

Read the following paragraph on athletes' nutrition and, as you read, underline words that have a strong positive or negative connotation.

> Athletes tend to eat either too much or too little protein, depending on their health consciousness, accuracy of nutrition education, or lifestyle. Some athletes fill up on too much meat. Others proclaim themselves vegetarian, yet they sometimes neglect to replace the beef with beans and are, in fact, only non-meat-eaters—and often protein deficient, at that. Although slabs of steak and huge hamburgers have no place in any athlete's diet—or anyone's diet—adequate amounts of protein are important for building muscles and repairing tissues.
>
> —Clark, *Nancy Clark's Sports Nutrition Guidebook*, pp. 21–22

Did you mark words such as *fill up on*, *neglect*, *deficient*, *slabs*, and *huge*?

EXERCISE **9-1** **Examining Connotative Meanings**

Directions: For each of the following pairs of words, underline the word with the more positive connotation.

1. _____   demand

2. _____   neglect

3. ridicule   ____

4. _____   stare

5. _____   expose

6. garment   ____

7. gaudy   _____

8. clumsy   _____

9. _____   fake

10. token   _____

EXERCISE **9-2**   **Writing Positive Connotations**

Directions: For each word listed below, write a word that has a similar denotative meaning but a negative connotation. Then write a word that has a positive connotation. Use your dictionary or thesaurus, if necessary.

	Negative	Positive
Example: eat	gobble	dine
1. take	_____	_____
2. ask	_____	_____
3. look at	_____	_____
4. walk	_____	_____
5. dress	_____	_____
6. music	_____	_____
7. car	_____	_____
8. laugh	_____	_____
9. large	_____	_____
10. woman	_____	_____

IMPLIED MEANINGS

2 LEARNING GOAL

Make inferences about what you read

An **inference** is an educated guess or prediction about something unknown based on available facts and information. It is the logical connection that you draw between what you observe or know and what you do not know.

Suppose that you arrive ten minutes late for your sociology class. All the students have papers in front of them, and everyone is busily writing. Some students have worried or concerned looks on their faces. The instructor is seated and is reading a book. What is happening? From the known information you can make an inference about what you do not know. Did you figure out that the instructor had given the class a surprise quiz? If so, then you made a logical inference.

While the inference you made is probably correct, you cannot be sure until you speak with the instructor. Occasionally a logical inference can be wrong. Although it is unlikely, perhaps the instructor has laryngitis and has written notes on the board for the students to copy. Some students may look worried because they do not understand what the notes mean.

Here are more everyday situations. Make an inference for each.

- You are driving on an expressway and you notice a police car with flashing red lights behind you. You check your speedometer and notice that you are going ten miles an hour over the speed limit.
- A woman seated alone in a bar nervously glances at everyone who enters. Every few minutes she checks her watch.

In the first situation, a good inference might be that you are going to be stopped for speeding. However, it is possible that the officer only wants to pass you to get to an accident ahead or to stop someone driving faster than you. In the second situation, one inference is that the woman is waiting to meet someone who is late.

The following paragraph is taken from a book by Jenny Lawson called *Let's Pretend This Never Happened: (A Mostly True Memoir)*. First, read it for factual content.

When I was little, my father used to sell guns and ammo at a sporting goods store, but I always told everyone he was an arms dealer, because it sounded more exciting. Eventually, though, he saved up enough money to quit his job and build a taxidermy shop next to our house (which was tiny and built out of asbestos back when people still thought that was a good thing). My dad built the taxidermy shop himself out of old wood from abandoned barns and did a remarkable job, fashioning it to look exactly like a Wild West saloon, complete with swinging doors and gaslights and a hitching post for horses. Then he hired a bunch of guys to work for him, many of whom looked to me as if they were fresh from prison or just about to go back in. I can't help feeling sorry for the confused strangers who would wander into my father's taxidermy shop, expecting to find a bar and a stiff drink, and who instead found several rough-looking men my father had hired, covered in blood and elbow deep in animal carcasses. I suspect, though, that the blood-covered taxidermists probably shared their personal flasks with the baffled stranger, because although they seemed slightly dangerous, they also were invariably good-hearted, and I'm fairly certain they recognized that anyone stumbling onto that kind of scene would probably need a strong drink even more than when they'd first set out looking for a bar to begin with.

—Lawson, *Let's Pretend This Never Happened: (A Mostly True Memoir)*, p. 18

The paragraph is primarily factual—it tells who did what, when, and where. However, some ideas are not directly stated and must be inferred from the information given. Here are a few examples. Some are fairly obvious inferences; others are less obvious.

- The author sometimes exaggerates.
- Asbestos is dangerous.
- The author's father had building skills.
- People mistook the taxidermy shop for a bar.
- Taxidermy involves removing the innards from animal carcasses.
- Taxidermy can be an upsetting process to watch.

Although none of the above ideas are directly stated, they can be inferred from clues provided in the passage. Some of the statements could be inferred from actions, others by adding facts together, and still others by the writer's choice of words.

Now read the following passage to find out what has happened to Katja's brother.

Due to her own hardship, Katja was not thrilled when her younger brother called her from Warsaw and said that he was going to join her in the U.K. Katja warned him that opportunities were scarce in London for a Polish immigrant. "Don't worry," he said in an effort to soothe her anxiety. "I already have a job in a factory."

An advertisement in a Warsaw paper had promised good pay for Polish workers in Birmingham. A broker's fee of $500 and airfare were required, so her brother borrowed the money from their mother. He made the trip with a dozen other young Polish men.

The "broker" picked the young men up at Heathrow and piled them in a van. They drove directly to Birmingham, and at nightfall the broker dropped the whole crew off at a ramshackle house inside the city. He ordered them to be ready to be picked up in the morning for their first day of work. A bit dazed by the pace, they stretched out on the floor to sleep.

Their rest was brief. In the wee hours of the night, the broker returned with a gang of 10 or so thugs armed with cricket bats. They beat the young Polish boys to a pulp and robbed them of all their valuables. Katja's brother took some heavy kicks to the ribs and head, then stumbled out of the house. Once outside, he saw two police cars parked across the street. The officers in the cars obviously chose to ignore the mayhem playing out in front of their eyes. Katja's brother knew better than try to convince them otherwise; the police in Poland would act no differently. Who knows, maybe they were part of the broker's scam. Or maybe they just didn't care about a bunch of poor Polish immigrants "invading" their town.

—Batstone, "Katja's Story," as appeared in *Sojourners Magazine*, June 2006

If you made the right inferences, you realized that Katja's brother became a victim of a scam. Let's look at the kinds of clues the writer gave that led to this inference.

1. **Description.** By the way the writer describes what happened to Katja's brother, you begin to understand the situation. He is promised a well-paying job, but is told that job opportunities are scarce for Polish immigrants. A broker's fee of $500 is charged. The house they are taken to on arrival is described as *ramshackle*. The young men slept on the floor.

2. **Conversation.** The brother sounded very confident, perhaps over-confident: "Don't worry. I already have a job in a factory."

3. **Action.** The actions make it clear what is happening. The brother is "piled" into a van with 12 other workers. They are robbed and brutally beaten after arriving at the house. The police do not respond.

4. **Writer's commentary/details.** As the writer describes the situation, he provides numerous clues. The trip was made with a dozen other men. The word *broker* is placed in quotation marks, suggesting the term is inaccurate or questionable. The men's rest was described as *brief*, suggesting that something is about to change. The broker returns with people the writer calls a "gang of . . . thugs." The police are described as having obviously chosen "to ignore the mayhem."

How to Make Inferences

Making an inference is a thinking process. As you read, you are following the author's thoughts. You are also alert for ideas that are suggested but not directly stated. Because inference is a logical thought process, there is no simple step-by-step procedure to follow. Each inference depends entirely on the situation, the facts provided, and the reader's knowledge and experience.

However, here are a few guidelines to keep in mind as you read. These will help you get in the habit of looking beyond the factual level to the inferential.

Making Inferences

1. **Be sure you understand the literal meaning.** You should have a clear grasp of the key idea and supporting details of each paragraph.

2. **Notice details.** Often a detail provides a clue that will help you make an inference. When you spot a striking or unusual detail, ask yourself, Why did the writer include this piece of information?

(Continued)

3. **Add up the facts.** Consider all the facts taken together. Ask yourself, What is the writer trying to suggest from this set of facts? What do all these facts and ideas point toward?

4. **Watch for clues.** The writer's choice of words and detail often suggest his or her attitude toward the subject. Notice, in particular, descriptive words, emotionally charged words, and words with strong positive or negative connotations.

5. **Be sure your inference is supportable.** An inference must be based on fact. Make sure there is sufficient evidence to justify any inference you make.

EXERCISE 9-3   Making Inferences

Directions: Read each of the following passages. Then answer the questions that follow. You will need to reason out, or infer, the answers.

Passage A

Schmoozing

If we want to be successful, we need to develop and enhance our conversational prowess in the face to face space. Schmooze or lose is the rule for both personal and professional success. Schmooze means relaxed, friendly, easygoing conversation. Period. End of story. There is no end result that is preplanned as a goal. Formal research from Harvard to Stanford and places in between indicates that the ability to converse and communicate is a key factor of successful leaders. Oral communication skills are consistently rated in the top three most important skill sets in surveys by universities and workplace specialists.

While we're able to communicate digitally, we must still be proficient in the face to face shared space as well as in cyberspace. As corporations continue to merge, jobs disappear and industries are offshored, we need conversation and communication more than ever before.

—RoAne, *Face to Face*, pp. 2–3

1. What is the author's attitude toward digital communication?

_____

2. Not everyone loves to schmooze. Why does the author think it is essential for success?

_____

3. What information sources does the author trust?

_____

4. What do you think the author considers success to be?

_____

_____

Passage B

Government Surveillance

Governments have long relied on . . . spying. What is new about today's surveillance is the ease with which it can be conducted; over the past several decades, technological advances have vastly expanded the government's monitoring ability. Wiretapping and bugging have been joined by space-age eavesdropping and computer-hacking techniques that make interception of oral and written communications infinitely easier than in J. Edgar Hoover's day. Observation of physical activities, once reliant on naked eye observation and simple devices like binoculars, can now be carried out with night scopes and thermal imagers, sophisticated telescopic and magnification devices, tracking tools and "see-through" detection technology. Records of transactions with hospitals, banks, stores, schools, and other institutions, until the 1980s usually found only in file cabinets, are now much more readily obtained with the advent of computers and the Internet.

A second difference between the surveillance of yesteryear and today is the strength of the government's resolve to use it. Especially since September 11, 2001, the United States government has been obsessed, as perhaps it should be, with ferreting out national security threats, and modern surveillance techniques— ranging from data mining to global positioning systems—have played a major role in this pursuit. But the new surveillance has also increasingly been aimed at ordinary criminals, including those who represent only a trivial threat to public safety. And more than

Which surveillance technique does this image illustrate?

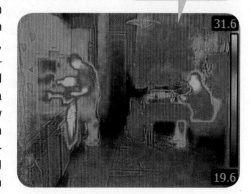

occasionally it has also visited significant intrusion on large numbers of law-abiding citizens—sometimes inadvertently, sometimes not.

Sophisticated surveillance technology and a powerful government eager to take advantage of it make a dangerous combination—a recipe for continuous mass surveillance. While surveillance can be a valuable law enforcement tool, it also poses a significant threat to our legitimate freedoms—to express what we believe, to do what we want to do, to be the type of person we really are. In short, it can diminish our privacy and autonomy.

—Slobogin, *Privacy at Risk*, pp. 3–4

5. What is the author's attitude toward the government?

_____

6. Why should the government be more interested in monitoring the behavior of its citizens today?

_____

7. How are surveillance techniques being misused?

_____

8. Where do you think the author stands on the issue of right to privacy? (What rights to privacy do we or should we have?)

_____

Passage C

UFOs

There should be little doubt that many claimed sightings of ghosts, UFOs, angels, and monsters by sincere witnesses are a result of the way our vision works. Contrary to what you may have assumed, we don't really "see" what we look at. What happens when you aim your eyes at something is that your brain "tells" you what you see. And your brain never tells you with 100 percent accuracy. It does this to be efficient and it really does help us function in a world with far too much detail and movement to take in. But sometimes this causes us to "see" things that were never there or at least not there in the form presented to us. It can also cause us to miss things that really are there. Sometimes things that our vision misses might have been the critical pieces of information that would have revealed to us that the UFO or ghost hovering out there is really just a bird or a patch of fog, for example.

—Harrison, *50 Popular Beliefs that People Think Are True*, p. 31

9. What do most people who see UFOs, ghosts, or angels believe about their sightings?

_____

10. What relationship does the brain have to the eyes?

_____

11. How is it helpful to not see everything?

_____

12. How does the brain cause us to see things that are not real?

_____

_____

_____

Passage D

Personal Comfort Zone

It's an uncomfortable fact of life, but there are people in this world who simply can't live in peace with their fellow human beings. You try to cultivate a love your neighbor philosophy, and then some mutant wrecks it by killing you. Regrettably, one violent encounter can cut short a lifetime of altruism. So you must make a personal decision either to be wholly trusting (and vulnerable) or ever vigilant. Vigilance doesn't mean you have to walk around angry. Indeed, if you take the emotion out of it, vigilance merely becomes a relaxed, practical exercise for fully participating in life.

For example, establish a personal comfort zone that no stranger is allowed to enter. This is not paranoia, just good practical sense. You need a trigger that allows you to stay relaxed most of the time. At a minimum, the zone is about as far as you can extend your arm or leg.

—Perkins et al., *Attack Proof*, p. 7

13. What attitude would you predict the author would have toward his co-workers?

_____

14. How realistic is it to keep a stranger-proof comfort zone the distance of our outstretched arm?

_____

15. Does the author anticipate that not all readers will agree with his ideas? How do you know?

_____

_____

16. How would the author define the term *comfort zone*?

_____

EXERCISE **9-4**   **Making Inferences**

Directions: Read each of the following passages and answer the questions that follow.

Passage A

Working Moms

Always a career woman, Sharon Allen panicked when she had her first child. "I thought, 'How can I have my career and a child?'" recalls the now-longtime law enforcement official. "The minute I held her, I knew she was the most important thing in my life."

Thus began Allen's personal and professional journey as a working mother and wife (she's been married to her husband for 28 years) that blended child care with police work. Whether she was a detective or now the assistant police chief, she had irregular hours and at one time worked a 4–10 shift giving her three days off—one day to take care of the house, one to be at the kids' school, and one for herself. During that time, she earned her BS and Masters Degree in Education at a local college, and even worked part-time as a security guard at a mall to make ends meet.

"I was doing well with my career even as a working mother before it was in style . . . and yes, sometimes I felt I had to work twice as hard. I made mistakes, too, such as when my son was in high school, and I badgered him to cut his long hair. 'Mother,' he said, 'I am a good person . . . I follow your rules and stay out of trouble . . . If I have long hair, it's not a big deal;' I learned to compromise. (He's now at West Point!)

"That 'S' on my chest can fade sometimes. I used to crash and burn and sleep on the weekends. People say I am so successful—I say if my children have grown up to be self-sufficient, good citizens, I've been a pretty good mom. Half the battle in life is choosing something you love to do. You need to have that sense of accomplishment in your heart and to serve people the way you would like to be served. That's key."

—Greenberg and Avigdor, *What Happy Working Mothers Know*, p. 97

1. What is Sharon Allen's attitude toward working mothers?

   _____

2. What does the "S" on her chest stand for?

   _____

3. Why do you think the author chose to profile Sharon Allen for a book about happy working mothers?

   _____

   _____

4. Why might Sharon have had to work twice as hard as others?

   _____

   _____

Passage B

Why Manners Matter

When we leave home, driven by the overwhelming need to earn a living or go to the January sales or eat good Italian food, our apprehension about what we might encounter in the world proves to be negatively reinforcing. We put on our dark glasses and avoid eye contact. Increasingly we plug in our iPods: less for tuning into the music than tuning out the people around us. We talk or text on our cell phones constantly, on the train or bus, in the shops and cinemas, on the street. It's as if we deprive ourselves of immediate sensory stimulation—shade our eyes, block our ears, stop our mouths—in order to experience the world through a protective mask.

Finally, when with reluctant resignation we do interact with a stranger—with say, a taxi driver or a coffee barista or a checkout person at the super-market—we do it all with sign language and half sentences, often still talking on the phone to someone (anyone!) else as if to distract our attention away from the irritations inherent in any physical, material encoun-ter with untested individuals. People we need, and upon whose goodwill we depend.

> What idea in the passage does this photograph illustrate?

In our efforts to avoid all the latent rudeness and unpleasantness in the world, we, too, have become harder, and ruder, and less pleasant. Yet the more we distrust each other, the more we are confused and irritated by each other, the greater the risk that we abandon the task of finding a common language with which to peacefully interact.

In my block of units there's a different but connected problem. We share the same building, we see each other regularly, we pass close by each other in the foyer and on the stairs. But because we don't have manners, we have no formula for successfully relating to each other. Living in the noisy hubbub of the city, each one of us wants to protect our privacy, especially at home. Me, too. I consider myself something of an urban hermit. I don't want to be friends with people purely because we live in close proximity. On the other hand, it's rather strange to pretend you have no knowledge of someone who lives across the hall.

So when we cross paths we all shut our eyes or mumble Hi—but it's awkward. No one wants to cross that dreaded threshold into cozy familiarity or, God forbid, mutual obligation. Here is where manners would come in handy. In a more mannered world, we'd simply get the introductions over with, have a cup of tea and then return to pleasant but formal distance. Good morning Lovely day, isn't it? we would say. But instead we scuff and shuffle and we're not sure whether to smile or not and the whole process is uncomfortable. The fear of over familiarity with our neighbors has led to an inability to relate to each other in any way at all.

—Holdforth, *Why Manners Matter*, pp. 16–17

5. What assumption does the author make about anyone who ventures out in public?

_____

6. Why does the author think that people want to isolate themselves?

_____

7. The author infers that people feel uncomfortable around close neighbors because they scuff and shuffle. Is this a reasonable inference?

_____

8. How and why would manners be helpful?

_____

9. The author states we talk on phones to avoid talking to people face-to-face. Do you agree with this assumption?

_____

EXERCISE **9-5**   **Making Inferences**

Working Together

Directions: Bring a magazine ad to class. Working in groups of three or four students, make as many inferences as possible about each ad. For example, answer questions such as "What is happening?" "How does each person feel?" and "How will this ad sell the product?" Group members who differ in their opinions should present evidence to support their own inferences. Each group should then state to the class, as clearly as possible, the purpose of each ad. Be specific; try to say more than "To sell the product."

FIGURATIVE LANGUAGE

3 LEARNING GOAL

Understand figurative language

Read each of the following statements:

> The cake tasted like a moist sponge.
> The wilted plants begged for water.
> Jean wore her heart on her sleeve.

You know that a cake cannot really have the same taste as a sponge, that plants do not actually request water, and that a person's heart cannot really be attached to her sleeve. However, you know what message the writer is communicating in each sentence. The cake was soggy and tasteless, the plants were extremely dry, and Jean revealed her feelings to everyone around her.

Each of these sentences is an example of figurative language. **Figurative language** is a way of describing something that makes sense on an imaginative level but not on a factual or literal level. Notice that while none of the above expressions is literally true, each is meaningful. In many figurative expressions, one thing is compared with another for some quality they have in common. Take, for example, the familiar expression in the following sentence:

> Sam eats like a horse.

The diagram below shows the comparison being made in this figurative expression:

> A horse eats large amounts of food.

> Sam eats large amounts of food.

> Sam eats like a horse.

You can see that two unlike things—Sam and a horse—are compared because they are alike in one particular way—the amount they eat.

The purpose of figurative language is to paint a word picture—to help you visualize how something looks, feels, or smells. Figurative language is a device writers use to express an idea or feeling and, at the same time, allow the reader the freedom of imagination. Since it is not factual, figurative language allows the writer to express attitudes and opinions without directly stating them. Depending on the figurative expression chosen, a writer can create a variety of impressions.

When reading an article that contains figurative language, be sure to pay close attention to the images and feelings created. Be sure you recognize that the writer is shaping your response to the topic or subject.

Figurative language is used in many types of articles and essays. It is also used in everyday speech and in slang expressions. Various types of literature, especially poetry, also use figurative language. Notice its use in the following excerpt from a play by William Shakespeare.

> All the world's a stage,
> And all the men and women merely players;
> They have their exits and entrances;
> And one man in his time plays many parts.
>
> —Shakespeare, *As You Like It*, II, vii, 139

Here are a few more examples from other sources. Notice how each creates a visual image of the person, object, or quality being described.

> The red sun was pasted in the sky like a wafer.
>
> —Stephen Crane, *The Red Badge of Courage*
>
> In plucking the fruit of memory,
> one runs the risk of spoiling its bloom.
>
> —Joseph Conrad
>
> "I will speak daggers to her, but use none."
>
> —Shakespeare, *Hamlet*
>
> Life, like a dome of many-colored glass,
> Stains the white radiance of Eternity.
>
> —Shelley, "Adonais"

EXERCISE **9-6**   ## Analyzing Figurative Expressions

Directions: Each of the following sentences includes a figurative expression. Read each sentence and explain in your own words what the expression means.

1. My psychology quiz was a piece of cake.

   _____

2. My life is a junkyard of broken dreams.

   _____

3. "Life is as tedious as a twice-told tale." (Shakespeare, *King John III*)

   _____

4. "A sleeping child gives me the impression of a traveler in a very far country." (Ralph Waldo Emerson)

   _____

5. "I refuse to accept the cynical notion that nation after nation must spiral down a militaristic stairway into the hell of thermonuclear destruction." (Martin Luther King, Jr.)

   _____

EXERCISE **9-7**   ## Analyzing Passages

Directions: Read each of the following passages and answer the questions that follow.

Passage A

Doing Time Together

1   Toward the end of visiting hours today, Grace, who is married to a man serving a life sentence, came out of the prison.[1] I've seen Grace visiting San Quentin since 1995. She always greets me warmly but has never really opened up to me about her personal life—so I was particularly intrigued when she said excitedly, "I have a present in the gift shop! Come on, you can come get it with me." The gift shop (or "hobby shop" as is it officially called by the San Quentin authorities) is located just outside the main gate of the prison and is staffed by one highly trusted inmate decked out in a blindingly bright yellow jumpsuit (an outfit mandated after a hobby

_____
[1]Grace is a pseudonym, as are the names of all the participants.

What does this photograph reveal about the man and woman?

shop worker wearing the customary prison attire of a chambray shirt and blue jeans walked away from his post and into the "free" world unnoticed). This particular store consists of a dimly lit sallow room with three long display cases arranged like a horseshoe. Inside the cases and hanging on the walls are hundreds of objects crafted by prisoners, available for purchase by anyone who takes a fancy to them: paintings, drawings, earrings, note cards, clocks, and other trinkets produced by those inmates lucky enough to be permitted to engage in such "hobbies" behind the walls.

2   As we strolled the short distance to the shop, Grace explained that her wedding anniversary was this week and her husband had made a gift for her that she could now retrieve. Before I could ask any questions we reached the front of the shop and came upon the prisoner–worker standing outside the door, smoking. Visibly eager to claim her present, Grace told the worker that she had a gift to collect but added kindly, "You can finish your cigarette first." The man smiled shyly and took a few more self-conscious puffs, then stubbed out the cigarette and headed into the shop. Once inside he seemed a little uncertain of what to do, so Grace coached him through the process of giving her the correct form to fill out and of locating her gift, noting wryly, "I've done this a few times before." She signed the paperwork, and the inmate handed over a package about double the size of a shoe box, which Grace clutched to her chest. "I already know what it is," she told me, her voice quickening with anticipation. "Come on, we can go to the car and open it."

3   We walked over to the parking lot, and she set the gift on the hood of her car, unlocked the vehicle's door and threw her jacket inside, then pulled a pocket knife out of the glove compartment and began slitting open the box. Tearing away the protective packaging, Grace lifted out a wooden jewelry box, the general style of which I recognized from the others on display in the hobby shop. It was beautifully made, and Grace commented happily on the luster of the orange-colored wood and the obvious attention to detail. We both stood there admiring it, and then she opened the lid, revealing that it doubled as a music box: a tune began to tinkle, and I recognized it as a popular ballad for lovers, "Unchained Melody": "Oh, my love, my darling/I've hungered for your touch, a long lonely time/And time goes by so slowly and time can do so much."

4   While I was listening to the little chimes, I stole a glance at Grace and saw that she was teary eyed. Without saying anything, she set down the box and turned and wrapped her arms around me. We stood there hugging each other, much harder and longer than I had ever hugged her before, and the tightness of her clutch overwhelmed me with sadness. My melancholy was keenly intensified by the gray misty December weather, a fitting backdrop for the bleak scene: a lonely woman with only a graduate student conducting her fieldwork for company, opening her

anniversary gift on the hood of a car in a deserted prison parking lot, having just said goodbye to her husband before leaving him to be locked back into his cell . . . as he likely would be for a great many anniversaries to come.

—Comfort, *Doing Time Together: Love and Family in the Shadow of the Prison*, pp. 1–2

1. Answer each of the following questions by making an inference.

   a. How does wearing a yellow jumpsuit prevent the inmate from escaping?

   _____

   b. Why is it odd to call the activities the prisoners engage in "hobbies"?

   _____

   c. Why did Grace let the prisoner finish his cigarette?

   _____

   _____

   d. How does the reader know that Grace is familiar with the prison?

   _____

   _____

   e. Why is Grace's pocket knife in her car and not in her purse or on her person?

   _____

   f. What does the music say about Grace's relationship with her husband?

   _____

   g. What is unusual about the way Grace is celebrating her anniversary?

   _____

   _____

2. List several words with negative connotations that suggest how the writer feels about the prison.

   _____

3. List several words with positive connotations that suggest how the writer feels about the woman she is with.

   _____

4. What main point do you think the writer is trying to make?

   _____

Passage B

Avatar Fantasy Life: The Blurring Lines of Reality

1   Dissatisfied with your current life? Would you like to become someone else? Maybe someone rich? Maybe someone with no responsibilities? You can. Join a world populated with virtual people and live out your fantasy.

2   For some, the appeal is strong. *Second Life*, one of several Internet sites that offer an alternative virtual reality, has exploded in popularity. Of its 8 million "residents," 450,000 spend twenty to forty hours a week in their second life.

3   To start your second life, you select your avatar, a kind of digital hand puppet, to be your persona in this virtual world. Your avatar comes in just a basic form, although you can control its movements just fine. But that bare body certainly won't do. You will want to clothe it. For this, you have your choice of outfits for every occasion. Although you buy them from other avatars in virtual stores, you have to spend real dollars. You might want some hair, too. For that, too, you'll have your choice of designers. And again, you'll spend real dollars. And you might want to have a sex organ. There is even a specialty store for that.

4   All equipped the way you want to be?

5   Then it is time to meet other avatars, the virtual personas of real-life people. In this virtual world, they buy property, open businesses, and interact with one another. They share stories, talk about their desires in life, and have drinks in virtual bars.

6   Avatars flirt, too. Some even date and marry.

7   For most people, this second life is just an interesting game. They come and go. Some people, though, get so caught up in their virtual world that their real world shrinks in appeal, and they neglect friends and family. That is, they neglect their real friends and family, but remain attentive to their virtual friends and family. As the virtual replaces the real, the virtual becomes real and the real fades into nonreality.

—Henslin, *Sociology: A Down-to-Earth Approach*, p. 153

5. What is the author's attitude toward avatars?

_____

6. Explain why the phrase "digital hand puppet" is an example of figurative language.

_____

_____

7. Why does the author put the word "residents" in quotation marks?

_____

_____

8. What kind of tone is the author using when he says, "But that bare body certainly won't do"?

_____

9. When the author says, "All equipped the way you want to be?" what is the author suggesting about the choices available for avatars?

_____

_____

_____

10. What does the author think about how avatars affect people's perception of reality?

_____

_____

UNDERSTAND THE AUTHOR'S PURPOSE

4 **LEARNING GOAL**
Discover the author's purpose

Writers have many different reasons or purposes for writing. Read the statements below and try to decide why each was written:

> 1. About 14,000 ocean-going ships pass through the Panama Canal each year. This averages about three ships per day.
> 2. *New Unsalted Dry Roasted Almonds.* Finally, a snack with a natural flavor and without salt. We simply shell the nuts and dry-roast them until they're crispy and crunchy. Try a jar this week.
> 3. Man is the only animal that blushes or has a need to.
> 4. If a choking person has fallen down, first turn him or her face up. Then knit together the fingers of both your hands and apply pressure with the heel of your bottom hand to the victim's abdomen.
> 5. If your boat capsizes, it is usually safer to cling to the boat than to try to swim ashore.

Statement 1 was written to give information, 2 to persuade you to buy almonds, 3 to amuse you and make a comment on human behavior, 4 to explain, and 5 to give advice.

In each of the examples, the writer's purpose was fairly clear, as it will be in most textbooks (to present information), newspaper articles (to communicate daily events), and reference books (to provide facts). However, in many other types of writing, authors have varied, sometimes less obvious, purposes. In these cases, an author's purpose must be inferred.

Often a writer's purpose is to express an opinion indirectly. Or the writer may want to encourage the reader to think about a particular issue or problem. Writers achieve their purposes by manipulating and controlling what they say and how they say it. This section will focus on techniques writers use and features of language that writers control to achieve the results they want.

Style and Intended Audience

Are you able to recognize a friend just by his or her voice? Can you identify family members by their footsteps? You are able to do so because each person's voice and footsteps are unique. Have you noticed that writers have unique characteristics as well? One author may use many examples; another may use few. One author may use relatively short sentences; another may use long, complicated ones. The characteristics that make a writer unique are known as **style**. By changing style, writers can create different effects.

Writers may vary their styles to suit their intended audiences. A writer may write for a general-interest audience (anyone who is interested in the subject but is not considered an expert). Most newspapers and periodicals, such as *Time* and *The Week*, appeal to a general-interest audience. On the other hand, a writer may have a particular interest group in mind. A writer may write for medical doctors in the *Journal of American Medicine*, for skiing enthusiasts in *Skiing Today*, or for antique collectors in *The World of Antiques*. A writer may also target his or her writing for an audience with particular political, moral, or religious attitudes. Articles in the *New Republic* often appeal to a particular political viewpoint, whereas the *Catholic Digest* appeals to a specific religious group.

Depending on the group of people for whom the author is writing, he or she will change the level of language, choice of words, and method of presentation. One step toward identifying an author's purpose, then, is to ask yourself the question, Who is the intended audience? Your response will be your first clue to determining why the author wrote the article.

EXERCISE **9-8**   **Analyzing Intended Audience**

Directions: Read each of the following statements and decide for whom each was written. Write a sentence that describes the intended audience.

1. If you are worried about the state of your investments, meet with a broker to figure out how you can still reach your financial goals.

_____

_____

2. Think about all the places your drinking water has been before you drink another drop. Most likely it has been chemically treated to remove bacteria and chemical pollutants. Soon you may begin to feel the side effects of these treatments. Consider switching to filtered, distilled water today.

_____

_____

3. The new subwoofers from Gilberton put so much bass in your ride that they are guaranteed to keep your mother out of your car.

_____

4. Bright and White laundry detergent removes dirt and stains faster than any other brand.

_____

5. As a driver, you're ahead if you can learn to spot car trouble before it's too late. If you can learn the difference between drips and squeaks that occur under normal conditions and those that mean big trouble is just down the road, then you'll be ahead of expensive repair bills and won't find yourself stranded on a lonely road.

_____

_____

TONE

5 LEARNING GOAL

Recognize tone

The **tone** of a speaker's voice helps you interpret what he or she is saying. If the following sentence were read aloud, the speaker's voice would tell you how to interpret it: "Would you mind closing the door?" In print you cannot tell whether the speaker is polite, insistent, or angry. In speech you could tell by whether the speaker emphasized the word *would*, *door*, or *mind*.

Just as a speaker's tone of voice tells how the speaker feels, so does a writer convey a tone, or feeling, through his or her writing. Tone refers to the attitude or feeling a writer expresses about his or her subject. A writer may adopt a sentimental tone, an angry tone, a humorous tone, a sympathetic tone, an instructive tone, a persuasive tone, and so forth. Here are a few examples of different tones. How does each make you feel?

- Instructive

> When purchasing a piece of clothing, one must be concerned with quality as well as with price. Be certain to check for the following: double-stitched seams, matched patterns, and ample linings.

- Sympathetic

> The forlorn, frightened-looking child wandered through the streets alone, searching for someone who would show an interest in helping her find her parents.

- Persuasive

> Child abuse is a tragic occurrence in our society. Strong legislation is needed to control the abuse of innocent victims and to punish those who are insensitive to the rights and feelings of others.

- Humorous

> ACQUAINTANCE, n. A person whom we know well enough to borrow from, but not well enough to lend to.
> CABBAGE, n. A familiar kitchen-garden vegetable about as large and wise as a man's head.
> CIRCUS, n. A place where horses, ponies and elephants are permitted to see men, women and children acting the fool.
> LOVE, n. A temporary insanity curable by marriage or by removal of the patient from the influences under which he incurred the disorder.
>
> —Ambrose Bierce

- Nostalgic

> "Framed in gold is an old inscription for my great grandmother in the living room of the Miranda house in Roswell, NM. My grandma-grandma died, but it still hangs in the very same spot her daughter, my grandmother, had placed it in her honor decades ago. Ever since my sisters and I were infants our grandmother claimed us as her own. Every weekend she would make the 3-hour trek from Roswell to Mountainair to visit us and our single parent father. Long after she had returned home, the smell of Elizabeth Taylor perfume would linger on our clothes, fried potatoes and refried beans in our kitchen. Never have we called anyone else 'mother.'"
>
> —Montoya, "A Collection for My Mother and Father," *Tribal College Journal*

In the first example, the writer offers advice in a straightforward, informative style. In the second, the writer wants you to feel sorry for the child. This is done through description. In the third example, the writer tries to convince the reader that action must be taken to prevent child abuse. The use of such words as *tragic*, *innocent*, and *insensitive* establish this tone.

The tone of an article directly affects how the reader interprets and responds to it. If, as in the fourth example, the writer's tone is humorous and you do not recognize this, you will miss the point of the entire selection. If the writer's tone is nostalgic, as in the fifth example, it is important to recognize this and the feelings it provokes in you the reader. From these examples, you can see, then, that you may not receive an objective, unbiased treatment of a subject.

The author's tone is intended to rub off on you, so to speak. If a writer's tone is humorous, the writer hopes you will be amused. If a writer's tone is persuasive, the writer hopes you will accept his or her viewpoint. You can see how tone can be important in determining an author's purpose. Therefore, a second question to ask when trying to determine an author's purpose is, What tone does the writer use? Or, How is the writer trying to make me feel about the subject?

EXERCISE 9-9   Analyzing Tone

Directions: Read each of the following statements, paying particular attention to the tone. Then write a sentence that describes the tone. Prove your point by listing some of the words that reveal the author's feelings.

1. No one says that nuclear power is risk free. There are risks involved in all methods of producing energy. However, the scientific evidence is clear and obvious. Nuclear power is at least as safe as any other means used to generate electricity.

   _____

   _____

2. The condition of our city streets is outrageous. The sidewalks are littered with paper and other garbage—you could trip while walking to the store. The streets themselves are in even worse condition. Deep potholes and crumbling curbs make it unsafe to drive. Where are our city tax dollars going if not to correct these problems?

   _____

   _____

3. I am a tired American. I am tired of watching criminals walk free while they wait for their day in court. I'm tired of hearing about victims getting as much as or more hassle than criminals. I'm tired of reading about courts of law that even accept a lawsuit in which a criminal sues his or her intended victim.

   _____

   _____

4. Cross-country skis have heel plates of different shapes and materials. They may be made of metal, plastic, or rubber. Be sure that they are tacked on the ski right where the heel of your boot will fall. They will keep snow from collecting under your foot and offer some stability.

_____

_____

5. A parent often must reduce her work hours to take care of a sick or disabled child, to take the child to therapy or treatments, and to handle crisis situations. With a child with significant special needs, it can be very difficult, if not impossible, for the primary caregiver parent to maintain full-time employment and provide the care the child needs. The caregiver parent often must take part-time status at work to avoid being fired completely. When the parent becomes a part-time employee, she also usually loses her health insurance, retirement and other benefits. Often part-time employees are ineligible to participate in these benefits. These restrictions present a financial loss to this parent.

—Price, *The Special Needs Child and Divorce*, p. 4

_____

_____

_____

6. I fondly remember the summers I spent in Maine. The coziness of the cabin, the long summer days, and the gentleness of the ocean breezes. It was a time for our family to be together and to simply enjoy each other and our surroundings. Each day was special and slightly magical. Walks on the beach, trips to pick blueberries, and quiet moments with just the seagulls and the rushing tides filled the days and made me never want to leave.

_____

_____

EXERCISE 9-10   Identifying Tone

Directions: Bring to class an advertisement, photograph, newspaper or Web headline, or paragraph that clearly expresses tone. Working in groups, students should agree on the tone each piece expresses. Then groups should exchange materials and identify the tone of each new piece. Groups should compare findings.

LANGUAGE

6 LEARNING GOAL
Examine language

One important feature that writers adjust to suit their purpose is the kind of language they use. There are two basic types of language: objective and subjective.

Objective and Subjective Language

Objective language is factual, whereas **subjective language** expresses attitudes and feelings.

Read each of the following descriptions of the death penalty. As you read, decide how they differ.

> The death penalty is one of the most ancient of all types of formal punishment for crime. In early criminal codes, death was the penalty for a wide range of offenses, such as kidnapping, certain types of theft, and witchcraft. Today, in the United States, the death penalty is reserved for only the most serious of crimes—murder, kidnapping, and treason.

> The death penalty is a prime example of man's inhumanity to man. The death penalty violates the Eighth Amendment to the Constitution, which prohibits cruel and unusual punishment.

You probably noticed that the first paragraph gave facts about the death penalty and that the second paragraph seemed to state a case against it. These two paragraphs are examples of two different types of writing.

The first paragraph is an example of objective language. The writer reports information without showing feelings. You cannot tell whether the writer favors or is opposed to the death penalty.

The second paragraph is an example of subjective language. Here, the writer expresses freely his or her own attitudes and feelings. You know exactly how the author feels about the death penalty. Through choice of words and selection of facts, a tone of moral disapproval is evident. Such words as *inhumanity*, *violates*, and *cruel* have negative connotations.

EXERCISE 9-11 **Writing Using Objective and Subjective Language**

Directions: Choose a topic that interests you, or use one of the topics listed below. On a separate sheet of paper, write two brief paragraphs. In the first, use only objective, factual information. In the second, try to show your feelings about the topic by using subjective language.

1. One of your college instructors

2. Managing your time

3. Current fashion fads

Descriptive Language

Descriptive language is a particular type of subjective language. It is the use of words that appeal to one or more of the reader's senses. Descriptive words help the reader create an imaginary picture of the object, person, or event being described. Here is a paragraph that contains numerous descriptive words and phrases. As you read, underline words and phrases that help you to imagine what Yellowstone is like.

> The river edges near the mountains are prime feeding and gathering grounds for herds of elk and bison that roam the park freely. We dismount near the river and watch elk graze and sleep on the opposite river bank. They are unconcerned with us, as are bison we encounter just a mile up the river, the jagged 8,235-foot Mt. Haynes casting its shadow over the valley. The giant hairy beasts create an almost prehistoric scene as the bison bury their faces in the snow searching for food, and then wander methodically toward the river for water. Bron says bison are not unlike cattle in a field, pretty melancholy most of the time, although YouTube shows us they can get riled up and punt people who get too close. These animals routinely weigh in around 2,000 pounds, they know they are the ones in control, not us on our puny snowmobiles. We gave them a respectful amount of space.
>
> —Savage, "Inside Yellowstone," *American Snowmobiler*

Through descriptive language, a writer often makes you feel a certain way about the topic. In the preceding paragraph, the writer is trying to suggest that Yellowstone is wild and peaceful. Did you notice such words and phrases as *roam freely, jagged, hairy, wander*?

EXERCISE 9-12   Using Descriptive Language

Directions: Work with a partner to expand each of the following sentences to include as many descriptive details as possible.

1. The movie was enjoyable.

2. The restaurant serves terrible food.

3. The classmate was annoying.

EXERCISE **9-13** **Analyzing Language, Tone, and Purpose**

Directions: Read each of the following passages and answer the questions that follow.

Passage A

Americans and the Land

I have often wondered at the savagery and thoughtlessness with which our early settlers approached this rich continent. They came at it as though it were an enemy, which of course it was. They burned the forests and changed the rainfall; they swept the buffalo from the plains, blasted the streams, set fire to the grass, and ran a reckless scythe through the virgin and noble timber. Perhaps they felt that it was limitless and could never be exhausted and that a man could move on to new wonders endlessly. Certainly there are many examples to the contrary, but to a large extent the early people pillaged the country as though they hated it, as though they held it temporarily and might be driven off at any time.

—Steinbeck, *America and Indians*, pp. 127–128

1. Is this selection an objective or subjective account of the early settlement of America? Give examples to support your choice.

   _____

   _____

   _____

2. Describe the writer's tone. How does it make you feel?

   _____

   _____

3. Why do you think the author wrote this selection?

   _____

   _____

Passage B

Malaysia Up Close

The first time you fly into Kuala Lumpur International Airport, you might be surprised. It is stunningly beautiful, modern in every sense. You board the gleaming Aerotrain for a quick, smooth ride from your plane to the main terminal. The terminal is a dazzling structure of glass and steel, with soaring architecture. The use of information and computer technologies pervades every aspect of the airport's systems, from the information boards to the baggage claim processes, to the handling of customs and immigration. When you express surprise, a proud Malaysian tells you that this airport, built in 1998, is ranked as the second best airport in the world.

But it is not just the airport. As you arrive by a sleek train into "KL" (Kuala Lumpur, capital of Malaysia), the night skyline is even more breathtaking—the many towering skyscrapers in a variety of postmodern shapes glow in a kaleidoscope of bright colors. The roads are full of late model cars. You find huge, multistory malls are overflowing with expensive, high-quality goods from all the major brands and labels that you recognize. There are elegant restaurants with every type of cuisine. The teenage Malaysians are using cell phones that have more capabilities than yours does! Except for the differences in dress and language, you might think you were in New York or Paris, except Kuala Lumpur seems more modern and sophisticated. This is the "Third World"?

As you spend more time in Malaysia, you discover more of its complexity. You visit the Petaling Street night market—hundreds of little outdoor stalls hawking everything from T-shirts and cheap jewelry to inexpensive household staples, to a cornucopia of fresh spices, vegetables and fish, to some risky-looking street food. Many of the locals at the market seem very traditional in terms of dress and behavior. You find other parts of KL—slums with old tenement houses, teeming with young kids who seem impoverished in their minimal, worn clothes. You also notice many older buildings from the colonial period under the British.

And as you get away from the major cities and the luxurious hotels along the beautiful tourist-centric beaches, you see more of this other Malaysia. Rural areas where homes and roads are ramshackle and in disrepair, cable TV service and even electricity are pirated from public lines, and trash and decay seem everywhere. Locals travel mainly on foot, bicycle, or in rickety old buses. Most people here do have cell phones, but they do not appear either prosperous or cosmopolitan. Many people don't even look very healthy, with bad teeth and various afflictions. All this more closely matches your image of a less-developed country.

—Danziger, *Understanding the Political World*, pp. 350–351

4. What is the author's purpose?

_____

_____

5. For whom is this article written?

_____

_____

6. Describe the tone of this article.

   _____

7. List several words or phrases that have a positive connotation. List several words
   or phrases with negative connotations.

   _____

   _____

   _____

   _____

   _____

   _____

8. Explain the figurative expression "the many towering skyscrapers . . . glow in a
   kaleidoscope of bright colors."

   _____

   _____

9. This reading is an excerpt from a longer chapter. What do you expect the rest of
   the chapter to contain?

   _____

   _____

LEARNING STYLE TIPS

If you tend to be a(n) . . .	Then build your interpretive reading skills by . . .
Applied learner	Asking these questions: How can I use this information? Of what value is this information?
Conceptual learner	Studying to see how the ideas fit together, looking for connections, relationships, and inconsistencies

SELF-TEST SUMMARY

1 **What are connotative meanings?**	Connotative meanings are the shades of meaning a word may have in addition to its literal (denotative) meaning.
2 **What are implied meanings?**	Implied meanings are those suggested by facts and information given by the author, but not directly stated. Readers must infer these implied meanings by noticing details, adding up the facts, watching for clues, and making sure the inference is supportable.
3 **What is figurative language?**	Figurative language is a way of describing things that makes sense on an imaginative level but not on a factual level.
4 **How can you identify the author's purpose?**	Analyzing the writer's style and identifying the intended audience are the first steps toward identifying the writer's purpose. A writer will change his or her style (level of language, choice of words, and method of presentation) to suit the intended audience.
5 **What is tone?**	A writer's tone (serious, humorous, angry, sympathetic) is a clue to how the writer wants you to feel about the topic.
6 **What types of language provide clues about the author's purpose?**	A writer's language may be objective or subjective, depending on whether the writer is simply presenting facts (objective) or expressing an opinion or feelings (subjective). This language can be helpful in identifying the writer's purpose.

GOING ◉ ONLINE

1. **Examining Political Web Sites**

   Political Web sites are often filled with rich, connotative, and sometimes biased language. Conduct a Web search for sites that focus on political matters. (You might choose a political party's Web site, for example.) Closely examine the language used on the home page and throughout the site. Identify words with strong connotations and look for implied meanings. Is the language used objective or subjective? Provide examples.

2. **Types of Figurative Language**

   This chapter provides an overview of figurative language, which comes in many types. Conduct a Web search to identify three different types of figurative language (for example, simile, metaphor, personification). Provide a definition and an example of each. Working with classmates, compile a table that lists as many different types of figurative language as possible (along with definitions and examples).

MASTERY TEST 1 Reading Selection

The Doctor Will E-mail You Now

Consumer Reports

Before Reading

This selection was taken from the Web site of *Consumer Reports*, a nonprofit organization dedicated to consumer rights and protection.

Previewing the Reading

Using the steps listed on page 49, preview the reading selection, including the boldfaced headings. When you have finished, indicate whether each statement is true (T) or false (F).

_____ 1. More doctors are e-mailing their patients, and this trend appears to be growing.

_____ 2. E-mailing with your doctor means you will likely get faster feedback.

_____ 3. Online patient portals are intended as a substitute for visits to the doctor's office.

Predicting and Connecting

1. What do you think are the pros and cons of e-mailing your doctor rather than going to his or her office?

2. Would you be able to list five benefits of e-mailing with your doctor just by previewing the selection? If so, how?

> **Vocabulary Preview**
> **screenings** (par. 3) evaluations
> **chronic** (par. 6) persistent; long-term
> **outcomes** (par. 6) results
> **via** (par. 10) by way of

1   Though they may be late to the party, this year you can expect your doctors to join your bank, your credit-card company, your insurance company, and probably even your supermarket and hairdresser in connecting with you online. In fact, you may find your doctor actively encouraging you to send her an e-mail.

2   Why? Starting this year, doctors and certain other health care providers are eligible for financial incentives under a program run by the Centers for Medicare and Medicaid Services if they make electronic health records available to patients online—and if they communicate with them online. What's more, they have to make sure that at least 5 percent of their patients use the technology.

3   You're most likely to get that information through a patient portal, a secured Web site that gives you access to portions of your medical records and can allow you to make appointments, request prescription refills, pay bills, view lab reports, e-mail your doctor, and add information to your health record. Some provide patient education information, health monitoring tools (such as food diaries, body mass index calculators, and depression screenings), and personalized health plans to help you, for example, quit smoking or lose weight.

4   Patient portals aren't perfect, and there are bound to be glitches as more doctors and patients start using them. And the government program is voluntary, so not all health care professionals will have one. Still, if a portal is available to you, there are good reasons for you to give it a try.

5   **Portals put your health in your hands.** Electronic health records and patient portals "break down the hierarchical doctor–patient relationship, where the patient's health information goes to the doctor and the doctor controls when and how the patient sees it," said Julie Hollberg, M.D., chief medical information officer at Emory Health Care in Atlanta. "The hope is that portals will engage patients in their own health care and change the relationship to be more of a patient–provider partnership."

6   Managing chronic diseases such as diabetes, high blood pressure, asthma, and congestive heart failure is easier when doctors and patients have access to the same data. "Putting information in the hands of the patient creates a bit of a drive for them to get more involved in tracking their numbers than maybe they have been previously," Hollberg said. In a study in the *New England Journal of Medicine*, people with diabetes seen by doctors who used electronic health records were 35 percent more likely to get all of the recommended screening measures, such as eye exams and blood sugar tests, than patients whose doctors relied on paper records. What's more, they were 15 percent more likely to have favorable outcomes on those measures.

7   Another study, by Kaiser Permanente researchers, found that patients with diabetes who e-mailed their doctors received better care compared with those who didn't. And just being able to access your health data whenever you want can help you remember details about your health or improve understanding.

8   Of course, doctors often have their own language, so interpreting those medical records can pose challenges. A small study from Kings College in London found that a third of patients who accessed their electronic health records had difficulty understanding the content. To overcome that, some portals have a glossary or information that explains common tests or procedures, or the physician may have created a list of reliable Web sites where patients can get information.

You can also use the portal to send an e-mail asking about things that aren't clear to you, or of course, you can get information the old-fashioned way: on the phone or at a follow-up appointment.

9   **They're convenient.** You can get the information you need when it's convenient for you, not your doctor. "Patients spend more time outside the doctor's office than in it, and they have health care needs that arise outside of the office," says Daniel Sands, M.D., M.P.H., a practicing physician at Beth Israel Deaconess Medical Center in Boston and former chief medical informatics officer at Cisco. Avoiding phone tag—either when making an appointment or getting information—is another perk. "If you can look up your lab results in the portal or e-mail me to ask about your medication, it saves you a phone call," Sands says. "If I can answer a question over e-mail, it may save you an office visit."

10   Depending on the doctor or system her office uses, all e-mails may go to administrative staff members, who then direct them to the appropriate person or department. Or you may be able to send e-mails individually to the front desk for appointments, the doctor's nurse or assistant for prescription refills, the billing office if you have a payment question, or directly to your doctor. If you use the portal to schedule appointments, you should get a confirmation e-mail and maybe even a reminder a day or so before your visit. (Some doctors are even asking patients to outline what they want to cover during the visit beforehand via e-mail.) And if you are using the system for the first time and have any concerns about whether your appointment request went through, check by phone the first time or two that you book the appointment on the portal.

11   **Accurate records.** Patients remember less than half of what they're told in the office or on the phone, experts say. But if the information is in your electronic health record or an e-mail, you can read it, digest it, and refer back to it when needed. If you spot any errors, you can alert your doctor. In addition, Sands points out an often overlooked downside of phone calls. "It's a scary fact, but the majority of phone conversations don't get documented in the patient's medical record," he says. "E-mail is self-documenting."

12   **Faster feedback.** Under the government guidelines, lab results must be posted in the patient portal within 96 hours of the doctor's office receiving them, whether your doctor has seen the results or not. That means no more waiting for him to call you with results or send them to you by snail mail. It also eliminates the practice some doctors have of notifying you only if something is wrong or just leaving you with a vague "everything looks good." For the most part, seeing the actual values is empowering, but there is the chance that misunderstanding the results could cause you worry. To head off confusion, you might want to talk to your doctor when you have the test about how to interpret the results and what to do if you're concerned about them.

13   **More-rewarding visits.** It may seem impersonal, but online interactions can improve the doctor–patient relationship. Portals let you stay in touch with him more frequently. It can even "extend" the office visit. "I might treat a patient

and say, 'I'm not sure we solved the problem. I want you to check in with me in two days.' It's easier to do that by e-mail," Sands says.

14   "In our experience, having open records and doctors' notes enhances trust between patients and doctors," says Jan Walker, R.N., M.B.A., a member of the research faculty of the Division of General Medicine and Primary Care at Beth Israel Deaconess Medical Center and Harvard Medical School. She is also co-director of OpenNotes, an initiative that goes beyond allowing patients to see lab results and medication lists and invites them to also see the notes clinicians write about the patient's office visits. Patient portals are not meant to replace face-to-face visits, though. Even for the most tech-savvy patient, there will always be times when that office visit or phone call is best. Those options aren't going away.

After Reading

Checking Your Comprehension

_____ 1. What is the key reason that more doctors are going online?
   a. They believe that doing so will benefit their patients.
   b. They are trying to be more accessible to a younger generation.
   c. They receive financial incentives from the government.
   d. They are trying to become more like doctors in other countries.

_____ 2. The online space through which patients can retrieve information related to their health care is called a(n)
   a. HealthCheck app.
   b. patient portal.
   c. e-wellness initiative.
   d. Medicare supplement.

_____ 3. The selection lists all of the following as reasons you should consider accessing your health information online *except*
   a. convenience and quick response.
   b. an improved relationship between patient and health-care provider.
   c. more control over your health.
   d. less-expensive medical care.

_____ 4. To help their patients understand key terms in their medical records, doctors' offices sometimes provide a(n) _____ on their Web site.
   a. index
   b. link to Wikipedia
   c. glossary
   d. link to the *New England Journal of Medicine*

_____ 5. According to government guidelines, doctors' offices must post test results within _____ hours of receiving them.

a. 2
b. 6
c. 24
d. 96

Applying Your Skills: Interpreting the Writer's Message and Purpose

_____ 6. The author's purpose in writing this selection is to

a. persuade doctors to put patients' medical records online.
b. explain why readers should consider using an online patient portal.
c. criticize insurance companies that have too much control over doctor–patient relationships.
d. help readers understand key medical conditions, such as diabetes and asthma.

_____ 7. Following is a list of words found in the reading. Which one has the most positive connotation?

a. hierarchical (par. 5)
b. old-fashioned (par. 8)
c. overlooked (par. 11)
d. empowering (par. 12)

_____ 8. In the last sentence of paragraph 8, the author states, "you can get information the old-fashioned way: on the phone or at a follow-up appointment." The author is implying that

a. older people usually prefer voice or in-person communication.
b. doctors' offices are set up to keep patients from talking with the doctor.

c. sometimes older methods of communication work just as well or better than new methods.
d. those who choose to visit doctors' offices are those who are retired or chronically ill.

_____ 9. Paragraph 8 begins by stating, "Of course, doctors often have their own language." The author means that

a. doctors use medical vocabulary that the average person may not understand.
b. doctors write their prescriptions in Latin.
c. U.S. doctors now come from all over the world.
d. doctors ask administrative staff to convey medical information to patients.

_____ 10. The tone of this selection would best be described as

a. informative.
b. humorous.
c. saddened.
d. frustrated.

Studying Words

_____ 11. The word *glitch* (par. 4) means

a. problem.
b. selection.
c. limit.
d. crowd.

_____ 12. The word *hierarchical* (par. 5) means

a. pleasant.
b. professional.
c. ranked.
d. medical.

_____13. The word *perk* (par. 9) means
     a. benefit.
     b. cost.
     c. solution.
     d. need.

_____14. The word *downside* (par. 11) means
     a. bottom.
     b. expense.
     c. threat.
     d. drawback.

_____15. The word *vague* (par. 12) means
     a. gray.
     b. unclear.
     c. fast.
     d. simple.

> For more practice, ask your instructor for an opportunity to work on the mastery tests that appear in the Test Bank.

Thinking Visually

1. What does the photograph on page 361 contribute to the reading overall?

2. Suppose this reading were to appear in a magazine for retired adults, *Modern Maturity*. What types of photos should the author include? Now suppose that the reading were to appear in a magazine for young female readers, such as *Elle* or *Marie Claire*. What types of photos should the author include?

Thinking Critically About the Reading

1. Does the author use a great deal of figurative language in this reading, or is the language mostly straightforward? What does your answer imply about the audience for the selection?

2. What clues in the reading tell you that the intended audience is adults over, say, age 40?

3. Would you describe the author's language as objective, subjective, or descriptive? Explain.

4. Do you see any bias in this selection? That is, does the author present only one side of the story, or is an attempt made to present multiple perspectives? Explain

Academic Application: Summarizing the Reading

Directions: Suppose you are taking an exam. You have 15 minutes to complete the following essay question: "Write a brief summary of 'The Doctor Will E-mail You Now.'" Complete the following summary of the reading. The first sentence is provided; you will have to write the rest of the summary.

This year, more doctors may actively begin using e-mail to communicate with their patients.

_____

_____

_____

_____

_____

_____

_____

_____

_____

MASTERY TEST 2 Reading Selection

You Must Be This Old to Die

Nicholas St. Fleur

Before Reading

This selection originally appeared in *The Atlantic*, a respected magazine known for the quality of its writing.

Previewing the Reading

Using the steps listed on page 49, preview the reading selection. As part of your preview, read the first sentence of each paragraph. When you have finished, complete the following items.

1. Cassandra C. is suffering from what disease? _____

2. Indicate whether each item is true (T) or false (F).
    _____ a. Cassandra is voluntarily undergoing chemotherapy.
    _____ b. Chemotherapy greatly increases a cancer patient's chance of survival.
    _____ c. In the United States, all 16- and 17-year-olds have the right to bodily integrity.

Predicting and Connecting

1. Have you ever known someone who has suffered from cancer? What types of treatment did that person have (if any), and how did he or she respond?

2. Do you expect the reading to be fairly easy to understand, of moderate difficulty, or challenging? Why?

> **Vocabulary Preview**
> **stewardship** (par. 2) care
> **expedited** (par. 4) sped up
> **pundits** (par. 6) experts
> **doctrine** (par. 7) principle
> **impediment** (par. 7) obstacle

During Reading

As you read the selection, complete each of the following. When highlighting, use a different color highlighter for each task.

a. Highlight the topic sentence of each paragraph. If the main idea is unstated, write a sentence that states it.

b. Highlight the most important details in each paragraph.

c. Highlight useful transitional words and phrases that help you understand and connect the author's ideas.

d. Read and respond to the questions in the margin.

Predict the thesis of the reading from the subheading.

What feeling does this photograph create?

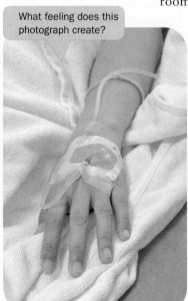

Just nine months from her 18th birthday, a Connecticut girl is fighting against forced chemo.

1   A 17-year old Connecticut girl is currently confined to a hospital room against her will and receiving life-saving treatment that she does not want.

2   The girl, identified only as Cassandra C., was diagnosed with a type of cancer called Hodgkin's lymphoma in September. The disease infiltrates essential components of the body's immune system, specifically weakening the lymphatic tissue, which helps fight infection. Though fatal, patients often have a high survival rate with early treatment. Yet, Cassandra was adamantly against treatment from the beginning, according to the *Hartford Courant*. Her mother, Jackie Fortin, supported the teenager's decision and allowed her to miss several appointments for treatment. Cassandra's doctors then informed Connecticut's Department of Children and Families (DCF), accusing Fortin of neglect. The DCF removed Cassandra from her mother's stewardship and put her into temporary state custody.

3   In Cassandra's case, the chemotherapy gives her an 85 percent chance of survival. Without it, she has two years to live, according to doctors. Yet, she and her mother do not want to subject her to the treatments, which can often be painful and traumatic. They argue that Cassandra is fully aware of the consequences of her decision, and should be allowed to make it. "She has always—even years ago—said that if ever she had cancer she would not put poison into her body," Fortin told NBC. According to her mother, Cassandra feels that the chemotherapy would do as much harm to her body as the cancer.

4   According to court documents, the state forced Cassandra to undergo two chemotherapy sessions in November, after which she ran away. When she returned a week later, Cassandra was placed in Connecticut Children's

Medical Center in Hartford, where she currently continues to receive unwanted treatment. After trying unsuccessfully to stop the government from administering treatment to Cassandra, her mother and lawyers have filed an appeal with the state's highest court. Because of its urgency to Cassandra's life, the appeal has been expedited and will take place on Thursday, according to the court documents. Now, the Connecticut Supreme Court is mired in a legal battle over whether a 17-year-old can make medical decisions about her own body. With Cassandra turning 18 in September, the question becomes whether she can legally make the same choice today as she could in nine months.

5   "Give us the chance to prove that she has the maturity to do this," assistant public defender Joshua Michtom told the Associated Press. "One has a right to bodily integrity. It doesn't matter if it's harmful. An adult's right to refuse care is without limitation, provided they're not incompetent."

Why does the author quote the public defender?

6   In the U.S., adults have the right to bodily integrity, meaning they can refuse life-saving medical treatment. For many adults, ending life-prolonging treatment is an issue to be discussed much later in life. But when young people choose to die, like 29-year-old Brittany Maynard, pundits make impassioned pleas. Maynard, who had terminal brain cancer, chose to end her own life in November of last year rather than undergo treatment that would extend her life, but reduce its quality. The right to refuse life-prolonging treatment is even more contentious for minors.

Underline the definition of "bodily integrity."

7   Only a few states allow the "mature minor doctrine" which lets 16- and 17-year-olds argue in court whether they are mature enough to make medical decisions. In 1989, Illinois had a case where a 17-year-old Jehovah's Witness with leukemia was allowed to refuse life-saving blood transfusions. Normally this doctrine is used when children want to receive treatment that their parents are refusing, but in this case the girl's parents also agreed in accordance with their religious beliefs. The court decided in favor of her right to refuse treatment under the mature minor doctrine. Ironically, the girl survived her bout with leukemia because she had already received a transfusion before the court made its decision. It's unclear if Cassandra's appeal, which will be Connecticut's first case calling for the "mature-minor doctrine," will face similar judicial impediments.

Underline the definition of "mature minor doctrine."

8   Considering her high chances of death without treatment, the state is arguing that it is rational for them to take over. According to the Associated Press, the DCF justified its actions by saying that when experts inform them a child will die because a parent decided not to treat her, the state has a responsibility to take control. Fortin continues to stand with her daughter, telling NBC, "My daughter and I have a close connection, and I have always said—since she was a baby—no matter what you do in life, I will be here for you and I will be by your side."

How does this paragraph summarize both sides of the controversy?

—St. Fleur, *The Atlantic*, January 7, 2015

After Reading

Checking Your Comprehension

_____ 1. Hodgkin's lymphoma is a type of
   a. cancer.
   b. heart disease.
   c. mental illness.
   d. invasive treatment.

_____ 2. Without chemotherapy treatment, Cassandra is likely to live about
   a. six months.
   b. one year.
   c. two years.
   d. three years.

_____ 3. The right to bodily integrity means the ability to
   a. donate organs.
   b. use birth control.
   c. refuse medical treatment.
   d. take prescription medications.

_____ 4. The legal battle over Cassandra's right to bodily integrity is strictly a matter of her
   a. sex.
   b. state of residence.
   c. mental health.
   d. age.

_____ 5. According to the selection, "mature minors" are _____ years old.
   a. over 16
   b. 16 or 17
   c. under 21
   d. over 19

Applying Your Skills: Interpreting the Writer's Message and Purpose

_____ 6. The author's purpose in writing this selection is to
   a. convince Cassandra's mother that her daughter has the right to live.
   b. criticize the Connecticut health and social-welfare systems.
   c. support mature minors in their quest for medical rights.
   d. present both sides of a controversial issue.

_____ 7. Paragraph 5 contains all of the following words. Which has the most negative connotation?
   a. maturity
   b. defender
   c. integrity
   d. incompetent

_____ 8. From paragraph 2, you can infer that the Connecticut authorities consider Jackie Fortin to be
   a. mentally ill.
   b. an unfit parent.
   c. a drug addict.
   d. a threat to the children of America.

_____ 9. Which of the following phrases from the reading uses language that is the _least_ slanted or subjective?
   a. "Cassandra was adamantly against treatment" (par. 2)
   b. "treatments, which can often be painful and traumatic" (par. 3)
   c. "impassioned pleas" (par. 6)
   d. "court decided in favor of her right" (par. 7)

_____10. The tone of the selection is best described as
   a. serious.
   b. comedic.
   c. nostalgic.
   d. insensitive.

Studying Words

Using context or a dictionary, define each of the following words as it is used in the reading.

11. infiltrate (par. 2) _____

12. adamant (par. 2) _____

13. traumatic (par. 3) _____

14. mired (par. 4) _____

15. contentious (par. 6) _____

Thinking Visually

1. How does the photo on page 366 illustrate the content of the selection? Write a caption that ties the photo to the content of the selection.

2. Create a map that summarizes both sides of the argument in the selection.

3. The reading does not include photographs of Cassandra C., Brittany Maynard, or the young woman described in paragraph 7. Why do you think these photos are *not* included?

Thinking Critically About the Reading

1. Are the two quotations from Joshua Michtom in paragraph 5 facts or opinions? Explain.

2. How would you describe the author's approach to the topic?

3. For what type of audience is "You Must Be This Old to Die" written?

4. How does the title of the selection relate to the key controversy being discussed?

Academic Application: Writing a Paraphrase

Directions: Your instructor asks you to paraphrase paragraph 6 to ensure that you understand the concept of bodily integrity. Write the paraphrase below. The first sentence is provided for you, but you must write the rest.

The right to bodily integrity means that adults can make the decision not to have medical care that would keep them alive. _____

_____

_____

_____

Evaluating: Asking Critical Questions

LEARNING GOALS

This chapter will show you how to

1 Identify and examine sources

2 Evaluate the authority of the author

3 Evaluate Internet sources

4 Examine assumptions

5 Recognize bias

6 Recognize slanted writing

7 Examine supporting ideas

8 Distinguish between fact and opinion

9 Identify value judgments

Focusing on . . . Evaluating What You Read

CAR SALE

HOT PRICES!
BEST CHOICES!
NEW, USED, ORIGINAL MODELS!

How would you go about shopping for a used car? Certainly you would ask about its make, model, and year. But to be a savvy consumer you would also want to evaluate its gas mileage, its mechanical soundness, its ownership history (single owner or many, for example), its body and interior condition, its maintenance history, and whether it was ever involved in an accident. Written material needs to be similarly evaluated for worth, value, accuracy, and delivery technique. This chapter will show you how to read and evaluate persuasive material.

When it comes to buying something, most of us have learned the motto "Buyer beware." We have learned to be critical, sometimes suspicious, of a product and its seller. We realize that salespeople will often tell us only what will make us want to buy the item. They will not tell what is wrong with the item or whether it compares unfavorably with a competitor's product.

Readers need to adopt a similar motto: *Reader beware*. You can think of some writers as sellers and their written material as the product to be sold. Just as you would ask questions about a car before buying it, so should you ask questions about what you read before you accept what is said. You should ask questions about who wrote the material and where it came from. You need to decide whether the writer is selling you a one-sided, biased viewpoint. You should evaluate whether the writer provides sufficient support for his or her ideas. This chapter will discuss these critical issues and show you how to apply them to articles, essays, and Internet resources.

WHAT IS THE SOURCE OF THE MATERIAL?

1 LEARNING GOAL

Identify and examine sources

A first question to ask before you even begin to read is, What is the source? That is, from what book, magazine, newspaper, or Web site was this taken? Knowledge of the source will help you judge the accuracy and soundness of what you read. For example, in which of the following printed sources would you expect to find the most accurate and up-to-date information about computer software?

- An advertisement in *Time*
- An article in *Reader's Digest*
- An article in *Software Review*

The article in *Software Review* would be the best source. This is a magazine devoted to computers and computer software. *Reader's Digest*, on the other hand, does not specialize in any one topic and often reprints or condenses articles from other sources. *Time*, a weekly newsmagazine, does contain information, but a paid advertisement is likely to provide biased information on only one line of software.

Knowing the source of an article will give clues to the kind of information the article will contain. For instance, suppose you went to the library to locate information for a research paper on the interpretation of dreams. You found the following sources of information. What do you expect each to contain?

- An encyclopedia entry titled "Dreams"
- An article in *Psychological Review* titled "An Examination of Research on Dreams"
- An entry on a blog titled "The Interpretation of Dreams"

You can predict that the encyclopedia entry will be a factual report. It will provide a general overview of the process of dreaming. The blog will likely report personal experience and contain little or no research. The article from *Psychological Review*, a journal that reports research in psychology, will present a primarily factual, research-oriented discussion of dreams.

As part of evaluating a source or selecting an appropriate source, be sure to check the date of publication or posting. For many topics, it is essential that you work with current, up-to-date information. For example, suppose you have found an article on the safety of over-the-counter (nonprescription) drugs. If the article was written four or five years ago, it is already outdated. New drugs have been approved and released; new regulations have been put into effect; packaging requirements have changed. The year a book was published can be found on the copyright page. If the book has been reprinted by another publisher or has been reissued in paperback, look to see when it was first published and check the year(s) in the copyright notice. Web sites often include the date on which the material was posted. (For further information about evaluating Internet sources, see Learning Goal 3 on page 374.)

EXERCISE 10-1   Evaluating Sources

Directions: For each set of sources listed below, choose the one that would be most useful for finding information on the stated topic. Then, in the space provided, give a reason for your choice.

_____ 1. **Topic:** gas mileage of American-made cars

   Sources
   a. A research report in *Car and Driver* magazine on American car performance
   b. A newspaper article titled "Gas-Eating American Cars"
   c. The U.S. Department of Energy's fuel economy site: http://www .fueleconomy.gov/

   Reason: _____

_____ 2. **Topic:** viruses as a cause of cancer

   Sources
   a. A textbook titled *Well-Being: An Introduction to Health*
   b. An article in *Scientific American* magazine on controlling viruses
   c. An issue of the *Journal of the American Medical Association* devoted to a review of current research findings on the causes of cancer

   Reason: _____

_____ 3. **Topic:** the effects of aging on learning and memory

   Sources
   a. An article from *Forbes* magazine titled "Fountain of Youth"
   b. A psychology textbook titled *A General Introduction to Psychology*
   c. A textbook titled *Adult Development and Aging*

   Reason: _____

WHAT IS THE AUTHORITY OF THE AUTHOR?

2 LEARNING GOAL
Evaluate the authority of the author

Another clue to the reliability of the information is the author's qualifications. If the author lacks expertise in or experience with a subject, the material may not be accurate or worth reading.

In textbooks, the author's credentials may appear on the title page or in the preface. In nonfiction books and general market paperbacks, a summary of the author's life and credentials may be included on the book jacket or back cover. Web sites may provide a brief biography of the author, along with his or her contact information. In many cases, however, the author's credentials are not given. You are left to rely on the judgment of the editors, publishers, or Webmasters about an author's authority.

If you are familiar with an author's work, then you can anticipate the type of material you will be reading and predict the writer's approach and attitude toward the subject. If, for example, you found an article on world banking written by former President Clinton, you could predict it will have a political point of view. If you were about to read an article on John Lennon written by Ringo Starr, one of the other Beatles, you could predict the article might possibly include details of their working relationship from Ringo's point of view.

EXERCISE 10-2   **Evaluating the Authority of the Author**

Directions: Read each statement and choose the individual who would seem to be the best authority on the subject.

_____ 1. Print newspapers are becoming obsolete.
   a. Michael Denton, a former *New York Times* print subscriber
   b. Todd Gitlin, professor, Columbia University School of Journalism
   c. Bill O'Reilly, television journalist

_____ 2. The president's recent news conference was a success.
   a. Katie Couric, a well-known news commentator
   b. David Axelrod, one of the president's advisors
   c. Howard Summers, a professor of economics

_____   3. Amy Tan is one of the most important modern American novelists.
   a. Wayne Wang, director of the film adaptation of Tan's book *The Joy Luck Club*
   b. Nancy Pearl, former librarian, author, and commentator on books
   c. David Gewanter, professor of modern literature at Georgetown University

IS AN INTERNET SOURCE APPROPRIATE, ACCURATE, AND TIMELY?

3 LEARNING GOAL

Evaluate Internet sources

Although the Internet contains a great deal of valuable information and a great many resources, it also contains rumor, gossip, and misinformation. Literally anyone can post literally anything on the Internet. Web sites can be here today, gone tomorrow. URLs can go dead or change with no notice or for no apparent reason. Anyone can say anything, whether it's completely true, utterly false, or somewhere in between. Gossip Web sites may have no basis in reality, and Web sites may be intended as big jokes. Even Wikipedia may be unreliable, because there are no limitations on who may add to or subtract from any Wikipedia entry. For example, there are Web sites devoted to all of the following:

- male pregnancy
- the dangers of dihydrogen monoxide to treat DSACDAD
- the prescription drug Havidol

Of course you realize that men cannot get pregnant. The Dihydrogen Monoxide Web site lists dangers including "death due to accidental inhalation" as a reason to ban the substance—misleading when you consider that "Dihydrogen Monoxide" is merely a technical term for water. There is no such drug as Havidol ("have it all"), and the disorder that it is supposed to treat (DSACDAD, or Dysphoric Social Attention Consumption Deficit Anxiety Disorder) is completely fictional.

These are extreme examples, but they prove a point. Attractive Web design and serious-sounding words do not mean that a source is reliable. You must evaluate each source before accepting it.

Discovering the Purpose of a Web Site

There are thousands of Web sites, and they vary widely in purpose. Table 10-1 on the next page summarizes five primary types of Web sites.

TABLE 10-1   Types of Web Sites

Type	Purpose	Description	URL Suffix
Informational	To present facts, information, and research data	May contain reports, statistical data, results of research studies, and reference materials	.edu or .gov
News	To provide current information on local, national, and international news	Often supplements print newspapers, periodicals, and television news programs	.com
Advocacy	To promote a particular cause or point of view	May be concerned with a controversial issue; often sponsored by nonprofit groups	.org
Personal	To provide information about an individual and his or her interests and accomplishments	May list publications or include the individual's résumé	URL will vary. May contain .com or .org or may contain a tilde (~)
Commercial	To promote goods or services	May provide news and information related to a company's products	.com

Evaluating Content

When evaluating the content of a Web site, evaluate its appropriateness, its sponsor, its level of technical detail, its presentation, its completeness, and its links.

Evaluate a Site's Appropriateness   To be worthwhile, a Web site should contain the information you need. It should answer one or more of your search questions. If the site only touches upon answers to your questions but does not address them in detail, check the links on the site to see if they lead to more detailed information. If they do not, search for a more useful site.

Evaluate the Sponsor   Another important step in evaluating a Web site is asking yourself, "Who is the sponsor?" and "Why was this site put up on the Web?" The sponsor of a Web site is the person or organization who paid for it to be created and placed on the Web. The sponsor will often suggest the purpose of a Web site. For example, a Web site sponsored by Nike is designed to promote its products, while a site sponsored by a university library is designed to help students learn to use its resources more effectively.

Evaluate the Level of Technical Detail   Some sites may provide information that is too sketchy for your search purposes; others assume a level of background knowledge or technical sophistication that you lack. For example, if you are writing a short, introductory-level paper on threats to the survival of marine animals, the Web site of the Scripps Institution of Oceanography may be too technical and contain more information than you need. Unless you have some previous knowledge in that field, you may want to search for a different Web site.

Evaluate the Presentation   Information on a Web site should be presented clearly and should be well written. If you find a site that is not clear and well written, you should be suspicious of it. If the author did not take time to present ideas clearly and correctly, he or she may not have taken time to collect accurate information either.

Evaluate the Completeness   Determine whether the site provides complete information on its topic. Does it address all aspects of the topic that you feel it should? For example, if a Web site on important twentieth-century American poets does not mention Robert Frost, then the site is incomplete. If you discover that a site is incomplete, search for sites that provide a more thorough treatment of the topic.

Evaluate the Links   Many reputable sites supply links to other related sites. Make sure that the links work and are current. Also check to see whether the sites to which you were sent are reliable sources of information. If the links do not work or the sources appear unreliable, you should question the reliability of the site itself. Also determine whether the links provided are comprehensive or only present a representative sample. Either is acceptable, but the site should make clear the nature of the links it is providing.

EXERCISE 10-3   **Evaluating the Content of Web Sites**

Directions: Suppose you are writing a research paper on species extinction and you need to determine which species are currently in danger of becoming extinct. Use a search engine to locate at least three Web sites that address the topic. Evaluate the content of the sites. Explain why you would either trust or distrust the content on each site.

Evaluating Accuracy

When using the Web to research an academic paper, it is important to find accurate information. One way to determine the accuracy of a Web site is to compare it with print sources (periodicals and books) on the same topic. If you find a wide discrepancy between the Web site and the printed sources, do not trust the Web site. Another way to determine accuracy is to compare the site with other sites that address the same topic. If discrepancies exist, further research is necessary.

The site itself will also provide clues about the accuracy of its information. Ask yourself the following questions:

Evaluating a Web Site's Accuracy

1. **Are the author's name and credentials provided?** A well-known writer with established credentials or affiliations is likely to write only reliable, accurate information. If no author is given, you should question whether the information is accurate.

2. **Is contact information for the author included on the site?** Often, a site provides an e-mail address where the author may be contacted.

3. **Is the information complete, or in summary form?** If it is a summary, use the site to find the original source. Original information has less chance of containing errors and is usually preferred in academic papers.

4. **If opinions are offered, are they clearly presented as opinions?** Authors who disguise their opinions as facts are not trustworthy.

5. **Does the site provide a list of works cited?** As with any form of research, the sources of information included on a Web site must be documented. If sources are not credited, you should question the site's accuracy.

6. **Is the information available in print form?** If it is, try to obtain the print version. Errors may occur when the article, essay, or information is put up on the Web.

EXERCISE 10-4 **Evaluating the Accuracy of Web Sites**

Directions: Suppose you are preparing for a class discussion on surveillance cameras and the right to privacy. Use a search engine to locate at least three Web sites that address the topic. Evaluate the accuracy of the sites. Explain why you would either trust or distrust the content on each site.

Evaluating Timeliness

Although the Web often provides up-to-the-minute information, not all Web sites are current. Evaluate the timeliness by checking

- the date on which the information was posted (put on the Web)
- the date when the document you are using was created
- the date when the site was last revised
- the date when the links were last checked

This information is usually provided at the end of the site's home page or at the end of the document you are using.

EXERCISE **10-5** **Evaluate the Timeliness of Web Sites**

Directions: Suppose you are writing an essay on the use of cell phones as a teaching tool in classrooms. Use a search engine to locate at least three Web sites that address the topic. Evaluate the timeliness of the sites. Explain why you would either trust or distrust the content on each site.

DOES THE WRITER MAKE ASSUMPTIONS?

4 LEARNING GOAL
Examine assumptions

An **assumption** is an idea, theory, or principle that the writer believes to be true. The writer then develops his or her ideas based on that assumption. Of course, if the assumption is not true or is one you disagree with, then the ideas that depend on that assumption are of questionable value. For instance, an author may believe that the death penalty is immoral and, beginning with that assumption, develop an argument for the best ways to prevent crime. However, if you believe that the death penalty *is* moral, then from your viewpoint, the writer's argument is invalid.

Read the following paragraph. Identify the assumption the writer makes, and write it in the space provided.

> Everyone suffers during an economic crisis. No one can come through unscathed, let alone better off. High unemployment and the unavailability of credit hurt all members of society as their negative effects trickle through the economic system. People who are not working cut back on their spending, which causes small businesses to close, which creates more unemployment. Closed businesses contribute to urban blight, which feeds crime and weakens our cities. Everyone across all levels suffers.

Assumption: _____

Here the assumption is stated in the first sentence—the writer assumes that an economic crisis negatively affects everyone. He makes no attempt to address how those who are independently wealthy or those who have not lost their jobs might not be suffering. He also fails to mention certain industries that thrive during troubled economic times, such as thrift stores.

EXERCISE **10-6**   **Identifying Assumptions**

Directions: For each of the following paragraphs, identify the assumption that is made by the writer and write it in the space provided.

1.   In high school, course selection is simple. Once all the mandatory courses are dropped into your schedule, you get to choose between art, drama or music. Then everything is put together automatically. In the university, things get a bit more complicated. You have some control over what day of the week each class is, or whether you take a course in three one-hour lectures a week or one three-hour lecture a week. You can even take into account who the instructor is. For incoming first-year students, choosing the right courses and putting together a schedule can seem like an impossible task.

—Dobson-Mitchell, "Beat the Clock," *Maclean's*

Assumption: _____

_____

2.   Rather than traveling for rest and relaxation, you can join more and more of the world's population in traveling for sports-related reasons. Sports tourism has exploded in the last ten years and is now seen as a major form of special-interest tourism. Sports tourism is "travel away from home to play sport, watch sport, or to visit a sport attraction including both competitive and noncompetitive activities" (p. 229). Think of the vast array of travel that is included in this definition. Sport team members traveling to out-of-town tournaments are included; booster and alumni clubs trekking to "bowl" games are included; golf fans traveling to the British Open are included; a snowboard/skiing club traveling to the Rockies for spring break is included!

—Cook et al., *Tourism*, p. 55

Assumption: _____

_____

IS THE AUTHOR BIASED?

5 LEARNING GOAL

Recognize bias

As you evaluate any piece of writing, determine whether the author is objective (fair) or one-sided (**biased**). Does the author present an objective view of the subject, or is a particular viewpoint favored? An **objective** article presents all sides of an issue, while a biased one presents only one side.

You can decide whether a writer is biased by asking yourself these questions:

1. Is the writer acting as a reporter by presenting facts, or as a salesperson by providing only favorable information?

2. Are there other views toward the subject that the writer does not discuss?

Use these questions to determine whether the author of the following paragraph is biased:

> In order for children to become literate, they need to be exposed to good storytelling. Television is a great source of good storytelling. Because of the short time frame of many programs, television shows must deliver a structured, logical, interesting, visually captivating story in about 20 minutes. In fact, a study published in 2009 in the *British Journal of Development Psychology* showed that preschoolers from economically disadvantaged homes develop literacy skills from watching television. Since some minority children already suffer from literacy difficulties and sometimes do not have the opportunity to hear librarians or parents read to them, television can be an important tool in their education.

The subject of this passage is the development of children's literacy skills through television viewing. The passage makes a positive connection between literacy and television and reports evidence that suggests that some children should watch television as part of their education. The other side of the issue—the negative effects of television viewing—is not mentioned. There is no discussion of the possible negative effects of watching TV: for example, childhood obesity, children's exposure to commercials and marketing messages, and the effects of watching TV violence. The author is biased and expresses only a positive attitude toward television.

IS THE WRITING SLANTED?

6 LEARNING GOAL

Recognize slanted writing

Slanting refers to the inclusion of details that suit the author's purpose and the omission of those that do not. Suppose you were asked to write a description of a person you know. If you wanted a reader to respond favorably to the person, you might write something like this:

> Alex is tall, muscular, and well-built. He is a friendly person and seldom becomes angry or upset. He enjoys sharing jokes and stories with his friends.

On the other hand, if you wanted to create a less positive image of Alex, you could omit the above information and emphasize these facts instead:

> Alex has a long nose and his teeth are crooked. He talks about himself a lot and doesn't seem to listen to what others are saying. Alex wears rumpled clothes that are too big for him.

While all of these facts about Alex may be true, the writer decides which to include, and which to omit.

Much of what you read and hear is slanted. For instance, advertisers tell only what is good about a product, not what is wrong with it. Talk-show hosts often have a strong political agenda and do not report information that would support alternative viewpoints.

As you read material that is slanted, keep these questions in mind:

1. **What types of facts has the author omitted?**

2. **How would the inclusion of these facts change your reaction or impression?**

EXERCISE 10-7 **Identifying Slanted Writing**

Working Together

Directions: Below is a list of different types of writing. Working in pairs, decide whether each item has little slant (L), is moderately slanted (M), or is very slanted (V). Write *L*, *M*, or *V* in the space provided.

_____ 1. Help-wanted ads

_____ 2. An encyclopedia entry

_____ 3. A newspaper editorial

_____ 4. A biology textbook

_____ 5. A letter inviting you to apply for a credit card

_____ 6. A college admissions Web site

_____ 7. An autobiography of a famous person

_____ 8. An online use agreement

_____ 9. *Time* magazine

_____ 10. *Catholic Digest* magazine

HOW DOES THE WRITER SUPPORT IDEAS?

7 LEARNING GOAL
Examine supporting ideas

Suppose a friend said he thought you should quit your part-time job immediately. What would you do? Would you automatically accept his advice, or would you ask him why? No doubt you would not blindly accept the advice but would inquire why. Then, having heard his reasons, you would decide whether they made sense.

Similarly, when you read, you should not blindly accept a writer's ideas. Instead, you should ask why she believes them by checking to see how she supports or explains those ideas. Then, once you have examined the supporting information, you decide whether you accept the idea.

Evaluating supporting evidence involves using your judgment. The judgment you make depends on your purpose and background knowledge, among other things. In judging the quality of supporting information a writer provides, you should watch for the use of (1) generalizations, (2) personal experience, and (3) statistics as evidence.

Generalizations

What do the following statements have in common?

> Dogs are vicious and nasty.
> College students are more interested in having fun than in learning.
> Parents want their children to grow up to be just like them.

These sentences have one thing in common: each is a **generalization** that makes a broad statement about a group—dogs, college students, parents. Generalizations necessarily involve the writer's judgment. For example, the first statement says that dogs are vicious and nasty. Yet the writer could not be certain that this statement is true unless he or she had seen *every* existing dog. No doubt the writer felt this statement was true based on his or her observation of and experience with dogs.

The question that must be asked about all generalizations is whether they are accurate. How many dogs did the writer observe, and how much research did he or she do to justify the generalization? Try to think of exceptions to the generalization—in this instance, a dog that is neither vicious nor nasty.

As you evaluate supporting evidence, be alert for generalizations that are presented as facts. A writer may, on occasion, support a statement by offering unsupported generalizations. When you encounter such statements, treat the writer's ideas with a critical, questioning attitude.

EXERCISE **10-8**   **Identifying Generalizations**

Directions: Read each of the following statements and decide whether it is a generalization. Place a check mark next to the statements that are generalizations.

_____ 1. My sister wants to attend the University of Chicago.

_____ 2. Most engaged couples regard their wedding as one of the most important occasions in their lives.

_____ 3. Senior citizens are a cynical and self-interested group.

_____ 4. People do not use drugs unless they perceive them to be beneficial.

_____ 5. Warning signals of a heart attack include pain or pressure in the left side of the chest.

EXERCISE **10-9**   **Identifying Generalizations**

Directions: Read the following passages and underline the generalization(s) in each.

1. Child care workers are undereducated in relation to the importance of their jobs. A whole generation of children is being left day after day in the hands of women with little more than high-school-level education. These children will suffer in the future for our inattention to the child-care employment pool.

2. For the past few years, drivers have been getting worse. Especially guilty of poor driving are the oldest and youngest drivers. There should be stricter tests and more classes for new drivers and yearly eye exams and road tests for drivers once they hit age 60. This is the only way to ensure the safety of our roads.

3. The things that attract men and women to each other have not changed a lot over the years. Throughout history and even to this day, men and women are valued for different qualities. Men are traditionally prized for their ability to hunt and gather (i.e., provide and achieve status in the group). Women, on the other hand, are valued for their youth and beauty, because this represents an ability to produce genetically desirable children.

—Papadopoulos, *What Men Say, What Women Hear*, p. 22

EXERCISE 10-10 Evaluating Generalizations

Directions: Work in groups of three or four students. For each of the following generalizations, discuss what questions you would ask and what types of information you would need to evaluate the generalization.

1. Vegetarians are pacifists and they do not own guns.

2. Most crimes are committed by high school dropouts.

3. It always rains in Seattle.

4. Private school students get a better education than public school students.

5. Scientists don't believe in any kind of higher power.

Personal Experience

Writers often support their ideas by describing their **personal experiences**. Although a writer's experiences may be interesting and reveal a perspective on an issue, do not accept them as proof. Suppose you are reading an article on drug use and the writer uses his personal experience with particular drugs to prove a point. There are several reasons why you should not accept the writer's conclusions about the drugs' effects as fact. First, the effects of a drug may vary from person to person. The drugs' effects on the writer may be unusual. Second, unless the writer kept careful records about times, dosages, surrounding circumstances, and so on, he is describing events from memory. Over time, the writer may have forgotten or exaggerated some of the effects. As you read, treat ideas supported only through personal experience as *one person's experience*. Do not make the error of generalizing the experience.

Statistics

People are often impressed by **statistics**—figures, percentages, averages, and so forth. They accept these as absolute proof of an assertion. Actually, statistics can be misused, misinterpreted, or used selectively to give other than the most objective, accurate picture of a situation.

Here is an example of how statistics can be misused. Suppose you read that magazine A increased its readership by 50 percent, while magazine B had only a 10 percent increase. From this statistic, some readers might assume that magazine A has a wider readership than magazine B. The missing but crucial statistic is the total readership of each magazine prior to the increase. If magazine A had a readership of 20,000 and this number increased by 50 percent, its readership would total 30,000. If magazine *B*'s readership was already 50,000, a 10 percent increase, bringing the new total to 55,000, would still give it the larger readership despite the smaller increase.

Here is another example:

> Americans in the workforce are better off than ever before. The average household income is $71,000.

At first the statement may seem convincing. However, a closer look reveals that the statistic given does not really support the statement. The term *average* is the key to how the statistic is misused. An average includes all salaries, both high and low. It is possible that some Americans earn $4,000 while others earn $250,000. Although the average salary may be $71,000, the average does not mean that *everyone* earns $71,000.

EXERCISE **10-11 Evaluating the Use of Statistics**

Directions: Read each of the following statements and decide how the statistic is misused. Write your explanation in the space provided.

1. Classrooms on our campus are not overcrowded. There are ten square feet of floor space for every student, faculty member, and staff member on campus.

   _____

   _____

   _____

2. More than 14,000 people bought a Prius last year, so it is a popular car.

   _____

   _____

   _____

3. The average water pollution by our local industries is well below the hazardous level established by the Environmental Protection Agency.

   _____

   _____

   _____

IS IT FACT OR OPINION?

8 LEARNING GOAL

Distinguish between fact and opinion

Facts are statements that can be verified. They can be proven true or false. **Opinions** are statements that express a writer's feelings, attitudes, or beliefs. They are neither true nor false. Here are a few examples of each:

FACTS

1. My car insurance costs $1,500 per year.
2. The theory of instinct was formulated by Konrad Lorenz.
3. Greenpeace is an organization dedicated to preserving the sea and its animals.

Opinions

1. My car insurance is too expensive.
2. The slaughter of baby seals for their pelts should be outlawed.
3. Population growth should be regulated through mandatory birth control.

The ability to distinguish between fact and opinion is an essential part of evaluating information. Factual statements from reliable sources can usually be accepted as correct. Opinions, however, must be considered as one person's viewpoint that you are free to accept or reject.

EXERCISE 10-12 Distinguishing Between Fact and Opinion

Directions: Identify each of the following statements as either fact or opinion.

_____ 1. Alligators provide no physical care for their young.

_____ 2. Humans should be concerned about the use of pesticides that kill insects at the bottom of the food chain.

_____ 3. There are 24 more humans living on Earth now than there were ten seconds ago.

_____ 4. We must bear greater responsibility for the environment than our ancestors did.

_____ 5. Nuclear power is the only viable solution to our dwindling natural resources.

_____ 6. Between 1850 and 1900 the death rate in Europe decreased due to industrial growth and advances in medicine.

_____ 7. Dogs make the best pets because they can be trained to obey.

_____ 8. Solar energy is available wherever sunlight reaches Earth.

_____ 9. By the year 2020, many diseases, including cancer, will be preventable.

_____ 10. Hormones are produced in one part of the body and carried by the blood to another part of the body where they influence some process or activity.

Judgment Words

When a writer or speaker expresses an opinion, he or she often uses words or phrases that can tip you off that a judgment or opinion is being offered. Here are a few examples.

> Professor Rodriguez is a *better* teacher than Professor Harrigan.
> My sister's behavior at the party was *disgusting*.

Here is a list of words that often suggests that the writer is interpreting, judging, evaluating, or expressing feelings.

bad	good	worthless	amazing	frightening
worse	better	worthwhile	wonderful	
worst	best	disgusting	lovely	

EXERCISE 10-13 **Identifying Judgment Words**

Directions: For each of the following statements, underline the judgment word or phrase that suggests the statement is an opinion.

1. Purchasing a brand new car is a _____.

2. Many _____ vegetarian cookbooks are available in bookstores.

3. Of all the film versions of Victor Hugo's novel *Les Miserables*, the 1935 version starring Charles Laughton is _____.

4. The introductory biology textbook comes with an _____ DVD.

5. Volunteers for Habitat for Humanity are engaged in a _____ activity.

Informed Opinion

The opinion of experts is known as **informed opinion**. For example, the Surgeon General is regarded as an authority on the health of Americans and his or her opinion on this subject is more trustworthy than that of casual observers or nonprofessionals.

Here are a couple of examples of expert opinions:

- Carol Dweck, Ph.D., Stanford University psychologist: *"One of the main jobs of parents is building and protecting their children's self-esteem."*
- Jane Goodall, primate expert: *"Chimps are in massive danger of extinction from dwindling habitats—forests are being cut down at an alarming rate."*

Textbook authors, too, often offer informed opinion. As experts in their fields, they may make observations and offer comments that are not strictly factual. Instead, these observations are based on years of study and research. Here is an example from a cultural anthropology textbook:

> What induces anthropologists to choose so broad a subject for study? In part, they are motivated by the belief that any suggested generalization about human beings, any possible explanation of some characteristic of human culture or biology, should be shown to apply to many times and places of human existence. If a generalization or explanation does not prove to apply widely, anthropologists are entitled or even obliged to be skeptical about it. The skeptical attitude, in the absence of persuasive evidence, is our best protection against accepting invalid ideas about humans.
>
> —Ember and Ember, *Cultural Anthropology*, pp. 3–4

The authors of this statement have reviewed the available evidence and are providing their expert opinion on what the evidence indicates about the approach anthropologists take. The reader, then, is free to disagree and offer evidence to support an opposing view.

Some authors are careful to signal the reader when they are presenting an opinion. Watch for words and phrases such as:

apparently	this suggests	in my view	one explanation is
presumably	possibly	it is likely that	according to
in my opinion	it is believed	seemingly	

In the following excerpt from a sociology textbook, notice how the authors carefully distinguish factual statements from opinion by using qualifying words and phrases (underlined here for easy identification).

After studying the urban poor in the Bronx, New York, and other cities around the world, anthropologist Oscar Lewis (1959, 1966) <u>concluded that</u> many poor people were held back by a **culture of poverty**, a set of norms, beliefs, values, and attitudes that trap a small number of the urban poor in a permanent cycle of poverty. <u>Lewis believed that</u> some of the distinctive attitudes and values of the "hard-core poor" include immediate gratification, apathy, and distrust, which encourages people to "blow" their earnings and live for the moment, making it hard to respond to opportunity.

Most <u>sociologists disagree</u> with Lewis' argument that the poorest of the poor have distinctive values, and most are opposed to the idea that the "culture of poverty" is structural and therefore highly resistant to change.

—Thompson and Hickey, *Society in Focus*, p. 216

EXERCISE 10-14 Identifying Informed Opinion

Directions: Read the following statements. In each, underline the word or phrase that suggests that the author is offering an informed opinion.

1. _____ that parents who would bring a young child to an R-rated movie are putting their own interests ahead of what's best for the child.

2. Voters rejected the proposed rapid transit system connecting the southern and northern suburbs, _____ racial issues.

3. _____, school uniforms lead to improved behavior and fewer disruptions in the classroom.

4. _____ low attendance at professional sporting events is the high price of tickets.

5. _____ that most people practice some form of recycling in their daily lives.

EXERCISE **10-15** **Distinguishing Between Fact and Opinion**

Directions: Each of the following paragraphs contains both facts and opinions. Read each paragraph and label each sentence as fact or opinion.

Paragraph 1

¹Flowering plants that are native to the South include purple coneflower and rose verbena. ²In the view of many longtime gardeners, these two plants are an essential part of the Southern landscape. ³Trees that are native to the South include a variety of oaks, as well as flowering dogwoods and redbuds. ⁴Dogwoods are especially lovely, with their white, pink, or coral blossoms announcing the arrival of spring. ⁵For fall color, the deep red of Virginia willow makes a spectacular show in the native Southern garden.

Sentences

1. _____   4. _____

2. _____   5. _____

3. _____

Paragraph 2

¹Today, many companies provide child care assistance, either on- or off-site, for their employees. ²This suggests that employers are becoming aware that their workers' family concerns can affect the company's bottom line. ³The Eli Lilly pharmaceutical company, for example, has built two child-development centers with a total capacity of more than 400 children. ⁴In addition to assistance with daily child care, Bank of America reimburses employees for child-care expenses related to business travel. ⁵It seems clear that other, less progressive employers will have to follow these companies' leads in order to attract and retain the best employees.

Sentences

1. _____   4. _____

2. _____   5. _____

3. _____

Paragraph 3

¹Preparing a will is an important task that millions of people ignore, presumably because they prefer not to think about their own death. ²However, if you die without a will, the courts will determine how your assets should be distributed, as

directed by state law. [3]Even more important than establishing a will, in my opinion, is expressing your willingness to be an organ donor upon your death. [4]Each year, 25,000 new patients are added to the waiting list for organ transplants. [5]The legacy of an organ donor is far more valuable than any material assets put in a will.

Sentences

1. _____

2. _____

3. _____

4. _____

5. _____

DOES THE WRITER MAKE VALUE JUDGMENTS?

9 LEARNING GOAL

Identify value judgments

A writer who states that an idea or action is right or wrong, good or bad, desirable or undesirable is making a **value judgment**. That is, the writer is imposing his or her own judgment on the worth of an idea or action. Here are a few examples of value judgments:

> Divorces should be restricted to couples who can prove incompatibility.

> Hunting animals is wrong.

> Welfare applicants should be forced to apply for any job they are capable of performing.

> Social drinking is acceptable.

You will notice that each statement is controversial. Each involves some type of conflict or idea over which there is disagreement:

1. Restriction versus freedom
2. Right versus wrong
3. Force versus choice
4. Acceptability versus nonacceptability

As you read, be alert for value judgments. They represent one person's view *only* and there are most likely many other views on the same topic. When you identify a value judgment, try to determine whether the author offers any evidence in support of the position.

EXERCISE 10-16 **Answering Critical Questions**

Directions: Read the following essay and answer the questions that follow.

I was at McDonald's on the West Side of Buffalo when the guy in front of me tried to order a double cheeseburger.

The cashier spoke Spanish with the workers behind the counter, who wrapped and stuffed food into white paper bags.

When the guy said, "No pickles," the cashier replied, "No understand."

The man raised his voice, as if talking to his half-deaf grandmother, and shouted: "No pickles!"

My mind jumped to a chat I once had with an old Chinese woman. I was teaching an English class at Buffalo's International Institute. The woman approached me in the lobby with a question burning on her lips. She smiled, allowing a thousand tiny wrinkles to gobble up her face.

"Teacher, I have question," she began. "Pizza in America. It have cheese and small meat on top . . . small circle meat. Very red. What is call this meat?"

"Pepperoni," I answered. She looked at me in awe, as if my ability to pronounce this word was magical. "Pep-per-o-ni," I said, sounding it out again.

She gave it a whirl, at first failing and laughing at herself. Then she tried again, insisting that she get it right. Who knows? Maybe all this was prompted by a messed-up pizza order.

That night, I found myself wondering how to say pepperoni in Chinese. I'd been studying the language for a couple of years, but hadn't come across it (the meat is not common in Chinese cuisine). I hopped on Google Translate and typed it in. Seven characters appeared, and in Chinese, each character has meaning by itself. The literal translation was: "Meaning Big Advantage Spicy Flavor Scented Intestines." Taken as a whole, it meant "pepperoni."

This was not very appetizing to me and made little sense to my Western mind. The first three characters, "Meaning Big Advantage," had no apparent connection to pork, but then I remembered that in Chinese, the characters make the sounds Yi Da Li. This is how Mandarin speakers say "Italy." I was on to something.

The remaining four characters translated into English as "Spicy Flavor Scented Intestines," a very descriptive way of getting about "sausage." So pepperoni, when uttered in Chinese, is Italian spicy sausage, roughly.

I felt just as perplexed as the old woman who had asked me about America's favorite pizza topping. Our concepts of the same food were worlds apart. She must have been wondering what small red circular meat has to do with peppers—and "oni," whatever that is.

I pondered this as I waited in line for coffee. The man in front of me continued to bark "No pickles!" in vain at the blank-faced cashier.

As an ESL instructor, I felt the need to butt in. I thought about how a seemingly simple word like pepperoni gets broken up into multiple concepts in Chinese. I tried doing the same for the word pickle in English. When you break it down, what is a pickle, really?

"A pickle is a sour green vinegar vegetable," I said, exaggerating a sour expression with my lips and drawing one of the small round McDonald's pickles in the air with my index finger.

"Ah!" exclaimed the cashier, smiling. "Thank you."

She had pieced together a pickle. The work of an off-duty Buffalo ESL instructor was done.

—Stone, "Simple Explanations Ease Communication," *The Buffalo News*

1. The subject of this essay is cross-cultural communication. How does the writer support his ideas?

   _____

2. Is the author qualified to write on the topic of cross-cultural communication? Give your reasons.

   _____

   _____

3. This essay contains both fact and opinion. Give an example of each.

   _____

   _____

   _____

4. Does the author make any value judgments? If so, explain at least one.

   _____

   _____

   _____

5. Does the author state any generalizations? If so, identify at least one.

   _____

   _____

6. Does this article express bias?

   _____

   _____

EXERCISE **10-17** **Answering Critical Questions**

Directions: Read the following passage and answer the questions that follow.

Consumer Privacy

1. To what extent should a consumer's personal information be available online? This is one of the most controversial ethical questions today. Scott McNealy, CEO of Sun Microsystems, said in 1999: "You already have zero privacy—get over it." Apparently many consumers don't agree: A study of 10,000 Web users found that 84 percent object to reselling of information about their online activity to other companies. One of the highest profile cases is that of DoubleClick Inc., a company that places "cookies" in your computer to let you receive targeted ads. The trouble began when DoubleClick bought Abacus Direct, a 90-million-name database, and began compiling profiles linking the two sets of data so clients would know who was receiving what kinds of ads.

2. DoubleClick's ability to track what you choose to buy and where you choose to surf is just one isolated example, though. Many companies can trace choices you make online and link them to other information about you. For example, when you register online for a product a Globally Unique Identity (GUID) is linked to your name and e-mail address. That means firms like RealJukebox, with 30 million registered users, can relay information to its parent company RealNetworks about the music each user downloads. Comet Systems, which creates customized cursors for companies featuring characters ranging from Pokemon to Energizer bunnies, reports each time a person visits any of the 60,000 Web sites that support its technology. Still other privacy violations are committed by consumers themselves: A site called disgruntledhousewife.com features a column to which women write to describe in excruciating detail the intimate secrets of former lovers. Be careful how you break off a relationship!

3. How can these thorny ethical issues be solved? One solution is an "infomediary"; an online broker who represents consumers and charges marketers for access to their data. As a Novell executive observed, "Slowly but surely consumers are going to realize that their profile is valuable. For loaning out their identity, they're going to expect something in return." Or, perhaps the solution is to hide your identity: Zero-Knowledge Systems of Montreal sells a software package called Freedom that includes five digital pseudonyms to assign to different identities.

4. All of these precautions may be irrelevant if regulations now being considered are ever implemented. One now being discussed is an "opt in" proposal that would forbid a Web site from collecting or selling personal data unless the user checked a box letting it do so. These efforts are being resisted by the online commerce lobby, which argues these safeguards would drastically reduce ad revenues.

—Solomon, *Consumer Behavior*, p. 19

1. What is the main point of the passage?

   _____

2. What is the author's attitude toward women who use the disgruntled housewife site?

   _____

3. This passage appeared in a consumer behavior college text. Evaluate it as source for
   a. a business marketing term paper
   b. computer users who want to learn more about privacy issues on the Internet

   _____

   _____

4. Is the passage biased? Explain your answer.

   _____

   _____

5. What types of supporting evidence does the author provide? Mark several
   examples of each type in the passage.

   _____

6. What assumptions does the author make?

   _____

   _____

   _____

7. Describe the tone of the passage.

   _____

8. Identify the generalization that is contained in the first paragraph. How is it
   supported?

   _____

9. Identify a statement of opinion in the first paragraph.

   _____

10. Identify a value judgment made in the passage.

   _____

EXERCISE 10-18 **Asking Critical Questions**

Working Together

Directions: Bring to class a brief (two- or three-paragraph) newspaper article, editorial, film review, blog entry, etc. Working in groups of three or four students, each student should read his or her piece aloud. The group can then discuss and evaluate (1) assumptions, (2) bias, (3) slanted writing, (4) methods of support, and (5) value judgments for each article. Each group should choose one representative article and submit its findings to the class or instructor.

LEARNING STYLE TIPS

If you tend to be a . . .	Then build your critical reading skills by . . .
Creative learner	Asking "What if . . .?" and "So what?" questions to free new ideas and new ways of looking at the subject
Pragmatic learner	Writing marginal notes, recording your thoughts, reactions, and impressions

---

SELF-TEST SUMMARY

1	**How do you identify and examine sources?**	Source refers to the place the material was originally published. Be sure to use trustworthy and reliable sources and check to be sure they are current.
2	**How can you evaluate the authority of the author?**	Evaluate the author's credentials and qualifications to write about the topic. Also evaluate the author's expertise with the subject matter as a further indication of the reliability of the information presented.
3	**How can you evaluate Internet sources?**	To evaluate a Web site's content, examine its appropriateness, sponsor, level of technical detail, presentation, completeness, and links. Also check the site for accuracy and timeliness.

4 What are assumptions, and how can you identify them?	Assumptions are ideas that the author believes to be true and upon which further ideas are based. If an author makes no attempt to establish the accuracy or validity of a statement, it may be an assumption.
5 What is bias, and how can you identify it?	Bias is present in a one-sided viewpoint; alternative viewpoints are not presented. To identify bias, look for statements that present only one side of an issue and do not present opposing or alternative ideas.
6 What is slanted writing, and how can you recognize it?	Slanted writing refers to an author's selection of details that suit his or her purpose. To identify slanted writing, ask yourself what facts have been omitted and how inclusion of these details might change your response to the material.
7 How does the writer support his or her ideas?	Writers may support their ideas using generalizations, statements about an entire group based on experience with some members of the group. Writers may also use personal experience or statistics, as well as facts and opinions.
8 How can you distinguish between facts and opinions?	Facts are verifiable statements; opinions express beliefs, feelings, and attitudes. Facts provide information that can be verified to be true. Judgment words suggest that an author is expressing an opinion.
9 What are value judgments, and how can you identify them?	Value judgments are statements that express the author's view of what is good or bad, or right or wrong. Look for statements on a controversial issue that indicate the author's moral or religious values.

GOING  ONLINE

1. **Evaluating Blogs**

   A *blog* (short for *Web log*) is a Web site on which a person posts his or her thoughts on a topic of interest (for example, pet care, gardening, parenting). Many blogs mix fact and opinion. Conduct a Web search for a blog that interests you, and print out a post or two. Identify the facts, opinions, and expert opinions in the posts. What types of information (if any) does the author provide to support his or her main ideas? Does the author exhibit any bias?

2. **Evaluating a Wiki**

   A *wiki* is a Web site that allows any user to post to or modify it. Wikis are very popular but often controversial. Working with a group of classmates, identify the pros and cons of wikis. Some questions to consider include, How reliable is the material provided on the wiki? How qualified are the people who post to wikis?

MASTERY TEST 1 Reading Selection

Reality Check: Reality TV Does Not Make You Feel Better

Rosie Molinary

Before Reading

This selection appeared on a blog by a woman who teaches about body image and self-acceptance.

Previewing the Reading

Using the steps listed on page 49, preview the reading selection. When you have finished, complete the following items.

1. What is the topic of the selection? _____

2. What is the writer's job? _____

3. Indicate whether each statement is true (T) or false (F).
    _____ a. The author is opposed to all reality TV shows.
    _____ b. The author wants readers to take charge of their own lives.

Predicting and Connecting

1. Do you watch reality TV? Which reality TV shows do you like, and which do you dislike? Why?

2. The reading does not contain headings. Suggest some effective ways for reading and studying the content.

> **Vocabulary Preview**
> **contrived** (par. 1) made up
> **faux** (par. 3) artificial or fake
> **predicated** (par. 7) dependent on
> **vulnerable** (par. 7) able to be hurt
> **authenticity** (par. 7) genuineness

1   "I watch reality television because it makes me feel better about myself, and I can just escape reality for little bit," my students often tell me. As they see young adults start a fight in a bar, women break each other down over some man they are in a contrived competition over, or see people make bad choices over and over again in their lives, my students feel vindicated.

2   "I may not be that rich, but I would never make that decision."

3   "I may not be that pretty, but I would never act so foolish." I may not have this or that or the other, but at least I've got sense, they tell themselves over and over again. And that, to many people, not just my students, is the primary gift we get from these faux-documentaryish reality television shows: the ability to believe that while we don't have the trappings of that pretty life, we at least have these other things going for us. And those things, we tell ourselves, really are what matter most to us.

4   But, here's the thing. If you are sucked into a reality television show and what you feel while you watch it is "Oh, at least I am not that much of a train wreck," then I would argue that maybe there is a value conflict going on. Maybe it really isn't that good for your self-esteem at all.

5   When we need to compare ourselves to others—whether we see those others at the mall, at a party, in class, at the office, or on a reality television show—to determine our worth, to have it vindicated and articulated, then two things are true:

6   1. What the show has going on really does matter to us in some way because we are giving it some of our precious, finite time and our limited energy. If you give the Kardashians 30 minutes of your time, five days a week for 50 weeks a year then you have given them 7500 minutes, which is 125 hours (and over 5 days of your life). I'm sorry, but you can't give away 5 days of your life accidentally without the thing that you are giving it to mattering to you in some way. So, if you are voting with your time, you are also voting with your values. You are saying, "This show and its messages matter enough to me that the trade-off is worth it. It is worth 5 whole days of my life."

7   2. You are on a slippery slope with your self-acceptance. If our ability to feel positively about ourselves is predicated by how we feel about other people and their choices, then we are always vulnerable to how we feel in a moment, what we see at any given time, who we are with at the moment of judgment, etc. And none of that is rooted in our authenticity, truth, and depth. At the end of the day, you actually do not feel better about yourself when you say, "At least, I am not that much of a train wreck." You actually feel like "all I have going for me is that I haven't done that—yet."

8   When a reality show—or anything or anyone else other than you—is your standard for your worth, then you are vulnerable, malleable, dependent on someone else's failures to articulate or even begin to recognize your own

successes. Our scale, our model, our measure isn't ours and it doesn't come from an empowered place. It comes from an "at least" place and that's never a place of power.

9   We need to quit fooling ourselves. If we watch these shows and think, "well, I am better than that," then we really must quit believing that these shows have no impact on us and are just for fun and we have to face the truth. We have to come to understand that they are exploiting us by giving us low standards and slippery foundations and we can't stand on either of those.

10   I am not saying that every reality show is bad or that I never watch them. I love the talent competition shows like *So You Think You Can Dance*, *The Voice*, and *Project Runway*. I do know that if you are looking at some of those faux-reality shows to make yourself feel better, then you are building your esteem on a house of cards. Turn off the television and focus on who you are and how you want to be in the world. Reality TV has destroyed many a life among its stars. Don't let it take you down, too.

—Molinary, www.rosiemolinary.com

After Reading

Checking Your Comprehension

_____ 1. The purpose of this selection is to
a. discuss how reality TV affects self-esteem.
b. express admiration for reality competition TV shows.
c. explain how reality TV harms the people in the shows.
d. show ways in which reality TV benefits watchers.

_____ 2. The author believes people watch reality TV because they think that it
a. sets new standards for behavior.
b. offers a peek at wealthy lifestyles.
c. makes them feel better about themselves.
d. helps them analyze human behavior.

_____ 3. The main idea of paragraph 6 is that reality TV shows
a. are too long.
b. overemphasize celebrity fashion.
c. are highly entertaining.
d. use up valuable time and energy.

_____ 4. The main idea of paragraph 7 is that self-acceptance
a. must come from yourself, not in comparison to others.
b. never happens on reality TV shows.
c. requires hours of work per week.
d. helps you make better TV viewing choices.

_____ 5. The author believes reality shows are harmful because they
a. do not have honest competitions.
b. are uncensored.
c. give us low standards.
d. show people behaving badly.

Applying Your Skills: Evaluating: Asking Critical Questions

_____ 6. The author's tone throughout this selection can best be described as
  a. hopeful.
  b. objective.
  c. critical.
  d. apologetic.

_____ 7. An example of *objective* language in this selection is
  a. "If you are sucked into a reality television show and what you feel while you watch it is 'Oh, at least I am not that much of a train wreck,' then I would argue that maybe there is a value conflict going on."
  b. "If you give the Kardashians 30 minutes of your time, five days a week for 50 weeks a year, then you have given them 7500 minutes which is 125 hours (and over 5 days of your life)."
  c. "You are on a slippery slope with your self-acceptance."
  d. "We need to quit fooling ourselves."

_____ 8. Because the source of this selection is a personal blog, you can anticipate that it
  a. will contain opinion.
  b. has been fact-checked.
  c. contains research.
  d. is a paid advertisement.

_____ 9. The author's intended audience is most likely
  a. reality TV stars.
  b. people interested in reality TV.
  c. television executives.
  d. psychologists.

_____ 10. The statement that is used by the author to indicate that she is not biased is
  a. "What the show has going on really does matter to us in some way because we are giving it some of our precious, finite time and our limited energy."
  b. "Maybe it really isn't that good for your self-esteem at all."
  c. "I am not saying that every reality show is bad or that I never watch them."
  d. "Our scale, our model, our measure isn't ours and it doesn't come from an empowered place."

Studying Words

_____ 11. The word *vindicated* (par. 1) means
  a. compromised.
  b. ignored.
  c. affected.
  d. justified.

_____ 12. The word *articulated* (par. 5) means
  a. explained.
  b. altered.
  c. destroyed.
  d. proven.

_____ 13. The word *finite* (par. 6) means
  a. gradual.
  b. excessive.
  c. limited.
  d. popular.

_____14. The word *malleable* (par. 8) refers to
an ability to be
   a. changed.
   b. noticed.
   c. included.
   d. distracted.

_____15. The word *exploiting* (par. 9) means
   a. encouraging expression.
   b. allowing honesty from.
   c. taking advantage of.
   d. denying freedom to.

For more practice, ask your instructor for an opportunity to work on the mastery tests that appear in the Test Bank.

Thinking Visually

1. How does the photo on page 400 enhance your understanding of the selection?

2. Describe at least two other photos, graphs, or visual aids that could be used to emphasize the reading's key points.

Thinking Critically About the Reading

1. Evaluate the effectiveness of the title and the first few lines of the article in capturing your interest. Why does the author call this a reality check?

2. How might subheadings enhance the readability of this article? Try to come up with several subheadings that could be placed at different points in the reading.

3. What types of facts has the author omitted in this article? How would these facts change your reaction or opinion?

4. What is your opinion about how reality shows affect self-acceptance? If you feel strongly one way or the other, make a case in favor of your side.

5. In its online form, this article allows readers to make comments about the content, agreeing, disagreeing, or offering another viewpoint. Do you think this aspect of online writing is helpful? Why or why not?

Academic Application: Summarizing the Reading

Directions: Suppose you are taking an essay exam and you encounter this question: "Write a summary of the reading 'Reality Check: Reality TV Does Not Make You Feel Better.'" Use the opening below as your starting point.

Reality TV is harmful. _____

_____

_____

MASTERY TEST 2 Reading Selection

Vigilantes: When the State Breaks Down

James M. Henslin

Before Reading

This selection appeared in an introductory sociology textbook in a chapter titled "Deviance and Social Control." What does *deviance* mean? What does *social control* mean?

Previewing the Reading

Using the steps listed on page 49, preview the reading selection. When you have finished, complete the following items.

1. What term means "people taking the law into their own hands"? _____

2. What country does the author use as a main example? _____

Predicting and Connecting

1. Have you ever felt "watched" by the government, or by security cameras in public places (such as stores, banks, or street corners)?

2. Do you expect the reading to be fairly easy to understand, of moderate difficulty, or challenging? Why?

> **Vocabulary Preview**
>
> **coercive** (par. 1) using force or threats
>
> **chafe** (par. 2) be angry or annoyed
>
> **mount** (par. 8) rise
>
> **blockades** (par. 10) barricades

During Reading

As you read the selection, complete each of the following. When highlighting, use a different color highlighter for each task.

a. Highlight the topic sentence of each paragraph. If the main idea is unstated, write a sentence that states it.

b. Highlight the most important details in each paragraph.

c. Highlight useful transitional words and phrases that help you understand and connect the author's ideas.

d. Read and respond to the questions in the margin

---

1   Many of us chafe under the coercive nature of the state: the IRS, Homeland Security, the many police agencies from the CIA, FBI, and NSA to who knows how many other groups summarized with three capital letters. Little cameras litter society, seemingly watching our every move.

> What does "the state" mean?

2   We certainly have given up a lot of freedoms—and we are likely to give up many more in the name of security. We can chafe and complain all we want. This is the wave of the future, seemingly an unstoppable one.

3   There is another side to what is happening. As many fear, the many guns that the many uniformed and plainclothes men and women are carrying can be trained on us. But for now, they bring security. They indicate that the state is operating; perhaps overreacting, but operating effectively nonetheless.

> Underline the sentence that tells you that the author is shifting to a new idea.

4   What happens when the state fails, when men and women in an official capacity carry guns and shields but can't be effective in protecting citizens from the bad guys who are carrying guns—and using them to enforce their way?

5   One reaction is vigilantism, people taking the law into their own hands. This is what happened in what we call the Wild West. Citizens armed themselves, formed posses, chased the bad guys, and dispensed quick justice at the end of a rope. You've seen the movies.

6   And this is what is happening in Mexico right now.

7   The state in Mexico has failed at all levels, from the local to the national. Citizens live in fear since the bad guys, in this case the drug lords, have

A boy walks past a member of the unofficial "community police" in Cruz Grande, Guerrero, Mexico.

gained much control. They have infiltrated the police, from the local cops to the *federales*. Even the head of Mexico's national drug enforcement agency was on the drug lords' payroll. Army generals, supposedly part of the war against drugs, take money to protect drug deals. They even use army vehicles to transport drugs. The corruption goes beyond belief, reaching even into the presidential palace. (But why the rush to judgment? Perhaps the president's brother was given a billion-dollar tip by some taxi driver who said he was a good passenger.)

> What is the author really saying?

8   The arrests are countless, the executions (shooting deaths by the police and the army) in the thousands. The death toll continues to mount, now over 60,000 police, drug dealers, and regular citizens.

9   The result, other than the many deaths? Failure to secure the people's safety.

> Why is this example included?

10   The Mexican people, then, have begun to take the law into their own hands. In the state of Guerrero, country folk have grabbed their old hunting rifles, put on masks, raided the homes of drug dealers, and put them in makeshift jails. They have set up blockades on the roads leading to their little towns. They won't let drug dealers, or any strangers, in. They won't even let the federal police, the state police, or the army in. These "enforcers of the law" are too corrupt, they say. We can trust only the neighbors we grew up with.

11   The reaction of the local police, the honest ones? "Maybe they can do something about the problem. We can't. If we try, the drug dealers will go to our homes and kill our families. They don't know who these masked men are."

> Summarize the attitudes expressed in paragraphs 11, 12, and 13.

12   The reaction of the state governor? "Good job."

13   The reaction of the regular citizens? Relief. And pleasure at being able to go out at night again and drink a little tequila and dance in the town square.

> What does this paragraph accomplish?

14   The masked men are going to hold their own trials. They haven't strung anyone up yet. But what will they do? If they send the men they convict to prison, well, the prison guards and administrators are corrupt, too. In one prison (in Gomez Palacio), the administrators even loaned the prisoners their guns and cars, and let the prisoners out to kill members of a rival drug gang. Afterward, the men dutifully returned to the prison, turned in the cars and guns, and went back to their cells. Incredible, I know. But true. (Based on Sheridan 1998; Malkin 2010; Archibold 2012; Casey 2013.)

After Reading

Checking Your Comprehension

_____ 1. According to the author, what do we give up in order to obtain more security?
  a. money
  b. freedom
  c. opportunity
  d. peace of mind

_____ 2. Vigilantism occurs when
  a. governments give law-enforcement rights to ordinary people.
  b. members of extremist groups engage in terrorist attacks.
  c. people take the law into their own hands.
  d. lawyers attempt to protect the guilty.

_____ 3. What is the chief purpose of the blockades in Guerrero?
  a. They allow the local people to raise money by taxing the roads.
  b. They prevent the children from leaving the country.
  c. They stop the flow of illegal immigration into Mexico.
  d. They help protect the people of Guerrero from outsiders.

_____ 4. How do the local police feel about the vigilantes in Guerrero?
  a. They believe the Guerrero vigilantes are criminals.
  b. They believe the Guerrero vigilantes are terrorists.
  c. They want to elect the leader of the Guerrero vigilantes to national office.
  d. They believe the Guerrero vigilantes are more effective than the police are.

_____ 5. What group of criminals now runs Mexico?
  a. the Mafia
  b. drug lords
  c. slave traders (human traffickers)
  d. Al Qaeda

Applying Your Skills: Evaluating: Asking Critical Questions

_____ 6. The source of this reading is a _____, which means that it is most likely _____ of information.
  a. Web site, an unreliable source
  b. textbook, a reliable source
  c. blog, a biased source
  d. magazine article, an accurate source

_____ 7. Paragraph 2 states, "This is the wave of the future, seemingly an unstoppable one." This sentence is
  a. a fact.
  b. a statistic.
  c. a generalization.
  d. based on the author's personal history as a drug dealer.

_____ 8. Paragraph 7 begins, "The state in Mexico has failed at all levels, from the local to the national." This statement is
  a. an assumption.
  b. a fact.
  c. unslanted.
  d. an uninformed opinion.

_____ 9. The last two sentences of paragraph 7 read, "But why the rush to judgment? Perhaps the president's brother was given a billion-dollar tip by some taxi driver who said he was a good passenger." The tone of these two sentences is

a. nostalgic.
b. weary.
c. sarcastic.
d. curious.

_____ 10. The only statistic used in the reading refers to

a. the number of drug dealers in Mexico.
b. the population of Guerrero.
c. the size of the local police force.
d. the death toll in Mexico.

Studying Words

Using context or a dictionary, define each of the following words as it is used in the reading.

11. posse (par. 5) _____

12. dispense (par. 5) _____

13. infiltrate (par. 7) _____

14. makeshift (par. 10) _____

15. string up (par. 14) _____

Thinking Visually

1. How does the photo on page 405 illustrate the content of the selection? What feeling does it create?

2. Describe at least two other photos, graphs, or visual aids that could be used to emphasize the reading's key points.

Thinking Critically About the Reading

1. Identify at least three opinions in the reading.

2. How would you describe the author's attitude toward the IRS, CIA, FBI, and other agencies mentioned in the first paragraph?

3. The article focuses on the positive effects of vigilantism. What are some possible negative effects of vigilantism?

4. Evaluate the effectiveness of the title and the first few lines of the selection in capturing your interest.

Academic Application: Summarizing the Reading

Directions: You receive the following assignment: "Write a summary of the article by summarizing each paragraph into just one sentence." Write your one-sentence summary of each paragraph on the lines below. Taken together, the sentences will be a complete summary of the reading.

1. _____

2. _____

3. _____

4. _____

5. _____

6. _____

7. _____

8. _____

9. _____

10. _____

11. _____

12. _____

13. _____

14. _____

A Fiction Mini-Reader

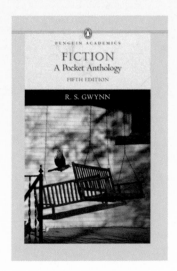

READING AND INTERPRETING SHORT STORIES

A short story is a creative or imaginative work describing a series of events for the purpose of entertainment and/or communicating a serious message. It has six basic elements. The next section describes each. But first, read the following short story, "The Story of an Hour," and then refer back to it as you read about each of the six elements.

The Story of an Hour

Kate Chopin

1   Knowing that Mrs. Mallard was afflicted with heart trouble, great care was taken to break to her as gently as possible the news of her husband's death.

2   It was her sister Josephine who told her, in broken sentences; veiled hints that revealed in half concealing. Her husband's friend Richards was there, too, near her. It was he who had been in the newspaper office when intelligence of the railroad disaster was received, with Brently Mallard's name leading the list of "killed." He had only taken the time to assure himself of its truth by a second telegram, and had hastened to forestall any less careful, less tender friend in bearing the sad message.

3   She did not hear the story as many women have heard the same, with a paralyzed inability to accept its significance. She wept at once, with sudden, wild abandonment, in her sister's arms. When the storm of grief had spent itself she went away to her room alone. She would have no one follow her.

4   There stood, facing the open window, a comfortable, roomy armchair. Into this she sank, pressed down by a physical exhaustion that haunted her body and seemed to reach into her soul.

5   She could see in the open square before her house the tops of trees that were all aquiver with the new spring life. The delicious breath of rain was in the air. In the street below a peddler was crying his wares. The notes of a distant song which someone was singing reached her faintly, and countless sparrows were twittering in the eaves.

6   There were patches of blue sky showing here and there through the clouds that had met and piled one above the other in the west facing her window.

7   She sat with her head thrown back upon the cushion of the chair, quite motionless, except when a sob came up into her throat and shook her, as a child who has cried itself to sleep continues to sob in its dreams.

8   She was young, with a fair, calm face, whose lines bespoke repression and even a certain strength. But now there was a dull stare in her eyes, whose gaze was fixed away off yonder on one of those patches of blue sky. It was not a glance of reflection, but rather indicated a suspension of intelligent thought.

9   There was something coming to her and she was waiting for it, fearfully. What was it? She did not know; it was too subtle and elusive to name. But she felt it, creeping out of the sky, reaching toward her through the sounds, the scents, the color that filled the air.

10   Now her bosom rose and fell tumultuously. She was beginning to recognize this thing that was approaching to possess her, and she was striving to beat it back with her will—as powerless as her two white slender hands would have been.

11   When she abandoned herself a little whispered word escaped her slightly parted lips. She said it over and over under her breath: "free, free, free!" The vacant stare and the look of terror that had followed it went from her eyes. They stayed keen and bright. Her pulses beat fast, and the coursing blood warmed and relaxed every inch of her body.

12   She did not stop to ask if it were or were not a monstrous joy that held her. A clear and exalted perception enabled her to dismiss the suggestion as trivial.

13   She knew that she would weep again when she saw the kind, tender hands folded in death; the face that had never looked save with love upon her, fixed and gray and dead. But she saw beyond that bitter moment a long procession of years to come that would belong to her absolutely. And she opened and spread her arms out to them in welcome.

14   There would be no one to live for her during those coming years; she would live for herself. There would be no powerful will bending hers in that blind persistence with which men and women believe they have a right to impose a private will upon a fellow-creature. A kind intention or a cruel intention made the act seem no less a crime as she looked upon it in that brief moment of illumination.

15   And yet she had loved him—sometimes. Often she had not. What did it matter! What could love, the unresolved mystery, count for in face of this possession of self-assertion which she suddenly recognized as the strongest impulse of her being!

16   "Free! Body and soul free!" she kept whispering.

17   Josephine was kneeling before the closed door with her lips to the keyhole, imploring for admission. "Louise, open the door! I beg; open the door—you will make yourself ill. What are you doing, Louise? For heaven's sake open the door."

18   "Go away. I am not making myself ill." No; she was drinking in a very elixir of life through that open window.

19   Her fancy was running riot along those days ahead of her. Spring days, and summer days, and all sorts of days that would be her own. She breathed a quick prayer that life might be long. It was only yesterday she had thought with a shudder that life might be long.

20   She arose at length and opened the door to her sister's importunities. There was a feverish triumph in her eyes, and she carried herself unwittingly like a goddess of Victory. She clasped her sister's waist, and together they descended the stairs. Richards stood waiting for them at the bottom.

21   Someone was opening the front door with a latchkey. It was Brently Mallard who entered, a little travel-stained, composedly carrying his grip-sack and umbrella. He had been far from the scene of the accident, and did not even know there had been one. He stood amazed at Josephine's piercing cry; at Richards' quick motion to screen him from the view of his wife.

22   But Richards was too late.

23   When the doctors came they said she had died of heart disease—of joy that kills.

Plot

The **plot** is the basic story line—the sequence of events as they occur in the work. The plot focuses on conflict and often follows a predictable structure. The plot frequently begins by setting the scene, introducing the main characters, and providing the background information needed to follow the story. Next, there is often a complication or problem that arises. Suspense builds as the problem or conflict unfolds. Near the end of the story, events reach a climax—the point at which the outcome (resolution) of the conflict will be decided. A conclusion quickly follows as the story ends.

The plot of "The Story of an Hour" involves a surprise ending: Mrs. Mallard learns that her husband has been killed in a railroad disaster. She ponders his death and relishes the freedom it will bring. At the end of the story, when Mrs. Mallard discovers that her husband is not dead after all, she suffers a heart attack and dies.

Setting

The **setting** is the time, place, and circumstances under which the action occurs. The setting provides the mood or atmosphere in which the characters interact. The setting of "The Story of an Hour" is the Mallards' home and takes place during the course of one hour.

Characterization

Characters are the actors in a narrative story. The characters reveal themselves by what they say—the dialogue—and by their actions, appearance, thoughts, and feelings. The **narrator,** or person who tells the story, may also comment on or reveal information about the characters. As you read, analyze the characters' traits and motives. Also analyze their personalities and watch for character changes. Study how the characters relate to one another.

In "The Story of an Hour" the main character is Mrs. Mallard; her thoughts and actions after learning of her husband's supposed death are the crux of the story.

Point of View

The **point of view** refers to the way the story is presented or the person from whose perspective the story is told. Often the story is not told from the narrator's perspective. The story may be told from the perspective of one of the characters, or that of an unknown narrator. In analyzing point of view, determine the role and function of the narrator. Is the narrator reliable and knowledgeable? Sometimes the narrator is able to enter the minds of some or all of the characters, knowing their thoughts and understanding their actions and motivations. In other stories, the narrator may not understand the actions or implications of the events in the story.

"The Story of an Hour" is told by a narrator not involved in the story. The story is told by a third-person narrator who is knowledgeable and understands the characters' actions and motives. In the story's last line, the narrator tells us that doctors assumed Mrs. Mallard died of "joy that kills."

Tone

The **tone** or mood of a story reflects the author's attitude. Like a person's tone of voice, tone suggests feelings. Many ingredients contribute to tone, including the author's choice of detail (characters, setting, etc.) and the language that is used. The tone of a story may be, for example, humorous, ironic, or tragic. The author's feelings are not necessarily those of the characters or the narrator. Instead, it is through the narrator's description of the characters and their actions that we infer tone. In "The Story of an Hour," the tone might be described as serious. Serious events occur that dramatically affect Mrs. Mallard's life. The story also has an element of surprise and irony. We are surprised to learn that Mr. Mallard is not dead after all, and it is ironic, or the opposite of what we expect, to learn that Mrs. Mallard dies "of joy that kills."

Theme

The **theme** of the story is its meaning or message. The theme of a work may also be considered its main idea or main point. Themes are often large, universal ideas dealing with life and death, human values, or existence. To establish the theme, ask yourself, "What is the author trying to say about life by telling the story?" Try to explain it in a single sentence. One theme of "The Story of an Hour" is freedom. Mrs. Mallard experiences a sense of freedom upon learning of her husband's supposed death. She sees "a long procession of years to come that would belong to her absolutely." There is also a theme of rebirth, suggested by references to springtime; her life without her husband was just beginning. The author also may be commenting on the restrictive or repressive nature of marriage during the time the story was written. After Mr. Mallard's death, "There would be no powerful will bending hers. . . ." Mrs. Mallard, after all, dies not from losing her husband but from the thought of losing her newly found freedom.

If you are having difficulty stating the theme, try the following suggestions:

1. **Study the title.** Now that you have read the story, does it take on any new meanings?
2. **Analyze the main characters.** Do they change? If so, how and in reaction to what?
3. **Look for broad general statements.** What do the characters or the narrator say about life or the problems they face?
4. **Look for symbols,** figurative expressions, meaningful names (example: Mrs. Goodheart), or objects that hint at larger ideas.

The Tell-Tale Heart

Edgar Allan Poe

Edgar Allan Poe was born in Boston in 1809 and was orphaned at the age of two. He was raised by wealthy foster parents who provided him with a privileged upbringing, including education and travel. He embarked upon a successful literary career as both editor and contributor to several major journals. However, after his wife died in 1847, Poe's personal problems and heavy drinking became worse. This led to unemployment, poverty, and eventually to his death in Baltimore at the age of 40. Poe is most famous for his macabre poems and short stories, and he is considered by many to be the inventor of the modern detective story.

Vocabulary Preview

hearken (par. 1) listen, pay attention

dissimulation (par. 3) disguising one's true intentions

profound (par. 3) insightful

sagacity (par. 4) wisdom

suppositions (par. 7) assumptions or beliefs

crevice (par. 8) a narrow opening or crack

scantlings (par. 13) small pieces of lumber

suavity (par. 14) pleasantness; showing politeness and charm

deputed (par. 14) assigned or delegated

audacity (par. 15) boldness

gesticulations (par. 17) gestures or movements

derision (par. 17) ridicule or contempt

1   True!—nervous—very, very dreadfully nervous I had been and am; but why *will* you say that I am mad? The disease had sharpened my senses—not destroyed—not dulled them. Above all was the sense of hearing acute. I heard all things in the heaven and in the earth. I heard many things in hell. How, then, am I mad? Hearken! and observe how healthily—how calmly I can tell you the whole story.

2   It is impossible to say how first the idea entered my brain; but once conceived, it haunted me day and night. Object there was none. Passion there was none. I loved the old man. He had never wronged me. He had never given me insult. For his gold I had no desire. I think it was his eye! Yes, it was this! One of his eyes resembled that of a vulture—a pale blue eye, with a film over it. Whenever it fell upon me, my blood ran cold; and so by degrees—very gradually—I made up my mind to take the life of the old man, and thus rid myself of the eye for ever.

3   Now this is the point. You fancy me mad. Madmen know nothing. But you should have seen *me*. You should have seen how wisely I proceeded—with what caution—with what foresight—with what dissimulation I went to work! I was never kinder to the old man than during the whole week before I killed him. And every night, about midnight, I turned the latch of his door and opened it—oh, so gently! And then, when I had made an opening sufficient for my head, I put in a dark lantern, all closed, closed, so that no light shone out, and then I thrust in my head. Oh, you would have laughed to see how cunningly I thrust it in! I moved it slowly—very, very slowly, so that I might not disturb the old man's sleep. It took me an hour to place my whole head within the opening so far that I could see him as he lay upon his bed. Ha!—would a madman have been so wise as this? And then, when my head was well in the room, I undid the lantern cautiously—oh, so cautiously—cautiously (for the hinges creaked)—I undid it just so much that a single thin ray fell upon the vulture eye. And this I did for seven long nights—every night just at midnight—but I found the eye always closed; and so it was impossible to do the work; for it was not the old man who vexed me, but his Evil Eye. And every morning, when the day broke, I went boldly into the chamber, and spoke courageously to him, calling him by name in a hearty tone, and inquiring how he had passed the night. So you see he would have been a very profound old man, indeed, to suspect that every night, just at twelve, I looked in upon him while he slept.

4   Upon the eighth night I was more than usually cautious in opening the door. A watch's minute hand moves more quickly than did mine. Never before that night had I *felt* the extent of my own powers—of my sagacity. I could scarcely contain my feelings of triumph. To think that there I was, opening the door, little by little, and he not even to dream of my secret deeds or thoughts. I fairly chuckled at the idea; and perhaps he heard me; for he moved on the bed suddenly, as if startled. Now you may think that I drew back—but no. His room was as black as pitch with the thick darkness, (for the shutters were close fastened, through

fear of robbers), and so I knew that he could not see the opening of the door, and I kept pushing it on steadily, steadily.

5   I had my head in, and was about to open the lantern, when my thumb slipped upon the tin fastening, and the old man sprang up in bed, crying out—"Who's there?"

6   I kept quite still and said nothing. For a whole hour I did not move a muscle, and in the meantime I did not hear him lie down. He was still sitting up in the bed, listening;—just as I have done, night after night, hearkening to the death watches* in the wall.

7   Presently I heard a slight groan, and I knew it was the groan of mortal terror. It was not a groan of pain or of grief—oh, no!—it was the low stifled sound that arises from the bottom of the soul when overcharged with awe. I knew the sound very well. Many a night, just at midnight, when all the world slept, it has welled up from my own bosom, deepening, with its dreadful echo, the terrors that distracted me. I say I knew it well. I knew what the old man felt, and pitied him, although I chuckled at heart. I knew that he had been lying awake ever since the first slight noise, when he had turned in the bed. His fears had been ever since growing upon him. He had been trying to fancy them causeless, but could not. He had been saying to himself—"It is nothing but the wind in the chimney—it is only a mouse crossing the floor," or "It is merely a cricket which has made a single chirp." Yes, he had been trying to comfort himself with these suppositions; but he had found all in vain. *All in vain*; because Death, in approaching him, had stalked with his black shadow before him, and enveloped the victim. And it was the mournful influence of the unperceived shadow that caused him to feel—although he neither saw nor heard—to *feel* the presence of my head within the room.

8   When I had waited a long time, very patiently, without hearing him lie down, I resolved to open a little—a very, very little crevice in the lantern. So I opened it—you cannot imagine how stealthily, stealthily—until, at length, a single dim ray, like the thread of the spider, shot from out the crevice and fell upon the vulture eye.

9   It was open—wide, wide open—and I grew furious as I gazed upon it. I saw it with perfect distinctness—all a dull blue, with a hideous veil over it that chilled the very marrow in my bones; but I could see nothing else of the old man's face or person: for I had directed the ray as if by instinct, precisely upon the damned spot.

10   And now have I not told you that what you mistake for madness is but over-acuteness of the senses?—now, I say, there came to my ears a low, dull, quick sound, such as a watch makes when enveloped in cotton. I knew *that* sound well, too. It was the beating of the old man's heart. It increased my fury, as the beating of a drum stimulates the soldier into courage.

---

death watches: beetles that infest timbers. Their clicking sound was thought to be an omen of death.

11   But even yet I refrained and kept still. I scarcely breathed. I held the lantern motionless. I tried how steadily I could maintain the ray upon the eye. Meantime the hellish tattoo of the heart increased. It grew quicker and quicker, and louder and louder every instant. The old man's terror *must* have been extreme! It grew louder, I say, louder every moment!—do you mark me well? I have told you that I am nervous: so I am. And now at the dead hour of the night, amid the dreadful silence of that old house, so strange a noise as this excited me to uncontrollable terror. Yet, for some minutes longer I refrained and stood still. But the beating grew louder, louder! I thought the heart must burst. And now a new anxiety seized me—the sound would be heard by a neighbor! The old man's hour had come! With a loud yell, I threw open the lantern and leaped into the room. He shrieked once—once only. In an instant I dragged him to the floor, and pulled the heavy bed over him. I then smiled gaily, to find the deed so far done. But, for many minutes, the heart beat on with a muffled sound. This, however, did not vex me; it would not be heard through the wall. At length it ceased. The old man was dead. I removed the bed and examined the corpse. Yes, he was stone, stone dead. I placed my hand upon the heart and held it there many minutes. There was no pulsation. He was stone dead. His eye would trouble me no more.

12   If still you think me mad, you will think so no longer when I describe the wise precautions I took for the concealment of the body. The night waned, and I worked hastily, but in silence. First of all I dismembered the corpse. I cut off the head and the arms and the legs.

13   I then took up three planks from the flooring of the chamber, and deposited all between the scantlings. I then replaced the boards so cleverly, so cunningly, that no human eye—not even *his*—could have detected anything wrong. There was nothing to wash out—no stain of any kind—no bloodspot whatever. I had been too wary for that. A tub had caught all—ha! ha!

14   When I had made an end of these labors, it was four o'clock—still dark as midnight. As the bell sounded the hour, there came a knocking at the street door. I went down to open it with a light heart,—for what had I *now* to fear? There entered three men, who introduced themselves, with perfect suavity, as officers of the police. A shriek had been heard by a neighbor during the night; suspicion of foul play had been aroused; information had been lodged at the police office, and they (the officers) had been deputed to search the premises.

15   I smiled,—for *what* had I to fear? I bade the gentlemen welcome. The shriek, I said, was my own in a dream. The old man, I mentioned, was absent in the country. I took my visitors all over the house. I bade them search—search *well*. I led them, at length, to *his* chamber. I showed them his treasures, secure, undisturbed. In the enthusiasm of my confidence, I brought chairs into the room, and desired them *here* to rest from their fatigues, while I myself, in the wild audacity of my perfect triumph, placed my own seat upon the very spot beneath which reposed the corpse of the victim.

16   The officers were satisfied. My *manner* had convinced them. I was singularly at ease. They sat, and while I answered cheerily, they chatted of familiar things, But, ere long, I felt myself getting pale and wished them gone. My head ached, and I fancied a ringing in my ears: but still they sat and still chatted. The ringing became more distinct:—it continued and became more distinct: I talked more freely to get rid of the feeling: but it continued and gained definitiveness—until, at length, I found that the noise was *not* within my ears.

17   No doubt I now grew *very* pale—but I talked more fluently, and with a heightened voice. Yet the sound increased—and what could I do? It was *a low, dull, quick sound—much such a sound as a watch makes when enveloped in cotton.* I gasped for breath—and yet the officers heard it not. I talked more quickly—more vehemently; but the noise steadily increased. I arose and argued about trifles, in a high key and with violent gesticulations; but the noise steadily increased. Why *would* they not be gone? I paced the floor to and fro with heavy strides, as if excited to fury by the observations of the men—but the noise steadily increased. Oh God! what *could* I do? I foamed—I raved—I swore! I swung the chair upon which I had been sitting, and grated it upon the boards, but the noise arose over all and continually increased. It grew louder—louder—*louder!* And still the men chatted pleasantly and smiled. Was it possible they heard not? Almighty God!—no, no! They heard!—they suspected!—they *knew!*—they were making a mockery of my horror!—this I thought and this I think. But anything was better than this agony! Anything was more tolerable than this derision! I could bear those hypocritical smiles no longer! I felt that I must scream or die!—and now—again!—hark! louder! louder! louder! *louder!*—

18   "Villains!" I shrieked, "dissemble no more! I admit the deed!—tear up the planks!—here, here!—it is the beating of his hideous heart!"

Directions: Select the choice that best completes each of the following statements.

Checking Your Comprehension

_____ 1. In this story, the main character describes how
     a. an old man tried to murder him.
     b. he prevented an old man's murder.
     c. he caught and arrested a murderer.
     d. he murdered an old man.

_____ 2. The character was inspired to kill the old man because
     a. he wanted the old man's gold.
     b. the old man had wronged him.
     c. the old man had insulted him.
     d. he was disturbed by one of the old man's eyes.

_____ 3. Once the character decided to kill the old man, he
   a. killed him later that day.
   b. waited until the next day to kill him.
   c. waited a whole week before killing him.
   d. waited almost a year and then changed his mind.

_____ 4. The reason the killer waited was that he
   a. wanted to find someone to help him kill the old man.
   b. could not kill the old man unless the old man's eye was open.
   c. needed to find a weapon.
   d. was afraid of being caught.

_____ 5. When the police came to the house, they
   a. immediately found the old man's body and arrested the killer.
   b. searched for clues but left without making an arrest.
   c. were suspicious of the man's story and took him in for questioning.
   d. were satisfied with the man's story.

The Elements of a Short Story

_____ 6. The tone of the story can best be described as
   a. suspenseful.
   b. humorous.
   c. ironic.
   d. sad.

_____ 7. The setting of the story is
   a. the old man's house.
   b. the police station.
   c. prison.
   d. an insane asylum.

_____ 8. This story is told from the perspective of
   a. the old man.
   b. the police.
   c. the killer.
   d. a neighbor.

_____ 9. The title is a reference to how the
   a. killer imagined the old man's heart beating so loudly that it gave him away.
   b. old man knew that he was going to be murdered.
   c. police officers found the old man's heart and knew he had been murdered.
   d. killer gave himself away by the loud beating of his own heart.

_____ 10. Which statement best expresses the theme of the story?
   a. Murder is immoral.
   b. Madness is a social disease.
   c. Law enforcement personnel deserve respect.
   d. Guilt is powerful and self-destructive.

Discussion Questions

1. How does Poe create feelings of suspense in this story?

2. How does Poe convince us that the narrator is mad?

3. What do you think is the relationship between the old man and his killer?

4. Why do you think Poe chose to tell this story from the killer's point of view?

Little Brother™

Bruce Holland Rogers

Bruce Holland Rogers is an American writer of award-winning fiction. This story appeared in *Strange Horizons*, a weekly online magazine that features science fiction and fantasy.

1   Peter had wanted a Little Brother™ for three Christmases in a row. His favorite TV commercials were the ones that showed just how much fun he would have teaching Little Brother™ to do all the things that he could already do himself. But every year, Mommy had said that Peter wasn't ready for a Little Brother™. Until this year.

2   This year when Peter ran into the living room, there sat Little Brother™ among all the wrapped presents, babbling baby talk, smiling his happy smile, and patting one of the packages with his fat little hand. Peter was so excited that he ran up and gave Little Brother™ a big hug around the neck. That was how he found out about the button. Peter's hand pushed against something cold on Little Brother™'s neck, and suddenly Little Brother™ wasn't babbling any more, or even sitting up. Suddenly, Little Brother™ was limp on the floor, as lifeless as any ordinary doll.

3   "Peter!" Mommy said.

4   "I didn't mean to!"

5   Mommy picked up Little Brother™, sat him in her lap, and pressed the black button at the back of his neck. Little Brother™'s face came alive, and it wrinkled up as if he were about to cry, but Mommy bounced him on her knee and told him what a good boy he was. He didn't cry after all.

6   "Little Brother™ isn't like your other toys, Peter," Mommy said. "You have to be extra careful with him, as if he were a real baby." She put Little Brother™ down on the floor, and he took tottering baby steps toward Peter. "Why don't you let him help open your other presents?"

7   So that's what Peter did. He showed Little Brother™ how to tear the paper and open the boxes. The other toys were a fire engine, some talking books, a wagon, and lots and lots of wooden blocks. The fire engine was the second-best present. It had lights, a siren, and hoses that blew green gas just like the real thing. There weren't as many presents as last year, Mommy explained, because Little Brother™ was expensive. That was okay. Little Brother™ was the best present ever!

8   Well, that's what Peter thought at first. At first, everything that Little Brother™ did was funny and wonderful. Peter put all the torn wrapping paper in the wagon, and Little Brother™ took it out again and threw it on the floor. Peter started to read a talking book, and Little Brother™ came and turned the pages too fast for the book to keep up.

9   But then, while Mommy went to the kitchen to cook breakfast, Peter tried to show Little Brother™ how to build a very tall tower out of blocks. Little Brother™ wasn't interested in seeing a really tall tower. Every time Peter had a few blocks stacked up, Little Brother™ swatted the tower with his hand and laughed. Peter laughed, too, for the first time, and the second. But then he said, "Now watch this time. I'm going to make it really big."

10   But Little Brother™ didn't watch. The tower was only a few blocks tall when he knocked it down.

11   "No!" Peter said. He grabbed hold of Little Brother™'s arm. "Don't!"

12   Little Brother™'s face wrinkled. He was getting ready to cry.

13   Peter looked toward the kitchen and let go. "Don't cry," he said. "Look, I'm building another one! Watch me build it!"

14   Little Brother™ watched. Then he knocked the tower down.

15   Peter had an idea.

16   When Mommy came into the living room again, Peter had built a tower that was taller than he was, the best tower he had ever made. "Look!" he said.

17   But Mommy didn't even look at the tower. "Peter!" She picked up Little Brother™, put him on her lap, and pressed the button to turn him back on. As soon as he was on, Little Brother™ started to scream. His face turned red.

18   "I didn't mean to!"

19   "Peter, I told you! He's not like your other toys. When you turn him off, he can't move but he can still see and hear. He can still feel. And it scares him."

20   "He was knocking down my blocks."

21   "Babies do things like that," Mommy said. "That's what it's like to have a baby brother."

22   Little Brother™ howled.

23   "He's mine," Peter said too quietly for Mommy to hear. But when Little Brother™ had calmed down, Mommy put him back on the floor and Peter let him toddle over and knock down the tower.

24   Mommy told Peter to clean up the wrapping paper, and she went back into the kitchen. Peter had already picked up the wrapping paper once, and she hadn't said thank you. She hadn't even noticed.

25   Peter wadded the paper into angry balls and threw them one at a time into the wagon until it was almost full. That's when Little Brother™ broke the fire engine. Peter turned just in time to see him lift the engine up over his head and let it drop.

26   "No!" Peter shouted. The windshield cracked and popped out as the fire engine hit the floor. Broken. Peter hadn't even played with it once, and his best Christmas present was broken.

27   Later, when Mommy came into the living room, she didn't thank Peter for picking up all the wrapping paper. Instead, she scooped up Little Brother™ and turned him on again. He trembled and screeched louder than ever.

28   "My God! How long has he been off?" Mommy demanded.

29   "I don't like him!"

30   "Peter, it scares him! Listen to him!"

31   "I hate him! Take him back!"

32   "You are not to turn him off again. Ever!"

33   "He's mine!" Peter shouted. "He's mine and I can do what I want with him! He broke my fire engine!"

34   "He's a baby!"

35   "He's stupid! I hate him! Take him back!"

36   "You are going to learn to be nice with him."

37   "I'll turn him off if you don't take him back. I'll turn him off and hide him someplace where you can't find him!"

38   "Peter!" Mommy said, and she was angry. She was angrier than he'd ever seen her before. She put Little Brother™ down and took a step toward Peter. She would punish him. Peter didn't care. He was angry, too.

39   "I'll do it!" he yelled. "I'll turn him off and hide him someplace dark!"

40   "You'll do no such thing!" Mommy said. She grabbed his arm and spun him around. The spanking would come next.

41   But it didn't. Instead he felt her fingers searching for something at the back of his neck.

Directions: Select the choice that best completes each of the following statements.

Checking Your Comprehension

_____ 1. At the start of the story, Peter can best be described as
    a. the oldest of several children.
    b. the youngest of several children.
    c. an only child.
    d. a teenager.

_____ 2. Peter's initial reaction to Little Brother was
    a. excitement.
    b. disappointment.
    c. jealousy.
    d. fear.

_____ 3. When Peter hugged Little Brother, he discovered that Little Brother
    a. was able to talk.
    b. cried when he was held.
    c. was made of plastic.
    d. had a button on his neck.

_____ 4. Peter's mother became angry when
    a. Little Brother broke Peter's new fire engine.
    b. Peter did not pick up the wrapping paper as she had asked.
    c. Peter turned off Little Brother.
    d. Little Brother knocked down Peter's blocks.

_____ 5. At the end of the story, we find out that
    a. Peter's mother planned to take Little Brother back.
    b. Peter's father would be coming home soon.
    c. Little Brother was actually a real baby.
    d. Peter also had a button on his neck.

The Elements of a Short Story

_____ 6. This story is told from the perspective of
    a. Peter's mother.
    b. Little Brother.
    c. Peter.
    d. a knowledgeable narrator.

_____ 7. One possible theme of the story is
    a. Technology is replacing human relationships.
    b. Family is more valuable than material possessions.
    c. It is important to be patient with small children.
    d. Brothers should look out for each other.

_____ 8. The climax of the story occurs when
   a. Peter first hugs Little Brother.
   b. Peter's mother leaves the room to cook breakfast.
   c. Peter's mother reaches around to switch him off.
   d. Little Brother breaks the fire engine.

_____ 9. The setting of the story is
   a. a store at the mall.
   b. Peter's birthday party.
   c. Little Brother's birthday party.
   d. Christmas day at Peter's house.

_____ 10. The tone of this story can best be described as
   a. serious.
   b. comical.
   c. ironic.
   d. tragic.

Discussion Questions

1. Were you surprised by the ending of this story? Discuss what you think will happen next.

2. Why did the author include the trademark symbol (TM) in the title and throughout the story?

3. How would the story be different if it were told from the mother's point of view?

4. In addition to Little Brother, what other clues does the author give to reveal that the story is taking place in the future?

5. Evaluate the effectiveness of the story's title. Can you think of other titles that would work for this story?

READING AND INTERPRETING NOVELS

A **novel** is a full-length piece of fiction. In college, you will be expected to read novels in literature classes or for supplemental assignments in any of a wide variety of disciplines. In everyday life, you may choose to read them for fun and relaxation.

Why Read Novels?

Novels can be amusing, engaging, entertaining, and educational. But a novel is also an experience—an opportunity to get involved in a different world. Think of reading a novel as similar to watching a movie. (Many movies are actually based on novels. *The Girl with the Dragon Tattoo* movies, for example, were novels before they became movies.) In a novel, you can become lost in the lives of the characters—you sympathize with them, you feel sadness for them, you share their emotions and life problems. The experience of reading a novel can be uplifting; it can be an escape from day-to-day life worries and stress; it can be educational. Through reading novels, you can learn a great deal about the ways other people live and have relationships, discover different cultures and ways of seeing and understanding the world, and "visit" different geographic places and historical periods.

How to Read a Novel

A **novel** is an extended story that can tell about several generations of a family, or an entire historical period, or can take place in the space of a day. Like a short story, it contains the following elements. Refer to pages 413–415 for a review of these elements.

- Plot
- Setting
- Characterization
- Point of view
- Tone
- Theme

Here are a few tips for reading a novel.

Before Reading

1. **Study the title.** Make some guesses about what the story might be about.
2. **Preview before reading.** Spend a few minutes reading the inside front cover flap and the back cover and studying the table of contents. Discover who the author is and what he or she typically writes about. Flip through the novel, and read the first paragraph. This will give you a sense of the setting and possibly of the main characters.

While Reading

3. **Reread the first paragraph.** Many opening paragraphs immediately engage you in an event or with a critical person or people.
4. **Watch the plot evolve.** Notice the development of events. Often the story leads up to a crisis or critical point that involves suspense, and its resolution leads to changes in the life of the main character and often of the people he or she is involved with.

5. **Determine the narrator's role.** Find out if the person telling the story is functioning as a reporter, reporting facts, or as a commentator, commenting and interpreting actions and events from his or her own point of view.

6. **Study the characters.** Pay attention to physical characteristics, as well as to dialogue and actions. Notice what other characters think of the main character(s) and what the narrator tells you about him- or herself.

7. **Highlight or make notes as you read.** When a character makes a meaningful statement or the narrator makes an insightful comment, highlight it. Also highlight important or significant actions, interesting descriptions, and unique uses of language. Make note of possible developing themes.

8. **Pay attention to language.** Writers often use figurative expressions (p. 339) and descriptive language to convey meaning.

9. **Watch for clues.** Writers often give you clues about what is going to happen next. (This is called foreshadowing.)

After Reading

10. **Reread the title.** Think about what it means now that you have read the book.

11. **Analyze the themes.** Determine the author's message: what is he or she trying to convey to the reader through telling the story? Reread your highlighting or notes for clues to why the author wrote the novel.

Reading and Analyzing the Prologue from *Water for Elephants*

Water for Elephants, by Sara Gruen, is a popular novel about a critical series of events that occurred when the main character dropped out of school and joined the Benzini Brothers circus. Below is the **prologue** (the introduction) to the novel. Read it now before continuing with this section.

Prologue from *Water for Elephants*

Sara Gruen

1   Only three people were left under the red and white awning of the grease joint: Grady, me, and the fry cook. Grady and I sat at a battered wooden table, each facing a burger on a dented tin plate. The cook was behind the counter, scraping his griddle with the edge of a spatula. He had turned off the fryer some time ago, but the odor of grease lingered.

2   The rest of the midway—so recently writhing with people—was empty but for a handful of employees and a small group of men waiting to be led to the cooch tent. They glanced nervously from side to side, with hats pulled low and hands thrust deep in their pockets. They wouldn't be disappointed: somewhere in the back Barbara and her ample charms awaited.

3   The other townsfolk—rubes, as Uncle Al called them—had already made their way through their menagerie tent and into the big top, which pulsed with frenetic music. The band was whipping through its repertoire at the usual ear-splitting volume. I knew the routine by heart—at this very moment, the tail end of the Grand Spectacle was exiting and Lottie, the aerialist, was ascending her rigging in the center ring.

4   I stared at Grady, trying to process what he was saying. He glanced around and leaned in closer.

5   "Besides," he said, locking eyes with me, "it seems to me you've got a lot to lose right now." He raised his eyebrows for emphasis. My heart skipped a beat.

6   Thunderous applause exploded from the big top, and the band slid seamlessly into the Gounod waltz. I turned instinctively toward the menagerie because this was the cue for the elephant act. Marlena was either preparing to mount or was already sitting on Rosie's head.

7   "I've got to go," I said.

8   "Sit," said Grady. "Eat. If you're thinking of clearing out, it may be a while before you see food again."

9   That moment, the music screeched to a halt. There was an ungodly collision of brass, reed, and percussion—trombones and piccolos skidded into cacophony, a tuba farted, and the hollow clang of a cymbal wavered out of the big top, over our heads and into oblivion.

10   Grady froze, crouched over his burger with his pinkies extended and lips spread wide.

11   I looked from side to side. No one moved a muscle—all eyes were directed at the big top. A few wisps of hay swirled lazily across the hard dirt.

12   "What is it? What's going on?" I said.

13   "*Shh*," Grady hissed.

14   The band started up again, playing "Stars and Stripes Forever."

15   "Oh Christ. Oh shit!" Grady tossed his food onto the table and leapt up, knocking over the bench.

16   "What? What is it?" I yelled, because he was already running away from me.

17   "The Disaster March!" he screamed over his shoulder.

18   I jerked around to the fry cook, who was ripping off his apron. "What the hell's he talking about?"

19   "The Disaster March," he said, wrestling the apron over his head. "Means something's gone bad—real bad."

20   "Like what?"

21   "Could be anything—fire in the big top, stampede, whatever. Aw sweet Jesus. The poor rubes probably don't even know it yet." He ducked under the hinged door and took off.

22   Chaos—candy butchers vaulting over counters, workmen staggering out from under tent flaps, roustabouts racing headlong across the lot. Anyone and everyone associated with the Benzini Brothers Most Spectacular Show on Earth barreled toward the big top.

23   Diamond Joe passed me at the human equivalent of a full gallop. "Jacob—it's the menagerie," he screamed. "The animals are loose. Go, go, *go!*"

24   He didn't need to tell me twice. Marlena was in that tent.

25   A rumble coursed through me as I approached, and it scared the hell out of me because it was on a register lower than noise. The ground was vibrating.

26   I staggered inside and met a wall of yak—a great expanse of curly-haired chest and churning hooves, of flared red nostrils and spinning eyes. It galloped past so close I leapt backward on tiptoe, flush with the canvas to avoid being impaled on one of its crooked horns. A terrified hyena clung to its shoulders.

27   The concession stand in the center of the tent had been flattened, and in its place was a roiling mass of spots and stripes—of haunches, heels, tails, and claws, all of it roaring, screeching, bellowing, or whinnying. A polar bear towered above it all, slashing blindly with skillet-sized paws. It made contact with a llama and knocked it flat—boom. The llama hit the ground, its neck and legs splayed like the five points of a star. Chimps screamed and chattered, swinging on ropes to stay above the cats. A wild-eyed zebra zigzagged too close to a crouching lion, who swiped, missed, and darted away, his belly close to the ground.

28   My eyes swept the tent, desperate to find Marlena. Instead I saw a cat slide through the connection leading to the big top—it was a panther, and as its lithe black body disappeared into the canvas tunnel I braced myself. If the rubes didn't know, they were about to find out. It took several seconds to come, but come it did—one prolonged shriek followed by another, and then another, and then the whole place exploded with the thunderous sound of bodies trying to shove past other bodies and off the stands. The band screeched to a halt for a second time, and this time stayed silent. I shut my eyes: *Please God let them leave by the back end. Please God don't let them try to come through here.*

29   I opened my eyes again and scanned the menagerie, frantic to find her. How hard can it be to find a girl and an elephant, for Christ's sake?

30   When I caught sight of her pink sequins. I nearly cried out in relief—maybe I did. I don't remember.

31   She was on the opposite side, standing against the sidewall, calm as a summer day. Her sequins flashed like liquid diamonds, a shimmering beacon between the multicolored hides. She saw me, too, and held my gaze for what seemed like forever. She was cool, languid. Smiling even. I started pushing my way toward her, but something about her expression stopped me cold.

32   That son of a bitch was standing with his back to her, red-faced and bellowing, flapping his arms and swinging his silver-tipped cane. His high-topped silk hat lay on the straw beside him.

33   She reached for something. A giraffe passed between us—its long neck bobbing gracefully even in panic—and when it was gone I saw that she'd picked up an iron stake. She held it loosely, resting its end on the hard dirt. She looked at me again, bemused. Then her gaze shifted to the back of his bare head.

34   "Oh Jesus," I said, suddenly understanding. I stumbled forward, screaming even though there was no hope of my voice reaching her. "Don't do it! *Don't do it!*"

35   She lifted the stake high in the air and brought it down, splitting his head like a watermelon. His pate opened, his eyes grew wide, and his mouth froze into an O. He fell to his knees and then toppled forward into the straw.

36   I was too stunned to move, even as a young orangutan flung its elastic arms around my legs.

37   So long ago. So long. But still it haunts me.

38   I DON'T TALK MUCH about those days. Never did. I don't know why—I worked on circuses for nearly seven years, and if that isn't fodder for conversation, I don't know what is.

39   Actually I do know why: I never trusted myself. I was afraid I'd let it slip. I knew how important it was to keep her secret, and keep it I did—for the rest of her life, and then beyond.

40   In seventy years, I've never told a blessed soul.

This prologue helps you get ready to read the novel and demonstrates many of the characteristics of a novel:

- **The setting is clearly established.** A place—the circus—is described in vivid detail.

- **The main characters are introduced.** You meet the main character of the novel, the narrator. You are also introduced to other principal characters, including Marlena (the woman the narrator falls in love with) and the evil ringmaster ("that son of a bitch").

- **Action immediately engages you.** You learn that the Disaster March is played because there is a crisis—the circus animals have escaped. You learn that someone has split someone's head open.

- **Suspense builds.** You are instantly dropped right into an action-packed story. While you learn much about the plot, there is much you do not know and you wonder about. You don't know how the animals escaped. You do not know who killed the man, who the man was, or why he was killed. You wonder what secret the narrator refers to in the last paragraph and why he has never told anyone.

- **The language is descriptive and engaging.** You can hear (the earsplitting band, the "thunderous applause" of the audience, and the screaming of the animals), smell (the odor of grease), and see (the terrified chimps, yak, polar bear, and lion) what is going on. Notice the use of figurative language—the polar bear has "skillet-sized paws," and the person's head was "split like a watermelon." Can you easily visualize the confusion and mayhem occurring as the animals escaped and the audience panicked and ran?

Based on the prologue, aren't you interested in reading the novel?

PART VI

A Contemporary Issues Mini-Reader

Reading About Controversial Issues

READING ABOUT CONTROVERSIAL ISSUES

A controversial issue is one about which people disagree and hold different opinions. This section offers suggestions for how to read articles about controversial issues. But first, read "The High Cost of Having Fun," below, and then refer back to it as you read the guidelines that follow it.

The High Cost of Having Fun

A majority of Americans follow at least one professional sport. Unfortunately, rising costs are making it impossible for the average fan to watch his or her favorite athlete or team in person. According to *Team Marketing Report*, the average ticket price in the NFL is $58.95, and in the NBA it's $45.28. For professional baseball, the average ticket price is $22.21, while in hockey, it's $43.13. Some argue that the high prices are justified. After all, they say, in order to please fans, teams must win more games than they lose. The best way to win is to have the top players, but teams must spend large amounts of money to get these players. These costs are passed on to the fans through ticket prices and merchandising. However, instead of raising ticket prices, team owners should raise the fees paid by corporations who sponsor stadiums and put their logo on the TV next to the score or advertise in the arena, making use of the real money in the hands of big business. The love of sports cuts across socioeconomic lines; the ability to enjoy a game in person should too.

Guidelines for Reading About Controversial Issues

Use the following suggestions when reading about controversial issues:

1. **Plan on reading the article several times.** Read the article once to get a first impression. Read it another time to closely follow the author's line of reasoning. Read it again to analyze and evaluate it.

2. **Identify the issue.** The issue is the problem or controversy that the article discusses. In "The High Cost of Having Fun," the issue is the high cost of tickets to sporting events.

3. **Identify the author's position on the issue.** In many articles, the author takes one side of the issue. In the paragraph above, the author's position is that the cost of tickets is too high. A different author could take the opposite view—that tickets are reasonably priced for the level of entertainment provided. Or another article could examine and discuss both sides of the issue, explaining why some people feel the cost is too high and why others think it is reasonable.

4. **Examine the reasons and evidence.** As you read, look closely at the reasons and types of evidence the author provides in support of the position or positions presented in the article. In "The High Cost of Having Fun," the author presents statistics about the cost of tickets and

recognizes that running a professional sports team is expensive. The author argues that the costs are being unfairly passed on to the fans and suggests an alternative means of financing the teams—passing the costs on to sponsors. The author also argues that sports should not be only for wealthy people who can afford high ticket prices.

5. **Evaluate the evidence.** Once you have examined the evidence offered, decide whether it is of good quality and whether there is enough evidence to be convincing. In "The High Cost of Having Fun," the statistics about the cost of tickets are useful. However, the author does not present any information about how much cost sponsors already assume and what additional costs they would need to assume in order to maintain or lower ticket prices.

6. **Opposing viewpoints.** If the writer presents only one viewpoint on the issue, be sure to consider the opposing viewpoints. The author will sometimes recognize opposing viewpoints, and sometimes even refute (present arguments against) them. In "The High Cost of Having Fun," the writer does recognize that some feel the high ticket prices are justified in order to get and keep top players.

Issue 1: Celebrities and Athletes as Activists

The following two selections discuss the involvement of Hollywood celebrities and famous athletes in political causes. As you read, identify each writer's position on the issue, and evaluate the evidence offered in support of the position. Consider the differences between each author's opinion on the topic, and think critically about which selection you agree with more.

Why Celebrity Activism Does More Harm Than Good

Andres Jimenez

Vocabulary Preview

NGO (par. 2) nongovernmental organization

righteous (par. 4) virtuous, moral

UNHCR (par. 5) United Nations High Commissioner for Refugees

paternalistic (par. 5) limiting people's rights on the assumption that restricting these rights is in the people's best interests

deterred (par. 6) discouraged

embolden (par. 6) make brave

Prereading

1. What do you predict the author's approach to celebrity activism is?

   _____

2. In what country is Gulu located? _____

1   As I sat in the stands of Pece Stadium in the northern Uganda town of Gulu on a sunny Sunday morning, a couple of young men made their way close to where I was sitting. We struck up a conversation, and they said that it was a pity that I had not witnessed the event that had taken place not long before my arrival in town a few weeks earlier.

2   My new friends began to describe how there had been a massive gathering in the stadium for the screening of a video put together by a foreign NGO. The video had profoundly upset a significant amount of those present that evening, and a riot broke out. I realized that, of course, they were talking about the launch of the first Kony 2012 video campaign by the U.S.-based organization Invisible Children. The video's portrayal of the over two-decade-long conflict had deeply angered many of those who had endured it firsthand. The crowd ended up having to be dispersed by police and tear gas.

3   As I listened to the men's account of how the crowd's anger turned to violence, I could hardly keep myself from thinking how emblematic and representative such an event was of countless celebrity-fueled, do-good awareness campaigns that I had already had the misfortune to witness over the years.

4   The tragedy behind these sorts of campaigns is that they are motivated by the belief that problems around the world remain unresolved due to the lack of international awareness of their existence or global commitment to resolve them. If only enough people knew and cared about a certain conflict or problem, the assumption goes, then the combined energy and support could be harnessed in order to trigger an immediate flood of solutions. Any action taken toward this end is therefore righteous and will put us a step closer to fixing the problem; surely any little bit of help must be better than nothing.

5   It is this mindset that has motivated celebrities like the rock star Bono to take up the causes of debt cancelation, the increase in foreign aid and the promotion of the Millennium Development Goals. Actor George Clooney has taken great interest in Darfur; Madonna and Oprah Winfrey have embraced the fight for girls' education in Africa, while Angelina Jolie knocks at the doors of the major centers of power as a UNHCR Goodwill Ambassador to promote support for humanitarian relief. Unfortunately, many of the policies and remedies promoted by this ever-growing influx of celebrity activists have been heavily criticized for being paternalistic, detached from reality and often dangerously counterproductive.

Bono, lead singer of U2 and anti-poverty activist, tells a story during a meeting with President Obama on development policy.

6   However, far from being deterred, celebrity activists find solace in the assurances of so-called experts, specialists and analysts who fill the ranks of leading international organizations, Washington think tanks and Ivy League universities. These people are the Nicholas Kristofs and the Jeffrey Sachses of the world who often find their self-assurance and sense of certainty in their Ivy League educations, in the power that their positions grant them or in the titles that they hold. Their almost complete confidence in their predictions and analyses, combined with the allure of celebrity, emboldens them to leap at the opportunity to promote what they consider to be the solutions for conflicts whose complexities they only superficially grasp.

7   Celebrity-led campaigns do often prove to be highly successful in generating broad public support. This is because they draw on the self-serving guilt trips that lead many people to believe that their privileged position has invested them with the burden and the responsibility to save those less fortunate from their plight. Celebrity activists provide us with a powerful outlet for our guilty consciences and our self-serving views of history. What better way to liberate ourselves from this burden than by taking up a global cause in a far-away land, and who better to show us the way to do it than our favorite celebrities?

8   My experience working with armed conflicts and humanitarian crises has shown me the disastrous effects that such views tend to have on the ground. Away from the fantasy world of easy-to-understand, black-and-white, single-story views of a conflict lays a world of complexity, depth and uncertainty. With the embrace of complexity we are able to discover that the way we seek to approach and work within a conflict must be incredibly flexible and diverse.

9   We need to distance ourselves from the powerful desire to follow simple solutions drafted by experts in conference rooms half a world away. We should begin, above all, by focusing on the creative energy already present among the local actors in a conflict in order to discover context-specific strategies that can help us to transform it.

10   Sadly, this approach does not fit well in a five-minute YouTube video or an inspirational TED Talk. Our fascination with pre-packaged solutions and our short attention spans are incompatible with appreciation for true complexity, humility and unpredictability.

11   If you feel invested in a cause, engage it with all your passion, but tread carefully. Ask yourself why you even care about this conflict in the first place. Whose

voices are you listening to about it? Whose interests are they serving? What is already being tried by local actors on the ground? And, most importantly, why should you become involved?

12   If you do decide to take that leap, then start by listening rather than preaching, facilitating rather than commanding, cooperating rather than defeating, creating organically rather than planning mechanically, and seeking to unsettle the status quo rather than trying to control it in its entirety. Being told that you have an urgent responsibility to act in order to help solve a conflict that you hardly even knew existed in the first place is the first step down a slippery slope of continuous despair, wasted goodwill and neo-colonialism.

—http://wagingnonviolence.org/feature/why-celebrity-activism-does-more-harm-than-good/

Checking Your Comprehension

1. What is the main point of this reading?

    _____

    _____

    _____

2. According to the author, what motivates "awareness campaigns" like that created by the Invisible Children organization?

    _____

    _____

    _____

3. Which two celebrities have embraced the fight for girls' education in Africa?

    _____

4. What are three key criticisms of celebrity involvement in international causes?

    _____

    _____

5. What is a key benefit to celebrity activism?

    _____

    _____

6. Summarize the author's advice for becoming involved in a cause in a positive way.

    _____

    _____

    _____

7. What does the author mean by "neo-colonialism" (the last word of the reading)?

_____

_____

_____

_____

Critical Reading and Thinking

1. What is the author's purpose for writing this selection?

_____

_____

_____

_____

_____

2. What is the author's attitude towards celebrity activists?

_____

_____

_____

3. How does the author's opinion of celebrity activists compare to his opinion of government specialists and experts like Nicholas Kristof and Jeffrey Sachs?

_____

_____

4. How does the author support his idea that many people oversimplify complicated international issues?

_____

_____

_____

5. List at least four words or phrases in paragraph 12 that have a negative connotation.

_____

_____

6. What is the tone of the reading?

_____

7. Is the author biased or objective? How biased or objective is he?

_____

_____

8. What is the purpose of the photo?

_____

_____

Words in Context

Directions: Locate each word in the paragraph indicated and reread that paragraph. Then, based on the way the word is used, write a synonym or brief definition. You may use a dictionary, if necessary.

1. **dispersed** (par. 2) _____

2. **influx** (par. 5) _____

3. **solace** (par. 6) _____

4. **plight** (par. 7) _____

5. **status quo** (par. 12) _____

Vocabulary Review

Directions: Match each word in Column A with its meaning in Column B.

Column A	Column B
_____ 1. endured (par. 2)	a. whole
_____ 2. emblematic (par. 3)	b. lived through
_____ 3. harnessed (par. 4)	c. symbolic
_____ 4. counterproductive (par. 5)	d. naturally
_____ 5. allure (par. 6)	e. walk, proceed
_____ 6. superficial (par. 6)	f. put to use
_____ 7. humility (par. 10)	g. modesty
_____ 8. tread (par. 11)	h. having the opposite effect
_____ 9. organically (par. 12)	i. surface
_____ 10. entirety (par. 12)	j. appeal

Summarizing the Reading Selection

Directions: Write a summary of the reading "Why Celebrity Activism Does More Harm than Good" on a separate sheet of paper.

Writing Exercises

1. Why do you think so many celebrities donate their time to international causes rather than to domestic causes (that is, problems within the United States)?

2. Watch the first Kony 2012 video (par. 2) on YouTube. Write a summary of it.

3. The author lists almost no positive aspects of celebrity activism. List and explain at least three ways that celebrity activism may have positive effects.

4. If you were going to volunteer for a human-rights organization, which one would you choose and why? (You may want to do some Internet research before deciding.)

After Ferguson, Staten Island, Cleveland, Athletes Are Becoming Activists Again

Dave Sheinin

> **Vocabulary Preview**
> **anthropologist** (par. 1) one who studies mankind
> **disseminated** (par. 4) spread, dispersed
> **in the wake of** (par. 17) after

Prereading

1. How do you predict the author will develop his article? (Hint: What do the title and the first paragraph tell you?)

   _____

   _____

2. Name at least four athletes or teams that will be discussed in the reading.

   _____

   _____

   _____

   _____

1   The past quarter-century has been great for athletes as corporations and "brands," with salaries exploding, endorsement opportunities multiplying and awareness of how to groom their images for maximum marketability growing. But it has not been a very good period for the notion of athletes as activists. Political expression and social activism, hallmarks of the sports landscape of the 1960s and '70s, had

LeBron James wears a T-shirt honoring Eric Garner after the controversial Staten Island grand jury decision.

come to be seen as too risky, bad for business. "The era of the activist athlete is dead," a Duke University cultural anthropologist wrote in 2008.

2   But that accepted wisdom appears to be changing. As the United States confronts anew its racial polarization, prominent athletes are no longer avoiding these sensitive topics—and in some cases are leading the public discourse.

3   On Sunday, five St. Louis Rams players took the field together during pregame introductions with a "Hands Up, Don't Shoot" gesture meant to show solidarity with Michael Brown, the black teenager shot dead by a white police officer in August in the St. Louis suburb of Ferguson.

4   Three days later, following another controversial non-indictment by a grand jury of a white police officer who killed an unarmed, 43-year-old African American man with a chokehold in Staten Island, University of Maryland wide receiver Deon Long took part in a peaceful protest on the College Park campus, holding up a handwritten sign—widely disseminated on social media—that said, "Are we still 'thugs' when you pay to watch us play sports?" The sign had the popular Twitter hashtag "#blacklivesmatter."

5   "It's extremely tough to take a stand one way or another [as an athlete]. In our position, it's very easy to not have an opinion on anything—because if you don't have an opinion on anything, you draw no scrutiny to yourself," said Washington Redskins safety Ryan Clark, speaking of the Rams players. "I think it was really cool that those guys felt strongly enough and felt the solidarity among one another—whether you agree with their stance or not—to go out and actually try to say, 'Okay, this is how we feel.'"

6   At least in St. Louis, the Rams' gesture had a polarizing effect. The St. Louis Police Officers Association criticized the players involved, demanding

punishment for them, and a bitter public debate ensued over whether the team had apologized to the police department for the players' actions.

7   But in any case, the days when athletes were expected to "shut up and play" appear to be over. "It's a sensitive subject right now," Cleveland Cavaliers star LeBron James told reporters during practice in New York on Thursday. "Violence is not the answer, and retaliation isn't the solution," he said, discouraging violent protests. "As a society, we just have to do better. I pray for the families of the lost ones."

8   On Thursday night, Amare Stoudemire's New York Knicks played a home game at Madison Square Garden against James and the Cavaliers, while more than 200 people were arrested in the city during protests of the Staten Island grand jury decision. Stoudemire said he would have been outside with the protesters if he didn't have a game to play. "I think it's something that's . . . very alarming in our country," Stoudemire told reporters. "We have to be more conscientious of what the law enforcement's job is, and that's to protect and serve. Those two words are very strong when you think about that. Your first job is to protect, and your second job is to serve. Obviously it's not happening that way."

9   Watching from afar, one man who understands like few others the intersection of sports and activism has been watching the current events and smiling. "I'm delighted," John Carlos said. "I always knew it was going to come." Carlos, 69, is considered the godfather of modern-day athlete activism. The gesture he and U.S. teammate Tommie Smith made on the medal stand at the 1968 Mexico City Olympics—a single black-gloved fist raised in the air, meant to signal "Black Power"—became one of the decade's iconic images.

10   Cultural anthropologist Orin Starn, the one who wrote in 2008 that athlete activism was dead, said there are "echoes" of Carlos and Smith's 1968 protest today, though it is still too early to say whether there has been a revival of that tradition. "To me, these still feel like isolated incidents rather than a shift in sporting culture," Starn said.

11   Carlos and Smith, who were kicked out of the Olympics for their gesture, were hardly alone in using the platform of sports stardom to advocate for social change during those decades of upheaval. Boxer Muhammad Ali protested against the Vietnam War. NBA star Bill Russell spoke out against racism. Tennis icons Arthur Ashe and Billie Jean King advocated for equality for blacks and women.

12   By the 1990s, generally speaking, that sense of activism among athletes was all but gone, replaced by a sense of the athlete as a marketing vessel. This stance was most vividly seen when Chicago Bulls star Michael Jordan reportedly explained his refusal to endorse a Democratic Senate candidate in his home state of North Carolina by saying, "Republicans buy shoes, too." Jordan "was the alpha model for the new kind of athlete who never took controversial stands," Starn said, "and Tiger Woods followed in his footsteps."

13   Perry Wallace, an American University law professor who in 1967 became the first black basketball player in the Southeastern Conference, believes the rise in social activism among athletes is in part a reaction to the criticism heaped on African American superstars such as Jordan and Woods for not "contributing to the cause."

14   "Jordan was criticized a lot inside and outside the African American community for not playing a more active role in helping the community," said Wallace, the subject of a new biography, "Strong Inside." "Some of that criticism has had an impact on some of these younger players. . . . I'm glad to see it because, among other things, I hope it reflects that they're looking around and thinking about the broader society rather than just themselves and their sneaker sales."

15   If there was one turning point in returning social activism to big-time sports, it may have come in 2012, when James and his Miami Heat teammates donned black "hoodies" and posed together for a team picture with their heads bowed and their hands in their pockets. The gesture, which James tweeted along with the hashtag "#WeWantJustice," was meant to show solidarity with Trayvon Martin, the black teenager shot and killed by a white/Hispanic man in Florida while wearing a similar hooded sweatshirt.

16   A year later, punter Chris Kluwe was released by the Minnesota Vikings, allegedly because of his outspoken support for same-sex marriage. Although the team denied that allegation, as well as Kluwe's claims he was subjected to homophobic behavior by team officials and coaches, the team reached a settlement with Kluwe that included a donation to charities that support lesbian, gay, bisexual and transgender causes.

17   But the spate of recent high-profile and polarizing police killings—in Ferguson, in Staten Island and in Cleveland, where a white police officer shot a 12-year-old African American boy after mistaking his pellet gun for a more lethal one—appears to have pushed the notion of athletes-as-activists to a new threshold. In part, this is because social media has made it easier than ever for athletes to voice their opinions. In the wake of the Ferguson grand jury's decision not to indict officer Darren Wilson for the killing of Brown, many high-profile athletes took to Twitter and Instagram to speak out. They included James, Los Angeles Lakers legend Magic Johnson, Redskins wide receiver DeSean Jackson and tennis superstar Serena Williams.

—https://www.washingtonpost.com/sports/after-ferguson-staten-island-cleveand-athletes-are-becoming-activists-again/2014/12/05/5ed5d61e-7c8d-11e4-8241-8cc0a3670239_story.html

Checking Your Comprehension

1. What is the main point of this reading?

_____

_____

2. What type of polarization in U.S. society does the author claim is motivating more professional athletes to take a stand?

_____

3. How did the St. Louis police react to the Rams' "hands up, don't shoot" pregame gesture?

_____

4. Which athlete said that he'd be outside with protesters if he didn't have a game to play?

_____

5. Why were John Carlos and Tommie Smith kicked out of the 1968 Olympics?

_____

6. Does anthropologist Orin Starn believe that professional athletes today are becoming much more activist?

_____

7. Which tennis stars advocated for equality for black people and for women?

_____

8. Which two athletes are considered the "alpha models" of star players who will not get involved in controversial issues?

_____

9. For which minority group has football player Chris Kluwe expressed support?

_____

Critical Reading and Thinking

1. What is the author's purpose for writing this selection?

_____

_____

_____

2. What kinds of evidence does the author present?

_____

_____

3. What is the tone of the reading?

_____

4. Is the author biased or objective? Does he present alternative viewpoints?

_____

_____

_____

_____

5. In paragraph 12, the author uses the term "marketing vessel." What does this figurative language mean?

_____

_____

6. What is the purpose of the first paragraph?

_____

_____

7. What is the purpose of the photo?

_____

_____

Words in Context

Directions: Locate each word in the paragraph indicated and reread that paragraph. Then, based on the way the word is used, write a synonym or brief definition. You may use a dictionary, if necessary.

1. groom (par. 1) _____

2. polarization (par. 2) _____

3. ensued (par. 6) _____

4. upheaval (par. 11) _____

5. donned (par. 15) _____

Vocabulary Review

Directions: Match each word in Column A with its meaning in Column B.

	Column A	Column B
_____	1. anew (par. 2)	a. discussion
_____	2. discourse (par. 2)	b. inspection

	Column A	Column B
_____	3. solidarity (par. 3)	c. deadly
_____	4. scrutiny (par. 5)	d. supposedly
_____	5. stance (par. 5)	e. again
_____	6. allegedly (par. 16)	f. viewpoint, opinion
_____	7. retaliation (par. 7)	g. accusation
_____	8. allegation (par. 16)	h. revenge
_____	9. spate (par. 17)	i. unity
_____	10. lethal (par. 17)	j. cluster

Summarizing the Reading Selection

Directions: Write a summary of the reading "After Ferguson, Staten Island, Cleveland, Athletes Are Becoming Activists Again" on a separate sheet of paper.

Writing Exercises

1. Do you think athletes should take part in social protests or political activism? Or do you think they are entertainers who should stay out of the political arena? Explain.
2. Amare Stoudemire states that law enforcement's job is to "protect and serve." What exactly does that phrase mean?
3. Is there any athlete you particularly admire? If so, is he or she politically active—and if so, how?
4. Have there been any political protests on your campus or in your neighborhood or city recently? If so, what were the reasons for the protests?

Analyzing and Synthesizing Ideas

1. On what one key idea do the authors of these two readings disagree strongly?
2. In each reading, identify at least three words with a positive connotation and three words with a negative connotation.
3. In each reading, identify three facts and three opinions.
4. Which reading is more balanced? Which is more biased?
5. What do you think each author would say about the other author's topic? That is, what would Dave Sheinin say about celebrity activists, and what would Andres Jimenez say about professional athletes who make political statements?

Issue 2: The Marketing of Human Organs

Many sick people will die while they wait for organ transplants. Most donated organs come from dead bodies. In recent years, some have begun questioning whether living people should be allowed to sell their organs to those who are willing to buy them. The following two selections examine the debate. As you read, identify the writers' positions and evaluate the evidence they provide. Before you begin reading, think about any knowledge you may already have about organ transplants and organ donation.

Is Selling Human Organs Really So Unethical?

Andrew Crane and Dirk Matten

Vocabulary Preview

borne (par. 4) carried

safeguards (par. 4) protections

euthanasia (par. 5) mercy killing; the painless killing of someone suffering from an incurable or painful disease or coma

codify (par. 5) arrange into a systematic code

concerted (par. 7) vigorous

mandatory (par. 10) required

bastion (par. 11) defender

advocate (par. 11) argue in favor of

Prereading

1. How are the buyers and sellers of human organs at risk?

   _____

   _____

2. What is the only country that has a legalized system for buying and selling human organs? _____

1   Recently, the World Health Organization (WHO) reported on the rise in the illegal trade in human organs. The WHO estimates that more than 10,000 black market operations involving purchased human organs are now carried out every year. There are serious ethical and medical concerns associated with the practice. Sellers risk being exploited, buyers may be victims of scams, and both parties face far higher risks of medical complications due to the lack of proper medical care.

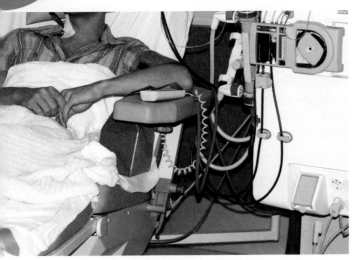

According to the National Kidney Foundation, over 100,000 people await lifesaving organ donations in the United States in 2015. The majority await kidney transplants.

2   The problem is that, although the commercial trade in organs is in many respects morally repugnant, many of the problems associated with the illegal trade in organs are actually directly a result of its illegality. Backstreet operations, black market trading—these are the critical risk factors here, not its dubious moral status. Plus, for all the important concerns about the problem of poor people being exploited to sell their organs to the rich, it is important not to mix up what are two different ethical issues here—one about exploitation of organ sellers and one about whether the commercial trade in organs is something that is acceptable in society at all. Both of these are worth examining in a little more detail.

3   First off, let's bracket for a moment the problem of exploitation and just consider the ethics of commercial organ trading. Sure, we know the practice has been made illegal in almost every country—but is selling human organs really so bad? One major issue that we have to consider here is that, like it or not, the sale of human organs saves lives. Donations of organs from the deceased are simply too limited to meet demand almost everywhere. In the U.S., more than 100,000 people are currently waiting for organ donations. In China, it is estimated that a million people are currently in need of a kidney . . . yet last year only something like 5000 actually received one. Most countries are facing a severe supply problem. So from a simple societal cost–benefit perspective, then, providing the seller stays in relatively good health, and the buyer is able to live longer or better than they would have otherwise, the benefits would appear to exceed the costs. Without sufficient supply from other sources, commercial organ trade can make society as a whole better off.

4   That is not to deny that there are indeed very significant costs that have to be borne by the seller here in terms of potential health risks. Even if society can be shown to benefit in aggregate, not everyone benefits equally. After all, the seller is potentially putting their own life at risk here. But if we can imagine a situation where the seller is provided with suitable safeguards to minimize these risks— through a guaranteed level of decent medical care for example—then the cost– benefit argument could certainly prevail. In fact, that is precisely why we do often permit some forms of voluntary non-paid donation: under the right conditions, live organ donation can make a net positive benefit to society. In principle, that cost-benefit equation should not be materially changed by introducing a commercial transaction . . . except of course we have thrown some actual financial costs and benefits into the mix.

5   To be sure, few of us are comfortable with the idea of selling organs for money. For critics, it only makes sense from a cost–benefit point of view if we ignore the more ambiguous costs involved, such as the loss of basic humanity involved in such an act. Simply put, it is not something we want to accept in a civilized society. A similar argument is also raised in relation to other "unacceptable" practices, such as euthanasia, prostitution and drug use. Legalization might well create benefits, minimize harms, or simply enable greater personal freedoms, but the law also has to codify the principles of human society that we want to establish and live up to. And commercial trade in live organs, so the argument goes, is against those basic principles.

6   Let's be clear though: those principles come at a cost—the cost of human lives. People are literally dying waiting for suitable organ donors. At a time when the illegal trade is actually growing, shouldn't we be revisiting the question of whether the commercial organ trade is really so unacceptable that it's worth letting people die for our principles? Isn't it time we asked whether the legal prohibition route is actually working?

7   The exploitation question is a different but no less important question. The prospect of the most disadvantaged in society selling their own body parts just to get by assaults our most basic principles of human dignity. Obviously we need to tackle poverty itself in a more concerted fashion to get to the heart of this problem. But in the meantime, the big question we have to ask is whether the decision to make the commercial trade in organs illegal is actually benefiting or further exacerbating the exploitation of the poor.

8   Regardless of its legal status, people will continue to do whatever they can to escape poverty, and for the truly desperate, their organs may be their most valuable asset. Pushing such people into the hands of criminals and unlicensed medical practitioners, however, is a recipe for adding yet more exploitation onto an already unfair situation.

9   Legalization by itself would not solve the problem. But if we were to accept that, in principle at least, the trade in human organs might be socially acceptable, the real question then becomes: how could we do it in a responsible way so that people do not get exploited?

10   There's no easy answer to this, but it is possible to conceive of a tightly regulated system that could eliminate most if not all of the worst forms of exploitation. Price controls for organ donations, strict rules for participation as donors and recipients, mandatory counseling for prospective donors, enforcement of medical follow-up, quality control checks, a transparent system to ensure clear organ provenance—these are the kind of arrangements that a serious regulator might want to put in place.

11   Many governments probably won't have the will or the capability to do this effectively, and it's hardly a very encouraging sign that the only country currently operating a legalized system is that great bastion of freedom and security, Iran. But a few years ago the Singaporean government was apparently also

considering the issue, although nothing seems to have come of it. Who's to say that China won't be the next, especially given that they are currently operating a widely condemned practice of harvesting organs from executed prisoners? A voluntary system could hardly be more controversial. But who these days would really be brave enough to advocate legalization given the international consensus against the trade? Maybe it's time for those on the interminable organ waiting lists to start getting organized.

—http://craneandmatten.blogspot.com

Checking Your Comprehension

1. What is the main point of this reading?

   _____

   _____

2. The authors divide the controversy into two different ethical issues. What are they?

   _____

   _____

3. What is the cause of the serious organ shortage?

   _____

   _____

4. Which "unacceptable" practices do the authors list as activities not acceptable in a civilized society?

   _____

5. What do the authors identify as the "main cost" of preventing people from selling organs legally?

   _____

6. Which group of people is most likely to sell their organs?

   _____

7. List at least five ways the legal system might help protect people who choose to sell their organs.

   _____

   _____

   _____

Critical Reading and Thinking

1. What is the authors' purpose for writing this selection?

_____

_____

_____

_____

2. Is this reading fact based, opinion based, or a mixture of both?

_____

_____

_____

3. What is the tone of the reading?

_____

4. How would you describe the authors' description of Iran as "that great bastion of freedom and security"?

_____

5. Identify two uses of statistics in the reading.

_____

_____

_____

6. What is the purpose of the photo?

_____

_____

Words and Phrases in Context

Directions: Locate each word or phrase in the paragraph indicated and reread that paragraph. Then, based on the way the word or phrase is used, write a synonym or brief definition. You may use a dictionary, if necessary.

1. black market (par. 1) _____

2. dubious (par. 2) _____

3. potential (par. 4) _____

4. materially (par. 4) _____

5. provenance (par. 10) _____

Vocabulary Review

Directions: Match each word in Column A with its meaning in Column B.

Column A	Column B
____ 1. repugnant (par. 2)	a. banning
____ 2. deceased (par. 3)	b. general agreement
____ 3. aggregate (par. 4)	c. unclear, debatable
____ 4. prevail (par. 4)	d. disgusting
____ 5. ambiguous (par. 5)	e. endless
____ 6. prohibition (par. 6)	f. total
____ 7. assault (par. 7)	g. used for profit
____ 8. exploitation (par. 7)	h. attack
____ 9. consensus (par. 11)	i. triumph, win
____ 10. interminable (par. 11)	j. dead

Summarizing the Reading Selection

Directions: Write a summary of the reading "Is Selling Human Organs Really So Unethical?" on a separate sheet of paper.

Writing Exercises

1. Do you think any of the controversial issues mentioned in paragraph 5 (euthanasia, prostitution, drug use) should be legalized? Why or why not?

2. Under what circumstances would you donate or sell one of your organs?

3. What is your opinion of China's practice of harvesting organs from executed prisoners? Explain.

4. Do you believe buying and selling organs in the United States should be legal? Why or why not?

Ethicists, Philosophers Discuss Selling of Human Organs

Corydon Ireland

Vocabulary Preview
monitor (par. 6) keep track of, watch

Prereading

1. Which key human organ will the reading discuss? _____

2. What main type of evidence do you anticipate that the author will offer to support his thesis? _____

1   In nearly every country in the world, there is a shortage of kidneys for transplantation. In the United States, around 73,000 people are on waiting lists to receive a kidney. Yet 4,000 die every year before the lifesaving organ is available.

2   Worldwide, about 66,000 kidney transplants are performed annually. By far, that's too slow a rate to help an estimated 1 million people who have end-stage renal disease. Is a global market for organ sales the answer? Can a for-profit system exist, save lives, and still not exploit the poor? A series of experts—medical doctors, international health experts, and ethicists—looked at the issue during a series of Harvard conferences on current controversies in global health.

3   "It's an extremely sensitive and troubling topic," said symposium Chairman Daniel E. Wikler, who is on the steering committee of Harvard's Program in Ethics and Health. "We have here the elements of tragedy." On one side, he said, are patients for whom "life hangs in the balance." On the other, there are the desperately poor whose organs now have monetary value, and who are vulnerable to exploitation in a growing industry known as "transplant tourism."

4   Kidney transplantation was the focus of the three-hour conference. In the case of kidneys, said Wikler, even the poorest person in the Philippines or India has "a couple of gemstones—diamonds—on each hip."

5   Even in the face of desperate illness, there are moral standards to protect, said the one-time chief ethicist for the World Health Organization (WHO). But "with life hanging in the balance," said Wikler of organ markets, "we need very convincing moral reasons to get in the way."

6   Medical systems across the world are far from meeting the needs of kidney-transplant candidates, said Luc Noël, who tracks transplantation issues for WHO in Geneva. But there is also an urgent need for global resolve, he said. In the past decade, WHO and other groups have called for international standards that will protect the poor, monitor transplantation quality, keep the process transparent, and ban commercialization (now driven largely by the Internet).

Most often the poor and vulnerable sell organs for cash.

7   In the present global hodgepodge of transplant tourism, thousands of patients—from the United States, Israel, Saudi Arabia, and other prosperous nations—get the kidneys they need, he said. But their donors (some of them exploited by organized crime) frequently get the short and sharp end of the stick. Noël cited one survey of kidney donors in Pakistan's for-profit market, where two-thirds of the operations are performed on foreigners. The survey showed that almost 70 percent of donors were slaves or bonded laborers; 90 percent were illiterate; 88 percent had no improvement in economic status from the donation; and 98 percent reported a subsequent decline in health, including chronic pain from large incisions.

8   WHO and its decision-making body, the World Health Assembly, have taken stands against commercialized kidney transplantation. Their goal is to establish within a decade a binding international document that protects the poor.

9   Prevention is one way of reducing the need for kidney transplants, acknowledged Noël. But in the meantime, waiting lists could shorten through more cadaver donations and more by living donors (a step he called "a civic gesture"). In the United States alone, said Noël, one additional donated kidney a month to each of 58 donation service areas would create equilibrium—an equal number of waiting patients and available organs—in 2013.

10   Meanwhile, there have been country-by-country improvements, he said. Egypt is debating tighter laws; so is Pakistan. China recently cracked down on medical tourism, reducing the number of operations by one-third between 2006 and 2007. (Practices in China also add another layer of moral complexity: All 8,000 kidneys transplanted there in 2006 came from executed prisoners.) In the Philippines, kidney transplants are officially restricted, with only 10 percent of operations supposed to go to foreigners. But the reality is different. One slum of Manila is known as "Kidneyville" for the high number (3,000) of organ donors living there. Worse, Philippine health officials last December wrote a health policy that would make organ sales open and legal. That would mean sick patients would "descend on Manila [like] predators," said Harvard Medical School (HMS) professor of surgery Francis L. Delmonico. A transplant surgeon, he's medical director of the New England Organ Bank in Newton, Mass., and travels worldwide as a member of the ethics committee of The Transplantation Society, a scientific group.

11   Even in a regulated, government-run version of transplant tourism, "unethical realities" lead to exploitation of the poor and the vulnerable, said Delmonico. Waiting lists of sick patients are a concern, he acknowledged—but studies suggest that a profit-based international transplantation market "will destroy altruism" and reduce the number of kidney donations from both live donors and from cadavers. To put waiting lists in perspective, he added, half of all patients on the lists are "medically ineligible" for transplants anyway—too sick for the required surgery.

12   A market-based system for kidneys is "workable and defensible," argued conference presenter Julio J. Elias, an economist at the State University of New York, Buffalo. Elias is co-author of a widely circulated paper that shows—with a flurry of economics formulas and cost-benefit analyses—that market incentives would increase the supply of organs available for transplanting, and would shorten waiting lists. Still, he added, "The market may work, but some people may feel it's repugnant." And the effect of this repugnance on markets was the focus of his talk. This culturally shared form of extreme dislike can sometimes mean certain transactions become illegal, said Elias. Horsemeat is widely illegal to sell, for instance, though it shares the same nutritional properties as the flesh of cows. Liquor used to be illegal, and so was life insurance. "Repugnance," he said, "is associated with social costs."

13   But the good news, in economic terms, is that perceptions of repugnance can shift along with other cultural norms, said Elias. If the price of beef goes up, he speculated, maybe the shared disgust at eating horsemeat will disappear—as the disgust at drinking did very soon after Prohibition. Attitudes will change regarding legal transplantation markets for kidneys, he predicted, "when it is shown how efficiently prices will solve this problem."

14   Two philosophers presenting at the conference disagreed. Nir Eyal, an instructor in social medicine in HMS's Division of Ethics, argued that "dignitary harm" (an insult and/or injury to the dignity of a person) results from exploiting the economically vulnerable—a harm that unfairly spreads out and compromises every member of the same group.

15   Philosopher Samuel Kerstein, post-doctoral fellow in Harvard's Program in Ethics and Health, was wary of markets for organs because of Immanuel Kant's "Formula of Humanity"—in summary, "Act always in a way that expresses respect for the value of humanity."

16   "To have value as a person is to have incomparable worth," said Kerstein—so a market for organs that treats the poor as "tools available for the right price" is wrong. Organ transplantation was something Kant had a direct opinion of, though he died in 1804. In 18th-century Europe, the poor were being exploited for their teeth, which were transplanted into the jaws of the willing rich. Today, said Kerstein, "selling organs is wrong in the current context it is likely to occur." That is—with little respect for human dignity, particularly for the dignity of the poor.

17   But perhaps there are permissible alternatives to buying and selling organs, he said. Opt-out programs for organ donation, for instance, which have increased the number of cadaver donations in Spain, might be a possibility. Or even an "organ draft," suggested Kerstein, provocatively—a lotterylike system that would require a random set of the healthy to donate organs. "If we're not willing to do that sort of thing," he said, "we have to ask ourselves, 'Why not?"

—http://news.harvard.edu/gazette/story/2008/02/ethicists
-philosophers-discuss-selling-of-human-organs/

Checking Your Comprehension

1. What is the main point of this reading?

2. About how many people in the world suffer from kidney diseases?

3. What is the key force that is commercializing the sale of human organs?

4. What is the social class of the Pakistanis who have sold their organs? What happened to them after selling their organs?

5. According to Luc Noël, what would solve the problem of the kidney shortage?

6. Where does China get its donated organs?

7. What does Julio J. Elias believe will make people feel less repugnance at the idea of selling human organs?

8. What is "dignitary harm"?

Critical Reading and Thinking

1. What is the author's purpose for writing this selection?

   _____

   _____

2. Daniel Wikler states that even the poorest people in the Philippines or India have "a couple of gemstones—diamonds—on each hip" (par. 4). *Gemstones* and *diamonds* are figurative language for what?

   _____

3. What kinds of evidence does the author provide?

   _____

4. What is the tone of this reading?

   _____

5. Does the author present only one side of the issue, or does he explore multiple viewpoints?

   _____

   _____

6. What is the purpose of the photo?

   _____

   _____

Words in Context

Directions: Locate each word in the paragraph indicated and reread that paragraph. Then, based on the way the word is used, write a synonym or brief definition. You may use a dictionary, if necessary.

1. **renal** (par. 2) _____

2. **hodgepodge** (par. 7) _____

3. **chronic** (par. 7) _____

4. **altruism** (par. 11) _____

5. **incomparable** (par. 16) _____

Vocabulary Review

Directions: Match each word in Column A with its meaning in Column B.

Column A	Column B
_____ 1. urgent (par. 6)	a. series
_____ 2. resolve (par. 6)	b. cut
_____ 3. prosperous (par. 7)	c. pressing
_____ 4. subsequent (par. 7)	d. suspicious
_____ 5. incision (par. 7)	e. successful or wealthy
_____ 6. cadaver (par. 9)	f. public, community
_____ 7. civic (par. 9)	g. guess
_____ 8. flurry (par. 12)	h. corpse
_____ 9. speculate (par. 13)	i. following
_____ 10. wary (par. 15)	j. decision, resolution

Summarizing the Reading Selection

Directions: Write a summary of the reading "Ethicists, Philosophers Discuss Selling of Human Organs" on a separate sheet of paper.

Writing Exercises

1. The author describes "transplant tourism," which involves wealthy people getting organs from people around the globe. For what other services or products do people go to other countries? Provide and explain one or two examples.

2. Which criteria should humanitarian organizations use to determine who should receive a donated kidney? For example, should young people have priority over older people? Should kidneys be given to people who live in the same city or state as the donor?

3. The author cites an expert who talks about changing attitudes toward alcohol, which was once against the law (during the U.S. Prohibition period). On what other topics do you see society's attitudes changing? Explain.

Analyzing and Synthesizing Ideas

1. Highlight the words in each reading that have strong negative and positive connotations.
2. Which reading is more balanced? Which is more biased?
3. Evaluate the support used in each reading. Which reading offers more support for its main ideas?
4. Did reading these selections affect your thinking in any way about organ sales and donations? For example, are you now more likely to donate organs after your death? Do you now feel more in favor of (or more against) the idea of a commercial market for human organs?
5. Both readings use the word *repugnant*. What other practices do you think many human beings or societies consider repugnant?

Issue 3: The Internet and Technology

In the United States, many of us take the Internet for granted. Like most technologies throughout history, the Internet has helped many people while creating some unexpected (and negative) consequences. The following two selections examine some of technology's effects on people and society. Before you read, think about how you use technology and how your life would change without it.

Is Internet Addiction a Real Thing?

Maria Konnikova

> **Vocabulary Preview**
>
> **colleague** (par. 2) coworker
> **behest** (par. 4) requirement
> **impairment** (par. 7) handicap
> **maladaptive** (par. 7) not providing adequate adjustment to circumstances
> **A.D.H.D.** (par. 7) attention deficit hyperactivity disorder
> **O.C.D.** (par 7.) obsessive-compulsive disorder
> **endemic** (par. 8) within

Prereading

1. Predict some questions that the reading will answer.

_____

_____

2. About what percentage of Dr. Potenza's patients come to him for Internet addiction?

_____

1   Marc Potenza, a psychiatrist at Yale and the director of the school's Program for Research on Impulsivity and Impulse Control Disorders, has been treating addiction for more than two decades. Early in his career, he, like most others studying addiction at the time, focused on substance-abuse problems—cocaine and heroin addicts, alcoholics, and the like. Soon, however, he noticed patients with other problems that were more difficult to classify. There were, for example, the sufferers of trichotillomania, the inescapable urge to pull your hair until it falls out. Others had been committed for problem gambling: they couldn't stop no matter how much debt they had accumulated. It was to this second class of behaviors—at the time, they were not called addictions—that he turned his attention. Were they, he wondered, fundamentally the same?

2   In some sense, they aren't. A substance affects a person physically in a way that a behavior simply cannot: no matter how severe your trichotillomania, you're not introducing something new to your bloodstream. But, in what may be a more fundamental way, they share much in common. As Potenza and his colleague Robert Leeman point out in a recent review of the last two decades of research, there are many commonalities between those two categories of addiction. Both behavioral and substance addictions are characterized by an inability to control how often or how intensely you engage in an activity, even when you feel the negative consequences. Both come with urges and cravings: you feel a sudden and debilitating need to place a bet or to take a hit in the middle of a meal. Both are marked by an inability to stop.

3   In recent years, however, Potenza has been increasingly treating a new kind of problem: people who come to him

In terms of the Internet and technology, how much is too much?

because they can't get off the Internet. In some ways, it seems exactly like the behavioral addictions that he has been treating for years, with many of the same consequences. "There are core features that cut across those conditions," Potenza says. "Things like the motivation to engage in the behaviors and put aside other important elements of life functioning, just to engage in them." Or, in other words, "behavior for behavior's sake."

4   There's something different, and more complicated, about Internet addiction, though. Unlike gambling or even trichotillomania, it's more difficult to pin down a quantifiable, negative effect of Internet use. With problematic gambling, you're losing money and causing harm to yourself and your loved ones. But what about symptoms like those of a woman I'll call Sue, who is a patient of Potenza? A young college student, Sue first came to Potenza at the behest of her parents, who were becoming increasingly concerned about the changes in their daughter. A good—and social—student in high school, she found herself depressed, skipping or dropping classes, foregoing all college extracurricular activities, and, increasingly, using the Internet to set up extreme sexual encounters with people she had never met in real life. Sue spends the majority of her time online social networking, but does that mean that she has a problem with the Internet or with managing her social life and her sex life? What if she were obsessively online, for the rest of her life, but learning languages or editing Wikipedia?

5   The Internet, after all, is a medium, not an activity in and of itself. If you spend your time gambling online, maybe you have a gambling addiction, not an Internet addiction. If you spend your time shopping online, maybe it's a shopping addiction. "Some people have posited that the Internet is a vehicle and not a target of disorder," Potenza said. Can you be addicted to a longing for virtual connectivity in the same way that you can be addicted to a longing for a drink?

6   As far back as 1997, before the days of ubiquitous smartphones and laptops, when dial-up and AOL dominated the landscape, psychologists were already testing the "addictive potential" of the World Wide Web. Even then, certain people were exhibiting the same kinds of symptoms that appeared with other addictions: trouble at work, social isolation, and the inability to cut back. And, to the extent that there was something that people referred to as an addiction, it appeared to be to the medium itself—the feeling of connectedness to something—rather than to an activity that could be accomplished via that medium.

7   The realization that the Internet may be inducing some addictive-seeming behaviors in its own right has only grown more widespread. One study, published in 2012, of nearly twelve thousand adolescents in eleven European countries, found a 4.4 percent prevalence of what the authors termed "pathological Internet use" or using the Internet in a way that affected subjects' health and life. That is, through a combination of excessive time spent online and that time interfering with necessary social and professional activities, Internet use would result in either mental distress or clinical impairment, akin to the type of inability to function associated with pathological gambling. For maladaptive Internet

use—a milder condition characterized by problematic but not yet fully disruptive behavior—the number was 13.5 percent. People who exhibited problematic use were also more likely to suffer from other psychological problems, such as depression, anxiety, A.D.H.D., and O.C.D.

8   Sue wasn't the first patient that Potenza had seen for whom the Internet was causing substantial, escalating problems; that number had been rising slowly over the last few years, and his colleagues were reporting the same uptick. He had been working with addicts for decades, and her problems, as well as those of her fellow sufferers, were every bit as real as those of the gambling addicts. And it wasn't just an iteration of college angst in a new form. It was something endemic to the medium itself. "I think there are people who find it very difficult to tolerate time without using digital technologies like smartphones or other ways of connecting via the Internet," Potenza said. It's the very knowledge of connectivity, or its lack, that's the problem.

9   Internet addiction remains a relatively minor part of Potenza's work—he estimates that fewer than ten out of every forty patients he sees come in for an Internet problem. These patients tend to be younger, and there seems to be a gender divide: male patients are more likely to be addicted to activities like online gaming; women, to things like social networking. But it's hard to make generalizations, because the nature of the problem keeps changing. "The truth is, we don't know what's normal," Potenza says. "It's not like alcohol where we have healthy amounts that we can recommend to people." In other words, just because you're online all day doesn't mean you're an addict: there are no norms or hard numbers that could tell us either way.

—*The New Yorker*, November 26, 2014

Checking Your Comprehension

1. What is the main point of this reading?

   _____

   _____

   _____

   _____

2. What psychological term is used for the condition in which people have a desire to pull their hair until it falls out?

   _____

3. What does a substance like alcohol or cocaine do that the Internet cannot?

   _____

2. The author quotes Toby Shapshak as saying that mobile technology is a "technology leapfrog." What does this figurative language mean in the context of this reading selection?

_____

_____

_____

3. What is the tone of the reading?

_____

4. Is the author biased? Does he present alternative viewpoints?

_____

_____

_____

_____

_____

5. What kinds of evidence does the author present?

_____

6. What purpose does the last paragraph serve?

_____

_____

7. What is the purpose of the photo?

_____

Words in Context

Directions: Locate each word in the paragraph indicated and reread that paragraph. Then, based on the way the word is used, write a synonym or brief definition. You may use a dictionary, if necessary.

1. infrastructure (par. 2)

_____

2. trend (par. 3) _____

3. entrepreneur (par. 5) _____

4. legacy (par. 9) _____

5. pent-up (par. 11) _____

Vocabulary Review

Directions: Match each word in Column A with its meaning in Column B.

Column A	Column B
_____ 1. overcome (par. 2)	a. lightly populated and developed; opposite of urban
_____ 2. swath (par. 2)	b. conquer or defeat
_____ 3. rural (par. 2)	c. business
_____ 4. ingenious (par. 2)	d. broad area
_____ 5. commerce (par. 5)	e. far-reaching
_____ 6. spurring (par. 7)	f. adoption
_____ 7. uptick (par. 7)	g. common
_____ 8. widespread (par. 9)	h. brilliantly clever or inventive
_____ 9. profound (par. 10)	i. stimulating
_____ 10. trajectory (par. 12)	j. path

Summarizing the Reading Selection

Directions: Write a summary of the reading "Internet Use on Mobile Phones in Africa Predicted to Increase 20-Fold" on a separate sheet of paper.

Writing Exercises

1. The author makes it clear that people in sub-Saharan Africa prefer smartphones to landlines. Do you have a landline in your home? Why or why not?

2. What are the top three activities you do on your smartphone? List at least three other ways you might use your smartphone to improve your life.

3. If you were an investor, would you invest in cell-phone towers and technology in Africa? Why or why not?

Analyzing and Synthesizing Ideas

1. Compare the tones of the two readings.
2. Compare the intended audience for each reading. Who do you think comprises the intended readership for each selection?
3. What point might Maria Konnikova, author of "Is Internet Addiction a Real Thing?" make about the second reading in this pair?

4. Which reading is more critical? Which is more upbeat and optimistic?
5. In each reading, identify at least five words with strong negative or positive connotations.
6. Identify at least three facts and three opinions in each reading.

Issue 4: Reviving Extinct Species

The following two selections discuss the pros and cons of bringing extinct species back to life. As you read, identify each writer's position on the issue, and evaluate the evidence offered in support of the position.

Pro: The Case for Reviving Extinct Species

Stewart Brand

Vocabulary Preview

biodiversity (par. 4) many different types of animals and plants

ecosystems (par. 4) a community of organisms that creates a system in an environment

genomes (par. 9) sets of chromosomes or genes

bottleneck (par. 9) a situation in which no progress can be made

Achilles' heel (par. 10) vulnerable spot

keystones (par. 12) important things that other things depend on

herbivore (par. 13) an animal that eats only plants

boreal forest (par. 13) cold northern forest with pine trees

deciduous forest (par. 14) forest with trees that lose their leaves in the fall

icons (par. 15) symbols

Prereading

4. Identify at least one species the article discusses.

_____

_____

5. What types of evidence do you anticipate that the author will offer to support his position?

_____

A boy looks at a model of an extinct dodo at the Humboldt Museum in Germany.

1   Many extinct species—from the passenger pigeon to the woolly mammoth—might now be reclassified as "bodily, but not genetically, extinct." They're dead, but their DNA is recoverable from museum specimens and fossils, even those up to 200,000 years old.

2   Thanks to new developments in genetic technology, that DNA may eventually bring the animals back to life. Only species whose DNA is too old to be recovered, such as dinosaurs, are the ones to consider totally extinct, bodily and genetically.

3   But why bring vanished creatures back to life? It will be expensive and difficult. It will take decades. It won't always succeed. Why even try?

4   Why do we take enormous trouble to protect endangered species? The same reasons will apply to species brought back from extinction: to preserve biodiversity, to restore diminished ecosystems, to advance the science of preventing extinctions, and to undo harm that humans have caused in the past.

5   Furthermore, the prospect of de-extinction is profound news. That something as irreversible and final as extinction might be reversed is a stunning realization. The imagination soars. Just the thought of mammoths and passenger pigeons alive again invokes the awe and wonder that drives all conservation at its deepest level.

6   Then, there's the power of good news. The International Union for Conservation of Nature is adding to its famous "Red List" of endangered species a pair of "Green Lists."

7   One will describe species that are doing fine as well as species that were in trouble and are now doing better, thanks to effective efforts to help them. The other list will describe protected wild lands in the world that are particularly well managed.

8   Conservationists are learning the benefits of building hope and building on hope. Species brought back from extinction will be beacons of hope.

9   Useful science will also emerge. Close examination of the genomes of extinct species can tell us much about what made them vulnerable in the first place. Were they in a bottleneck with too little genetic variability? How were they different from close relatives that survived? Living specimens will reveal even more.

10   Techniques being developed for de-extinction will also be directly applicable to living species that are close to extinction. Tiny populations can have their genetic variability restored. A species with a genetic Achilles' heel might be totally cured with an adjustment introduced through cloning.

11   For instance, the transmissible cancer on the faces of Tasmanian devils is thought to be caused by a single gene. That gene can be silenced in a generation of the animals released to the wild. The cancer would disappear in the wild soon after, because the immune animals won't transmit it, and animals with the immunity will out-reproduce the susceptible until the entire population is immune.

12   Some extinct species were important "keystones" in their region. Restoring them would help restore a great deal of ecological richness.

13   Woolly mammoths, for instance, were the dominant herbivore of the "mammoth steppe" in the far north, once the largest biome on Earth. In their absence, the grasslands they helped sustain were replaced by species-poor tundra and boreal forest. Their return to the north would bring back carbon-fixing grass and reduce greenhouse-gas-releasing tundra. Similarly, the European aurochs (extinct since 1627) helped to keep forests across all of Europe and Asia mixed with biodiverse meadows and grasslands.

14   The passenger pigeon was a keystone species for the whole eastern deciduous forest, from the Mississippi to the Atlantic, from the Deep South clear up into Canada. "Yearly the feathered tempest roared up, down, and across the continent," the pioneer conservationist Aldo Leopold wrote, "sucking up the laden fruits of forest and prairie, burning them in a traveling blast of life."

15   Such animals can also serve as icons, flagship species inspiring the protection of a whole region. The prospect of bringing back the aurochs is helping to boost the vibrant European "rewilding" movement to connect tracts of abandoned farmland into wildlife corridors spanning national boundaries.

16   Similar projects to establish "wildways" joined across American eastern states could benefit from the idea of making the region ready for passenger pigeon flocks and flights of the beautiful Carolina parakeet, once the most colorful bird in the United States.

17   Wilderness in Tasmania is under pressure from loggers and other threats. The return of the marvelous marsupial wolf called the thylacine (or Tasmanian tiger), extinct since 1936, would ensure better protection for its old habitat.

18   The current generation of children will experience the return of some remarkable creatures in their lifetime. It may be part of what defines their generation and their attitude to the natural world. They will drag their parents to zoos to see the woolly mammoth and growing populations of captive-bred passenger pigeons, ivory-billed woodpeckers, Carolina parakeets, Eskimo curlews, great auks, Labrador ducks, and maybe even dodoes. (Entrance fees at zoos provide a good deal of conservation funding, and zoos will be in the thick of extinct species revival and restoration.)

19   Humans killed off a lot of species over the last 10,000 years. Some resurrection is in order. A bit of redemption might come with it.

—Brand, National Geographic News

Checking Your Comprehension

1. What is the main point of this reading?

_____

2. Why won't dinosaurs be brought back to life?

_____

3. List three extinct species that could be brought back.

_____

_____

4. How will extinct species that are brought back to life help prevent the extinction of other species?

_____

_____

5. How might restoring extinct animals affect plant growth?

_____

_____

6. How might the possibility of bringing back an extinct species change people's feelings about certain areas of land?

_____

_____

7. Describe how having revived extinct species at zoos could impact conservation.

_____

_____

Critical Reading and Thinking

1. What is the author's purpose for writing this selection?

_____

2. What kinds of evidence does the author present? _____

3. What purpose does the photograph have?

_____

4. What is the tone of the reading? _____

5. Are the negative effects of species revival discussed or refuted? _____

Words in Context

Directions: Locate each word in the paragraph indicated and reread that paragraph. Then, based on the way the word is used, write a synonym or brief definition. You may use a dictionary, if necessary.

1. extinct (par. 1) _____

2. irreversible (par. 5) _____

3. beacons (par. 8) _____

4. transmissible (par. 11) _____

5. susceptible (par. 11) _____

Vocabulary Review

Directions: Match each word or phrase in Column A with its meaning in Column B.

Column A	Column B
_____ 1. extinct (par. 1)	a. no longer alive
_____ 2. reclassified (par. 1)	b. unchangeable
_____ 3. diminished (par. 4)	c. made smaller
_____ 4. profound (par. 5)	d. successful
_____ 5. irreversible (par. 5)	e. bringing back to life
_____ 6. effective (par. 7)	f. relabeled
_____ 7. emerge (par. 9)	g. forgiveness
_____ 8. laden (par. 14)	h. appear
_____ 9. resurrection (par. 19)	i. heavily hanging
_____ 10. redemption (par. 19)	j. greatly important

Summarizing the Reading Selection

Directions: Write a summary of the reading "The Case for Reviving Extinct Species" on a separate sheet of paper.

Writing Exercises

1. Does reviving extinct species give you hope? How would it make you feel if an extinct species were brought back? Write a paragraph explaining your position.

2. Do you think the concept of "rewilding" is important? Why or why not? Discuss your opinion by writing a paragraph.

3. Should it matter whether a species became extinct due to something humans did or due to genetic problems within the species? Does the reason behind the extinction affect whether you think we should revive the species? Write a paragraph to explain your viewpoint.

Con: The Case Against Species Revival

Stuart Pimm

> **Vocabulary Preview**
>
> **paleobotanist** (par. 1) a scientist specializing in fossil plants
> **metaphorically** (par. 1) not literally, as a figure of speech
> **pollinators** (par. 1) animals that move pollen from one plant to another
> **symbiotic** (par. 1) interdependent
> **charismatic** (par. 2) charming, stand-out
> **touted** (par. 3) praised
> **cabrito** (par. 4) roasted goat
> **inherent** (par. 8) naturally occurring
> **gimmickry** (par. 12) using new or exciting gadgets
> **rapaciousness** (par. 12) greed

Prereading

1. Do you expect this author to present a reasoned argument or an emotional one? Why?

   _____

2. Name several species discussed in this article.

   _____

1   In the movie *Jurassic Park*, a tree extinct for millions of years delights the paleobotanist. Then a sauropod eats its leaves. This movie later shows us how to re-create the dinosaur but not how to grow the tree, which at that size would be perhaps a hundred or more years old, or how to do so metaphorically overnight. To sustain even a single dinosaur, one would need thousands of trees, probably of many species, as well as their pollinators and perhaps their essential symbiotic fungi.

2   De-extinction intends to resurrect single, charismatic species, yet millions of species are at risk of extinction. De-extinction can only be an infinitesimal part of solving the crisis that now sees species of animals (some large but most tiny), plants, fungi, and microbes going extinct at a thousand times their natural rates.

3   "But wait"—claim de-extinction's proponents. "We want to resurrect passenger pigeons and Pyrenean ibex, not dinosaurs. Surely, the plants on which these animals depend still survive, so there is no need to resurrect them as well!" Indeed, botanic gardens worldwide have living collections of an impressively large fraction of the world's plants, some extinct in the wild, others soon to be so. Their absence from the wild is more easily fixed than the absence of animals, for which de-extinction is usually touted.

4   Perhaps so, but other practical problems abound: A resurrected Pyrenean ibex will need a safe home, not just its food plants. Those of us who attempt to reintroduce zoo-bred species that have gone extinct in the wild have one question at the top of our list: Where do we put them? Hunters ate this wild goat to extinction. Reintroduce a resurrected ibex to the area where it belongs and it will become the most expensive *cabrito* ever eaten. If this seems cynical, then consider the cautionary tale of the Arabian oryx, returned to Oman from a captive breeding program. Their numbers have declined so much that their home, designated as a UNESCO World Heritage site, was summarily removed from the register.

The spotted owl's habitat is threatened by the logging of old-growth forests—an industry that has lawmakers inquiring about more high-tech measures to save the birds in an effort to justify more deforestation.

5   Yes, the set of plants alive a century or so ago when the passenger pigeon went extinct are probably still here. Is the pigeon's habitat intact? Surely not: The land use changes since then have been far too extensive.

6   In every case, without an answer to "where do we put them?"—and to the further question, "what changed in their original habitat that may have contributed to their extinction in the first place?"—efforts to bring back species are a colossal waste.

7   De-extinction is much worse than a waste: By setting up the expectation that biotechnology can repair the damage we're doing to the planet's biodiversity, it's extremely harmful for two kinds of political reasons.

8   Fantasies of reclaiming extinct species are always seductive. It is a fantasy that *real* scientists—those wearing white lab coats—are using fancy machines with knobs and digital readouts to save the planet from humanity's excesses. In this fantasy, there is none of the messy interaction with people, politics, and economics that characterizes my world. There is nothing involving the real-world realities of habitat destruction, of the inherent conflict between growing human populations and wildlife survival. Why worry about endangered species? We can simply keep their DNA and put them back in the wild later.

9   When I testify before Congress on endangered species, I'm always asked, "Can't we safely reduce the spotted owl to small numbers, keeping some in captivity as insurance?" The meaning is clear: "Let's log out almost all of western North America's old-growth forests because, if we can save species with high-tech solutions, the forest doesn't matter."

10   Or I'm asked, "Can't we breed in captivity the Cape Sable seaside sparrow?"—an obscure little bird whose survival requires the water in Everglades National Park to be the right amount in the right place at the right time. "Let's accommodate the

sugar growers and damage large areas of the Everglades. Let's tolerate a high risk of extinction because our white-lab-coated science rock stars can save the day!"

11   The second political problem involves research priorities. I work with very poor people in Africa, Brazil, and Madagascar. Rich only in the diversity of life amid which they eke out their living, they generate no money for my university. Too many other universities equate excellence with funds generated, not with societal needs met. Over my career, molecular biologists flourished as university administrators drooled over their large grants and their expensive labs. Field-based biology withered. Many otherwise prominent universities have no schools of the environment, no ecology departments, no professors of conservation. It was all too easy to equate "biology" with molecules and strip faculty positions and facilities from those who worked in the field. De-extinction efforts can only perpetuate that trend.

12   Conservation is about the ecosystems that species define and on which they depend. Conservation is about finding alternative, sustainable futures for peoples, for forests, and for wetlands. Molecular gimmickry simply does not address these core problems. At worst, it seduces granting agencies and university deans into thinking they are saving the world. It gives unscrupulous developers a veil to hide their rapaciousness, with promises to fix things later. It distracts us from guaranteeing our planet's biodiversity for future generations.

—Pimm, *National Geographic News*

Checking Your Comprehension

1. What is the main point of this reading?

   _____

2. What important information does *Jurassic Park* leave out about bringing a dinosaur to life? _____

3. If the Pyrenean ibex were resurrected, what would it need in addition to plants in order to survive? _____

4. How does the ability to revive extinct species change the way people think about protecting endangered species?

   _____

5. Instead of meeting societal needs, what do many universities see as excellence?

   _____

6. How will reviving extinct species impact the way university biology departments are set up in the future?

   _____

   _____

7. According to the last paragraph, what should scientists focus on rather than reviving extinct species? _____

Critical Reading and Thinking

1. What is the author's purpose in writing this selection?

   _____

2. What is the purpose of the first paragraph?

   _____

   _____

3. What kinds of evidence does the author provide?

   _____

4. Is the author biased or objective? _____

5. What is the purpose of the photograph?

   _____

   _____

Words in Context

Directions: Locate each word in the paragraph indicated and reread that paragraph. Then, based on the way the word is used, write a synonym or brief definition. You may use a dictionary, if necessary.

1. sustain (par. 1) _____

2. infinitesimal (par. 2) _____

3. cautionary (par. 4) _____

4. seductive (par. 8) _____

5. perpetuate (par. 11) _____

Vocabulary Review

Directions: Match each word in Column A with its meaning in Column B.

	Column A	Column B
_____	1. essential (par. 1)	a. huge
_____	2. proponents (par. 3)	b. between
_____	3. cynical (par. 4)	c. pessimistic
_____	4. habitat (par. 5)	d. treat as equal
_____	5. intact (par. 5)	e. necessary

Column A	Column B
_____ 6. colossal (par. 6)	f. unharmed and complete
_____ 7. obscure (par. 10)	g. advocates
_____ 8. amid (par. 11)	h. dishonest
_____ 9. equate (par. 11)	i. mysterious and little known
_____ 10. unscrupulous (par. 12)	j. a plant or animal's natural environment

Summarizing the Reading Selection

Directions: Write a summary of the reading "The Case Against Species Revival" on a separate sheet of paper.

Writing Exercises

1. Before you read this selection, what did you think about the movie *Jurassic Park*? How has that changed after reading this selection? Write a paragraph describing this.

2. The author is suggesting that if we can revive extinct animals, we will be less protective of them. Are there things in your own life that are easily replaced? What are they? Are there things that are not so easily replaced? Do you treat these items differently? Why? Describe this difference in one paragraph. Write a second paragraph describing how this same thinking could apply to animals and the environment.

3. What do you think should be more important: preserving habitats for endangered species or allowing development and commercial use of land? Why? Write a paragraph explaining your answer.

Analyzing and Synthesizing Ideas

1. Highlight words in each reading that have strong positive or negative connotations.
2. Compare the tones of the two readings.
3. Which argument is more persuasive? Explain your answer.
4. Are there things that both authors agree on? What are they?
5. Each selection includes a photograph that illustrates the author's position. Which one did you find to be more compelling? Why?
6. The authors take very different positions about how reviving extinct species could affect land and plants. Discuss these two different viewpoints. Could both positions be true, or is only one correct?

Credits

IMAGE CREDITS

CHAPTER 1
1: Corepics/Fotolia; **33:** Duncan Noakes/Fotolia.

CHAPTER 2
37: 06photo/Shutterstock; **51:** Jaren Wicklund/Fotolia; **61:** Mohd Suhail/Pearson; **61:** Pearson Education Ltd; **61:** Designua/Shutterstock; **61:** Borges Samuel/123RF; **62:** Imagedb.com/Shutterstock.

CHAPTER 3
80: Tlegend/Shutterstock; **084:** EpicStockMedia/Shutterstock; **92:** Jamie Grill/Blend Image/Getty Images; **105:** Doug Menuez/Photodisc/Getty Images; **113:** Matusciac Alexandru/123RF.

CHAPTER 4
117: Justin Case/Stone/Getty Images; **128:** Emily Parrino/Kentucky New Era/AP Images; **133:** Hugo Felix/ Shutterstock; **134:** Elke Van de Velde/Photodisc/Getty Images; **140:** Horizont21/Fotolia; **142:** Susan Watts/New York Daily News.

CHAPTER 5
146: Marzky Ragsac Jr/Fotolia; **165:** T-Design/Shutterstock; **183:** Pavel Losevsky/Fotolia; **183:** Wjarek/Fotolia.

CHAPTER 6
194: Justasc/Shuttterstock; **195:** Zakaz/Fotolia; **195:** Steve Gorton/Dorling Kindersley, Ltd; **195:** Cedrov/Fotolia; **199:** Perfect Match/Fotolia; **201:** Roman_23203/Fotolia; **209:** Msh Foto/Fotolia; **210:** Cartoonresource/Shutterstock; **221:** Dennisjacobsen/Fotolia; **221:** Mallivan/Fotolia; **229:** John Foxx/ Imagestate; **235:** bepsphoto/Fotolia; **235:** Ariane Citron/Fotolia; **236:** Nmedia/Fotolia.

CHAPTER 7
240: Papkin/Shutterstock; **249:** Dotshock/123RF; **249:** Sborisov/123RF; **265:** deviantART/Fotolia; **271:** Seanlockephotography/Fotolia.

CHAPTER 8
286: Mgkuijpers/Fotolia; **286:** Mgkuijpers/Fotolia; **293:** Justasc/Shutterstock; **297:** Christopher Dodge/ Fotolia; **301:** Michael Ireland/Fotolia; **302:** Diana Taliun/Shutterstock; **313:** Diane Bondareff/AP Images; **320:** Africa Studio/Shutterstock; **320:** Chris Wildt/www.CartoonStock.com; **321:** Kzenon/Fotolia.

CHAPTER 9
325: Cartoonresource/Shutterstock; **333:** Dario Sabljak/Fotolia; **337:** Auremar/Fotolia; **342:** Ed Kashi/VII/Corbis; **361:** Andrey Burmakin/Fotolia; **366:** Twobee/Fotolia.

CHAPTER 10

370: Lena Pan/Shutterstock; **400:** Berc/Fotolia; **405:** REUTERS/Henry Romero/LANDOV.

PART V

410: The Granger Collection, New York; **410:** Everett Historical/Shutterstock; **410:** Pearson Education; **410:** Charles Rex Arbogast/AP Images.

PART VI

432: Corepics/Fotolia; **432:** Duncan Noakes/Fotolia; **432:** 06photo/Shutterstock; **432:** Jaren Wicklund/Fotolia; **432:** Mohd Suhail/Pearson; **432:** Pearson Education Ltd; **432:** Designua/Shutterstock; **432:** Borges Samuel/123RF; **436:** Everett Collection/AGE Fotostock; **441:** USA Today Sports/Reuters/Corbis; **448:** Keki/Shutterstock; **454:** Creativemarc/Shutterstock; **460:** Gladskikh Tatiana/Shutterstock; **466:** Alistair Cotton/Fotolia; **472:** VPC Travel Photo/Alamy; **477:** Edmund Lowe Photography/Getty Images.

TEXT CREDITS

CHAPTER 1

16: Kunz, Jenifer, *THINK Marriages and Families*, 1st ed., p. 83, © 2011. Printed and electronically reproduced by permission of Pearson Education, Inc., Upper Saddle River, New Jersey; **16–17:** Lawrence G. Gitman and Chad J. Zutter, *Principles of Managerial Finance*, 12th/e., (c) Lawrence G. Gitman (Upper Saddle River: Pearson Education, 2008); **18–19:** Dahlman, Carl H., William H. Renwick, and Edward Bergman, *Introduction to Geography: People, Places, and Environment*, 5th ed., p. 175, © 2011. Printed and electronically reproduced by permission of Pearson Education, Inc., Upper Saddle River, New Jersey; **21:** Leon G. Schiffman; Leslie Lazar Kanuk; Joseph Wisenblit, *Consumer Bevavior* (Upper Saddle River: Pearson Education, Inc., 2008); **22:** Colleen Belk and Virginia Borden Maier, *Biology: Science for Life with Physiology*, 3/e. (Upper Saddle River: Pearson Education, Inc., 2010); **22:** John W. Hill; Terry W. McCreary; Doris K. Kolb, *Chemistry for Changing Times*, 12th/e (Upper Saddle River:, Pearson Education, Inc. 2010) **24:** Carl, John D., *THINK Sociology*, 1st ed., p. 197, © 2010. Printed and electronically reproduced by permission of Pearson Education, Inc., Upper Saddle River, New Jersey. Data source: "Historical Income Tables-People," U.S. Census Bureau, 2006; **26–27:** Patrick Frank, *Prebles' Artforms: An Introduction to the Visual Arts*, 9/e, p. 100. Upper Saddle River, NJ: Pearson Education, Inc., 2009; **27:** Stephen Kosslyn and Robin Rosenberg, *Fundamentals of Psychology*, 3/e, pp. 368–369. Boston: Pearson Education, Inc., 2007; **33–35:** Wilson, Eric G., "The Allure of Disaster," *Psychology Today* blog, March 13, 2012. © 2012 by Eric G. Wilson. Reprinted by permission of the author. Eric G. Wilson is author of *Everyone Loves a Good Train Wreck: Why We Can't Look Away* and *Against Happiness: In Praise of Melancholy*.

CHAPTER 2

47: Henslin, James M., *Sociology: A Down-to-Earth Approach*, 10th ed., p. G4, © 2010. Printed and electronically reproduced by permission of Pearson Education, Inc., Upper Saddle River, New Jersey; **50–53:** Devito, Joseph A., *The Interpersonal Communication Book*, 13th Ed., © 2013, pp. 114–118. Reprinted and Electronically reproduced by permission of Pearson Education, Inc., New York, NY.; **62:** "Physical Activity for a Healthy Weight: Why is physical activity important?" Atlanta, GA: U.S. Centers for Disease Control and Prevention, September 13, 2011, http://www.cdc.gov/healthyweight/physical_activity/index.html; **66–71:** Kunz, Jenifer, *THINK Marriages and Families*, 1st ed., pp. 118–120, © 2011. Printed and electronically reproduced by permission of Pearson Education, Inc., Upper Saddle River, New Jersey; **67:** Knapp, Mark, *Interpersonal Communication and Human Relationships*. (Boston: Allyn & Bacon, 1984); **75–77:** Colleen Belk and Virginia Borden Maier, Biology: Science for Life with Physiology, 4/e. (Upper Saddle River: Pearson Education, Inc., 2012) p 376–377; **76:** Belk, Colleen M.; Borden Maier, Virginia, Biology: *Science For Life With Physiology*, 4th Ed., © 2013, p. 376. Reprinted and electronically reproduced by permission of Pearson Education, Inc., New York, NY.

CHAPTER 3

83: John R. Walker, *Introduction to Hospitality Management* 3/e, (Upper Saddle River: Pearson Education, Inc., 2010) p.45.; **84–85:** Goldman, Thomas F.; Cheeseman, Henry R., *The Paralegal Professional*, 3rd Ed., © 2011, p. 745. Reprinted and electronically reproduced by permission of Pearson Education, Inc., New York, NY.; **86:** Ciccarelli, Saundra K.; White, J. Noland, *Psychology: An Exploration*, 1st Ed., © 2010, p. 454. Reprinted and electronically reproduced by permission of Pearson Education, Inc., New York, NY.; **87–88:** Edwards, George C.; Wattenberg, Martin P.; Lineberry, Robert L., *Government In America: People, Politics, And Policy*, 14th Ed., © 2009, p. 285. Reprinted and electronically reproduced by permission of Pearson Education, Inc., New York, NY.; **88–89:** Norman Christensen, *The Environment and You*, 1/e, (Upper Saddle River: Pearson Education, Inc., 2012); **90:** Joan Salge Blake, *Nutrition and You*, 2/e (Upper Saddle River: Pearson Education, Inc., 2012), Pearson Education; **92:** Donatelle, Rebecca J., *Health: The Basics*, Green Edition, 9th ed., pp. 94, 96, © 2011. Reprinted and electronically reproduced by permission of Pearson Education, Inc., Upper Saddle River, New Jersey; **93–94:** James Fagin, CJ 2011, *Criminal Justice*, (Upper Saddle River: Pearson Education, Inc., 2012); **104–106:** Ciccarelli, Saundra K. and J. Noland White, *Psychology*, 2nd ed., pp. 169–171, © 2009. Adapted and electronically reproduced by permission of Pearson Education, Inc., Upper Saddle River, New Jersey; **128:** Henslin, James M., *Sociology: A Down-to-Earth Approach*, 10th ed., p. 386, © 2010. Printed and electronically reproduced by permission of Pearson Education, Inc., Upper Saddle River, New Jersey.

CHAPTER 4

128: Solomon, Michael R., *Consumer Behavior*, 8th Ed., © 2009, pp. 19, 21, 35, 392–393. Reprinted and electronically reproduced by permission of Pearson Education, Inc., New York, NY.; **128/207:** Colleen Belk, Virginia Borden Maier, Biology: Science for Life with Physiology, 3/e, (Upper Saddle River: Pearson Education, 2010); **129:** Donatelle, Rebecca J., Health: The Basics, Green Edition, 9th ed., p. 57, © 2011. Printed and electronically reproduced by permission of Pearson Education, Inc., Upper Saddle River, New Jersey; **132–135:** Rebecca J. Donatelle, *Access to Health, Green Edition*, 11/e (Upper Saddle River: Pearson Education, 2010), 355–356; **140–143:** Gerald Audesirk, Teresa Audesirk, Bruce E. Byers, *Biology: Life on Earth* 9/e (Upper Saddle River: Pearson Education, Inc. 2011).

CHAPTER 5

164: James Rubenstein, *Contemporary Human Geography*, Pearson Education; **165:** Henslin, James M., *Sociology: A Down-to-Earth Approach*, 10th ed., p. 52, © 2010. Printed and electronically reproduced by permission of Pearson Education, Inc., Upper Saddle River, New Jersey; **165:** Michael R. Solomon, *Consumer Behavior: Buying, Having, and Being* 8/e, (Upper Saddle River: Pearson Education, Inc., 2009) p.62–63; **166:** Donatelle, Rebecca J., *Health: The Basics*, Green Edition, 9th ed., p. 34, © 2011. Printed and electronically reproduced by permission of Pearson Education, Inc., Upper Saddle River, New Jersey; **167:** James Rubenstein, *Contemporary Human Geography*, 1/e (Upper Saddle River: Pearson Education, Inc. 2010); **169:** Copyright © 2015 by Houghton Mifflin Harcourt Publishing Company. Reproduced by permission from the online edition of *The American Heritage Dictionary of the English Language*, Fifth Edition at ahdictionary.com; **172:** Copyright © 2015 by Houghton Mifflin Harcourt Publishing Company. Reproduced by permission from the online edition of *The American Heritage Dictionary of the English Language*, Fifth Edition at ahdictionary.com; **182–195:** Macionis, John J., *Society: The Basics*, 12th ed., pp. 121–122, © 2013. Adapted and electronically reproduced by permission of Pearson Education, Inc., Upper Saddle River, New Jersey; **188–191:** Brown, Stacia, "How Can You Study When You Can't Eat? The Invisible Problem of Hunger on Campus," Salon.com, November 2013. This article first appeared in Salon.com, at http://www.Salon.com An online version remains in the Salon archives. Reprinted with permission.

CHAPTER 6

199: Donatelle, Rebecca J., *Health: The Basics*, Green Edition, 9th ed., p. 424, © 2011. Printed and electronically reproduced by permission of Pearson Education, Inc., Upper Saddle River, New Jersey; **200:** Frederick K. Lutgens; Edward J. Tarbuck; Dennis Tasa., Essentials of Geology, 10/e, (Upper Saddle River: Pearson Education, Inc., 2009) p. 62. **200:** Solomon, Michael R., *Consumer Behavior*, 8th Ed., © 2009, pp. 19, 21, 35, 392–393. Reprinted and electronically reproduced by permission of Pearson Education, Inc., New York, NY.; **200–201:** Colleen Belk and Virginia Borden Maier, *Biology: Science for Life with Physiology*, 3/e. (Upper Saddle River: Pearson Education, Inc., 2010) p.438; **201:** Henslin, James M., *Sociology: A Down-to-Earth Approach*, 10th ed., p. 148, © 2010. Printed and electronically reproduced by permission of Pearson Education, Inc., Upper Saddle River, New Jersey; **201:** Solomon, Michael R., *Consumer Behavior*, 8th Ed., © 2009, pp. 19, 21, 35, 392–393. Reprinted and Electronically reproduced by permission of Pearson Education, Inc., New York, NY.; **202:** Donatelle, Rebecca J., *Health: The Basics*, Green Edition, 9e, Pearson Education, 2011. Reprinted with permission; **202:** Ronald J. Ebert and Ricky W. Griffin, Business Essentials, 7/e, (Upper Saddle River: Pearson Education, Inc., 2009) p.12; **202:** Carl, John D., *THINK Sociology*, 1st ed., p. 51, © 2010. Printed and electronically reproduced by permission of Pearson Education, Inc., Upper Saddle River, New Jersey; **202–203:** Roy A. Cook; Laura J. Yale; Joseph J. Marqua., *Tourism: The Business of Travel*, 4/e, (Upper Saddle River: Pearson Education,

2010) p.347; **203:** Peter Facione, Think Critically, 1/e (Upper Saddle River: Pearson Education, Inc., 2011) p. 90; **203/379:** A. Cook; Laura J. Yale; Joseph J. Marqua, *Tourism: The Business of Travel*, 4/e, (Upper Saddle River: Pearson Education, Inc. 2010) p.52; **205:** Walter Thompson and Joseph V. Hickey, *Society in Focus*, 4/e, (Boston: Allyn and Bacon, 1994); **205:** Patrick Frank, Prebles' Artforms: An Introduction to the Visual Arts, 9/e, (Upper Saddle River: Pearson Education, Inc., 2009) p. 5.; **206:** Carl, John D., *THINK Sociology*, 1st ed., p. 128, © 2010. Adapted and electronically reproduced by permission of Pearson Education, Inc., Upper Saddle River, New Jersey; **206:** Donatelle, Rebecca J., *Health: The Basics*, Green Edition, 9th ed., p. 18, © 2011. Printed and electronically reproduced by permission of Pearson Education, Inc., Upper Saddle River, New Jersey; **206–207:** Carl, John D., *THINK Sociology*, 1st ed., p. 122, © 2010. Adapted and electronically reproduced by permission of Pearson Education, Inc., Upper Saddle River, New Jersey; **207:** Frank Schmalleger, *Criminal Justice*, 9/e (Upper Saddle River: Pearson Education, Inc., 2012); **207:** George C. Edwards III, Martin P. Wattenberg, Robert L. Lineberry, *Government in America: People, Politics, and Policy*, 14/e, (Upper Saddle River: Pearson Education, 2009), p.306; **208:** Henslin, James M., *Sociology: A Down-to-Earth Approach*, 10th ed., p. 6, © 2010. Printed and electronically reproduced by permission of Pearson Education, Inc., Upper Saddle River, New Jersey; **208:** Colleen Belk and Virginia Borden Maier, Biology: *Science for Life with Physiology*, 3/e , Upper Saddle River: Pearson Education, Inc. 2010) p.305; **208:** Mark Krause and Daniel Corts, *Psychological Science: Modeling Science Literacy*, 1/e, (Upper Saddler River: Pearson Education, Inc., 2012); **208:** Solomon, Michael R., *Consumer Behavior*, 8th Ed., © 2009, pp. 19, 21, 35, 392–393. Reprinted and electronically reproduced by permission of Pearson Education, Inc., New York, NY.; **209:** Henslin, James M., *Sociology: A Down-to-Earth Approach*, 10th ed., p. 85, © 2010. Printed and electronically reproduced by permission of Pearson Education, Inc., Upper Saddle River, New Jersey; **209:** Frederick K. Lutgens; Edward J. Tarbuck; Dennis Tasa., *Essentials of Geology*, 10/e. (Upper Saddle River: Pearson Education, Inc., 2009) p.144.; **217:** Edward Bergman, William Renwick, *Introduction to Geography, People, Places, and Environment*, 3/e, (Upper Saddle River: Pearson Education, Inc., 2005); **217–218:** Hugh D. Barlow, *Criminal Justice in America*, 1/e (Upper Saddle River, NJ: Pearson Education, Inc., 2000.); **218:** Donatelle, Rebecca J., *Health: The Basics*, Green Edition, 9th ed., p. 280, © 2011. Printed and electronically reproduced by permission of Pearson Education, Inc., Upper Saddle River, New Jersey; **219:** Kathleen German and Bruce Gronbeck, Principles of Public Speaking, 14/e, (New York: Longman, 2001) p.190–191; **219:** Tim Curry; Robert Jiobu; Kent Schwirian., *Sociology for the 21st Century*, 3/e, (Upper Saddle River: Prentice-Hall, 2001) p. 138; **220:** Karen O'Connor, Larry Sabato, Alixandra B. Yanus, American Government: Roots and Reform, 2011 edition, (Upper Saddle River: Pearson Education, Inc. 2012) **220:** Steven A. Beebe and John T. Masterson, *Communicating in Small Groups: Principles and Practices*, 6/e, (New York: Longman, 2001) p.150; **221:** Robert A. Divine and T. H. Breen., *America: Past and Present*, Combined Volume, 9/e, (Upper Saddle River: Pearson Education, Inc., 2011) p449; **221:** Belk, Colleen, and Virginia Borden Maier, *Biology: Science for Life with Physiology*, 3rd ed. San Francisco: Pearson Benjamin Cummings, 2010, p. 236; **221:** Donatelle, Rebecca J., and Lorraine G. Davis, Access to Health, 6th ed. Boston: Allyn and Bacon, 2000, p. 42; **222:** April Lynch; Barry Elmore; Tanya Morgan, *Choosing Health*, 1/e, (Upper Saddle River: Pearson Education, Inc., 2012); **222:** Edwards III, George C., Martin P. Wattenberg, and Robert L. Lineberry, *Government in America: People, Politics, and Policy*, 14th ed. New York: Pearson Longman, 2009, p. 9; **222:** Henslin, James M., *Sociology: A Down-to-Earth Approach*, 10th ed., p. 46, © 2010. Printed and electronically reproduced by permission of Pearson Education, Inc., Upper Saddle River, New Jersey; **222–223:** Belk, Colleen, and Virginia Borden Maier, *Biology: Science for Life with Physiology*, 3rd ed. San Francisco: Pearson Benjamin Cummings, 2010, p. 447; **223:** Michael R. Solomon, *Consumer Behavior*, 8/e, (Upper Saddle River: Pearson Education, Inc., 2009) p. 189; **223:** Donatelle, Rebecca J., *Health: The Basics*, Green Edition, 9th ed., p. 71, © 2011. Printed and electronically reproduced by permission of Pearson Education, Inc., Upper Saddle River, New Jersey; **223–224:** Donatelle, Rebecca J. and Lorraine G. Davis, *Access to Health*, 6th ed. Boston: Allyn and Bacon, 2000, pp. 289–290; **224:** Bergman, Edward F. and William H. Renwick, *Introduction to Geography: People, Places, and Environment*, 3rd ed., p. 422, © 2005. Printed and electronically reproduced by permission of Pearson Education, Inc., Upper Saddle River, New Jersey; **224:** Colleen Belk, Virginia Borden Maier, *Biology: Science for Life with Physiology*, 3/e, (Upper Saddle River: Pearson Education, 2010), p. 509; **224:** Joseph A. DeVito, Messages: Building Interpersonal Communication Skills, 5/e, (Upper Saddel River: Pearson Education, Inc., 2002), p. 224–225; **227–228:** Joseph DeVito, *Human Communication: The Basic Course*, 11/e (Upper Saddle River: Pearson Education, Inc., 2009); **234–236:** Carl H. Dahlman and William H. Renwick, *Introduction to Geography*, 5/e (Upper Saddle River: Pearson Education, Inc. 2011)

CHAPTER 7

241: John Thill and Courtland Bovee, *Excellence in Business Communication*, 9/e © Bovee and Thill, LLC, (Upper Saddle River: Pearson Education, Inc., 2010); **243:** John D. Carl, *THINK Sociology*, 1st ed., p. 200, © 2010. Printed and electronically reproduced by permission of Pearson Education, Inc., Upper Saddle River, New Jersey; **244:** April Lynch; Barry Elmore; Tanya Morgan, *Choosing Health*, 1/e, (Upper Saddle

River: Pearson Education, Inc., 2012); **245:** Steve Mariotti; Caroline Glackin, *Entrepreneurship & Small Business Management*, 1/e (Upper Saddle River: Pearson Education, Inc. 2012); **246:** Hugh D. Barlow, Criminal Justice In America, 1/e, (Upper Saddle River, NJ: Pearson Education, Inc., 2000.) p. 238;. **249:** John R. Walker and Josielyn T. Walker, *Tourism: Concepts and Practices*, 1/e (Upper Saddle River: Pearson Education, Inc., 2011.) p. 11; **250:** George C. Edwards III, Martin P. Wattenberg, Robert L. Lineberry, *Government in America: People, Politics, and Policy*, 14/e, (Upper Saddle River: Pearson Education, Inc. 2009) p.239; **250:** Thomas F. Goldman and Henry R. Cheeseman, *The Paralegal Professional,* 3/e, (Upper Saddle River: Pearson Education, Inc., 2011) pp. 736–737; **250–251:** Saundra K. Ciccarelli, J. Noland White, *Psychology: An Exploration*, 1/e, (Upper Saddle River: Pearson Education, Inc., 2010) p.249; **251:** Thomas F. Goldman and Henry R. Cheeseman, *The Paralegal Professional*, 3/e, (Upper Saddle River: Pearson Education, Inc., 2011) p.81.; **251–252:** Colleen Belk, Virginia Borden Maier, *Biology: Science for Life with Physiology*, 3/e, (Upper Saddle River: Pearson Education, Inc. 2010); **252:** James M. Henslin, *Sociology: A Down-to-Earth Approach*, 10th ed., p. 383, © 2010, James Henslin. Printed and electronically reproduced by permission of Pearson Education, Inc., Upper Saddle River, New Jersey, p. 383, © 2010. Printed and electronically reproduced by permission of Pearson Education, Inc., Upper Saddle River, New Jersey; **252–253:** David H. Goldfield and Carl E. Abbott, *The American Journey*, Combined Volume, 6/e (Upper Saddle River: Pearson Education, Inc. 2011); **253:** Limmer, Daniel J. and Michael F. O'Keefe, *Emergency Care*, 12th ed. Boston: Pearson Brady, 2012, p. 581; **254:** George C. Edwards III, Martin P. Wattenberg, Robert L. Lineberry, *Government in America: People, Politics, and Policy*, 14/e, (Upper Saddle River: Pearson Education, Inc., 2009), p. 206–207; **254:** Frederick K. Lutgens; Edward J. Tarbuck; Dennis G. Tasa, *The Atmosphere: An Introduction to Meteorology*, 12/e (Upper Saddle River: Pearson Education, Inc., 2012; **255:** Stephen F. Davis and Joseph J. Palladino, *Psychology*, 3/e, (Upper Saddle RiverJ: Pearson Education, Inc., 2000) pp. 563, 564, 566; **255:** Rebecca J. Donatelle and Lorraine G. Davis, *Access to Health*, 7/e, (Upper Saddle River: Pearson Education, Inc., 2002); **255:** John A. Garraty and Mark C. Carnes, *The American Nation*, 10/e, (New York: Longman, 2000); **256:** Roy A. Cook, Laura J. Yale; Joseph J. Marqua., *Tourism: The Business of Travel*, 4/e, (Upper Saddle River: Pearson Education, Inc., 2010); **256–257:** Palmira Brummer, George Jewsbury, Neil J. Hackett et al., *Civilization: Past and Present,* 11/e (Upper Saddle River: Pearson Education, Inc., 2005); **258:** Edward H. Reiley and Carroll L. Shry, *Introductory Horticulture*, 1/e (Albany: Delmar Publishers, 1979.) p114; **264–266:** Bogard, Paul, "Let There Be Dark," Los Angeles Times, December 21, 2012. © 2012 by Paul Bogard. Reprinted by permission of the author; **269–271:** Henslin, James M., *Essentials of Sociology: A Down-to-Earth Approach*, 6th Ed., ©2006 Jeams Henslin, p. 213. Reprinted and Electronically reproduced by permission of Pearson Education, Inc., New York, NY.

CHAPTER 8

274: Map courtesy of The Weather Channel; **276:** Michael R. Solomon; Greg W. Marshall; Elnora W. Stuart, *Marketing: Real People, Real Choices*, 6/e, (Upper Saddle River: Pearson Education, 2009); **277:** Gary Armstrong; Philip Kotler, *Marketing: An Introduction* 10/e, (Upper Saddle River: Pearson Education, Inc. 2011); **277:** John Thill and Courtland Bovee, *Excellence in Business Communication*, 9/e © Bovee and Thill, LLC, (Upper Saddle River: Pearson Education, Inc., 2010); **277–278:** April Lynch; Barry Elmore; Tanya Morgan, *Choosing Health*, 1/e, (Upper Saddle River: Pearson Education, Inc., 2012); **278:** Gary Armstrong; Philip Kotler, *Marketing: An Introduction* 10/e, (Upper Saddle River: Pearson Education, Inc. 2011); **280:** Excerpt from The World Book Online Reference Center © 2010. www.worldbookonline.com. By permission of the publisher. All rights reserved. This content may not be reproduced in whole or in part in any form without prior written permission from the publisher; **281:** Robert W. Christopherson, *Elemental Geosystems*, 6/e (Upper Saddle River: Pearson Education, Inc., 2010); **281:** Samuel E. Wood, Ellen Green Wood and Denise Boyd, *Mastering the World of Psychology,* 4/e (Upper Saddle River: Pearson Education, Inc., 2011); **281–282:** Michael R. Solomon, *Consumer Behavior: Buying Having, and Being*, 8/e, (Upper Saddle River: Pearson Education, 2009); **286:** Krogh, David, *Biology: A Guide to the Natural World*, 4th ed., pp. 466–467, 474, © 2009. Printed and electronically reproduced by permission of Pearson Education, Inc., Upper Saddle River, New Jersey; **287:** Henslin, James M., *Sociology: A Down-to-Earth Approach*, 10th ed., p. 164, © 2010. Printed and electronically reproduced by permission of Pearson Education, Inc., Upper Saddle River, New Jersey; **288:** David Krogh, Biology: *A Guide to the Natural World*, 4/e, (Upper Saddle River: Pearson Education, Inc., 2009); **288–289:** Norman Christensen, *The Environment and You*, 1/e, (Upper Saddle River: Pearson Education, Inc., 2012); **291–292:** Roy A. Cook; Laura J. Yale; Joseph J. Marqua, *Tourism: The Business of Travel*, 4/e, (Upper Saddle River: Pearson Education, 2010), p.282; **292–293:** Saundra Ciccarelli and J. Noland White, *Psychology: An Exploration,* 1/e, (Upper Saddle River: Pearson Education, Inc., 2010), p.280; **293:** Henslin, James M., *Sociology: A Down-to-Earth Approach*, 10th ed., p. 37, © 2010. Printed and electronically reproduced by permission of Pearson Education, Inc., Upper

Saddle River, New Jersey; **293:** Frederick K. Lutgens; Edward J. Tarbuck; Dennis Tasa., *Foundations of Earth Science*, 6/e. (Upper Saddle River: Pearson Education, Inc., 2011); **296:** Krogh, David, *Biology: A Guide to the Natural World*, 4th ed., p. 429, © 2009. Printed and electronically reproduced by permission of Pearson Education, Inc., Upper Saddle River, New Jersey; **296:** Henslin, James M., *Sociology: A Down-to-Earth Approach*, 10th ed., pp. 109, 111, © 2010. Printed and electronically reproduced by permission of Pearson Education, Inc., Upper Saddle River, New Jersey; **297:** Michael R. Solomon, *Consumer Behavior: Buying Having, and Being*, 8/e, (Upper Saddle River: Pearson Education, 2009), P.132–133; **298:** Hugh D. Barlow, *Criminal Justice in America*, 1/e (Upper Saddle River, NJ: Pearson Education, Inc., 2000), p. 332; **299:** Roy A. Cook; Laura J. Yale; Joseph J. Marqua Tourism: *The Business of Travel*, 4/e, (Upper Saddle River: Pearson Education, 2010,) p.170; **299:** Goldman Thomas F. Goldman and Henry R. Cheeseman, *The Paralegal Professional*, 3/e, (Upper Saddle River: Pearson Education, Inc., 2011) p.266 and Cheeseman, The Paralegal Professional, Pearson Education.; **299–300:** Robert A. Divine and T.H. Breen, *America: Past and Present*, Combined Volume, 9/e, (Upper Saddle River: Pearson Education, Inc., 2011), p. 596; **300:** Saundra Ciccarelli and J. Noland White, *Psychology: An Exploration*, 1/e, (Upper Saddle River: Pearson Education, Inc., 2010) p. 321; **301:** Krogh, David, *Biology: A Guide to the Natural World*, 4th ed., p. 750, © 2009. Printed and electronically reproduced by permission of Pearson Education, Inc., Upper Saddle River, New Jersey; **301:** John R. Walker and Josielyn T. Walker, *Tourism: Concepts and Practices*, 1/e (Upper Saddle River: Pearson Education, Inc., 2011.) p. 53–54.; **301:** Thomas F. Goldman, Henry R. Cheeseman, *The Paralegal Professional*, 3, (Upper Saddle River: Pearson Education, 2011), p. 641.; **302:** Rebecca J. Donatelle, *Health: The Basics, Green Edition*, 9th ed., (Upper Saddle River: Pearson Education, Inc., 2011); **302:** Krogh, David, *Biology: A Guide to the Natural World*, 4th ed., p. 488, © 2009. Printed and electronically reproduced by permission of Pearson Education, Inc., Upper Saddle River, New Jersey; **302:** John W. Hill; Terry W. McCreary; Doris K. Kolb, *Chemistry for Changing Times*, 12/e (Upper Saddle River:, Pearson Education, Inc. 2010); **303:** Belk, Colleen, and Virginia Borden Maier, *Biology: Science for Life with Physiology*, 3rd ed. San Francisco: Pearson Benjamin Cummings, 2010, p. 451; **303:** John R. Walker and Josielyn T. Walker, *Tourism: Concepts and Practices*, 1/e (Upper Saddle River: Pearson Education, Inc., 2011), p. 241.; **303:** Phillip Kotler and Gary Armstrong, *Principles of Marketing*, 13/e, (Upper Saddle River: Pearson Education, Inc. 2010); **305:** Thomas F. Goldman, Henry R. Cheeseman, *The Paralegal Professional*, 3/e, (Upper Saddle River: Pearson Education, 2011), p. 183; **306:** James M. Henslin, Sociology: *A Down-to-Earth Approach*, 6/e, © James Henslin 2003 (Upper Saddle River: Pearson Education, 2003), p. 637; **306:** Samuel E. Wood, Ellen Green Wood and Denise Boyd, *Mastering the World of Psychology*, 4/e (Upper Saddle River: Pearson Education, Inc., 2011); **307:** Germann, William J. and Cindy L. Stanfield, *Principles of Human Physiology*. San Francisco: Pearson Benjamin Cummings, 2002, pp. 303–304; **311–313:** Solomon, Michael, *Better Business*, Pearson Education; **312–314:** White, Alton Fitzgerald, "Right Place, Wrong Face," The Nation, January 1 © 2000 The Nation Company, LLC. All rights reserved. Used by permission and protected by the Copyright Laws of the United States. The printing, copying, redistribution, or retransmission of this Content without express written permission is prohibited; **318–322:** Benokraitis, Nijole V., *Marriages And Families*, 8th Ed., © 2015, pp. 250–253. Reprinted and electronically reproduced by permission of Pearson Education, Inc., New York, NY.

CHAPTER 9

327: Clark, Nancy, *Nancy Clark's Sports Nutrition Guidebook*. Champaign, IL: Human Kinetics, 2008, pp. 21–22; **329:** Jenny Lawson, Let's Pretend This Never Happened: (A Mostly True Memoir). New York: Berkley, p.18.; **330:** Batstone, David, excerpt from "Katja's Story: Human Trafficking Thrives in the New Global Economy," *Sojourners Magazine*, June 2006. © 2006 David Batstone. Reprinted by permission of the author; **332:** RoAne, Susan, *Face to Face: How to Reclaim the Personal Touch in a Digital World*. New York: Simon & Schuster, 2008, pp. 2–3; **333–334:** Slobogin, Christopher, *Privacy at Risk: The New Government Surveillance and the Fourth Amendment*. Chicago: University of Chicago Press, 2007, pp. 3–4; **334:** Harrison, Guy, 50 *Popular Beliefs That People Think Are True*. Amherst, NY: Prometheus Books, 2012, p. 31; **335:** Perkins, John, Al Ridenhour, and Matt Kovsky, *Attack Proof: The Ultimate Guide to Personal Protection*. Champaign, IL: Human Kinetics, 2009, p. 7; **336:** Greenberg, Cathy L. and Barrett S. Avigdor, *What Happy Working Mothers Know*. Hoboken, NJ: John Wiley & Sons, 2009, p. 97; **337–338:** Holdforth, Lucinda, *Why Manners Matter: The Case for Civilized Behavior in a Barbarous World*. New York: Amy Einhorn Books/G. P. Putnam's Sons, 2009, pp. 16–17; **340:** William Shakespeare, *As You Like It*, Act II, Scene VII, 1623 First Folio; **340:** Crane, Stephen, *The Red Badge of Courage*. New York: D. Appleton and Company, 1895; **340:** Conrad, Joseph, *The Arrow of Gold*. London: T. F. Unwin, 1919; **340:** William Shakespeare, *Hamlet*, Act III, Scene II, 1599; **340:** Percy Bysshe Shelley, *Adonais: An Elegy on the Death of John Keats* (London: Charles Ollier, 1821); **341–343:** Comfort, Megan, *Doing Time Together: Love and Family in the Shadow of the Prison*, 2007. Republished with permission of University of Chicago Press, permission conveyed through Copyright Clearance Center, Inc.; **344:** James M. Henslin, *Sociology: A Down-to-Earth Approach*, 10th ed., p. 153, © 2010 James Henslin. Printed and electronically reproduced by permission of Pearson Education, Inc., Upper Saddle River, New Jersey; **348:** Montoya, Katrina, "A Collection for My Mother and Father," *Tribal College Journal of American Indian Higher Education*, vol. 24, no. 1 (Fall 2012), p. 52. © 2012 by Katrina Montoya. Reprinted by permission of the author; **348:** Amrbose Bierce, *The Devil's Dictionary*, (Neale Publishing, 1911); **350:** Price, Margaret S., *The Special Needs Child and Divorce: A Practical Guide to Evaluating and Handling Cases*. Chicago: American Bar Association, Section of Family Law, 2009, p. 4; **352:** Savage, Mark, "Inside Yellowstone," *American Snowmobiler*, vol. 27, no. 4 (2013), p. 58; **353:** Steinbeck, John, *America and Indians*. New York: Viking Press, 1966, pp. 127–128; **353–354:** James N. Danziger, *Understanding the Political World: A Comparative Introduction to Political Science*, 10th edition (Upper Saddler River: Pearson Education, Inc., 2011) p350–351; **358–361:** "The Doctor will E-mail you Now" Copyright 2014 Consumers Union of U.S., Inc. Yonkers, NY 10703–1057, a nonprofit organization. Reprinted with permission from the January 2014 issue of *Consumer Reports*® for educational purposes only. www.ConsumerReports.org; **365–367:** St. Fleur, Nicholas, "You Must Be This Old to Die," *The Atlantic*, January 7, 2015. © 2015 The Atlantic Media Co., as first published in *The Atlantic Magazine*. All rights reserved. Distributed by Tribune Content Agency, LLC

CHAPTER 10

379: Scott Dobson-Mitchell, "The three day week: living every 12-year old's dream", *Maclean's*, January 23, 2009; **383:** Linda Papadopoulos, *What Men Say, What Women Hear*, (New York: Simon Spotlight, 2009). P. 22.; **388:** Quote from Carol Dweck in Andrew Postman, "Raising a Good Loser," *Good Housekeeping*," January 2010, 250:1, p. 85.; **388:** Dame Jane Morris Goodall, DBE is a British primatologist, ethologist, anthropologist, and UN Messenger of Peace.; **388:** Carol R, Ember and Melvin R. Ember, *Cultural Anthropology*, 13/e, (Upper Saddle River: Pearson Education, Inc., 2011); **389:** Walter Thompson and Joseph V. Hickey, *Society in Focus*, 4/e, Boston: Allyn and Bacon, 1994; **392–393:** Stone, Danny, "Simple Explanations Ease Communication," *Buffalo News*, February 10, 2013. © 2013 by Danny Stone. Reprinted by permission of the author; **394:** Michael R. Solomon, *Consumer Behavior: Buying Having, and Being*, 8/e, (Upper Saddle River: Pearson Education, 2009); **399–401:** Molinary, Rosie, "Reality Check: Reality TV Does Not Make You Feel Better," rosiemolinary.com, February 18, 2013. Copyright © 2013 Rosie Molinary. Reprinted by permission of the author; **404–406:** James M. Henslin, *Essentials of Sociology, A Down to Earth Approach*, 9/e © 2011 James Henslin. (Upper Saddle River: Pearson Education, Inc., 2011).

PART V

411–413: Kate Chopin, "The Story of an Hour", St. Louis Life, January 5, 1895.; **415–419:** Edgar Allan Poe, "The Tell-Tale Heart", The Pioneer, Vol. 1, No. 1, Drew and Scammell, Philadelphia, January 1843.; **421–423:** Rogers, Bruce Holland, "Little Brother," October 30, 2000, *Strange Horizons*. Copyright © by Bruce Holland Rogers. Reprinted by permission of the author. All rights reserved; **427–430:** Gruen, Sara, *Water for Elephants* © 2011 by Sara Gruen. Reprinted by permission of Algonquin Books of Chapel Hill. All rights reserved; **427–430:** Excerpt from Gruen, Sara, *Water for Elephants* © 2006 Sara Gruen. Published by HarperCollins Publishers Ltd. All rights reserved.

PART VI

434–437: Jimenez, Andres, "Why Celebrity Activism Does More Harm Than Good," Waging NonViolence, July 29, 2013. Reprinted with permission; **440–443:** Sheinin, Dave, "After Ferguson, Staten Island, Cleveland, Athletes Are Becoming Activists Again," *The Washington Post*, December 5 © 2014 Washington Post Company. All rights reserved. Used by permission and protected by the Copyright Laws of the United States. The printing, copying, redistribution, or retransmission of this content without express written permission is prohibited; **447–450:** Crane, Andrew and Dirk Matten, "Is Selling Human Organs Really So Unethical," Sustainable Business Forum, June 1, 2012. Reproduced with permission from the Crane and Matten blog: http://craneandmatten.blogspot.com; **453–456:** Ireland, Corydon, "Ethicists, Philosophers Discuss Selling of Human Organs," *Harvard Gazette*, Feb 14, 2008. Reprinted with permission of the Harvard Gazette; **459–462:** Konnikova, Maria, "Is Internet Addiction a Real Thing?" *The New Yorker*, November 26, 2014. Reprinted with permission of The New Yorker; **465–467:** Smith, David, "Internet Use on Mobile Phones in Africa Predicted to Increase 20–Fold," *The Guardian*, June 2014. Copyright Guardian News & Media Ltd 2015. Reprinted with permission; **471–473:** Brand, Stewart, "The Case for Reviving Extinct Species," *National Geographic News*, March 11, 2013. © 2013 by Stewart Brand. Reprinted by permission of the author; **476–478:** Pimm, Stuart, "The Case Against Species Revival," *National Geographic News*, March 12, 2013. © 2013 by Stuart Pimm. Reprinted by permission of the author.

Index